CRIME & SOCIETY

Series Editor, John Hagan
University of North Carolina–Chapel Hill

Crime and Public Policy: Putting Theory to Work,
edited by Hugh D. Barlow

Control Balance: Toward a General Theory of Deviance,
Charles R. Tittle

Alternatives to Imprisonment: Intentions and Reality,
Ulla V. Bondeson

Inequality, Crime, and Social Control,
edited by George S. Bridges and Martha A. Myers

Rape and Society: Readings on the Problem of Sexual Assault,
edited by Patricia Searles and Ronald J. Berger

FORTHCOMING

Great Pretenders: Pursuits and Careers
of Persistent Thieves, *Neal Shover*

Poverty, Ethnicity, and Violent Crime,
James F. Short

Crime, Justice, and Public Opinion,
Julian Roberts and Loretta Stalans

Crime, Justice, and Revolution
in Eastern Europe, *Joachim J. Savelsberg*

Youth and Social Justice: Toward the Twenty-First Century,
Nanette J. Davis and Suzanne E. Hatty

The White Collar Offender,
Michael Benson and Francis T. Cullen

Crime and Public Policy

Putting Theory to Work

EDITED BY

Hugh D. Barlow

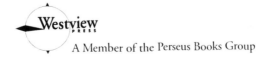
Westview
PRESS
A Member of the Perseus Books Group

Crime & Society

Copyright © 1995 by Westview Press, A Member of the Perseus Books Group

Published in 1995 in the United States of America by Westview Press, Inc., 5500 Central Avenue, Boulder, Colorado 80301-2877, and in the United Kingdom by Westview Press, 12 Hid's Copse Road, Cumnor Hill, Oxford OX2 9JJ

Library of Congress Cataloging-in-Publication Data
Crime and public policy : putting theory to work / edited by Hugh
  Barlow.
     p.   cm. — (Crime & society)
  Includes bibliographical references.
  ISBN 0-8133-2677-X — 0-8133-2678-8 (pbk.)
  1. Criminology—Philosophy.   2. Criminology—Methodology.
3. Crime—Government policy.   I. Barlow, Hugh D.   II. Series: Crime
& Society (Boulder, Colo.)
HV6035.C73   1995
364—dc20   95-37841
                                                                              CIP

The paper used in this publication meets the requirements of the American National Standard for Permanence of Paper for Printed Library Materials Z39.48-1984.

10   9   8

PERSEUS
POD
ON DEMAND

Crime and Public Policy

Contents

Foreword

The publication of *Crime and Public Policy: Putting Theory to Work* could not be more timely. The issues of crime, crime control, and criminal justice have recently dominated debates in the public arena. Media reports of drive-by shootings and carjackings around the nation fuel this debate. Moreover, the media coverage of a series of attacks against foreign white tourists in Florida by inner-city blacks increased the awareness of the random nature of violence. Although most murders and other violent crimes involve intimates, the sense that such crimes are being committed without provocation against strangers heightens anxiety and fear among the general public and the need to take action.

However, current public debates on what causes and how to control criminal activity have not been productive because they seek to assign blame rather than recognize and deal with the complex changing realities that produce criminal activity. As witnessed in the recent discussion of the national Crime Control Bill, the public framing of social outcomes involving criminal activity has profound implications for the proposals advanced by members of society to address them.

For all these reasons, there is increasing pressure on social scientists to enter the policy arena and use their informed opinions to improve our understanding of the crime problem and how to alleviate it. Yet, many social scientists continue to argue that we ought to wait until sufficient amounts of good data are accumulated before making any policy recommendations or entering the policy debate. If social scientists wait for more data before entering the policy arena, or if they avoid issues of public controversy because of lack of data even though their theoretical ideas or hypothesis would elevate the level of the debate and broaden perspectives, decisions will be made and policies will be formulated anyway—without their input.

In reading this excellent volume I am reminded that the contributions of social scientists to the policy arena need not be based solely on empirical studies or research findings. Their theories, ideas, and concepts may also help to shape the public perception of the nature of crime and how to address it.

As Carol Weiss (1993:39) has appropriately pointed out: "Although good data are useful and build credibility, equally important is the *sociological perspective* on entities, processes, and events. Participants in the policy process can profit from an understanding of the forces and currents that shape events, and from the structures of meaning that sociologists derive from their theories and research."

An important function of social science is to use existing theories or theoretical frameworks to provide an understanding of social processes and structures. In other words, social scientists can provide "enlightenment." Because of a narrow vision of the social sciences' approach to public policy, we often overlook the fact that the public discourse on issues such as persistent poverty and criminal justice has changed because of thought-provoking ideas from the social sciences. Theories of class conflict and mobility have influenced government policies in education, social services, and community development. Concepts such as labeling and concentration effects have been incorporated in policy discussion concerning criminal justice, mental health, poverty, and education. Indeed, it would not be unreasonable to argue that the ideas of the social scientists have done more than their specific research findings to influence the thinking of policy makers about the nature of social problems and the measures to confront them. Through these ideas social scientists "bring fresh perspectives into the policy arena, new understandings of cause and effect; they challenge assumptions that have been taken for granted and give credibility to options that were viewed beyond the pale. They provide enlightenment" (Weiss, 1993:28). It would be extremely shortsighted therefore to overlook the use of such knowledge to inform public policy debates as we wait for the compilation of "adequate" data.

Social scientists are plagued with feelings of insecurity and are concerned about and try very hard to avoid criticism. Many of them are therefore reluctant to become participants in the public policy debate before they have "adequate" information, even though their views on the issues are far more sophisticated and comprehensive than those of even some of the most influential opinion leaders.

However, resistance to the practical application of social science knowledge must be overcome. A more aggressive and positive orientation toward public agenda research and scholarship in the social sciences has to emerge. This includes expanding the domain of policy-relevant scholarship so that we recognize the important role of sociological theories, concepts, and ideas in the formulation and discussion of public policy issues. This volume of original essays by Hugh D. Barlow and his colleagues is an important step in that direction.

William Julius Wilson
Lucy Flower University Professor
of Sociology and Public Policy
University of Chicago

References

Weiss, Carol. 1993. "The Interaction of the Sociological Agenda and Public Policy." In William Julius Wilson (ed.), *Sociology and the Public Agenda*. Newbury Park, CA: Sage.

Preface

The idea for this book grew out of experiences I have had with students in a graduate criminology course. In that course the students are required to read, among other things, three books: Jack Katz's *Seductions of Crime: Moral and Sensual Attractions in Doing Evil*; John Braithwaite's *Crime, Shame and Reintegration*; and Michael Gottfredson and Travis Hirschi's *A General Theory of Crime*. In the discussions of these works, students inevitably get around to wondering about the policy implications of the theories they have struggled to understand. After all, they point out, doesn't the value of criminological theory lie ultimately in its usefulness in helping society deal with the problem of crime? And since the three assigned works are broad in scope, purporting to explain a wide range of criminal offenses, surely their practical implications for crime prevention are broad as well?

I do the best I can to help the students answer these important questions, and some guidance comes from the authors themselves, especially Braithwaite. However, our discussions always leave me unsatisfied, a feeling I suspect the students share. This is not a good feeling, especially these days, when crime seems to be on everyone's lips and people are anxious for guidance in dealing with it. When I try to guide the students to other sources, including other theorists, it turns out they have few places to go. Criminology has a lot more to say about the causes of crime than it does about solutions. And so I have found myself retreating, defensively, in the face of this question: If criminologists think they can explain crime, shouldn't they be sharing that wisdom with policymakers?

The reticence among many prominent theorists to get involved in policy questions reinforces the idea that theory and policy are distinct parts of the criminological enterprise, with little to connect them. Worse, it reinforces the idea that policy-oriented work is somehow less respectable than doing "pure" theory or research. My students have a quite different view of the value of their studies, for their concern, and the focus of most classroom discussions, is clearly with the question "What works?"

The question is important at any time, no doubt, but it seems to have special relevance these days. Criminology has passed its century mark, and the world is nearing a new millenium, with crime in many countries as serious a problem as ever. In America, the election of a Democratic president and a Republican Congress has brought the ideological conflicts underlying policy to the forefront of debate on all issues, no more so than on crime. The 1994 Crime Bill is long on ideology but very short on science. Where, one might well ask, was criminology when the bill's provisions were being crafted?

Against this background, therefore, I decided to make a contribution to bringing public policy and criminological theory together. As I broached the project with colleagues I was delighted by the encouragement I received. I was not alone, it appeared, in seeing value in asking theorists to think about the policy implications of their own and others' work. More important, some of the field's most respected criminologists with very busy schedules and plenty of projects already in the works were willing to sign on as contributing authors.

The result is this anthology of original essays. The central question that I asked contributors to consider was this: Where does contemporary criminological theory lead open-minded policymakers who are seeking to construct effective strategies for dealing with crime? Further, I encouraged them to move beyond the limits of current praxis, to speculate about what *could be*. Almost everyone who originally signed on to the project was able to contribute a chapter, and I believe that the results show just how well the effort paid off. All the major criminological theories and perspectives are represented, and in many cases we hear from authors who originated or refined what are now regarded as core criminological ideas.

With this book I can better answer my students' questions. But the effort must not end here. As we move into the twenty-first century, criminology must continue to get the word out: Policies purporting to do something about the crime problem must be linked directly with the explanation of crime. If they are not, why would we expect them to work?

Hugh D. Barlow

Acknowledgments

A book such as this involves contributions from many people. Let me begin by acknowledging my students and colleagues in criminology, without whose encouragement the project would surely have died. And, of course, the twenty-two authors who contributed their wisdom and time and put up with the editor's occasional hounding. The support and encouragement of the editorial board and Dean Birkenkamp at Westview Press are gratefully acknowledged, as is the work of assistant editor Jill Rothenberg, who has managed the project with patience and dedication. It has been a pleasure to work with the production staff at Westview Press, and I am especially grateful for the copyediting skills of Sarah Tomasek.

At Southern Illinois University at Edwardsville, I am certain that my colleagues and various members of the staff have been sorely tempted to lock me out of the building at different times during this project. To the following members of the departmental and university staff, I owe a special debt of gratitude for their help and patience: Rhonda Harper, Karen York, Norma Jean Hartlieb, Annette Peters, Sharon Wickham, Gina Wilton, Theresa Wasylenko, and Dennis Hostetler. Amy Milgrim helped with my end of the production process, and I am grateful for her efforts. Finally, I wish to thank my family for their love, patience, and understanding: Alison, Melissa, Colin, Chelsea, Eric, Kelsey, and Karen.

H.D.B.

1

Introduction: Public Policy and the Explanation of Crime

Hugh D. Barlow

As the twentieth century draws to a close, crime seems to be on everyone's mind, and both the media and politicians are having a fieldday with it. As this is being written, Americans are witnessing the first blow-by-blow nationally televised criminal trial in history. Meanwhile, politicians of every stripe are grappling noisily with how to fix their versions of the "crime problem." Crime policy for the twenty-first century is thus in the making, and what better time for criminologists to weigh in with expert testimony on the causes of crime and some suggestions for policymakers.

This introductory chapter begins with a brief discussion of recent trends in crime and public policy and their relationship to trends in the penal process. I then turn to a discussion of the relationship between policy and theories of crime. The final section consists of some observations on recent developments in criminological theory and the promise they may hold for construction of a just and effective public policy on crime.

Recent Trends in Crime, Policy, and the Penal Process

Annual editions of the *Sourcebook of Criminal Justice Statistics* provide the following official data on trends in the U.S. criminal process since the early 1980s: The adult prison population has more than doubled, to over 1 million inmates in 1994, while the number of people in jails and juvenile detention facilities has increased by over 200,000; the proportion of prison sentences over five years in length has increased steadily in both state and federal courts; the number of death row prisoners has more than tripled, to over 3,000 by the beginning of 1995; the rate of executions has grown from around one every two months to more than two each month; the number of felony court convictions

1

has increased steadily; and on the street, arrests have been increasing too, especially for violent crimes and particularly among juveniles and minorities.

These increases are due partly to changes in the shape of crime itself but arguably more so to an increasingly conservative, hard-line public policy. Although U.S. crime policy has always leaned more to the conservative right than to the liberal left, it clearly drifted further right during the Reagan and Bush administrations, and there is little likelihood of any turnaround in the foreseeable future. Indeed, the federal Crime Bill of 1994 was soon faulted by Republican leaders in Congress for its "liberal social programs," a term often applied to community-based treatment and prevention programs. Even so, the bill earmarked over two-thirds of its $30 billion budget for law enforcement and the penal system: $13.3 billion for federal, state, and local policing and $8.3 billion for corrections, most of it to build new prisons.

In addition, new "get-tough" federal laws were included in the package: The death penalty is expanded to more than fifty offenses, including terrorism, large-scale drug trafficking, drive-by shootings, and carjackers who murder; penalties are increased for a wide variety of other offenses, particularly those committed by juveniles and those involving drugs or weapons; and life imprisonment is mandated for persons convicted of three violent felonies or drug offenses—the so-called Three Strikes and You're Out provision (*Crime Prevention News*, August 12, 1994, pp. 1-3). Many states have already passed similar legislation, including "Truth in Sentencing" laws that require felony offenders to spend at least 85 percent of their prison sentences behind bars.

As for changes in the shape of crime itself, there is little dispute that the following trends have had an impact on the criminal process: The average age of offenders has declined and victimization of juveniles and young adults has increased; firearms are turning up more and more in homicides committed by youth, and more schools across the nation are reporting more violent crime problems than ever before; violent crimes involving strangers, including homicides, are also on the increase—the FBI claimed in 1994 that most of the nation's homicide victims are now killed by strangers (Federal Bureau of Investigation, 1994; but see also Riedel, 1993). And then there is the urban gang problem. Although an accurate count of gangs and gang membership—let alone their criminal activities—is virtually impossible, a 1991 survey of law enforcement agencies by the Centers for Disease Control indicates that gang involvement is growing across the nation, and this growth is said to be closely connected with rising rates of violent crime among teenagers and young adults, especially minority males living in the inner city.

Against a backdrop of overall *declines* in criminal victimization since the early 1980s (Bureau of Justice Statistics, 1993), these changes have come to symbolize the real crime threat and have fueled hard-line rhetoric. Specifically, the "true" crime danger in the United States has come to be associated with the urban minority male and more generally, the underclass. The purported "dangerous classes" that drove late eighteenth and early nineteenth century legislators into a frenzy of police and penal reform have been reinvented.

Or at least their presence has been reaffirmed. For in truth, the long-standing criminal stereotype is that of the urban street hoodlum whose offenses are muggings, rapes, burglaries, armed robberies, assaults, and homicides. Linked to this stereotype is an old and feared idea: that such criminals will find organization and eventually rule city streets. No law-abiding citizen will be safe. Small wonder, then, that the gang-banging and drive-by shootings of today are given so much press. People are encouraged to view inner-city streets as the unsafe turf of violent criminals. The task of any good government will therefore be to contain this threat—to get criminals off the streets or at least keep them from venturing into "decent" neighborhoods, the suburbs, and places where law-abiding citizens work and play.

Of course, the picture is incomplete without some mention of illicit drugs and drug trafficking. As discovered with alcohol during Prohibition, the profits from illicit drug business are a major incentive for criminals to organize, and cities provide large, anonymous populations of potential users. Concentrated populations of disadvantaged and disaffected individuals with little to lose may well constitute the prime target of this illicit enterprise, but few people are immune from the temptations of pleasure, especially youth. When the temptations are also opportunities for groups to make important identity claims—as in the case of marijuana and LSD during the 1960s—the demand grows, and user populations expand far beyond the groups first involved.

I believe that *containment* goes a long way toward explaining the so-called war on drugs: Keep them out of our backyard. Now more than ever is this true because the rise of crack cocaine—an inexpensive, extremely pleasurable drug—has been concentrated in the innercity, especially among minorities. Trafficking in crack can now be added to the sins of cities, and enforcement efforts are concentrated at containing it. Lo and behold, here is one more reason to paint the underclass as the true crime threat. During the 1980s, the proportion of drug arrests grew from under 6 to almost 10 percent of all arrests, with minority arrests rising faster than those of whites. In fact, among juveniles, white arrest rates for drug offenses actually declined throughout the 1980s (Blumstein, 1993:5). Between 1986 and 1990, convictions for drug trafficking increased 120 percent in state courts and 41 percent in federal courts (Bureau of Justice Statistics, 1994).

The explosive growth in the nation's prison population is largely due to the crackdown on drug offenses witnessed during the 1980s (Blumstein, 1993:5-6; see also Irwin and Austin, 1994). For example, Joyce (1992) shows that increases in Illinois crime account for only 9 percent of the recent growth in that state's prison population, demographic shifts for another 20 percent. However, a toughening of drug enforcement beginning in 1984 resulted in a 742 percent increase in the number of drug offenders sent to prison (from 518 to

4,361). She predicts that the prison population in Illinois will grow from 28,000 in 1992 to 45,900 in the year 2000 under current penal policy. The state will need to build twenty-three new prisons to keep up. The picture is not vastly different in Florida, New York, and other states (Blumstein, 1993).

Public Policy and the Causes of Crime

This brief review of current crime policy and its effects on the processing of street criminals hardly exhausts the subject, but space precludes a more complete analysis. The issue of drug policy, however, provides a convenient bridge to the central concern of this book, namely, the relationship between public policy and theories about crime.

In his presidential address to the American Society of Criminology, Alfred Blumstein (1993) observed that the so-called war on drugs was destined to fail inasmuch as it targets drug trafficking from the supply side and stresses severe penal sanctions. This is because none of the three major ways in which punishment is thought to prevent crime will work in this context: *Incapacitation* does not work because putting a drug pusher in prison "removes crimes from the street only if the crimes leave the street with the offender" (Blumstein, 1993:7). Besides, as everyone knows, drug trafficking in prison is widespread. *General deterrence* does not work because a strong market for drugs persists even when increasing numbers of traffickers are severely punished. This market coupled with the potentially severe penalties actually creates a "protective tariff" for those willing to take the risk. Journalist Walter Lippmann (1931:65-66) referred to this tariff more than sixty years ago: "The high level of lawlessness is maintained by the fact that Americans desire to do so many things which they also desire to prohibit. ... [They] have made laws which act like a protective tariff—to encourage the business of the underworld. Their prohibitions have turned over to the underworld the services from which it profits. ..." Finally, *rehabilitation* won't succeed, at least for drug pushers, because "there is nothing inherently irrational about their behavior, especially if they view themselves as having little economic potential in the legitimate economy" (Blumstein, 1993:8). Why change, drug pushers may well ask, when dealing is arguably the most promising strategy for economic survival in a world lacking any decent prospects?

One does not have to agree with Blumstein's analysis to appreciate the underlying point. To have hope of being effective, crime policy must be guided first by theory and research rather than by ideology. This is a tall order in almost any realm of government activity—even more so, one suspects, in a democracy—but especially when the topic is viewed with fear and apprehension and strikes at core values. Inciardi (in Trebach and Inciardi, 1993) is probably right when he claims that the American people want the war on drugs to continue, but that doesn't make it work. Indeed, it has been written that "ideology is the permanent hidden agenda of criminal justice" (Miller, 1973:142), and there is certainly no evidence that this characterization is now incorrect.

But this does not mean that criminal justice policy is unconnected with theories about why there are criminals or why crimes occur as they do. As a matter of fact, Miller (1973) showed over twenty years ago that there is considerable consistency between how people explain crime and what they propose should be done about it. Consider the following statements that Miller identified as "Right 3" or mainstream conservative (and for a similar but more contemporary statement of the classic conservative viewpoint, see Messner and Rosenfeld, 1994:94):

> *On the Causes of Crime and the Locus of Responsibility for It*: The root cause of crime is a massive erosion of the fundamental values which traditionally have served to deter criminality, and a concomitant flouting of the established authority which has traditionally served to constrain it. The most extreme manifestations of this phenomenon are found among...the young, minorities, and the poor. ...A major role in the alarming increase in crime and violence is played by certain elitist groups of left-oriented media writers, educators, jurists, lawyers and others who contribute directly to criminality by publicizing, disseminating, and support- ing these crime-engendering values.

> *On the Proper Operating Policies of Criminal Justice Agencies*: Law enforcement agencies must be provided all the resources necessary to deal promptly and decisively with crime and violence. ...The right of the police to stringently and effectively enforce the law must be protected from misguided legalistic interfer- ence. ...The scope of the criminal law must be expanded rather than reduced; the welfare of all law-abiding people and the moral basis of society itself are victim- ized by crimes such as pornography, prostitution, homosexuality, and drug use, and offenders must be vigorously pursued, prosecuted, and penalized. Attempts to prevent crime by pouring massive amounts of tax dollars into slum communi- ties are worse than useless, since such people absorb limitless welfare "benefits" with no appreciable effect on their criminal propensities. (Miller, 1973:156-157)

Although more moderate (and more extreme) conservative views can be found, the core of the conservative attack on criminality takes the shape of reasserting "traditional" values—those of family, religion, work, and obedience to authority—through a combination of moral exhortation and social isolation. "Just Say No" campaigns are one part of the exhortation package; reestablishing school prayer is another. Although clearly more moralistic and intolerant in their stance than moderate conservatives, the Religious Right has brought exhortation to a fine art, and claims many converts among the masses (for an insider's personal view, see White, 1994). In a marginally different but more humorous way, conservative commentators such as Rush Limbaugh pursue essentially the same strategy, also very successfully when measured by audience share.

The social isolation element in the conservative attack takes two forms: (1) an emphasis on the distinction between law-abiding, hard-working, tax-paying citizens on the one hand and the dangerous classes ("liberals," common criminals, welfare frauds, homosexuals, pornographers, and drug traffickers) on the other, and (2) attempts to identify and incapacitate as many of the latter as possible. In short, the purported causes of crime—immorality, low self-control, rejection of authority—mandate a counterattack that concentrates on controlling "dangerous" individuals, establishing and maintaining order, and enforcing moral rectitude.

The control and order-maintenance parts of this conservative counterattack complement the process of rationalization in law enforcement and the penal process that grew out of the authoritative reports of Lyndon Johnson's President's Commission on Law Enforcement and the Administration of Justice in the late 1960s. A managerial perspective emerged in which criminal justice was visualized as a system of agencies performing distinct but interrelated tasks whose measure of success was the coordinated and cost-effective identification and management of groups of offenders posing varying degrees of risk or danger. A "new penology" has been taking shape, argue Feeley and Simon (1992), that focuses on the management of unruly groups at minimum cost. Maximum-security prison lies at the hard end, for offenders classified as high-risk dangerous, but a growing list of low-cost "intermediate sanctions" are now available for offenders at midrange levels of risk, for whom traditional, often poorly supervised probation is deemed inappropriate: Boot camps, home confinement, secure drug treatment centers, and "intensive" probation are the most popular (see Parent, 1989; Gowdy, n.d.). Such programs permit much more surveillance and control than probation, but they are cheaper and more flexible than prison—and therein lies their value (Feeley and Simon, 1992:465).

Whether they have any crime-prevention value is another matter. For example, recent evaluations of boot camp programs show very mixed results. A study in Louisiana found that most boot camp inmates seemed to have responded positively to the experience when measured by their attitudes toward themselves and the program; however, the impact of the experience on recidivism was unclear, and the military atmosphere of hard labor and strict discipline presented opportunities for both accidents and staff abuse of inmates (MacKenzie, Shaw, and Gowdy, 1993; also MacKenzie and Souryal, 1994). Considering, furthermore, the decline in employment opportunities for the urban poor—the population from whom most boot camp inmates are likely to be drawn—and Feeley and Simon (1992:464) rightly question the applicability of military-style industrial discipline:

Even if the typical 90-day regime of training envisioned by proponents of boot camps is effective in reorienting its subjects, at best it can only produce soldiers without a company to join. Indeed, the grim vision of the effect of boot camp is that it will be effective for those who subsequently put their lessons of discipline and organization to use in street gangs and drug distribution networks.

Ironically, even as the conservative shift of the 1980s put's more offenders behind bars, the new penology described by Feeley and Simon lost interest in "correcting" offenders through rehabilitation and reintegration. Risk management and systems theory have replaced the long-standing criminological interest in assessing the causes of crime and designing the appropriate correctional response. Indeed, the pessimistic account of the urban underclass and its future developed by Wilson (1987) and documented in the street by recent ethnographies (e.g., Anderson, 1990) may seem to reinforce the new penology: The structural barriers and subcultural conditioning faced by the poor urban minority male suggest an intractable problem. Under these circumstances, the correctional system is encouraged to do little more than serve a "waste management function" (Feeley and Simon, 1992:469; see also Hudson, 1994). Whatever the causes of crime, the criminal justice system now has neither the time nor inclination to address them.

Bringing Criminology Back In

It can be argued that the penal end of the criminal process is not the place to begin crime prevention in any case. Perhaps not, but as Braithwaite (1989) and many others before him have shown, punishment cannot be divorced from crime itself. *How*, as well as *who*, we punish contributes to the shape of crime, and no adequate theory of one can exclude the other. That is why somewhere in all explanations of crime we find ideas about punishment, even if these are not always clearly expressed.

The problem with current crime policy is that a void exists where we should find instead the heart of the criminological enterprise—the explanation of crime. To place the onus differently, I believe that criminologists rarely contemplate the policy implications of our theories and when we do they are stated poorly and without confidence. Open-minded policymakers simply have little to guide them and have nothing with which to challenge vociferous colleagues with axes to grind. If the new penology is abandoning traditional criminology's interest in the etiology of criminality, it is to some extent our own fault. Unfortunately, as we have seen, an already marginal subpopulation of Americans once again comes out with the short end of the stick.

This is all the more unsettling because the past decade or so has been a particularly energetic period for criminological theory. For example, on a conceptual level we have the now-taken-for-granted distinction between *crime* and *criminality*. This distinction acknowledges that the propensity to commit crime (criminality—sometimes thought of as tendency or motivation) is only one element in crime, a second being the act or event itself (crime). People differ in their propensity to commit crime, but the likelihood of a particular crime occurring can vary independently of propensity. Put simply, if we find that criminality is greater in one person or group than in another, it does not necessarily mean that the former commit more crimes during a certain period, let alone more of a certain type of crime. Conditions relating to opportunity, guardianship, and skill can all influence the occurrence of a criminal event. There are therefore two distinct parts to the explanation of variations in crime rates: one accounting for variations in propensity, the other explaining variations in the occurrence of criminal events. This distinction was an important advance in criminological thinking and is incorporated in so-called rationality/opportunity theories of crime (e.g., Cohen and Felson, 1979; Clarke and Mayhew, 1980; Cornish and Clarke, 1986; Felson, 1994) as well as in the general theory of crime proposed recently by Gottfredson and Hirschi (1990).

If nothing else, the distinction between crime and criminality points to the inherent limitations of putting all our prevention eggs in either basket. Prevention strategies that target criminal events but ignore the conditions and structures that give rise to criminality and encourage its persistence may succeed in preventing some criminal events from taking place (a good thing) but will leave a criminally inclined population untouched. Or worse: It will leave them more frustrated, more angry, more innovative, more susceptible to criminal invitations and pressures, and even less hopeful about their futures. However, strategies that seek to reduce criminality but ignore the criminal event may produce long-term reductions in the prevalence of crime (a good thing), but their impact will not be nearly immediate and they will leave untouched the criminogenic influence of criminal events themselves. The clear policy implication is this: Crime prevention strategies of both sorts are needed, and when these are developed the task will be to figure out the balance.

Another major advance in contemporary criminological theory is represented by the so-called integrated theories of crime. Integrated theories take existing explanations of crime that were once viewed as distinct or even as competing theories and unite them into one theory. For example, theories that explain crime (or, more correctly, criminality) in terms of social structural factors have traditionally been kept distinct from those that explain criminality in terms of social process. Structural theories focus on the relationship of social organization and culture to the distribution of resources and opportunities and how these affect propensities to commit crime; social process theories, in contrast, consider how the interactions and experiences of individuals and groups influence how people behave and who they become. Thus, theories of criminality that focus on social disorganization, economic inequality, or blocked opportunities are examples of social structural theory; theories that focus on peer group associations, labeling, or social learning are examples of social process theories.

In reality, structure and process are connected: One way to think of that connection is to visualize structure as setting the stage for process, which in turn brings structure to life. Structure promotes, channels, and restrains criminal tendencies whereas process influences which individuals will become criminally active. Two questions are therefore relevant when considering why criminality varies from group to group: (1) How do the social structures to which they are exposed differ? and (2) How do their social interactions and experiences differ? By answering both these questions Laub and Sampson (1988) were able to develop an integrated model of delinquency in their reanalysis of data on 500 officially defined delinquents and 500 nondelinquents originally collected by Sheldon and Eleanor Glueck (1950). The model successfully explained differing rates of delinquency by showing how background structural factors such as economic dependency and irregular employment impact delinquency through their effect on the quality of parent-child relationships within the family.

Other integrated perspectives have incorporated more complex combinations of theories. Braithwaite's (1989) theory of reintegrative shaming comes to mind. This theory not only moves back and forth across the analytical line separating individual-level and aggregate-level explanation, but it also incorporates elements of five different sociological perspectives on criminal behavior: control theory, labeling theory, subcultural theory, opportunity (strain) theory, and social learning theory. Braithwaite (1989:107) actually claims only one element of originality for his theory—the notion that crime rates of individuals and groups are influenced directly by processes of shaming. Likewise, in their evolutionary-ecological theory of crime, Cohen and Machalek (1988) have integrated apparently disparate theories—in this case from biology, psychology, and sociology—and added one essential new element, the idea that crime is shaped by the alternative behavioral strategies that individuals adopt as they try to meet their needs under variable conditions.

These two theories, as well as that of Gottfredson and Hirschi (1990), also represent a third development that has taken place in criminological theory in the past decade: the rediscovery of general theory. General theories explain a broad range of facts and are not restricted to any one time or place. This does not mean that a general theory has to explain *all* crime, but the more exceptions allowed, the more limited the scope.

There are plenty of reasons to be pessimistic about the successful construction of an overarching general theory of crime. Quite apart from the many dimensions of crime and criminality, there is also considerable variation in the consequences that follow for offenders and victims and in the process of criminalization itself, from the declaration that certain activities are crimes all the way to the imposition of penalties. A general theory that explains all these variations would be impressive indeed, and even more so if it could explain variations at both individual and aggregate levels. The things that account for differences among individuals may not account for differences among neighborhoods or communities and vice versa. To use an example from Braithwaite (1989:104), "[T]here is some evidence...that while unemployment is a strong predictor of individual criminality, societies with high unemployment rates do not have high crime rates."

Another reason such an all-encompassing theory would be impressive relates to the conceptualization of crime as an event. In this conceptualization, crime occurs when opportunities and motivated offenders come together in the absence of capable guardians (Cohen and Felson, 1979). Another way to visualize crime as an event is in the form of a situated transaction that is constructed through the acts and reactions of participants as they occur *in situ*. Katz (1988) makes a distinction between "background" and "foreground" factors in crime, and this is relevant here. Background factors are the traditional focus of positivistic criminology: the biology underlying criminal behavior, the psychological determinants, the socioeconomic and cultural forces that push or pull people into criminal activity. Foreground factors have to do with the quality of the "lived experience" that is crime—in Katz's terms, the compulsions and seductions of crime felt by individuals as they live and breathe. From this vantage point, a general theory of crime would have to explain variations in the situational matrix that gives rise to criminal events. Furthermore, could a general theory of crime that accommodates background factors also explain the lived experience of crime?

The construction of an all-encompassing general theory of crime may well be an impossibility but a number of criminologists have recently published theories purporting to have wide scope. Theories developed by Wilson and Herrnstein (1985), Cohen and Machalek (1988), Katz (1988), Braithwaite (1989), Gottfredson and Hirschi (1990), and Sampson and Laub (1993) surely qualify. As one might imagine, none of these theories has escaped criticism, but in all the discussion little attention has been given to their policy implications.

All this theoretical activity, and the research that it has stimulated, provide an important opportunity for criminologists to take stock of the field's policy implications. And that is the purpose of this book. I do not limit the discussion only to these recent developments, but they certainly underscore the timeliness of the project. So, too, do recent events on the political front. As legislators in state houses and in the U.S. Congress grapple with the problem of crime, what can criminology offer them after more than a century of developing theories and conducting research on crime?

An objection might be heard that some of the new integrated and general theories of crime have not been adequately tested and therefore have no policy relevance. Designing policy around an untested theory could well be more damaging than having no theory at all. The easy answer is that any useful policy will include a substantial commitment to scientific exploration within its domain, including the testing and evaluation of new theory. Another answer is that a healthy field is a theoretically active field, where new ideas and new explanations build upon past thinking and research and encompass new facts relevant to the field. Policymakers benefit from that activity because it encourages discussion of alternative strategies and moves debate beyond existing practice. It invites policymakers to consider what *could* be done about crime and shows the grounding of those possibilities in a body of accumulated theory. To contemplate the policy implications of criminological theory is to think about its practical promise when people ask about hopeful strategies for dealing with crime.

What better place to start than with the theorists themselves, with those who create and interpret the ideas that drive the field? In the following chapters, prominent theorists write about their own and others' explanations of crime and criminality and contemplate the policy implications of the work they discuss. Some of the theories that are discussed have a long history, with many iterations; they will be recognized as the sociological pillars of criminological explanation: control theory, associational theory, conflict theory, subcultural theory, and strain theory. Others represent newly developed integrated theories, and some can rightly claim to be general theories of crime, though not all-encompassing.

Some of the chapters address crime policy in quite general terms whereas others focus on specific issues, for example, juvenile crime, violence, careers in crime, white-collar crime, and drugs. Often, when people think of crime, they have a particular version of it in mind. Domestic violence, perhaps, or gangs, or drugs, or consumer fraud. Or they have in mind a particular aspect of the crime scene that cuts across different types of criminal activity—minority involvement, perhaps, or the relationship between age, gender, or social class and crime. An entire book uniting criminological theory and public policy could be written on any one of these subjects. Each of these issues is addressed in this book, but not exclusively. My hope is that readers interested in a particular version or aspect of crime will find their appetite whetted by the essays that follow. I hope, furthermore, that the theories and related policy ideas that are discussed here will move all readers to new ways of thinking about the crime problem and its solution.

References

Anderson, Elijah. 1990. *Streetwise: Race, Class, and Change in an Urban Community*. Chicago: University of Chicago Press.

Blumstein, Alfred. 1993. "Making Rationality Relevant—The American Society of Criminology 1992 Presidential Address." *Criminology* 31:1-16.

Braithwaite, John. 1989. *Crime, Shame and Reintegration.* Cambridge: Cambridge University Press.

Bureau of Justice Statistics. 1993. *Highlights from Twenty Years of Surveying Crime Victims.* Washington, DC: U.S. Department of Justice.

———— 1994. *Felony Sentences in the United States, 1990.* Washington, DC: U.S. Department of Justice.

Clarke, Ronald V., and Patricia Mayhew, eds. 1980. *Designing Out Crime.* London: H.M.S.O.

Cohen, Lawrence E., and Marcus Felson. 1979. "Social Change and Crime Rate Trends: A Routine Activity Approach." *American Sociological Review* 44:588-608.

Cohen, Lawrence E., and Richard Machalek. 1988. "A General Theory of Expropriative Crime: An Evolutionary Ecological Approach," *American Journal of Sociology* 94: 465-501.

Cornish, Derek B., and Ronald V. Clarke. 1986. *The Reasoning Criminal: Rational Choice Perspectives on Offending.* New York: Springer-Verlag.

Federal Bureau of Investigation. 1994. *Crime in the United States, 1993.* Washington, DC: U.S. Department of Justice.

Feeley, Malcolm M., and Jonathan Simon. 1992. "The New Penology: Notes on the Emerging Strategy of Corrections and Its Implications." *Criminology* 30:449-474.

Felson, Marcus. 1994. *Crime and Everyday Life.* Thousand Oaks, CA: Pine Forge.

Glueck, Sheldon, and Eleanor Glueck. 1950. *Unraveling Juvenile Delinquency.* New York: Commonwealth Fund.

Gottfredson, Michael R., and Travis Hirschi. 1990. A General Theory of Crime. Stanford: Stanford University Press.

Gowdy, Voncile B. n.d. "Intermediate Sanctions." *NIJ Research in Brief:* 1-10.

Hudson, Barbara A. (1994). *Penal Policy and Social Justice.* Toronto: University of Toronto Press.

Irwin, John, and James Austin. 1994. *It's About Time: America's Imprisonment Binge.* Belmont, CA: Wadsworth.

Joyce, Nola M. 1992. "A View of the Future: The Effect of Policy on Prison Population Growth." *Crime and Delinquency* 38:357-368.

Katz, Jack. 1988. *Seductions of Crime: Moral and Sensual Attractions in Doing Evil.* New York: Basic Books.

Laub, John H., and Robert J. Sampson. 1988. "Unraveling Families and Delinquency: A Reanalysis of the Gluecks' Data." *Criminology* 26:355-380.

Lippmann, Walter. 1931. "The Underworld as Servant." In Gus Tyler (ed.), *Organized Crime in America.* Ann Arbor: University of Michigan Press.

MacKenzie, Doris L., James W. Shaw, and Voncile B. Gowdy. 1993. "An Evaluation of Shock Incarceration in Louisiana." *NIJ Research in Brief* (June): 1-7.

MacKenzie, Doris L., and Claire Souryal. 1994. *Multisite Evaluation of Shock Incarceration.* Washington, DC: U.S. Department of Justice.

Messner, Steven F., and Richard Rosenfeld. 1994. *Crime and the American Dream.* Belmont, CA: Wadsworth.

Miller, Walter B. 1973. "Ideology and Criminal Justice Policy: Some Current Issues." *Journal of Criminal Law and Criminology* 64:141-162.

Parent, Dale G. 1989. *Shock Incarceration: An Overview of Existing Programs.* Washington, DC: U.S. Department of Justice.

Riedel, Marc. 1993. *Stranger Violence*. New York: Garland.

Sampson, Robert J., and John H. Laub. 1993. *Crime in the Making: Pathways and Turning Points Through Life*. Cambridge: Harvard University Press.

Trebach, Arnold S., and James A. Inciardi. 1993. *Legalize It? Debating American Drug Policy*. New York: American University Press.

White, Mel. 1994. *Stranger at the Gate*. New York: Simon and Schuster.

Wilson, James Q., and Richard J. Herrnstein. 1985. *Crime and Human Nature*. New York: Simon and Schuster.

Wilson, William Julius. 1987. *The Truly Disadvantaged: The Inner City, the Underclass, and Public Policy*. Chicago: University of Chicago Press.

2

Transformation Versus Revolutionism and Reformism: Policy Implications of Conflict Theory

Austin T. Turk

A not uncommon view is that conflict theory has no policy implications or at least that conflict theorists have been unable or unwilling to bring their theory to bear on policy issues. The main purpose of this chapter is to demonstrate that policy implications can indeed be drawn from conflict theory. But to understand the demonstration requires that we first understand why so little attention has been given to the policy implications of conflict theory, which in turn requires understanding what conflict theory is and is not.

"Policy Irrelevance" of Conflict Theory

Serious consideration of the policy implications of conflict theory has been hindered by (1) traditional criminology's preoccupation with individual deviant behavior, (2) the confusion of nonpartisan conflict analysis with radical revolutionism, and (3) conflict theorists' aversion to piecemeal reformism.

Traditional criminology assumes that the person is the problem, so the objective is to explain what is wrong with the person that makes him or her do bad things. This fits well the common assumption that interpersonal relations and individual behavior are somehow more "real" than social structure and organizational behavior. Moreover, it also satisfies the political preference for "safe" problem definitions, explanations, and solutions—that is, those that do not question the way in which society is organized.

Conflict theory challenges every assumption of traditional criminology. First, social structure is the real problem, because it is the "root cause" of individual behavior patterns. Second, the aim is to determine how particular features of

15

social structure generate particular kinds of behavior, including illegal behavior. Social structure is assumed to be just as real as individual bodies and behavior. It follows that conflict theory is politically "unsafe" because it defines the crime problem as a structural problem, something wrong with the way in which society is organized. Instead of doing something with or to individuals, the emphasis is shifted to the politically nettlesome effort to specify what structural changes are needed and how to make them.

Because of their common emphasis on social structure as the real problem, and their common denigration of reformism, conflict theory and radical revolutionism tend to look pretty much the same to those who share the assumptions of traditional criminology. And indeed conflict theory and revolutionary theory do sometimes lead to similar conclusions. The essential difference is how their conclusions are reached: Simply put, what is problematic in conflict theory is assumed in revolutionary theory.

Radical revolutionism assumes that the only policy truly worth considering is how to bring about the destruction of the current social order. Whether the essential character of that order is thought to be capitalism, racism, sexism, militarism, or some other basis of social inequality, the impossibility of improving or transforming it is taken for granted. Some reforms may be defined tactically as "progressive" because they presumably have the direct or indirect effects of empowering the oppressed, raising their political consciousness, demystifying the political-legal system, or otherwise setting the stage for revolution. In that conflict theory does leave open the possibility that drastic structural changes may be required, the politically fearful are understandably wary.

Conflict theorists have generally been averse to debating the merits of piecemeal reforms aimed at changing persons but not structures. They point to the dismal historical record of reformism's failures—to rehabilitate serious offenders, to lower recidivism, to prevent the emergence of successive cohorts of serious lawbreakers, to reduce crime rates, or to effect lasting improvements in the administration of justice. Thus, viewing reformism as a political charade doomed to repeat past failures, conflict theorists have mostly excluded themselves from the forums and politics of reformist policymaking. The unsurprising consequence is that conflict theory has been widely regarded as irrelevant because it is seen as having no "feasible" policy implications.

Ironically, revolutionists also find conflict theory irrelevant, even pernicious, because it questions not only the assumptions of reformism but also those of revolutionism. While asserting the causal priority of social structure, conflict theory does not assume that structural problems can be solved only by revolutionary destruction of structures. Further, conflict theory raises the possibility that structural problems can *never* be solved by revolutionary destruction.

Questioning both the validity of revolutionary theory and the efficacy of revolutionary praxis, conflict theorists also largely exclude themselves from analyses and debates among radical revolutionists.

The bottom line is that conflict theory is unlikely to have a significant impact on reformist policymaking or on the strategic thinking of revolutionists—though some of its propositions may be deemed tactically useful. This is not a pessimistic conclusion but rather a "finding" that substantiates the need to clarify further the nature and aims of conflict theory in crime and justice studies.

Basics of Conflict Theory

To begin, conflict theory makes a sharp distinction between *crime* and *criminalization.*[1] Crime is the behavior of lawbreakers. More specifically, it is behavior defined as intolerably harmful in the law of a particular time and place. Criminalization is the behavior of law enforcers that produces criminality, the status of *defined* lawbreakers who may be guilty or innocent of the crime presumed to have been committed.

Because conflict theory posits the fundamental causal importance of social structure, its aims in criminology are to identify and explain variations in (1) the volume and patterns of crime and (2) the volume and patterns of criminalization in order to explain the relationship between (1) and (2). *Crime rates* are viewed as estimates (based on such sources as police and other reports, victimization surveys, self reports, or field observations) of the number of antisocial or antiauthority *acts* occurring in specified populations. *Criminality rates*, the output of criminalization, are viewed as estimates of the number of *conflicts* between law enforcers and offenders (actual or presumed), drawn from such data as arrests, detentions, reported investigations, citizen complaints, and observed encounters. Conflict analysis begins with the observation that the relationship between crime and criminalization is one of reciprocal causation. A major implication is that policing decisions and practices are not merely responses to crime rates and patterns but are also among the sources of crime.

The important point is that the ultimate objective is not to explain crime or the behavior of enforcers such as the police, but instead to explain the relationship—and changes in it—between offenders and enforcers. To do this requires understanding the ways in which class, ethnic, gender, and other structural relations affect, and are reflected in, patterns of offender-enforcer interactions. The general line of explanation is that structured inequalities lead to social conflicts, which generate both crime and criminalization and shape their relationship.

Explaining the criminal acts or law enforcement acts of particular individuals is left to clinicians, officials, and others who try to sort out the idiosyncratic and so far indeterminate interactions of biological, psychological, and social processes resulting in individual acts. It is taken for granted that the evidence by now is overwhelming that efforts to account for individual acts have virtually no significance for understanding such structural phenomena as variations in crime rates or law enforcement policies, much less the processes of reciprocal causation linking them.

The main features of conflict theory (at least one version of it) having been summarized, the task of deriving policy implications can now be sensibly undertaken.

Policy Implications:
A Program for Structural Transformation

General Principles

Major themes in the preceding discussion lead to the conclusion that sensible policymaking begins in recognizing five general principles:

1. *Policymaking is a political process, not merely the application of technical knowledge.* Even the most astute criminologists typically view the political obstacles to effective policymaking as the residue of ignorance and superstition. For instance, after a highly informed and convincing critique of prevalent misconceptions about crime control, Leslie Wilkins concludes that political and "metaphysical" concerns should be excised from the administration of justice, which ought to be a matter of applying models based on "the most sophisticated forms of management, not on the rituals of priests" (Wilkins, 1991:169).

Against such technocratic views, conflict theory accepts the political nature of law as, among other things, an exercise in the stating and defending of moralities. Policymaking is necessarily partisan. The making and implementation of laws constitute answers to the questions of whose interests and values are to be given priority and how less favored groups are to be handled. "Law and order" will be most valued by the socially and materially advantaged, not so much by the disadvantaged. Instead of merely trying to defend the social order as "given," effective policymaking will seek to alter structural barriers so that the inevitable clashes associated with unequal life chances will involve as few people as possible and result in minimum casualties.

2. *The focus has to be on changing structures and relationships, not persons, if crime and criminalization are to be reduced.* Without denying the possibility of reforming or rehabilitating some individual offenders, or of deterring or at least incapacitating others, conflict theory recognizes that such "end-point" measures do nothing to prevent or reduce crime or to restrain the ever more costly criminalization process. Pouring enormous resources into policing and penal institutions, especially at the expense of "early intervention" preventive programs, amounts to trying to cap a flooding waterpipe without turning off the valve. Instead of trying to find ways to improve reactive individual-centered

programs, policy research from the conflict perspective is aimed at identifying the structural sources of crime and criminalization—which means also identifying the political obstacles to change.

3. *Policies must fit within a broad strategy of change; piecemeal reform efforts cannot succeed.* The story of criminal justice reformism is one of experience ignored, fragmented experimentation, and avoidance of strategic planning. First, for example, long after learning how hopeless the rehabilitation ideal becomes when prisons are massive and overcrowded warehouses, policymakers persist in building and filling more big prisons and traditional criminologists persist in trying to find ways to improve the chances of individuals being reformed in such places. Second, the vast bulk of reformist research and policy experiments have been small-scale and short-term, featuring mostly unconnected reinventions and replications such as "saturation" policing, determinate and indeterminate sentencing, "diversion" of juveniles, and inmate "treatments" of all sorts. And third, despite the many impressive commissions set up to address all facets of "the crime problem,"[2] no overall strategy has ever resulted—especially not one that goes beyond lamenting racism, poverty, and other "social factors."

Conflict theory picks up where reformism leaves off. Instead of lamenting the obvious—that racism, poverty, materialism, selfishness, and other "root causes" of crime and criminalization exist—the point is to learn precisely how the causal associations are produced and maintained by the organization of social life, so as to determine what needs changing and how to make it happen. The task is to develop a strategy for bringing about the structural transformations needed to eliminate or minimize the causal significance of "social factors."

4. *Strategies emphasizing field controls are more efficient and effective than are strategies emphasizing command controls.* Policymaking and traditional policy research have been dominated by the notion that crime is the business of the state and therefore something to be handled solely or primarily through the enactment and enforcement of criminal laws. Even though more and more legislators, judicial and police spokespersons, journalists, and criminologists *say* that the "formal" social control exemplified by policing cannot succeed without "public support," significant policy changes have not been forthcoming. Instead, vague calls for more "community policing" and voluntary citizen crime prevention efforts such as Neighborhood Watch are far outweighed by the escalation of resources devoted to warring against crime. (The current "three strikes" mania across the country from California to the nation's capital belies the ostensible renewed appreciation of the importance of alternatives to busting individual offenders.)

The emphasis on command controls instead of field controls,[3] is both ineffective, indeed counterproductive, and extremely costly. Instead of promoting the emergence and strengthening of communities, top-down command and coerce policies typically aggravate the conflicts that obstruct community development. Threats have decreasing impact on people, especially young people, who see little or no hope of having a meaningful, rewarding life. Moreover, over time experiences of threat and coercion in the absence of experiences of support and opportunity generate the dangerous alienation increasingly evident among the "truly disadvantaged" of society (Wilson, 1987). Conflict theory asserts that the emphasis must be reversed from command to field controls, which means not only minimal reliance on direct repression but, most important, maximal dependence on measures to change the materially and/or spiritually blighted environments[4] that spawn ever higher and increasingly expensive levels of crime and criminalization. Contrary to a common misconception, applying conflict theory does not mean a Machiavellian strategy of deception. The "field control" measures needed to change blighted environments are not those of indirect manipulation through the scattering of "crumbs and carrots" while keeping the "big stick" always ready but are instead those directly and openly aimed at changing the "field" itself—that is, transforming the economic, political, and cultural structures responsible for such environments.

5. *The overriding aim of policymaking is a more viable society, not a more docile one.* To the powerful and privileged, the way in which social life is structured is the way it should and must be for society to be possible. Though life is inevitably hard for some, people virtually always get what they deserve according to the worth of their contributions to the general good. "Right-thinking" people understand this, so they go about their business without expecting rewards inappropriate to their "station in life." Because they are the crucial determinants of society's survival, the superior knowledge and abilities of the leading classes obviously deserve greater rewards. Challenges to their claims of deserved advantage are typically viewed as the hypocritical rhetoric of selfish dissidents who merely wish to replace them or else as anarchic threats to the very foundations of social order. Such challenges and threats clearly have to be suppressed.

Although accepting hierarchy as a universal feature of organized social life, conflict theory rejects the assumption that any particular "class structure" is either essential or equitable. Because people do not necessarily get what they deserve—and certainly not always what they feel they deserve—conflicts and challenges to the claims and demands of those "in authority" are inevitable. Attempts to make society docile, to impose stability by repressing challenges and threats, are seen to be ultimately futile. Instead of trying to make people docile, the goal should and must be to achieve a more viable society—one in which people are increasingly able to survive and prosper without having to exploit or destroy one another.

To summarize, policymaking based on conflict theory (1) is partisan on behalf of minimizing human casualties, (2) presupposes research that identifies the structural sources of crime and criminalization and the political obstacles to changing those sources, (3) gives priority to the development and implementation of a strategy for bringing about the necessary structural transformations, (4) recognizes the greater efficiency and effectiveness of field controls over command controls, and (5) aims toward a more viable society rather than a more docile one. The final step in the application of these general principles is to offer specific policy proposals that constitute a program of structural transformation to reduce crime and criminalization in America.

Specific Proposals

Prerequisite to all else, there must be a massive campaign to educate the public (and our politicians). Unless significant political support for structural transformation can be mobilized, there will be none. The flaws and limitations of traditional and politically safe notions about crime must be exposed as often and as publically as possible—as in Elliott Currie's dissection of the influential James Q. Wilson's conservative pronouncements (compiled in Stenson and Cowell, 1991:33-61). The real, structural sources of crime and criminalization must be identified and the policy implications clearly and repeatedly stated. People must be told exactly what is wrong, what changes are proposed, and whose interests are at stake. Because no one criminologist can speak with authority on every issue, and because not everyone is comfortable or effective in the activist role, the strategic need is for an organization of resources and efforts. Therefore,

Measure 1: *Establish a privately funded Public Information Resource Center on Crime and Justice to organize the collection, production, and dissemination of evidence and arguments favoring structural transformation.* Invariably, at least some governmental officials try to censor or otherwise influence the production and dissemination of information and viewpoints with which they are uncomfortable, especially when preferred policies are likely to be challenged. Many researchers and activists distrust assurances of objectivity in funding agency appointments, appropriations, grant awarding procedures, reviewer selection, and other aspects of governmental support programs. In any case, the point is not that governmental support totally precludes objectivity, or should not be welcomed by researchers, but that the credibility and thus the impact of the proposed Resource Center are likely to be greater if it is known to be funded by private donations "no strings attached."

Recognizing that they will have to be "sold" politically, several immediate and obvious steps must be taken in order to lay the foundation for the long-term measures proposed below to bring about structural changes in American society. Despite the politicking of the National Rifle Association, the Drug Enforcement Agency, and myriad other propagandists, the bulk of the evidence is overwhelmingly supportive of the following long-overdue reforms.

Measure 2: *Establish an effective nationwide system of gun control.* Minimally, this means (1) every firearm is registered; (2) no adult is allowed to own, possess, carry, use, or transfer any firearm without being licensed and registered; (3) license and registration are permanently invalidated by a violent crime or severe mental illness; (4) no minor is allowed to touch any firearm except on private property, with the permission and under the personal supervision of the adult owner; (5) automatic weapons, large-capacity magazines, and any firearm capable of being converted to automatic operation are available only to serving military and police personnel; (6) illicit production, importation, and transfers are severely penalized. The risks of homicide and the medical costs of treating gunshot wounds are clearly associated with easy access to firearms, especially among the young. Real gun control is essential to reduce casualties and costs and to help responsible people to "take back their streets" and go about the business of community building.

Measure 3: *Abolish capital punishment.* One, heinous crimes are not deterred by the chance of execution. Two, it costs far too much to process capital cases. Three, mistakes cannot be remedied. Fourth, of the relatively few death-eligible cases actually processed all the way, the losers are virtually always poor and disproportionately nonwhite. Eliminating the death penalty will remove one of the major symbols of historic and continuing oppression and thus a major source of the intergroup distrust and antagonism that promote social conflicts and resistance to change.

Measure 4: *Incarcerate heinous violent offenders for an indefinite period, at least until they are well into or past middle age.* Recognizing that predictions of individual dangerousness by psychiatrists and other experts are notoriously unreliable, failure to incapacitate those guilty—at whatever age—of repeated or onetime heinous acts of violence not only risks future attacks but is also, and much more important, morally confusing and corrosive. Although socialization of most offenders is clearly feasible given real social and material support, it is by now obvious that the "never habilitated" are extremely unlikely to be "rehabilitated". *Really* taking "the truly violent" out of circulation will not only prevent further crimes of violence by them but also help to reduce the fear of crime that fuels the nonsensical politics of "get tougher" crime control. And it will help deglamorize the violent acts that too often make the actors "pop heroes" and role models.

Measure 5: *Stop building prisons.* Economically and politically, this country cannot keep pouring billions of dollars into imprisoning an ever larger proportion of its people. Instead of continuing this clearly ineffectual and counterproductive end-point reactive program, the emphasis must shift to early intervention aimed at preventing the onset of serious criminal behavior as well as inhibiting progression from nonviolent to violent crimes. The vast majority of incarcerated offenders do not and cannot benefit from their imprisonment, so they eventually come out no better and probably less able to stay out of trouble. Community-based correctional programs encouraging and assisting offenders are far less expensive and far more likely to help them change their behavior. In any case, curtailing the prison-building and prison-filling boom will be a major step toward eliminating the gross disparities in the chances and severity of punishment that exacerbate class and ethnic antagonisms in American society.

Measure 6: *Create paid part-time community service jobs for all young people, not just young offenders.* Idleness is indeed "the devil's workshop." Although many poor young people certainly do need jobs, the basic problem is classless: Unsupervised youth are given no responsibilities and are encouraged to expect instant gratification. Volunteer neighborhood cleanups and other such occasional opportunities are laudable but insufficient. Rewarding and routinizing neighborly behavior is far more likely to inhibit youthful violence and other predatory activity. Moreover, neighborly behavior—community service work— should be *required* of every able young person not otherwise responsibly and routinely involved in supervised activities such as school, job, or old-fashioned "chores" at home. The goal must be to eliminate the conflicts arising from the youth-world/adult-world split, by giving young people a significant role to play in their communities, involving them in ongoing activities that are understood by everyone to be important—therefore worth rewarding materially as well as symbolically.

Measure 7: *Decriminalize drug possession and use and return substance abuse to the domain of medicine instead of the criminal law.* License the production and sale of all drugs (including "designer drugs"), requiring—as at present for legal drugs—the effects and potential hazards to be determined and made publicly known ("Surgeon General's Warning"). For especially hazardous drugs, a medical prescription should be required where a medical use has been established. Where no medical use has been found, the same warnings as for any poison should be on the label, with the seller required to inform the buyer of the danger. De-escalate the "war" with traffickers by eliminating the "crime tariff" (Packer, 1968) that makes trafficking profitable, while at the same time lessening the penalties for trafficking from maximum prison terms (possibly even death under current federal law) to heavy fines plus alternatives to prison, including community service. Illicit production, importation, or transfer of untested drugs or drugs known to be hazardous should be severely penalized. By medicalizing the drug abuse problem, legalizing the entire drug market, and punishing illicit operations, we will go far toward eliminating a major arena and source of class, racial, and intergenerational conflict.

Measure 8: *Decriminalize all consensual sexual activities.* Whatever one thinks of the concept of "victimless" crimes, the attempt to legislate morals by making crimes of consensual acts has not only failed but also diverted attention and policing resources from real (or at least far greater) threats such as violence, environmental destruction, and large-scale fraud and corruption. Even when the goal is noble, as in the radical feminist campaign against pornography, to call for criminalization is to play into the hands of the same moral absolutists and politicians who have tried both to legislate morals and to keep women "in their proper place." Education, persuasion, and tolerance—not repression—will erode sexism but will not necessarily reduce the market for pornography excepting, hopefully, its most brutal sexist forms. Attempts to impose particularistic moral norms sharpen class and other social divisions, making the reduction of structured inequalities harder to accomplish.

Measure 9: *Decriminalize all forms of recreational gambling.* The notion that gambling is or ought to be controlled by making it a crime is ludicrous: Governments compete for lottery dollars; casinos and racetracks are flourishing; churches, schools, and clubs raise funds through drawings and games; office betting pools are a tradition; and sweepstakes contest forms cram millions of mailboxes. Again, criminalization driven by moral absolutism and politics has proven to be ineffectual as well as pernicious in its impact. Class and ethnic conflicts are exacerbated by the inevitable discrimination resulting when the criminal law is used to distinguish between "good" and "bad" gambling.

Measure 10: *Declare a moratorium on all mandatory sentencing, "three strikes" laws, promoting of misdemeanors to felonies, and other indefensible legislative intrusions into the prosecutorial and judicial process.* In addition to ending the political assault on the courts' independence in interpreting laws, the moratorium will help to overcome the understandable distrust of those who have collectively experienced legalized discrimination and oppression. Insofar as the politics of crime legislation has meant a competition to look "tougher on crime," it is a major obstacle to implementing the structural changes necessary to reduce crime and criminalization. Attempts to "war" on crime have increased class and racial antagonisms, and made it ever more difficult to preserve or create the "community of concern" (Braithwaite's felicitous term, 1989:85) on which effective crime prevention strategies depend.

Measure 11: *Establish and prioritize community policing as an integral element in community-development programs.* The militaristic model of "professional" policing has proven to be one of the key sources of conflict in American society. Uniquely empowered to use deadly force to defend society's internal order, our police have too often and too long been encouraged to understand their job to be that of defending only the privileged in society. Consequently, instead of reinforcing social bonds law enforcement has more often further weakened those bonds. Unless the police role is not merely rhetorically but also institutionally redefined, policing will continue to be more a part—a key part—of "the crime problem" than of its solution. As Goldstein (1990), along with many others, has cogently argued, the most promising approach clearly is to restructure routine policing to make it "problem-oriented"—a helping resource for everyone, not only when citizens are threatened by street criminals but also when they are threatened by predators who live by economic and political exploitation. Moreover, community policing contributes to the strengthening of social bonds by supporting citizen-based efforts to prevent the physical and aesthetic decay that often signals the social decay of neighborhoods (cf. Skogan, 1990).[5]

These measures should be implemented without delay; in addition, long-term mechanisms are needed to institutionalize the process of structural transformation. Basically, this means setting up on-going agencies to initiate and monitor the social changes prerequisite to the prevention and reduction of crime.

Agency 1. A *National Governmental Oversight Commission*—organized at every level (federal, state, county, metropolitan, local) to ensure that citizens' complaints receive prompt and fair responses from all governmental agencies.

Agency 2. A *National Family Support Commission* to develop and promote programs at every level to ensure that everyone's basic health and economic needs are met regardless of circumstances.

Agency 3. A *National Education Commission* to establish and promote standards of educational excellence, including the ethics of civility and tolerance as well as academic skills, and to promote universal (cost-free) access to educational opportunities.

Agency 4. A *National Community Development Commission* to promote consultative and financial assistance to encourage and support local initiatives.

Agency 5. A *National Fair Taxation Commission* to promote the constitutional and other legal reforms needed to ensure progressive and eliminate regressive taxation. One of the primary goals of this agency would be to identify the kinds of financial speculation that drain needed capital from productive investment and to promote legal reforms to penalize and eliminate such speculation.

Agency 6. A *National Commission for Economic and Technological Development* to formulate and promote an "industrial strategy" that minimizes the human costs of social change. The priority would be legal reforms to require the planned *transition* of economic and technological innovations, with the explicit aim of minimizing the local, regional, and national costs of corporate policy and operational decisions. The long-range goal would be to ensure that profit- and power-oriented decisions do not threaten progress toward a more viable society by undermining and destroying families and communities.

Concluding Observations

The policy relevance of conflict theory has been questioned by conservatives because in rejecting reformism it implies too much. Radicals have questioned it because in rejecting revolutionism it implies too little. For conservatives and radicals alike, policy relevance is defined mainly by ideological assumptions and political preferences. In contrast, conflict theory assumes only that all assumptions are open to scrutiny and that political preferences are no substitute for hard evidence. Policy relevance is defined by the best available knowledge of what "the problem" is and of what does and does not "work" in dealing with it.

From the conflict perspective, the problem is not behavior but *relationships*. Against the traditional assumption that crime is the problem, as well as the radical assumption that criminalization is the problem, conflict theory says the immediate problem is the socially destructive linkage between crime (lawbreaking) and criminalization (law enforcement). That problem is, in turn, caused by the existence and persistence of social structures that pit classes and groups against one another instead of minimizing the conflicts among them.

Given the problem definition, it follows that structural changes are needed to eliminate or reduce the built-in inequalities that generate the class and other social conflicts producing the crime-and-justice problem. The extent and nature of the changes required depends on evidence, not ideology.

Whether the scale of needed change amounts to a massive transformation of society or something less, the evidence will not matter unless a determined effort is made to ensure that it cannot be ignored in the policymaking process. To this end, first, misinformation and misdirection have to be actively countered, not permitted to go unchallenged. Second, relevant evidence must be not only be accumulated but also be communicated as effectively as possible so as to influence policymaking—which means informing and supporting political figures willing to listen and learn. Perhaps the strongest implication of conflict theory is that progress will never be made without a fight—to eliminate despite resistance the structural barriers to including not just the privileged but all of us in what the renowned conflict theorist Ralf Dahrendorf (1985:98) calls "the edifice of citizenship."

Notes

1. From here on, "conflict theory" refers to the version formulated in my own work. See especially Turk, 1969, 1976, 1977, 1979, 1982a, 1982b, and 1984. Of course, the discussion below of policy implications has been informed by the relevant observations and findings of many other criminologists, irrespective of their theoretical orientations.

2. Authoritative reviews of the antecedents, findings, and impact of the landmark American Bar Foundation studies can be found in Ohlin and Remington (1993).

3. Feeley's (1976) distinction can be usefully extended to cover interventions at every level of social organization from local neighborhoods to societies and transsocietal structures. The important point is that control is sought primarily and indirectly through the manipulation of social environments. Instead of simply commanding people to be good, and threatening punishments if they are not, the emphasis shifts to making more "user friendly" the social environments in which they have to live.

4. Perhaps it needs emphasizing that conflict theory rejects "poverty determinism" and other materialistic explanations of why people commit crimes. Clearly people have nonmaterial as well as material needs, and their behavior will in many—probably most—instances be shaped more by their perceptions and values (or lack thereof) than

by their material circumstances. However, we must also keep in mind that nonmaterial needs are far less likely to be met when material needs are unsatisfied.

5. As conflict theory anticipates, local crime prevention efforts fail unless they are part of a broad program of community improvement (Rosenbaum, 1986) and community development programs fail unless they have external political and economic support (Bursik and Grasmick, 1993:157-180).

References

Braithwaite, John. 1989. *Crime, Shame and Reintegration.* Cambridge: Cambridge University Press.

Bursik, Robert J. and Harold G. Grasmick. 1993. *Neighborhoods and Crime: The Dimensions of Effective Community Control.* New York: Lexington Books.

Dahrendorf, Ralf. 1985. *Law and Order.* Boulder: Westview.

Feeley, Malcolm. 1976. "The Concept of Laws in Social Science: A Critique and Notes on an Expanded View." *Law and Society Review* 10:497-523.

Goldstein, Herman. 1990. *Problem-Oriented Policing.* New York: McGraw-Hill.

Ohlin, Lloyd E and Frank J. Remington, eds. 1993. *Discretion in Criminal Justice: The Tension Between Individualization and Uniformity.* Albany: State University of New York. Packer, Herbert L. 1968. *The Limits of the Criminal Sanction.* Stanford: Stanford University.

Rosenbaum, Dennis P., ed. 1986. *Community Crime Prevention: Does It Work?* Newbury Park, CA: Sage.

Skogan, Wesley G. 1990. *Disorder and Decline: Crime and the Spiral of Decay in American Neighborhoods.* New York: The Free Press.

Stenson, Kevin and David Cowell, ed. 1991. *The Politics of Crime Control.* Newbury Park: Sage.

Turk, Austin T. 1969. *Criminality and Legal Order.* Chicago: Rand McNally.

————. 1976. "Law as a Weapon in Social Conflict." *Social Problems* 23:276-291.

————. 1977. "Class, Conflict, and Criminalization." *Sociological Focus* 10:209-220.

————. 1979. "Analyzing Official Deviance: For Nonpartisan Conflict Analyses in Criminology." *Criminology* 16:459-476.

————. 1982a. *Political Criminality: The Defiance and Defense of Authority.* Newbury Park, CA: Sage.

————. 1982b. "Social Control and Social Conflict." In Jack P. Gibbs (ed.), *Social Control: Views From the Social Sciences.* Newbury Park: Sage.

————. 1984. "Criminology and Socio-Legal Studies." In Anthony N.Doob and Edward L. Greenspan, *Perspectives in Criminal Law.* Aurora, Ontario: Canada Law Book,Inc.

Wilkins, Leslie T. 1991. *Punishment, Crime and Market Forces.* Brookfield, VT: Dartmouth Publishing Co.

Wilson, William J. 1987. *The Truly Disadvantaged: The Inner City, the Underclass, and Public Policy.* Chicago: University of Chicago Press.

3

Rethinking Crime Theory and Policy: The New Sociology of Crime and Disrepute

John Hagan

Nearly two decades ago the political scientist James Q. Wilson (1975) turned his attention to *Thinking About Crime*. The book was a watershed in informed public discourse about crime policy and theory. Wilson noted that through three quarters of this century the great burden of theorizing and research about crime had been borne by sociologists who were intent on finding root causes of crime, which they most often located in conditions of social and economic disadvantage. Wilson argued that the evidence for this explanatory approach was mixed at best and that the policy implications of the conclusions that derived from this work were limited. He concluded that greater progress could be made if attention shifted from basic efforts focused on explaining crime and to efforts concentrated in a more applied fashion on ways of reducing or containing crime, for example, through a more selective use of imprisonment to deter and incapacitate criminal offenders.

The timing of Wilson's thinking about crime was significant. His thoughts came during the closing years of a post-war economic boom that had markedly enhanced the lives of Americans from many walks of life. Women were making new claims to nontraditional jobs and careers, minorities were exercising hard-won rights to housing, public services, and jobs, and perhaps most significant, young people from minority as well as majority group families were still confidently looking forward to improving upon the unprecedented postwar economic fortunes of their parents.

This paper was originally presented to the Alan Fortunoff Criminal Justice Colloquium at the Center for Research in Crime and Justice of the New York University School of Law, February 2, 1994.

Yet crime and violence persisted in the midst of this postwar American affluence and indeed began to increase in the 1960s. America already was uniquely violent among Western industrial nations, and the U.S. homicide rate nearly doubled between 1965 and 1975. The children of the post-war economic boom seemed more violent and criminal than any generation that living Americans could remember. This increase in crime and violence seemed to contradict the accepted sociological theories of crime that emphasized social and economic disadvantage as its root causes. The accompaniments of affluence seemed to be enervating instead of eliminating America's crime problems.

However, most of the rise in crime during this period probably resulted from the increased size of the postwar birth cohorts who were now in their teenage and young adult crime prone years. Yet this too was taken by Wilson as reason to question the relevance of sociological theories of crime and inequality, and he concluded that these theories were of doubtful utility for the formation of policies to reduce or even contain crime.

Of course, Wilson alone could not have changed American crime policy; nor could he have foreseen or much influenced the social and economic trends that surround crime and its punishment to this day. Nonetheless, his arguments were influential in policy circles and they were part of an era in which concerns about social inequality receded into the background of American politics. Interest in sociological theories of crime and inequality was replaced by renewed attention to political and economic formulations that emphasized the use of imprisonment to deter and incapacitate criminals who were assumed to be beyond any realistic hope of rehabilitation. The new consensus was that when it came to understanding the causes of crime and translating this understanding into rehabilitative treatment, "nothing worked" (Martinson, 1974).

In comparison with the failed rhetoric of rehabilitation, the new political economy of crime was seductive. It was so seductive that to this day it dominates the conventional wisdom of American electoral politics with its calls for increased investment in policing and prisons. Its lure continues to be the promise of near-term improvements if not solutions to the problems of crime. Grounded in assumptions of efficiency and choice, this policy imperative proposes that certain, swift, and severe punishments, including especially imprisonment but also the death penalty, can remove from the population those offenders who are most likely to reoffend while also dissuading prospective offenders who remain in the population from committing future anticipated crimes.

The logic of deterrence and incapacitation was applied with a sense of precision that led one economist of the 1970s, Isaac Ehrlich (1975), to estimate with time series data that each application of the death penalty in the United States could prospectively save the lives of eight potential victims of homicide. Similarly, in 1976 the National Academy of Sciences published a report which concluded that if prison use expanded there was a potential for a "two to fivefold decrease in crime." In an article in *The Public Interest,* Daniel Patrick Moynihan (1979) subsequently observed that this calculation was completely unrealistic.

Moynihan's skepticism was well justified, as the predicted declines in crime and violence proved an inaccurate guide to unfolding events. Although there were signs of stabilization and even decline in homicide rates over the next decade (from 1975 to 1985), in the mid-1980s, just as the full force of the American investment in imprisonment began to take full effect, homicide rates spiked upward again. More disconcerting still was the extent to which this upward trajectory was concentrated among nonwhite Americans, especially young African American males, the group most affected by the increased use of imprisonment and the accompanying economic slowdown. The upsurge in criminal violence in the face of an escalating severity of punishment clearly contradicted the optimistic expectations of the new political economy of crime.

It is useful to consider, against the background of these dashed expectations and with the advantages of hindsight, where the political economy of crime associated with Wilson's thoughts went wrong. I will argue that this new political economy of crime first failed as a result of ignoring social processes that surrounded the renewed resort to imprisonment as a policy priority. It is highly unlikely that those who advocated a renewed emphasis on punishment anticipated how receptive an audience they would find, or how extensive the American reliance on penal sanctions would become, and with what consequences in the most affected communities. I will suggest that in retrospect the inefficiencies of imprisonment can now easily be seen to outweigh the expected benefits, through processes that a social theory of punishment might well have anticipated.

Second, I will argue that the central failing of this approach most significantly involved its deflection of attention from the causal role of social inequality in the causation of crime. Wilson's *Thinking About Crime* was written at the end of an era of economic growth and declining economic inequality in America. It would have been difficult to imagine what the growth of this inequality would bring during the economic slowdown that followed. The passage of time now substitutes for this imagination, as I will describe in a brief discussion of policies and processes of what I will call capital disinvestment and subcultural recapitalization.

Third, I will argue that the new political economy of crime has accompanied an increasing reliance in America on ideologies and strategies of self-help in response to crime, most significantly but not only involving the acquisition of guns for self-protection. Guns not government, the new public thinking has seemed to suggest, must now help to protect Americans against crime. These ideologies and strategies, which put the burden of crime protection on the individual, are inefficient in ways not anticipated by those who otherwise encourage policies based on individual imperatives. These policies again neglect processes that social theories of crime should anticipate.

If my arguments are correct, they imply that the political economy of crime that emerged in the 1970s and that persists to this day contains its own inefficiencies that derive from a reluctance to acknowledge and develop a theoretical understanding of social processes associated with social inequality and the root causes of crime. A new sociology of crime and disrepute is renewing our attention to the importance of understanding these causes of crime.

The Political Economy of Prisons

The renewed interest in economic theories of punishment that emerged from the thinking of Wilson and others found a receptive audience among politicians seeking something to do in response to public concerns about crime. If patriotism is the last refuge of scoundrels, as Samuel Johnson suggested, then the politics of law and order cannot be far behind. At least since the difficulties of presidential candidate Michael Dukakis in answering a debate question about the preferred punishment for a person convicted of a hypothetical rape of his wife, the conventional political wisdom has been that only punitive responses to issues of crime can generate voter approval. In the 1992 presidential debates all three candidates, even the unconventional Ross Perot, could only agree that sterner measures were needed. President Clinton's "Three Strikes and You're Out" proposal is only the most recent in an unremitting politics of punishment. The result is a remarkable increase in the use of incarceration generally, and specifically for minority youths convicted of drug-related crime as much or more than violent crime. In a context of little apparent success in reducing reoffending or crime more generally, and in an era when contraction is expected of most public-sector activities and when most government agencies are expected to do more with less, prisons are an anomalous American growth industry.

It is difficult but nonetheless important to obtain some idea of how the use of imprisonment in the United States has grown and compares to that in other nations of the world. The per capita use of imprisonment in the United States has grown through most of the last century and a half, but it began to shoot upward in the 1970s, partially in response to the new political economy of crime and punishment.

Meanwhile, there is substantial variation in the current use of imprisonment in Western Europe. The United Kingdom hovers near the top of the list of West European countries, with rates of about 100 persons imprisoned per 100,000 population. Compare this to the way the former USSR and the United States stood out and changed in relative position over the decade from 1979 to 1989.

In 1979, the United States had an imprisonment rate that probably more than doubled any country in Western Europe, at 230 per 100,000, while the Soviet rate was 660 per 100,000 population. A decade later, in 1989, the Soviet rate is estimated to have dropped by nearly half to 353, while the U.S. rate increased to 426, about four times the highest West European figure (Christie, 1993). The U.S. figure was over 500 by 1991.

However, the most disconcerting comparisons are between the United States and South Africa, where in 1989 the imprisonment rate was 333 persons per 100,000 population. Not only is the U.S. rate higher, but it is more highly concentrated on blacks. The black rate of incarceration in the United States is well over 3,000 per 100,000 population, compared to about 681 in South Africa. In the decade following the publication of *Thinking About Crime*, the national rate of incarceration for African Americans was more than six times as high as the rate for white Americans (Chilton and Gavin, 1985). One might expect that this use of imprisonment was concentrated on violent offenders. Actually this incarceration was focused as much or more on drug-related crime as on violent crime. In 1991, more than half the inmates in federal prisons and more than a quarter of the inmates in state prisons were incarcerated on drug charges. A decade earlier less than 10 percent of prisoners were convicted of drug charges. In 1991, drug offenders represented nearly half of the new commitments to New York state prisons and about one-third of the overall state prison population (Blumstein, 1993).

How has our criminal justice system come to focus so extensively on drug crime? Malcolm Feeley and Jonathan Simon (1992) have argued that such trends are reflective of a new way of thinking about crime and punishment in America. This new focus is on subgroups or aggregations of individuals and their risks of crime, which are to be managed efficiently by means of selective incapacitation through imprisonment. This is the new political economy of crime, or what Feeley and Simon call the New Penology.

The key to this thoughtway is that target categories and subpopulations rather than individuals are singled out for penal attention. These target categories and subpopulations are sometimes identified technocratically as "high-rate offenders" or "career criminals" and at other times more substantively with terms such as the "underclass" or the "dangerous classes." In this way policies such as selective incapacitation can be directed at particular groups, including young African American drug offenders.

Often presumptive or prescriptive sentencing guidelines established along with or by federal and state sentencing councils and commissions have implemented policies that in effect target young black drug offenders as a high-risk population. These policies often require sentences for drug offenses that equal and surpass those for violent crimes, including homicide. A striking illustration is provided by a recent Minnesota Supreme Court ruling (cited in Blumstein, 1993:4n). This ruling declared unconstitutional a state statute that stipulated a presumptive sentence of four years for possession of three grams of crack cocaine. Elsewhere, possession of ten grams of powder cocaine was defined as warranting a presumptive sentence of only one year. These quantities of crack and powder cocaine are pharmacologically identical, but in 1988 all of those offenders sentenced in Minnesota under the crack cocaine statute were black, whereas two-thirds of those sentenced under the powder cocaine statute were white. Black defendants therefore received dramatically longer sentences under these presumptive provisions, and these were longer sentences than received by many or most violent offenders.

Even when sentencing guidelines and presumptive and prescriptive sentencing statutes are not so obviously slanted to treat minorities more severely, their cumulative effect is still to do so. That is, because so many young minority suspects are swept into the criminal justice system, even an increased punitiveness that is distributed to all convicted offenders who come before the court falls disproportionately on young minority males.

However, despite claims of efficiency, it cannot be said that this increased severity of punishment has reduced violent crime, even when it is imposed on violent offenders. A recent National Academy of Sciences report reveals that athough the time spent in prison by violent offenders nearly tripled in the United States between 1975 and 1989, violent crime did not decline. A social theory of crime and punishment can help to explain why this is the case.

Support for an increased use of imprisonment by advocates of the new political economy of crime seems largely to be based on an exaggerated optimism about the crime-reducing prospects of withdrawing a large proportion of very active offenders from the larger population. The logic is seductive. It reasons that if a large share of all recent crime is committed by a relatively small group of offenders, then removing a large share of these offenders from the population for a long time should substantially reduce crimes committed in the future.

A National Research Council panel on "Research on Criminal Careers" (Blumstein, Cohen, and Nagin, 1978) undertook an evaluation of research on such a policy and concluded that despite the concentration of much crime among some highly active offenders, it would not be possible to reduce crime significantly without very substantial increases in prison populations. This is because (1) the capacity to predict future careers in crime is limited (i.e., we are not able to predict very accurately who will continue in crime), (2) there is relatively little specialization by type of crime (i.e., offenders are more versatile than specialized), (3) most criminal careers are brief (i.e., offenders "age out" of crime quickly), and, most significant, (4) new offenders quickly replace those who are removed from the general population.

All of these factors are significant, but the last point involving replacement is especially telling with regard to the young minority drug offenders who are so often the current targets of imprisonment. Blumstein (1993:7) points out that imprisonment removes crimes from the street only if the targeted crimes leave the street with the imprisoned offender. He notes that this should happen, for example, with the pathological rapist. If, however, there continue to be buyers on the street, as there do in the underground economy of drugs, removing one drug dealer will simply mean that a substitute will move in to provide the service and meet the demand for the desired drugs. Recruitment and training may be required, but Padilla's (1992) work, discussed in more detail later, shows that there is a waiting stream of new recruits. Indeed, Anderson (1990:244) observes that "for many young men the drug economy is an employment agency. ... Young men who 'grew up' in the gang, but now are without clear opportunities, easily become involved; they fit themselves into its structure, manning its drug houses and selling drugs on street corners."

A social theory of the drug economy sees this as a clear instance of the operation of vacancy chains. In the more ordinary world of work, opportunity occurs in chains (White, 1970). For example, a retirement creates a vacancy to be filled by a new recruit. In turn, the new recruit creates a vacancy in his or her previous job, which pulls in a new person, and so on (Granovetter, 1992:250). In the illegal drug industry, imprisonment augments other sources of retirement (e.g., death, maturational reform) in expanding the vacancy chain. Each time a drug dealer or runner is taken off the streets through imprisonment, a vacancy is created in the hierarchy of this illicit industry. The higher the position in the industry, the longer the chain of vacancies. The chain of vacancies will end only if the job in which the vacancy appears is left unfilled. However, the previously discussed ethnographic studies indicate that this seldom happens because the demand for drugs is so persistent. In this context, government set rates of imprisonment can actually play a major role in the creation of vacancies and in the recruitment of new offenders.

Unfortunately, imprisonment of such offenders creates vacancies not only in the hierarchy of drug dealing, but also in the families from which prospective dealers and runners of drugs come. Current and prospective participants in the drug industry are often parents as well. Drug involvements impair parenting roles, and imprisonment can disrupt involvement in parenting altogether. Vacancy chains that end in imprisonment can create unfilled positions that lead all the way back to departures from family and parenting roles. One reflection of such vacancies is the scarcity of employed black males in distressed African American communities and families. In a study of over 150 U.S. cities, Sampson (1987) found that the scarcity of employed black males relative to black females was directly related to the prevalence of families headed by females in black communities and that black family disruption was in turn substantially related to rates of black murder and robbery, especially by juveniles (see also Messner and Sampson, 1991).

It is likely that vacancy chains stemming from imprisonment and leading through the hierarchy of the illegal drug industry are a source of continuing recruitment into this underground labor market, leaving the scale of this industry unaltered and actually increasing the numbers of young minority males in particular who are removed from potential legal employment and family roles. The result is increasing crime *and* punishment with intergenerational implications.

Thus far I have focused on the effects of imprisonment policy on crime, especially drug crime, in America. This, of course, begs the "root" question of why drug and related kinds of crime are so prominent in American life to begin with.

Community Disinvestment and Recapitalized Lives

The new political economy of crime that increased investment in American prisons, and increasingly took minority men out of their families and communities, is further associated, at least temporarily, with a process of capital disinvestment in America's most distressed minority communities. Of course, this is a kind of social and economic process that the new *Thinking About Crime* encouraged criminologists to ignore as unproductively involving unsubstantiated root causes of crime. Yet I will argue that just this process of disinvestment is vitally associated with a resurgence of crime and violence in distressed minority communities today.

The postwar economic boom that continued until about the time of Wilson's *Thinking About Crime* was a period that included some notable reductions in social and economic inequality in American life. However, the period that followed in the last quarter of this century has included, with peaks and troughs removed, a general slowdown that has about halved economic growth from the average of about 5 percent a year during the postwar boom. The economic slowdown that marks the last quarter of this century is characterized by increased unemployment and income inequality, led by the loss and only partial replacement of core-sector manufacturing jobs with less stable and poorer-paying service-sector jobs. Secure high-wage manufacturing jobs were lost permanently from the core sector of the American economy. In general, the poorest minority men and women in the United States lost most in this process, with actual declines in real incomes in the 1980s.

This economic slowdown was also a period in which policies of private businesses and government reallocated resources across the social and economic landscape of American life. For example, policies and processes of capital disinvestment increased the residential segregation that Douglas Massey calls "American Apartheid." This occurred with the help of private- and public-sector practices and policies. These including the "redlining" practices of banks and the "blockbusting" tactics of real estate agents. In addition, governments increased residential segregation through the location of freeway networks, .

public housing projects, and weakened enforcement of housing codes. Capital disinvestment policies also increased racial inequality through opposition in the courts to affirmative action laws and regulations and reductions in the real minimum wage.

The combined effects of deindustrialization, residential segregation, and increasing racial inequality were felt more generally in what William Julius Wilson (1987) calls a growing concentration of poverty in America. The cumulative effects of capital disinvestment and the concentration of poverty mean that individuals and families confront not only their own difficult situations but also the compounding effects of the situations that surround them. Individuals and groups who confront such situations are left in search of compensating means of recapitalizing their lives.

That is, processes of capital disinvestment are destructive of conventional forms of social and cultural life. They often produce subcultural adaptations, which are in effect forms of recapitalization, consisting of efforts to reorganize what resources are available, even if illicit, to reach attainable goals. This process of recapitalization often is linked to the development of and participation in what have been called deviant service industries and ethnic vice industries.

Throughout this century, and even as we approach its end, a great deal of law enforcement still is focused around the policing of deviance service centers (Clairmont, 1974) that are organized around ethnic vice industries (Light, 1977) and that disproportionately involve the urban and minority poor (Boritch and Hagan, 1987). This was true in the early part of this century, in areas like New Orlean's Basin Street, San Francisco's Barbary Coast, Denver's Market Street Line, and New York's Bowery and Five Points. And it remains true in relation to urban and ethnic vice industries concentrated in many of today's distressed minority neighborhoods.

The sociological concept of a deviance service center parallels in an ironic way the economic notion of a free enterprise zone, except for the very notable fact that a deviance service center is distinguished by its organization around illegal services and substances that form the base of vice industries. These centers are social locations in which activities otherwise defined as illegal (including prostitution, drugs, and alcohol) are allowed to develop and serve a clientele from within and outside the community. Such centers have existed throughout this century, but today they are concentrated in Hispanic and African American inner-city ghettos, the principal sites of the capital disinvestment I have described.

The process of recapitalization involved in the development of deviance service industries is partly indigenous to communities and partly a product of the actions of external authorities. The key to the development of these vice centers is that illegal markets emerge whenever desired substances and services—such as narcotic drugs, prostitution, and gambling—are made illegal.

Authorities with responsibility for the enforcement of such laws, whether they wish to or not, have the power to regulate the development and operation of these markets, and members of communities that are without adequate access and involvement in legal labor markets often pursue these illegal opportunities to accumulate criminal forms of social and cultural capital, that is, to develop criminal capital.

The linkage between deviance service industries and social mobility is given a historical grounding in the concept of ethnic succession, which refers to the fact that for lack of alternatives, first Irish, then Jews, later Italians, and most recently African and Hispanic Americans have sought to move upward in the American social structure through organized vice (Ianni, 1972, 1974). Earlier groups did this with some success, especially during the postwar boom. However, in the context of the economic slowdown that followed beginning in the mid-1970s, the loss of America's dominant place in the world economy, and the dire state of America's distressed minority communities, prospects for upward mobility through organized forms of urban vice are less promising and more hazardous.

Part of the hazard derives from the periodic crackdowns of law enforcement agencies on the operations of vice industries. These crackdowns probably reflect not only the ambivalence of public attitudes toward drugs, prostitution, and gambling but also the economic role these behaviors play in the social organization of inner-city American life and the fact that activities surrounding these vice industries have become more violent. In any case, at the end of this century as at the beginning, and now perhaps in a more concerted way, illegal sex and drugs are a central part of the capitalization of the social and economic life of America's distressed minority communities.

Lacking other sources of social and cultural capital, youth in low-income minority communities are today drawn to the promise of deviance service industries. Felix Padilla (1992) is explicit in drawing the connection between the concept of an ethnic vice industry and the activities of a Hispanic gang, the Diamonds, which he studied in northwest Chicago. He observes that "the business operated by the Diamonds parallels an 'ethnic enterprise': a distinctive entrepreneurial strategy historically developed and used by immigrants and their descendants in response to their marginal economic position" (Padilla, 1992:3).

Mercer Sullivan (1989), in his study of juvenile gang activity in three New York City neighborhoods, goes on to articulate the functional implications of this involvement in deviance service industries. In doing so, Sullivan emphasizes the reciprocal and redistributive roles that these activities can play in low-income minority communities, noting that the economic exchanges involved can sometimes function much like the selling of illegal alcohol beverages did during Prohibition. He writes: "Inner-city residents supply criminalized goods and services first to the local population and then to the wider community. ... Inner-city entrepreneurs risk violence and stigmatization in their personal careers in return for a flow of money back to them and into their neighborhoods. Respectability flows out and money flows back in" (Sullivan, 1989:241).

Sullivan's account makes clear that although deviance service centers promise to bring desperately needed additional resources into the inner city, they also play a role in maintaining the inner city on the moral as well as physical periphery of the economic system. So for communities as well as for the individuals who work within them, the ethnic vice industries of today are not the mobility ladders they once promised to be.

Until we confront the social and economic roles played by deviance service centers and vice industries in America's racial and ethnic ghettos, we will not be able to reduce the scale of their associated activities and stubborn persistence in these distressed minority settings. This is especially true in the context of the economic slowdown and transition that has characterized the last quarter of this century.

The Inefficiencies of Self-Help

Finally, I want to address the ways that many Americans feel they must respond to our contemporary plight. Confronted with the threat of a violent urban environment that seems increasingly impervious to policing and punishment, minority- and majority-group Americans are resorting in growing numbers to strategies of self-help. Many of us have become walking guidebooks to the rules and skills of urban life, attempting as in the title of Elijah Anderson's (1990) insightful ethnography to become *streetwise*. Of course, rules to navigate the streets of our cities are not sufficient for those of us fortunate enough to also possess coveted forms of property, and so we increasingly bar our doors, shutter our windows, surround our homes with sensing devices, acquire elaborate alarm systems, and more generally fortify our property against crime. But this too is not enough to guarantee a sense of personal security, and Americans who value and fear for their lives also are turning in increasing numbers to strategies of self-protection that include arming themselves through the acquisition of guns.

The number of guns in the United States has more than doubled over the past two decades, from less than 100 million prior to 1970 to about 200 million in 1990. In 1992, the citizens of Los Angeles County alone purchased over 100,000 guns. When illegal weapons are added in, we probably have more guns than citizens in the United States. A large share of these weapons are owned for self-protection and this kind of legal gun ownership increases with income and fear of crime (Smith and Uchida, 1988).

Unfortunately, guns purchased for self-protection are often used for other purposes. Research increasingly indicates that homes in which guns are present are at increased risk of accidents and suicides. In addition, legally acquired guns are frequently stolen and used for illegal purposes. In this way, guns acquired for protection are used for predation. As newer and more advanced weapons are acquired for self-protection, they increase the stock of more lethal weapons available for predation. No-one knows the exact extent to which this increasing lethality has contributed to the rising level of homicide in the United States. Nonetheless, there is good reason to suspect that the growing level of gun ownership in the United States is not only increasing the prevalence of suicides and accidents but that it is also escalating the terms of engagement in street crime in this country. This domestic arms race is a major source of inefficiency in the American response to crime. The circulation of guns is a social process that likely poses a greater threat to American society than the illegal drug industry with which these weapons are so often associated.

The New Sociology of Crime and Disrepute

We are left with a final question of how the new sociology of crime and disrepute that bills this discussion differs in its policy agenda from the political economy of crime and punishment that I have described. There is the obvious reminder from the sociological perspective that continuing inequalities cannot, as the political economy of crime recommends, so easily be set aside in the attempt to deal with America's crime problems. There is the further understanding that the problem of inequality is linked to a history of criminalizing the activities—especially sex, drugs, and gambling—that disadvantaged groups traditionally have explored as avenues of upward mobility in American society. There is an added awareness that the economic slowdown of the last two decades and the accompanying shift in the American economy from manufacturing to services has intensified links between inequality and disrepute in ways that provide less possibility for successful exits from involvements in crime and disrepute.

However, Wilson's *Thinking About Crime* at least was correct that a sociological focus on inequality frustrates the search for rapid improvements or even the near term containment of America's imposing crime problems. Changes in the social and economic inequalities of American life will come slowly at best, and the effects on crime would presumably also be indirect. As essential as these changes are to the longer-term health of American society, an even more immediate crisis is at hand that involves the perception and reality of public safety. A new sociology of crime and disrepute can also speak to these immediate concerns.

It does so by beginning with the understanding that we have focused too much as a nation on criminalizing and punishing drugs and too little on the more immediate problems of violence in America. Criminal violence is an immediate health as well as crime problem. Research indicates that more Americans will soon die of homicide than auto accidents. By focusing more specifically on violence and less exhaustively on drugs, we can better address our national needs.

The most direct opportunity to reduce violent crime involves banning the sale of guns and disarming the American public. It may be significant that when the U.S. government and to a lesser extent its public recently considered entering the conflict in Somalia, it debated the advisability of using the American military to disarm the Somalian public. Oddly, we have never had this debate with regard to the proliferation of guns in America. In addition to making Americans more aware that there are social and economic inequalities desperately in need of change and that are ultimately a key part of our national crime problems, a new sociology of crime and disrepute also recommends that it is time that we seriously consider the relative costs and benefits of the proliferation of guns in America. Indeed, I will close by suggesting that to have guns so freely available in a society with so much inequality is surely a recipe for continuing disaster that any social science should discern.

References

Anderson, Elijah. 1990. *Streetwise: Race, Class and Change in an Urban Community.* Chicago: University of Chicago Press.

Blumstein, Alfred. 1993. "Making Rationality Relevant." *Criminology* 31:1-16.

Blumstein, Alfred, Jacqueline Cohen and Daniel Nagin. 1978. *Deterrence and incapacitation: Estimating the Effects of Criminal Sanctions on Crime Rates.* Washington, DC: National Academy of Sciences.

Boritch, Helen, and John Hagan. 1987. "Crime and the Changing Forms of Class Control: Policing Public Order in 'Toronto the Good,' 1859-1955." *Social Forces* 66: 307-335.

Chilton, Roland, and J. Gavin. 1985. "Race, Crime and Criminal Justice." *Crime and Delinquency* 31:3-14.

Christie, Nils. 1993. *Crime Control as Industry.* London: Routledge.

Clairmont, Donald. 1974. "The Development of a Deviance Service Center." In Jack Haas and Bill Shaffir (eds.), *Decency and Deviance.* Toronto: McClelland and Stewart.

Ehrlich, Isaac. 1975. "The Deterrent Effect of Capital Punishment: A Question of Life and Death." *American Economic Review* 65:397-417.

Feeley, Malcolm, and Jonathan Simon. 1992. "The New Penology: Notes on the Emerging Strategy of Corrections and Implications." *Criminology* 30:449-474.

Granovetter, Mark. 1992. "The Sociological and Economic Approaches to Labour Market Analysis: A Social Structural View." In M. Granovetter and R. Swedberg (eds.), *The Sociology of Economic Life.* Boulder: Westview Press.

Ianni, Francis. 1972. *A Family Business.* New York: Russell Sage Foundation.
———. 1974. *Black Mafia.* New York: Simon & Schuster.
Light, Ivan. 1977. "The Ethnic Vice Industry, 1880-1944." *American Sociological Review* 42:464-479.
Martinson, Robert. 1974. "What Works? Question and Answers About Prison Reform." *The Public Interest* 35:22-54.
Messner, Steven, and Robert Sampson. 1991. "The Sex Ratio, Family Disruption, and Rates of Violent Crime: The Paradox of Demographic Structure." Social Forces 69: 693-713.
Moynihan, Daniel Patrick. 1979. "Social Science and the Courts." *The Public Interest* 54:12-31.
Padilla, Felix. 1992. *The Gang as an American Enterprise.* New Brunswick, NJ: Rutgers University Press.
Sampson, Robert. 1987. "Urban Black Violence: The Effect of Male Joblessness and Family Disruption." *American Journal of Sociology* 93:348-382.
Smith, Douglas A., and Craig D. Uchida. 1988. "The Social Organization of Self-Help: A Study of Defensive Weapon Ownership." *American Sociological Review* 53: 94-102.
Sullivan, Mercer. 1989. *Getting Paid: Youth Crime and Work in the Inner City.* Ithaca: New York: Cornell University Press.
White, Harrison. 1970. *Chains of Opportunity: System Models of Mobility in Organizations.* Cambridge: Harvard University Press.
Wilson, James Q. 1975. *Thinking About Crime.* New York: Basic Books.
Wilson, William J. 1987. *The Truly Disadvantaged: The Inner City, the Underclass, and Public Policy.* Chicago: University of Chicago Press.

4

Controlling Delinquency: Recommendations from General Strain Theory

Robert Agnew

The basic idea behind the general strain theory (GST) of crime and delinquency is a simple one: If you treat people badly, they may get mad and engage in crime (Agnew, 1992, 1995a). This idea is rooted in common sense and experience, has much indirect support, and the few direct tests of GST provide qualified support for it (Agnew and White, 1992; Paternoster and Mazerolle, 1994). The policy suggestions that flow from general strain theory are also very straightforward. First, reduce the likelihood that people will treat one another badly. Much data, described below, suggest that we can make some progress in this area. It is unlikely, however, that we can entirely eliminate negative treatment. Therefore, a second policy recommendation is that we reduce the likelihood that people will respond to negative treatment with delinquency.

This chapter begins with a brief overview of GST. The major types of negative treatment are described, and the factors that affect whether individuals respond to such treatment with delinquency are considered. Next, there is a discussion of programs that might reduce negative treatment by others. Most of these programs focus on the juvenile's family, school, and peer group. Certain programs, however, teach juveniles prosocial skills so that they will be less likely to provoke negative reactions from others. Third, there is a discussion of programs that try to reduce the likelihood that juveniles will respond to negative treatment with delinquency. Some programs try to increase the juvenile's level of social support, others attempt to improve the juvenile's own coping skills. The focus is on delinquency in the following discussion, since most of the research on GST has involved delinquency and most of the programs that are described have focused on delinquents. The arguments that are made, however, can easily be extended to adult crime.

All of the programs that are discussed have shown some signs of success, although they are in need of further evaluation (see Burchard and Burchard, 1987; Gendreau and Ross, 1987; Hollin, 1990a, 1990b; Kazdin, 1985, 1987; Morris and Braukmann, 1987; Pepler and Rubin, 1991). Data suggest that some of these programs are able to reduce delinquency in certain circumstances. Other of these programs affect factors that are associated with delinquency, and there is good reason to believe that with further modification they will be able to reduce delinquency as well. It is important to emphasize that none of these programs should be viewed as the definitive solution to the delinquency problem. None are able to substantially reduce delinquency in all circumstances. These programs, however, have much promise and there is good reason to believe that they will be able to have a significant impact on delinquency if they are used in combination and are properly implemented.

Finally, it should be noted that none of these programs are explicitly based on GST. They are not based on any theory or they have their origin in other theories. Many of these programs, for example, are based on social learning theory: They seek to reinforce prosocial behavior and punish deviant behavior *through appropriate means.* A common effect of all these programs, however, is to reduce negative treatment by others or increase the adolescent's capacity to cope with negative treatment through nondelinquent channels. These programs, then, are compatible with general strain theory. This is not surprising, since GST draws on many of the theories that inspired these programs, including social learning theory.

Overview of General Strain Theory

GST focuses on negative relationships with others: relationships in which the individual is not being treated as he or she would like to be treated. Such relations increase the likelihood that individuals will experience a range of negative emotions, with anger and frustration being especially important in GST. These emotions create pressure for corrective action, and delinquency is one possible response. Delinquency may be a method for reducing strain, seeking revenge, or managing negative emotions (through illicit drug use).

There are three major types of negative relations or strain. The first occurs when others try to prevent you from achieving positively valued goals.

Failure to achieve positively valued goals. Traditional strain theories, such as those of Merton (1938) and Cloward and Ohlin (1960), focus on the failure of individuals to achieve the goal of monetary success. In particular, adolescents who do not expect to achieve monetary success become frustrated, and they may turn to illegitimate channels of goal achievement such as theft as a result. Support for these versions of strain theory, however, is weak (Agnew, 1995b). Data suggest that adolescents pursue a variety of different goals and that the goal of monetary success may be unimportant to many adolescents. In particular, adolescents may be more concerned with achieving goals such as autonomy from adults and popularity with peers (see Agnew, 1995b; n.d.).

Further, much literature suggests that a central goal of all individuals is to be treated in a just or fair manner. Individuals, in particular, often like to have some say or voice in the rules that govern their behavior (known as "procedural justice"). And individuals are concerned that resources (e.g., money, grades, attention) are distributed in a fair manner (known as "distributive justice"). The definition of what constitutes "fair" may differ from situation to situation. A common view, however, is that individuals who contribute more to a relationship should receive more (known as the "equity" rule). So if my inputs to a relationship are greater than those of a similar other, my outcomes should be greater as well. Individuals may respond with delinquency when this is not the case. Delinquency may allow them to increase their outcomes (e.g., by theft), lower their inputs (e.g., truancy from school), lower the outcomes of others (e.g., vandalism, theft, assault), or increase the inputs of others (e.g., by being incorrigible). It should be noted that these arguments of GST have not been directly tested, although they have much indirect support.

The loss of positive stimuli and the presentation of negative stimuli. The second type of strain involves the removal or threatened removal of positively valued stimuli that are possessed. Examples include the loss of a boyfriend or girlfriend, moving to a new school district, and the divorce or separation of one's parents. The third type of strain involves the presentation or threatened presentation of negatively valued stimuli. Such stimuli may involve criminal victimization of various types, a wide assortment of stressful life events, and negative relations with parents, teachers, peers, and others—with such relations involving insults, verbal threats, and other noxious behavior.

Adolescents are especially likely to experience the above two types of strain. Adolescence is associated with a dramatic increase in the number of social relationships and the demands associated with these relationships. Adolescents leave elementary school and enter larger, more impersonal, and more diverse secondary schools. They typically change teachers and classmates several times during the day. Such schools are also more demanding than elementary school: They are subject to more rules, given more work, and graded in a more difficult manner. Adolescents also start to spend more time away from home, increasing their association with peers, including their romantic associations. Further, interaction with such peers comes to be governed by a more subtle set of social cues. All of these changes increase the likelihood that adolescents will be treated negatively by others. There are more people to negatively treat the adolescent. These people are freer to treat the adolescent in a negative manner since they are less likely to be under the supervision of adults and they often do not have strong ties to the adolescent. And interaction with these people is more demanding, so there is a greater likelihood that interactions will break down in ways that result in negative treatment. Adolescents, for example, may have difficulty meeting the academic demands of teachers or the emotional demands of romantic partners—resulting in poor grades or severed relationships (see Agnew, n.d., for a full discussion).

Certain individuals, of course, are more likely to experience negative treatment than others. Such individuals may be born into dysfunctional families, attend poor-quality schools, and grow up in neighborhoods plagued by a variety of social problems. Also, researchers argue that many individuals possess traits that increase their likelihood of negative treatment by others. Such traits include "difficult temperament" (moody, fussy, irritable, argumentative, stubborn), hyperactivity, impulsivity, attention deficit, insensitivity, limited problem-solving skills, and limited prosocial skills. These traits are a result of early social experiences in the family and, in some cases, biological factors. Individuals with these traits are more likely to provoke negative reactions from others and select themselves into adversive social environments—such as deviant peer groups (see Michaelson, 1987; Agnew, n.d.). The result is often high levels of delinquency on their part.

So there are three major types of strain or negative treatment, and adolescents may respond to such strain with delinquency. Delinquency may be a method for reducing strain; that is, for achieving positively valued goals, for protecting or retrieving positive stimuli, or for terminating or escaping from negative stimuli. Delinquency may also be used to seek revenge, and delinquency may occur as adolescents try to alleviate the negative emotions that result from strain through illicit drug use. Delinquency, however, is *not* the only possible response to strain.

Strategies for Coping with Strain

Adolescents may cope with strain in several ways, only some of which involve delinquency. The GST theory describes cognitive, behavioral, and emotional coping strategies.

Adolescents may cope with strain by *cognitively reinterpreting* negative treatment so as to minimize its impact. The GST lists three major cognitive coping strategies, summarized in the phrases "it's not important," "it's not that bad," and "I deserve it." Imagine, for example, an individual who is unable to achieve popularity with peers. This individual may minimize the failure to achieve this goal by arguing that such popularity is not important, perhaps claiming that other goals—such as good grades—are more important. Individuals may exaggerate their popularity with peers—claiming that they really are popular, even though most objective criteria suggest otherwise. Or individuals may state that they are to blame for their lack of popularity. This may not reduce feelings of depression or despair, but it is likely to reduce anger at others. Such cognitive coping strategies, then, may reduce the likelihood that individuals react to strain with delinquency.

Adolescents may also employ *behavioral* coping strategies, attempting to act in ways that reduce the strain they are experiencing. Certain of these strategies may involve nondelinquent behavior. Adolescents, for example, may try to avoid the peers who harass them or negotiate with the teachers who frustrate them. Other behavioral strategies for reducing strain, as indicated above, involve delinquency.

Finally, adolescents may engage in *emotional coping*. Rather than trying to reduce their negative treatment by others or cognitively reinterpret it, they act directly on the negative emotions that result from such treatment. They may attempt to alleviate their negative emotions through nondelinquent strategies such as exercise, deep breathing, or other relaxation techniques. Or they may employ delinquent strategies, such as the use of illicit drugs.

In sum, there are many ways of coping with strain—only some of which involve delinquency. Unfortunately, adolescents are not well equipped to cope with strain through nondelinquent channels. Adolescents do not have much experience at nondelinquent coping. They are often unaware of or unskilled at many of the nondelinquent cognitive, behavioral, and emotional coping strategies described above. Further, they often lack the power or resources to engage in many types of nondelinquent coping. Except under exceptional circumstances, they cannot move if they do not like their neighbors, they cannot leave school or change classes if their teachers harass them, and they cannot leave home if they do not get along with their parents. They may also lack the resources to effectively negotiate with adults. Finally, their increased independence from adults often means that they lack effective social supports. Their parents would often cope for them when they were children, but this diminishes during adolescence—meaning that they must increasingly cope on their own or rely on the support of similarly inexperienced friends.

In addition to their lack of legitimate coping skills, adolescents often find themselves in situations that are conducive to delinquent coping. They are then more likely to associate with delinquent peers (see Warr, 1993), who encourage the use of delinquent coping. Much of their negative treatment occurs before an audience or becomes known to peers, which increases the pressure to engage in "face-saving" responses involving delinquency. And adolescents are lower in many forms of social control. They are less subject to the familial controls that govern the lives of children but are not yet subject to adult controls. In particular, they are not yet subject to the sanctions of the adult justice system and have not yet formed close attachments to spouses or strong commitments to work. The negative consequences of delinquent coping, then, are lower.

Again, certain adolescents have more trouble coping through legitimate means than do others. Adolescents differ on a wide range of variables that affect coping, including their problem-solving abilities, their prosocial skills, their level of conventional social support, their association with delinquent peers, and their level of social control. Some adolescents, then, are more likely to respond to strain with delinquency.

Reducing Negative Treatment by Others

When adolescents are asked to describe the events or situations that upset or anger them, their responses inevitably focus on interpersonal problems. In particular, they usually describe interpersonal problems with parents, siblings, teachers, friends, and romantic partners. Their descriptions fall under the three categories of strain mentioned above, particularly the presentation of negative stimuli. For example, they indicate that these others have negatively evaluated them, disciplined or sanctioned them, pressured them, overburdened them, fought with or got into conflicts with them, and rejected them. Much data suggest that this negative treatment increases the likelihood of delinquency (Agnew, 1992; n.d.).[1]

There is good reason to believe, then, that reducing negative treatment by others will reduce delinquency. There are a variety of ways to reduce such treatment, and this review will highlight several programs that have shown some success in this area. The most promising programs focus on the family and involve parent management training and functional family therapy (for overviews of family programs, see Curry, Wiencrot, and Koehler, 1984; Farrington et al., 1990; Gendreau and Ross, 1987; Hollin, 1992; Kazdin, 1985, 1987; Morton, 1987; Morton and Ewald, 1987; Patterson, 1982; Rankin and Wells, 1987; Roberts and Camasso, 1991; Stumphauzer, 1986; Wahler, 1987).

Family-Based Programs

Numerous researchers have noted that the families of antisocial and delinquent children are often characterized by much adversity, including high levels of interpersonal conflict, harsh discipline, abuse and neglect, low rates of positive reinforcement and high rates of punishment, the indiscriminate use of reinforcement and punishment—with negative behavior sometimes being reinforced and positive behavior sometimes being ignored or punished, and ineffective communication patterns (Hollin, 1990a; Kazdin, 1985; Morton, 1987; Morton and Ewald, 1987; Patterson, 1982; Rankin and Wells, 1987).

The more effective family programs deal with these problems in several ways. Family members are taught how to better resolve interpersonal conflicts. Parents may negotiate behavioral contracts with their children, clearly specifying the responsibilities and privileges of family members. For example, adolescents may agree to go to school every day during the week in exchange for the privilege of staying out until midnight on Friday and Saturday night (see

Stumphauzer, 1986:91-102). The contract, then, specifies exactly what the adolescent needs to do to get specific privileges or rewards. The adolescent typically plays a major role in developing such contracts. Parents and children may also be taught how to negotiate agreements if additional conflicts arise or they may turn to the therapist to mediate such conflicts.

In addition, parents are taught how to more effectively discipline their children. They are taught how to better monitor their child's behavior, recognize both deviant and prosocial behavior, and properly sanction deviant behavior and reward prosocial behavior. Parents are encouraged to make greater use of positive reinforcements, such as praise and attention, and to make less use of punishments such as criticism and yelling. The preferred strategies of punishment involve time out (for children) and loss of privileges. Parents are taught these disciplinary techniques through a variety of strategies: They receive reading materials and/or direct instruction, they are exposed to models who display proper disciplinary and negotiation techniques, they rehearse such techniques themselves and receive feedback, and. they receive continued guidance when they apply such techniques in their homes. Special versions of these programs have also been developed to deal with problems such as child abuse and neglect (see Morton and Ewald, 1987).

Family programs have shown much promise in reducing undesirable behavior, although they are not effective with all families and there are still difficulties in inducing many families to participate—typically the families that need it most (Curry, Wiencrot, and Koehler, 1984; Hollin, 1990a; Kazdin, 1985, 1987). Efforts, however, are under way to deal with these problems (e.g., Hawkins et al., 1987; Morton, 1987; Morton and Ewald, 1987; Wahler, 1987). The effectiveness of these programs is undoubtedly due to a number of factors, most notably the fact that parents are taught to reward desirable behavior and *appropriately* sanction undesirable behavior. Another possible reason for the success of such programs, however, is that they substantially reduce the extent to which the adolescent is treated in a negative manner. Such programs, in particular, directly reduce several types of strain. Adolescents begin to have some say in the rules that govern their lives, and they are treated more fairly by parents—with parents more consistently rewarding prosocial behavioral and punishing negative behavior. Conflict with parents is reduced, adolescents are subject to less negative treatment, and they receive more positive stimuli. There is good reason to believe that the adolescent's level of anger and frustration is reduced as a result, and this may be another reason why such programs result in a reduction in delinquency.

If additional research confirms the promise of such programs, their use might be expanded in a number of ways. Versions of such programs might become part of the high school curriculum, a strategy that has already been tried in some areas (although its effectiveness is still uncertain). Parent training might also be offered to expectant and new parents. The intensity and cost of such programs suggest that they be limited to high-risk families, such as those families participating in preschool programs of the type discussed below (see Wilson, 1987; Hawkins et al., 1987; Wahler, 1987; Loeber, 1987).

Despite such efforts, it still may not be possible to significantly alter the family circumstances of certain delinquent youth. And it has been suggested that in extreme cases we may have to place these youth in surrogate families. One option, at least on a temporary basis, is group homes. Group homes are small residential facilities housing four to twelve juveniles. These juveniles often attend local schools and have some free time in the community. Group homes employing the "Teaching-Family" approach are directed by married couples called "teaching parents" and employ many of the behavioral techniques described above (see Braukmann and Wolf, 1987). Most notably, the teaching parents attempt to create a pleasant, nonaversive environment for the juveniles. They spend enjoyable time with the juveniles, regularly express interest in them, and attempt to help them deal with their problems. In fact, juveniles in one study were asked to list the behaviors of teaching parents they most liked or enjoyed, and this list was then used to guide the training of teaching parents. Youth also have some voice in how the group home is run. There is group decision-making on a wide range of issues, and a democratically elected peer manager plays a major role in the discipline process. Further, there is an attempt to explain the rationale behind all rules. Additional treatments, such as social skills training and problem-solving training, are also provided (see below). Such homes obviously reduce strain in several areas, and these homes seem to be effective in controlling disruptive behavior—although this effectiveness is lost when youths leave the home. These homes were not intended as a permanent replacement for the family, but it has been suggested that foster parents might be trained in many of the same techniques (also see Loeber, 1987:98). Certain of the juveniles leaving these homes might then be placed in long-term foster care.

School-Based Programs

The adversity of the school environment is also related to delinquency. Delinquency is related to school failure, the perceived relevance of school, attachment to teachers and school, and problems with teachers. And it is related to such features of the school environment as whether students have control over what happens to them at school; the fairness and consistency of discipline; the frequency that student achievement is recognized; the impersonality of school including contact between students and teachers; and the educational opportunities for students who are not college bound (see Agnew, 1985; Hawkins and Lam, 1987; Hawkins and Lishner, 1987a, 1987b).

Several strategies have been developed to reduce the adversity of school. Some of these strategies attempt to improve interpersonal relations between individuals in the school system, but most attempt to boost school performance. Improvements in performance increase one's level of social control, but they also reduce the adversity of school. Students who are doing poorly in school are likely to find school aversive for several reasons. School has little relevance for them, they are likely to find their classes boring, they may be embarrassed by their poor performance in the classroom, and their poor grades may function as negative stimuli. Improving adolescents' level of school performance, then, may significantly reduce their level of strain.

Evidence suggests that good preschool programs can both improve school performance and reduce delinquency (for overviews, see Schweinhart, 1987; Berrueta-Clement et al., 1987). Most such programs focus on preschool children in disadvantaged areas and attempt to promote the social and intellectual development of these children as well as increase their parents' involvement in the educational process. The best known of these programs is the Perry Preschool Program (Berrueta-Clement et al., 1877; Schweinhart, 1987). This program not only improved school performance and prevented delinquency but also was cost effective as well: It saved taxpayers money since program participants were more likely to obtain good jobs and less likely to be placed in special education programs, go on welfare, or engage in crime (Schweinhart, 1987). The impact of other preschool programs on delinquency has not been as well evaluated, although evidence suggests that good preschool programs are able to improve school performance (Schweinhart, 1987). The success of preschool programs is further enhanced if children continue to receive assistance once they have begun school (Zigler and Hall, 1987).

Other programs take place after school has begun and involve altering the classroom environment. Hawkins and associates have attempted to reduce delinquency through a number of such programs, including interactive teaching, proactive classroom management, and cooperative learning groups (Hawkins and Lam, 1987; Hawkins and Lishner, 1987b). Interactive teaching provides students with specific objectives they must master, employs objective grading, and bases grades on mastery of material and improvement over past performance—not on comparisons with other students. Interactive teaching is designed to increase the opportunities for students to succeed, and the grading methods increase perceptions of fairness and decrease competition/comparisons with other students. Teachers using proactive classroom management are taught to clearly state rules for classroom behavior, recognize and reward attempts to cooperate, make frequent use of encouragement and praise, and attempt to minimize the impact of disruptions. And cooperative learning groups involve small, heterogenous groups of students who help one another master classroom materials and who receive recognition as a team for their accomplishments. These groups serve to reduce alienation, reinforce cooperation, and promote attachment among students. The effect of these interventions was mixed, although there is reason to believe that their continued employment might have an impact on delinquency (Hawkins and Lam, 1987).

Additional examples of programs that reduce the adversity of the school environment are provided in Project PATHE Positive Action Through Holistic Education (Gottfredson, 1986). This project was implemented in seven schools and, among other things, attempted to better involve students in decision-making, improve disciplinary procedures, increase attachment to school, and generally make the school environment more satisfying. The following types of interventions were employed: Student leadership teams were formed to help plan and implement activities to improve the school, students were involved in the development of school disciplinary rules, teachers were taught innovative teaching and classroom management techniques, cooperative learning techniques were employed, students and teachers got involved in school pride campaigns, extra curricular activities were expanded, students were trained to hold peer counseling and rap sessions at which students could discuss topics of concern, and a special effort was made to increase the involvement and success experiences of high-risk students. Although the program did not reduce delinquency, it did reduce school disruption, alienation, and the frequency of punishment. It also increased attachment to school, the perceived rewards of school, the perceived fairness of school rules, and feelings of safety. And there is good reason to believe that the further development of the program may result in reductions in delinquency.

Still other programs have focused on peer relations in the school environment. Perhaps one of the most successful is the anti-bullying program in the Norwegian school system (Olweus, 1991). According to Olweus (1991:413), "a person is being bullied when he or she is exposed, repeatedly and over time, to negative actions on the part of one or more other persons." Negative actions are defined as those intentional actions that inflict or attempt to inflict injury or discomfort upon another. It was found that teachers did relatively little to stop bullying at school, and parents were largely unaware of the problem. A national campaign provided teachers and parents with information on the extent of bullying and advice on how to stop it. Teachers were encouraged to closely monitor student activities; to establish clear rules against bullying; to use nonhostile, nonphysical sanctions against bullies; and to support and protect victims. Surveys of students suggest that the program was quite successful, although it is of course unclear whether a similar program would work in the United States.

A variety of other programs with the potential for reducing school adversity have been employed. Behavioral contracting has been tried in the school as well as the family (see Lane and Murakami, 1987; Stumphauzer, 1986). Students and teachers will negotiate behavioral contracts, specifying the academic and behavioral goals that students will meet and the reinforcements they will obtain for meeting these goals. In many cases, parents are also involved in these negotiations. Other programs have tried to reduce the problems associated with large schools. Small groups of students, for example, are assigned to the same homeroom and same classes (Felner et al., 1982). Still other interventions are described in Lane and Murakami (1987) and Hawkins and Lishner (1987b).

Taken together, these interventions have the potential for significantly reducing the adversity of school: for better enabling students to achieve their goals, for giving students a say in the rules that govern their behavior, for treating students more fairly, for improving school success, and for improving interpersonal relations with teachers and peers.

It is still likely, however, that some students will find school adversive and turn to delinquency as a result. Toby (1983) proposes that we deal with this fact by making it easier for students to drop out of school; specifically, that we lower the drop out age to fifteen in all states. This would reduce the strain of these students and thereby lower their delinquency. This proposition has received mixed support (Bachman, O'Malley, and Johnston, 1981; Elliott and Voss, 1974; also see Thornberry, Moore, and Christenson, 1985). It would also make school more tolerable for those who remain. Toby does not advocate that we ignore those students who drop out: Rather, efforts should be made to secure them jobs and to help them reenter school at a later date if they so desire. Toby also proposes that we make it more difficult for outsiders to enter the school, noting that outside intruders are responsible for much of the violence in inner-city schools.

Programs Focusing on Peers

Peers occupy a central place in the lives of adolescents, and much data suggest that peer relations have a large effect on delinquency. Association with delinquent peers, in fact, is perhaps the best predictor of delinquency (next to prior delinquency). The effect of peers on delinquency is most often explained in terms of social learning theory: Peers reinforce the delinquency of the adolescent, model delinquency, and teach values conducive to delinquency (Akers, 1985). Peers, however, may also contribute to delinquency for reasons related to strain theory.

Although the topic of peer abuse has been largely neglected by researchers and policymakers, limited data suggest that peers frequently engage in physical, verbal, and other types of abuse against one another. A recent study, for example, asked a sample of college students about the sources of their happiness and unhappiness during childhood and adolescence (Ambert, 1994). Peers emerged as the main source of unhappiness, far surpassing parents in importance. Several forms of peer abuse emerged, involving "what peers said, did not say, did [and] did not do" (1994:172). Some of this abuse was racially motivated. Peer abuse, then, appears to be a major source of strain or negative affect. And many adolescents may choose to deal with this strain through delinquency. Evidence, for example, suggests that delinquents are more likely to have conflicts with and to be rejected by peers (Kazdin, 1987).

Most of the programs that attempt to improve peer relations occur in the school setting, given the fact that school is a convenient vehicle for reaching large numbers of youth. These programs, like cooperative learning and the anti-bullying program, have been described above. Other programs have attempted to increase the level of adult supervision over peer activities (Agnew and Petersen, 1989). Still other programs have attempted to treat delinquent youth by fostering association with pro social peers (Farrington et al., 1990; Feldman, Chaplinger, and Wodarski, 1983; Kazdin, 1987). And programs have been used to improve interpersonal relations, including peer relations, by teaching youth prosocial and problem-solving skills. It is clearly the case, however, that more research and policy initiatives need to focus on this neglected topic.

Programs Focusing on the Individual

As suggested above, it is possible to alter the individual's social environment in ways that reduce negative treatment by others. If we want to fully reduce negative treatment by others, however, we must also alter the behavior of the individual. Individuals play a role in creating their own social environment. Many juveniles act in ways that provoke negative reactions from others, and over the long term such juveniles often end up in adversive environments—such as delinquent peer groups, bad jobs, and bad marriages (see Michaelson, 1987; Agnew, n.d.). It is possible to alter the behavior of these juveniles in ways that reduce the likelihood of negative reactions from others. The primary method for doing so involves social skills training.

A variety of social skills training programs have been employed (see for example, Goldstein, Krasner, and Garfield, 1989; Henderson and Hollin, 1986; Hollin, 1990a, 1990b; Michaelson, 1987; Pepler et al., 1991; Stumphauzer, 1986). The skills taught in these programs allow juveniles to more effectively achieve their goals and reduce the likelihood of negative treatment by others. Certain of these skills are very specific, such as increasing the frequency of eye contact or reducing fidgeting movements; others are quite complex, like improving negotiation skills with adults or resisting peer pressure. As an illustration, the social skills training component of Aggression Replacement Training focuses on fifty skills (see Goldstein, Krasner, and Garfield, 1989) These skills are divided into six broad groups: (1) beginning social skills (e.g. listening, starting a conversation), (2) advanced social skills (e.g., asking for help, apologizing), (3) skills for dealing with feelings (e.g., dealing with someone else's anger), (4) skill alternatives to aggression (asking permission, responding to testing), (5) skills for dealing with stress (making a complaint, responding to failure), and (6) planning skills (e.g., deciding on something to do). Juveniles are not taught all fifty skills; only those skills in which they are deficient. Five or six juveniles with similar skill deficiencies are placed in the same training group. Each week the group and its trainers decide on what skill will be taught, with each of the fifty skills being divided into several steps. The skill of starting a conversation, for example, includes the following four steps: greet the other person, make small talk, decide if the other person is listening, and bring up the main topic.

The training typically involves direct instruction, modeling of the desired behaviors by the trainer or others, role playing by the youth (with feedback from the trainer and others), reinforcement for appropriate behavior, and homework assignments for which the social skills are used in real-life settings (Goldstein, Krasner, and Garfield, 1989; Hollin, 1990a, 1990b; Michaelson, 1987:295). Certain of the programs make special efforts to ensure that these skills will be used in the outside world, such as overlearning of the skill, making the training as similar to real-life as possible, and attempting to ensure that the new skills are reinforced in real-life settings (see especially Goldstein, Krasner, and Garfield, 1989; Henderson and Hollin, 1986).

The philosophy behind social skills training is perhaps best expressed by Michaelson, who developed the Behavioral Social Skills Training Program. According to Michaelson (1987:294), juveniles in this program "are encouraged to express themselves, but in ways that do not violate other peoples' rights or feelings and to engage in self-control procedures as a means of deflecting and redirecting anger, hostility, and aggressive behavior. ... The use of the term *social skills* refers to repertoires of social interaction and social knowledge that, when used interpersonally, tend to evoke positive reinforcement on both a short- and long-term basis, resulting in positive outcomes for *both* parties." A major impact of social skills training, then, is to reduce the likelihood of negative reactions from others and increase the likelihood of positive outcomes.

Limited data suggest that delinquent or antisocial juveniles are more likely to have deficits in the above sorts of skills, although this is certainly not true of all delinquents (Goldstein, Krasner, and Garfield, 1989; Henderson and Hollin, 1986; Hollin, 1990b; Kazdin, 1987; Michelson, 1987; Pepler et al., 1991). And data suggest that when properly implemented, programs of the above type are effective in improving social skills and *may* be effective in reducing antisocial behavior (see Cullen and Gendreau, 1989; Goldstein et al., 1989; Hollin, 1990a, 1990b, 1992; Michaelson, 1987; Quay, 1987). The effectiveness of these programs is enhanced if they are used in combination with other programs described in this chapter, especially the cognitive problem-solving programs described below. Social skills training may be used with delinquent youth or may be used on a preventive basis with at-risk youth (Michaelson, 1987).

It should be noted that the poor social skills of juveniles may be due to a number of factors, most notably the failure of the family to teach prosocial skills. Poor social skills, however, may also be related to a number of individual traits that emerge early in the life course—such as hyperactivity, impulsivity, and attention deficit. There is evidence that some of these traits may be influenced by biological factors, including poor prenatal nutrition, maternal drug use, complications during delivery, and exposure to toxic agents (Moffitt, 1993; Raine, 1993). And it has been suggested that programs designed to improve care during the prenatal/perinatal period may have an effect on later crime—although there have been no good evaluations in this area (Reiss and Roth, 1993:383).

Coping Through Nondelinquent Means

Even though the above programs may reduce the extent to which people treat one another badly, it is unlikely that we will be able to eliminate strain. As such, it is important that we also increase the ability of adolescents to cope with strain through nondelinquent means. In particular, most people would probably agree that it is important to teach people how to alleviate their strain by employing behavioral coping strategies of a nondelinquent nature. We might, for example, teach adolescents to be assertive rather than aggressive. The situation becomes more complex, however, when we deal with cognitive and emotional coping strategies. Such strategies teach adolescents to cognitively redefine situations in ways that do not provoke anger/frustration and teach them to deal with their anger in nondelinquent ways—such as through the use of relaxation techniques. Is it appropriate to teach adolescents such techniques when they are in fact being treated unfairly or unjustly by others? Such considerations should be kept in mind in the following discussion, although most of the programs discussed below seem to be on safe ethical ground. Those programs that emphasize cognitive reinterpretation, for example, focus on adolescents who tend to attribute hostile intentions to the benign or ambiguous acts of others. Such programs, then, do not cause adolescents to cognitively distort events—but rather to foster a more accurate interpretation of events. Likewise, those programs that focus on reducing anger do so in an effort to make it possible for the adolescent to engage in more effective behavioral coping.

Increasing Social Support

Parents and other adults typically help children cope with their problems, providing various types of support. Such social support, however, diminishes during adolescence. It diminishes, in part, because adolescents spend less time under the supervision of parents and are less likely to share their problems with parents. It also diminishes because of the expectation that adolescents should begin to cope on their own behalf, displaying the independence that characterizes adults. As argued above, however, adolescents confront a wide range of problems and they are often ill-equipped to cope on their own behalf. As a result, they often cope through delinquency. For example, they may attempt to resolve interpersonal conflicts through violence rather than negotiation. One solution to this problem is to increase the conventional social support available to adolescents.

Social support is narrowly defined in this chapter: It involves efforts to directly assist the juvenile in coping with specific problems. Such assistance may assume a variety of forms, including behavioral, emotional, and cognitive support (see Vaux, 1988, for typologies of social support). Behavioral support helps the juvenile act in ways that reduce or eliminate strain; such support may involve advice on how to act, the provision of resources necessary for action, and action by the supporter on behalf of the juvenile (e.g., a parent negotiating with the juvenile's teacher). Cognitive support helps the juvenile arrive at an appraisal of the strainful situation; for example, the teacher tells the juvenile that he or she was not deliberately insulted. Emotional support includes any effort designed to deal with the negative emotions that result from strain, such as advice on how to relax or expressions of comfort and affection.

There is indirect evidence that conventional social support may reduce delinquency (see the excellent review in Cullen, 1994). The literature on "resilient youth" focuses on juveniles who grow up in highly adversive environments but do not show any signs of maladaptation. One of the major findings to emerge from this literature is that such youth often had a close relationship with an adult who helped them cope with adverse events (Rutter, 1985; Grossman et al., 1992; also see Greene, 1993). Social support is a central component of many of the successful programs described above. Functional family therapy, for example, tries to improve communication among family members, including "the expression of emotion, support, and reciprocity" (Kazdin, 1985:112). There is also a concerted effort to teach family members to work together to better solve their problems. Recent evaluation research on rehabilitation finds that the more effective programs are those in which counselors are able to establish a warm relationship with clients (Andrews and Bonta, 1994; Andrews et al., 1990; Cullen and Gendreau, 1989). There are several possible reasons for this, one of which is that such counselors are able to more effectively provide social support. They may be more likely to become aware of the problems of clients, and clients might be more receptive to the informational, emotional, and behavioral support they provide. Broadly speaking, in fact, most rehabilitation efforts can be viewed as forms of social support. In this chapter, however, social support is distinguished from those programs that attempt to alter a major portion of the juvenile's environment (as described above) or teach juveniles how to cope on their own (as described below).

A range of strategies have been employed to increase social support. Some programs have professionals or volunteers provide support, some teach family members and teachers to provide more effective social support, and one innovative program teaches juveniles how to find their own social supports. Most programs focus on disadvantaged or delinquent youth, although some programs provide support to all adolescents during particularly stressful periods in the life course—such as the transition to high school. These programs have not been extensively evaluated, but the data are suggestive enough to support further experimentation. This is particularly true given the fact that our knowledge of social support is limited (see the excellent review in Vaux, 1988). As Vaux (1988) points out, it is not clear what types of support, administered in what ways, are most effective in dealing with what types of stress. Several examples of programs providing social support are provided below.

The Minnesota Youth Advocate Program focused on delinquents making the transition from correctional institutions to public schools (Higgins, 1978). Specially trained youth advocates provided behavioral, emotional, and perhaps cognitive support for these juveniles. Among other things, advocates spent time counseling the youth; working with others who served the youth, such as teachers; performing various services for the youth (e.g., driving them to job interviews, helping them reenroll in school); and "going to bat" for the youth in disputes with teachers, criminal justice officials, and others. Results suggest the program had a small, positive impact on adjustment, with youth in the program being more likely to stay in school and less likely to be sent to correctional institutions (see Coates, 1987, for a related discussion of individual and community advocates).

Other programs have employed lay volunteers. Such volunteer programs are often cheap to implement and volunteers are sometimes better able to relate to the youth they serve—particularly if they are from similar backgrounds. Stein (1987) examined nineteen evaluations of such programs, all of which paired disadvantaged or maladaptive children with older volunteers—usually undergraduates or adults. These volunteers typically visited the child in school once each week for one to three hours. The volunteers received little training and were simply encouraged to draw on their interpersonal skills to establish a warm, empathic relationship with the child. Tentative data suggest that this therapy resulted in a reduction in aggressiveness and acting out, as rated by teachers. This was especially true when the treatment was of long duration, when "sociable, outgoing" volunteers were used, and when adults rather than students were employed.

Another program attempted to help a broad range of adolescents cope with a particularly stressful event in the juvenile phase of the life-cycle: the transfer to high school (Felner, Ginter and Primavera, 1982). Among other things, the program tried to increase the behavioral, emotional, and perhaps cognitive support provided to students by teachers and peers. Students were assigned to one of four homerooms, which were staffed by homeroom teachers who provided academic and personal counseling and help with administrative matters. An effort was also made to assign these students to the same classes so that they would develop closer ties to one another. The impact of the program on delinquency was not evaluated, although the participants in the program had better grades, better attendance, higher perceptions of teacher support, and more positive perceptions of the school environment.

Mediation programs are yet another example of social support. A wide range of such programs are available, including community-based programs and programs run in the school system by students. Such programs provide youth with assistance in resolving interpersonal disputes and have shown some signs of success (see Coates, 1987; Fagan, 1987; Gronfors, 1989; Marshal, 1987). Juveniles are often pleased to meet with mediators and surprised that they have some voice in the deliberations.

In all of the above programs, someone who is willing to provide social support is made available to the juvenile. An alternative strategy is to equip juveniles with the skills to find their own social supports. And a central component of one skills training program is to teach youth to "seek out, identify, establish a relationship with, and maintain a relationship with prosocially-oriented adult or peer models" (Goldstein, Krasner, and Garfield, 1989:1-15; also see Vaux, 1988).

Training Juveniles to Cope on Their Own

In addition to increasing conventional social support, we can also attempt to teach juveniles to more effectively cope with strain on their own. This is part of the impetus behind the social skills programs described above. Such programs not only teach juveniles to behave in ways that evoke positive reactions from others but they also provide instruction in how to cope with interpersonal problems. Many programs, for example, include units on how to respond to teasing or barbs, deal with teachers' criticisms, behave during police encounters, and keep out of fights. Further, a central theme of many programs is to teach juveniles to be assertive rather than aggressive. Juveniles in one program, for example, are taught "Mental Kung-Fu," which includes standing tall (acting assertive and claiming one's rights), thinking smart (thinking about the consequences of one's behavior), and being self-controlled (Stumphauzer, 1986:89).

This instruction is based on data suggesting that delinquency often results from the fact that many juveniles "lack the knowledge and ability to ask rather than demand; negotiate, compromise, or otherwise respond appropriately to conflict rather than strike out physically; or exercise self-control in lieu of becoming highly aroused and aggressive. Furthermore, they may be deficient in the skills to handle frustration and failure by regrouping and trying again; to respond effectively to the complaints, anger, instructions, or accusations of others, or to behave competently in other important personal and interpersonal arenas" (Goldstein, Krasner, and Garfield, 1989:17).

Social skills training focuses on teaching juveniles how to *behave* in a prosocial manner. Juveniles, for example, are taught the steps involved in apologizing to others. Social skills training is limited, however, in that it is impossible to anticipate all the interpersonal problems that juveniles will face and teach them the behaviors necessary for dealing with these problems. Problem-solving training focuses on teaching juveniles how to *think*; specifically, it teaches juveniles the steps involved in generating effective solutions to any problem they might face. Dodge (1986) lists the following five steps in effective problem-solving: (1) search for cues in the environment; (2) interpret these cues; (3) generate possible responses to the situation; (4) consider the possible consequences of the responses; and (5) enact the chosen response (also see Kendall, Ronan, and Epps, 1991; Pepler et al., 1991; Spivack, Platt, and Shure, 1976). Data suggest that delinquents have problems at each of these steps. They attend to fewer environmental cues and tend to focus on aggressive cues, often attribute hostile intent when there is none, generate fewer alternative solutions, generate more aggressive responses, fail to recognize the negative consequences of delinquent behavior, and often lack the social skills to enact prosocial responses (Hollin, 1990b; Kazdin, 1985, 1987; Kendall, Ronan, and Epps, 1991; Michaelson, 1987; Pepler et al., 1991).

Problem-solving training teaches juveniles to carefully perform each of the steps necessary for effective problem solving, avoiding the mistakes listed above. The instructor will often model the steps in problem solving through a series of verbal statements. The children will then be asked to apply these steps to an imaginary problem, often making statements to themselves that call attention to the mental tasks that are to be performed. In the "Think Aloud" program, for example, children are taught to ask themselves a series of four questions: "What is my problem?" "What is my plan?" "Am I using my plan?" and "How did I do?" (Hollin, 1990a:66). The WISER way teaches youth to wait, identify the problem, generate solutions, evaluate the consequences, and self-reinforce (Hollin, 1990b:485). The instructor prompts the youth when necessary and provides feedback and reinforcement. Eventually, the youth apply the steps to real-life problems. In some programs, parents and teachers may be trained to teach children problem-solving skills.

Other programs focus on the anger and frustration often generated by strain. None of these programs try to reduce anger simply for its own sake. Rather, these programs are based on the observation that the anger and frustration generated by strain often leads to maladaptive behavior. The programs teach adolescents ways of limiting or controlling their anger with the goal of promoting more adaptive behavior. Most anger-control programs have several features in common. First, juveniles explore the causes and consequences of their anger. They may do this by keeping a diary or log of those events that made them angry and their reaction to these events. The causes of anger include not only external events but also the internal statements made about those events. As noted above, for example, aggressive individuals are more likely to interpret the ambiguous acts of others as hostile in intent. The diary may help identify such self-statements. It may also help identify the early warning signs of anger—such as tensed muscles or flushing. Second, the juveniles learn techniques for more effectively controlling their anger—such as counting backward, imagining a peaceful scene, deep breathing, muscle relaxation, and self-statements such as "calm down" and "cool off." Certain of the self-statements may be designed to counteract the internal self-statements that trigger anger (e.g., the juvenile may tell him/herself that "Joe didn't mean that as an insult"). Some programs also attempt to increase the juvenile's level of self-esteem and self-efficacy to further increase self-control. In addition to teaching juveniles to reduce or more effectively control their anger, these programs often teach social and problem-solving skills that allow for a more adaptive response to the situation. Finally, juveniles receive much practice applying the above techniques, first in response to imaginary provocations and eventually in real-life settings. As in the above programs, they receive much feedback and reinforcement (see Blackburn, 1993; Goldstein, Krasner, and Garfield, 1989; Hollin, 1990a, 1991; Howells, 1988; Novaco, 1975; Platt and Prout, 1987; Stumphauzer, 1986).

Problem-solving and anger-control training have not been well evaluated, but tentative results are promising—especially when these programs are used in conjunction with social skills training (Blackburn, 1993; Hollin, 1990a, 1990b; Michaelson, 1987; Platt and Prout, 1987; Kazdin, 1987).

A Note on the Larger Social Environment

Most of the work on general strain theory has been at the social-psychological level, focusing on the individual and the individual's immediate social environment. The nature of one's immediate environment, however, is strongly influenced by larger social forces (see Aneshensel, 1992). These forces play a major role in generating the problems that the above programs are designed to address—problems such as dysfunctional families, school failure, and inadequate social support. And these forces influence the success or failure of these programs, since they shape the context in which these programs operate. It is difficult for parent training programs to be successful, for example, when parents face multiple stressors such as the lack of good jobs, poor housing, and neighborhoods plagued by a host of social problems.

There are several excellent discussions of these larger social forces and strategies for dealing with them. At the most general level, Messner and Rosenfeld (1994) describe how the American Dream and the domination of the institutional sphere by the economy (1) fosters unrestrained competition between individuals and (2) impairs the functioning of noneconomic institutions, such as the family and school. They provide several suggestions for strengthening noneconomic institutions and weakening the hold of the American Dream. Recent work focuses on how changes in the stratification system in the United States may have increased strain at the individual level (among other effects) and may have increased the probability of reacting to strain with crime (see Bernard, 1990; Hagan, 1994; also see Currie, 1985). Cullen argues that the United States "is not *organized*, structurally or culturally, to be socially supportive" (1994:7). Cullen (1994) and Currie (1985) discuss effective strategies for increasing social support of various types. And Sampson (1992) describes how the organizational and cultural characteristics of the community have an impact on families in ways that are conducive to delinquency. He also describes certain interventions that may improve the lives of children and families. A detailed discussion of this literature is beyond the scope of this chapter, but it is clear that the ultimate success of any delinquency control program depends on our response to these larger forces.

Conclusion

In sum, there are a number of programs that try to reduce the extent to which individuals are negatively treated by others. These programs deal with the three major types of strain identified in GST. They try to increase the likelihood that individuals will be able to achieve positively valued goals, such as popularity with peers, school success, and treatment in a fair and just manner. They try to reduce the likelihood that individuals will lose valued possessions, such as friends. And they try to reduce the extent to which individuals are exposed to negative stimuli, such as verbal and physical abuse. Further, several programs try to reduce the likelihood that individuals will react to negative treatment by turning to delinquency. These programs all show some signs of success, although all are in need of further evaluation and none constitute anything close to a solution to the delinquency problem. Some of these programs, including most of the school interventions, can be made available to all youth at reasonable cost. Other programs are more intensive and may have to be limited to delinquent and at-risk youth.

The literature on prevention and rehabilitation contains many suggestions for the successful implementation of these programs (Andrews and Bonta, 1994). Programs should be multimodal, employing a variety of interventions since delinquent youth often suffer from a variety of problems. At the same time, programs should target the specific needs of the juveniles being served. Social skills training, for example, should not assume that all delinquents are deficient in all social skills. Rather, training should target those skills in which youth demonstrate a deficiency. Programs should target problems in the youth's social environment. If interventions such as social skills training are to have a lasting effect, for example, they must not be undermined by problems in the family or at school. Finally, evidence suggests that successful programs must be intensive and of long duration (also see Gendreau, 1995; Lipsey, 1992, for additional suggestions).

Although the above programs illustrate the approach that GST would take toward controlling delinquency, it should again be emphasized that none of these programs are based explicitly on GST. Many, in fact, are based on other theories and their impact on delinquency may be partly or even fully explained by these theories. Many of these programs, for example, are based on social learning and social control theory: They attempt to more effectively punish deviance, better reinforce prosocial behavior, and increase the adolescent's level of social control or stake in conformity. GST does not deny the importance of these strategies. In fact, such strategies are quite compatible with GST. As indicated above, GST argues that individuals are most likely to react to strain with delinquency when they are low in social control or when earlier delinquency has been reinforced. All of the above programs, however, *also* reduce negative treatment by others and/or reduce the likelihood that juveniles will react to negative treatment with delinquency. These programs, then, are compatible with GST. And we can argue that *one of the reasons* these programs reduce delinquency is because of their effect on strain or the reaction to strain. Compatibility of certain programs with more than one theory of delinquency is certainly desirable, since it means that these programs may be having an impact on multiple causes of delinquency. The extent to which the effect of these programs is explained in terms of GST or these other theories is, of course, an empirical question (for a discussion of strategies for testing between the different theories, see Agnew, 1995a).

Although the policy recommendations of GST overlap with those of other theories, GST does have a unique contribution to make. Unlike social control and social learning theory, GST focuses explicitly on negative relations with others and considers a much broader range of negative relations than these theories. Previous research on GST, for example, has considered a broad range of stressful life events and everyday "hassles" that have been largely neglected by control and learning theories (see Agnew, 1995a, n.d., for a fuller discussion). And GST is unique among sociological theories in the emphasis it places on the individual's ability to deal with negative treatment, focusing as it does on cognitive, behavioral, and emotional coping strategies. GST, however, is still in its infancy. With the exception of some family and school variables, we do not know much about those types of negative treatment that contribute to delinquency. Future research, it is hoped, will lead to inventories of negative treatment that affect delinquency among large groups of adolescents. Such inventories could then be used to design and direct treatment programs. We also do not know much about the types of social support and coping strategies that are best able to reduce the impact of strain on delinquency. Future knowledge in this area could be used to refine many of the programs described above.

Four tentative sets of recommendations for reducing delinquency summarize the above discussion. These recommendations reflect the central arguments of general strain theory: Some involve efforts to reduce the adversity of interpersonal relations and others involve efforts to cope with such adversity through nondelinquent means.

1. Reduce the adversity of the youth's social environment, including family, school, and peer group. Several general strategies were offered in this area. One is to provide youth with more "voice" in determining the rules that govern their lives. This will increase their sense of "procedural justice" and so should reduce strain and delinquency. Another strategy is to treat youth in a fair or just manner, which will increase their sense of "distributive justice." Progress toward this goal can be achieved by training parents and teachers in effective disciplinary techniques, which will help them better monitor and recognize prosocial and deviant behavior, and make use of appropriate rewards and punishments. The ability of youth to achieve other positively valued goals, such as academic success and popularity with peers should be increased. This might involve academic assistance of various sorts as well as social skills training. It should be made easier for youth to legally escape from adversive environments that cannot be altered. This might involve changing teachers or schools or, in extreme cases, allowing students to drop out of school or placing them in a surrogate family. The environment could be altered in other ways to reduce adversity. School-based strategies, for example, include reducing the size of schools, emphasizing cooperative learning strategies, and increasing the opportunities for success and participation in school activities.

2. Reduce the likelihood that youth will provoke negative reactions from others (and possibly end up in negative environments). A variety of social skills training programs can be used to achieve this goal.

3. Increase the social support available to adolescents, especially during highly stressful times—such as the switch to a new school, the transition from correctional institutions to public schools, or any period where several stressful events cluster together. Such support may involve the provision of advocates or counselors for youth, mediation programs, and the supervision of adolescent activities likely to result in interpersonal conflict.

4. Increase the ability of youth to cope with adversity through nondelinquent means. This involves social skills training, problem-solving training, and anger control programs.

Notes

1. These data do not prove that GST is correct. Negative relations with others may lead to delinquency for any one of several reasons. Physical abuse by parents, for example, may lead to delinquency not only because it angers and frustrates the adolescent but also because it reduces attachment to parents and implicitly teaches the

adolescent that violence is an acceptable means to deal with one's problems. Certain evidence, however, suggests that *one* of the reasons why negative treatment leads to delinquency is because it increases anger and frustration (Agnew, 1985).

References

Agnew, Robert. 1985. "A Revised Strain Theory of Delinquency." *Social Forces* 64:151-167.

———. 1992. "Foundation for a General Strain Theory of Crime and Delinquency." *Criminology* 30:47-87.

———. 1995a. "The Contribution of Social-Psychological Strain Theory to the Explanation of Crime and Delinquency." In Freda Alder and William S. Laufer (eds.), *Advances in Criminological Theory.* Vol. 6, *The Legacy of Anomie.* New Brunswick, NJ: Transaction.

———. 1995b. "Strain and Subcultural Theories of Criminality." In Joseph Sheley (ed.), *Criminology: A Contemporary Handbook.* Belmont, CA: Wadsworth.

———. n.d. "Stability and Change in Crime over the Life Course: A Strain Theory Explanation." In Terrence P. Thornberry (ed.), *Advances in Criminological Theory.* Vol. 7, *Developmental Theories of Crime and Delinquency.* New Brunswick, NJ: Transaction. Forthcoming.

Agnew, Robert, and David M. Petersen. 1989. "Leisure and Delinquency." *Social Problems* 36:332-350.

Agnew, Robert, and Helene Raskin White. 1992. "An Empirical Test of General Strain Theory." *Criminology* 30:475-499.

Akers, Ronald L. 1985. *Deviant Behavior: A Social Learning Approach.* Belmont, CA: Wadsworth.

Ambert, Anne-Marie. 1994. "A Qualitative Study of Peer Abuse and Its Effects: Theoretical and Empirical Implications." *Journal of Marriage and the Family* 56: 119-130.

Andrews, D. A., and James Bonta. 1994. *The Psychology of Criminal Conduct.* Cincinnati: Anderson. Andrews, D. A., Ivan Zinger, Robert D. Hoge, James Bonta, Paul Gendreau, and Francis T. Cullen. 1990. "Does Correctional Treatment Work? A Clinically Relevant and Psychologically Informed Meta-Analysis." *Criminology* 28:369-404.

Aneshensel, Carol S. 1992. "Social Stess: Theory and Research." *Annual Review of Sociology* 18:15-38.

Bachman, Jerald G., Patrick M. O'Malley, and Jerome D. Johnston. 1981. *Youth in Transition,* Vol. 3, *Dropping Out—Problem or Symptom?* Ann Arbor, MI: Institute for Social Research.

Bernard, Thomas J. 1990. "Angry Aggression Among the 'Truly Disadvantaged.'" *Criminology* 28:73-96.

Berrueta-Clement, John R., Lawrence J. Schweinhart, William Steven Barnett, and David P. Weikart. 1987. "The Effects of Early Educational Intervention on Crime and Delinquency in Adolescence and Early Adulthood." In John D. Burchard and Sara N. Burchard (eds.), *Prevention of Delinquent Behavior.* Newbury Park, CA: Sage.

Blackburn, Ronald. 1993. *The Psychology of Criminal Conduct.* Chichester: John Wiley.

Braukmann, Curtis J., and Montrose M. Wolf. 1987. "Behaviorally Based Group Homes for Juvenile Offenders." In Edward K. Morris and Curtis J. Braukmann (eds.), *Behavioral Approaches to Crime and Delinquency: A Handbook of Applications, Research, and Concepts*. New York: Plenum.

Burchard, John D., and Sara N. Burchard, eds. 1987. *Prevention of Delinquent Behavior*. Newbury Park, CA: Sage.

Cloward, Richard A. and Lloyd E. Ohlin. 1960. *Delinquency and Opportunity*. New York: Free Press.

Coates, Robert B. 1987. "Social Service and Citizen Involvement." In Elmer H. Johnson (ed.), *Handbook on Crime and Delinquency Prevention*. New York: Greenwwood.

Cullen, Frank T. 1994. "Social Support as an Organizing Concept for Criminology." *Justice Quarterly* 11:527-559.

Cullen, Francis T., and Paul Gendreau. 1989. "The Effectiveness of Correctional Rehabilitation: Reconsidering the 'Nothing Works' Debate." In Lynne Goodstein and Doris Layton MacKenzie (eds.), *The American Prison: Issues in Research and Policy*. New York: Plenum.

Currie, Elliott. 1985. *Confronting Crime: An American Challenge*. New York: Pantheon

Curry, John F., Steven I. Wiencrot, and Fran Koehler. 1984. "Family Therapy with Aggressive and Delinquent Adolescents." In Charles R. Keith (ed.), *The Aggressive Adolescent: Clinical Perspectives*. New York: Free Press.

Dodge, Kenneth A. 1986. *Social Competence in Children*. Chicago: University of Chicago Press.

Elliott, Delbert S., and Harwin Voss. 1974. *Delinquency and Dropout*. Lexington, MA: D. C. Heath.

Fagan, Jeffrey. 1987. "Neighborhood Education, Mobilization and Organization for Juvenile Crime Prevention." *Annals of the American Academy of Political and So cial Sciences* 494:54-70.

Farrington, David P., Rolf Loeber, Delbert S. Elliott, J. David Hawkins, Denise B. Kandel, Malcolm W. Klein, Joan McCord, David C. Rowe, and Richard E. Tremblay. 1990. "Advancing Knowledge about the Onset of Delinquency and Crime." In Benjamin B. Lahey and Alan Kazdin (eds.), *Advances in Clinical Child Psychology*. Vol. 13. New York: Plenum.

Feldman, Ronald A., T. E. Chaplinger, and J. S. Wodarski. 1983. *The St. Louis Conundrum: The Effective Treatment of Antisocial Youths*. Englewood Cliffs, NJ: Prentice-Hall.

Felner, Robert D., Melanie Ginter, and Judith Primavera. 1982. "Primary Prevention During School Transitions: Social Support and Environmental Structure." *American Journal of Community Psychology* 10:277-290.

Gendreau, Paul. 1995. "The Principles of Effective Intervention with Offenders." In A. Harland (ed.), *What Works in Community Corrections*. Newbury Park, CA: Sage.

Gendreau, Paul, and Robert R. Ross. 1987. "Revivification of Rehabilitation: Evidence from the 1980s." *Justice Quarterly* 4:349-407.

Goldstein, Arnold P., Leonard Krasner, and Sol L. Garfield. 1989. *Reducing Delinquency: Intervention in the Community*. New York: Pergamon.

Gottfredson, Denise G. 1986. *An Assessment of a Delinquency Prevention Demonstration with Both Individual and Environmental Interventions*. Baltimore: Center for Social Organization of Schools, Johns Hopkins University.

Greene, Michael B. 1993. "Chronic Exposure to Violence and Poverty: Interventions that Work for Youth." *Crime and Delinquency* 39:106-124.

Gronfors, Martti. 1989. "Mediation-Experiment in Finland." In Peter-Alexis Albrecht and Otto Backes (eds.), *Crime Prevention and Intervention: Legal and Ethical Problems.* Berlin: Walter de Gruyter.

Grossman, F.K., J. Beinashowitz, L. Anderson, M. Sakurai, L. Finnin, and M. Flaherty. 1992. "Risk and Resilience in Young Adolescents." *Journal of Youth and Adolescence* 21:529-550.

Hagan, John. 1994. *Crime and Disrepute.* Thousand Oaks, CA: Pine Forge.

Hawkins, J. David, Richard Catalano, Gwen Jones, and David Fine. 1987. "Delinquency Prevention Through Parent Training: Results and Issues from Work in Prog ress." In James Q. Wilson (ed.), *From Children to Citizens.* Vol. III, *Families, Schools, and Delinquency Prevention.* New York: Springer-Verlag.

Hawkins, J. David, and Tony Lam. 1987. "Teacher Practices, Social Development, and Delinquency." In John D. Burchard and Sara N. Burchard (eds.), *Prevention of Delinquent Behavior.* Newbury Park, CA: Sage.

Hawkins, J. David, and Denise Lishner. 1987a. "Etiology and Prevention of Antisocial Behavior in Children and Adolescents." In David H. Crowell, Ian M. Evans, and Clifford R. O'Donnell (eds.), *Childhood Aggression and Violence: Sources of Influence, Prevention, and Control.* New York: Plenum.

———. 1987b. "Schooling and Delinquency." In Elmer H. Johnson (ed.), *Handbook on Crime and Delinquency Prevention.* New York: Greenwood.

Henderson, Monika, and Clive R. Hollin. 1986. "Social Skills Training and Delinquency." In Clive R. Hollin and Peter Trower (eds.), *Handbook of Social Skills Training.* Vol. 1, *Applications Across the Life Span.* Oxford: Pergamon.

Higgins, Paul S. 1978. "Evaluation and Case Study of a School-Based Delinquency Prevention Program: The Minnesota Youth Advocate Program." *Evaluation Quarterly* 2:215-234.

Hollin, Clive R. 1990a. *Cognitive-Behavioral Interventions with Young Offenders.* New York: Pergamon.

———. 1990b. "Social Skills Training with Delinquents: A Look at the Evidence and Some Recommendations for Practice." *British Journal of Social Work* 20:483-493.

———. 1991. "Cognitive Behaviour Modification with Delinquents." In Martin Herbert (ed.), *Clinical Child Psychology.* Chichester: John Wiley.

———. 1992. *Criminal Behaviour: A Psychological Approach to Explanation and Prevention.* London: Falmer Press.

Howells, Kevin. 1988. "The Management of Angry Aggression: A Cognitive-Behavioural Approach." In Wendy Dryden and Peter Trower (eds.), *Developments in Cognitive Psychotherapy.* London: Sage.

Kazdin, Alan E. 1985. *Treatment of Antisocial Behavior in Children and Adolescents.* Homewood, Illinois: Dorsey.

———. 1987. "Treatment of Antisocial Behavior in Children: Current Status and Future Directions." *Psychological Bulletin* 102:187-203.

Kendall, Philip C., Kevin R. Ronan, and James Epps. 1991. "Aggression in Children/ Adolescents: Cognitive-Behavioral Treatment Perspectives." In Debra J. Pepler and Kenneth H. Rubin (eds.), *The Development and Treatment of Childhood Aggression.* Hillsdale, NJ: Lawrence Erlbaum Associates.

Lane, Theodore W. and Janice Murakami. 1987. "School Programs for Delinquency Prevention and Intervention." In Edward K. Morris and Curtis J. Braukmann (eds.), *Behavioral Approaches to Crime and Delinquency: A Handbook of Application, Research, and Concepts.* New York: Plenum.

Lipsey, Mark W. 1992. "Juvenile Delinquency Treatment: A Meta-Analytic Inquiry into the Variability of Effects." In Thomas D. Cook, Harris Cooper, David S. Corday, Heidi Hartmann, Larry V. Hedges, Richard J. Light, Thomas A. Louis, and Frederick Mosteller (eds.), *Meta-Analysis for Explanation.* New York: Russell Sage.

Loeber, Rolf. 1987. "What Policy Makers and Practitioners Can Learn from Family Studies of Juvenile Conduct Problems and Delinquency." In James Q. Wilson (ed.), *From Children to Citizens,* Vol. III, *Families, Schools, and Delinquency Prevention.* New York: Springer-Verlag.

Marshal, Tony F. 1987. "Mediation: A New Mode of Establishing Order in Schools." *Howard Journal of Criminal Justice* 26:33-46.

Merton, Robert. 1938. "Social Structure and Anomie." *American Sociological Review* 3:672-682.

Messner, Steven F. and Richard Rosenfeld. 1994. *Crime and the American Dream.* Belmont, CA: Wadsworth.

Michaelson, Larry. 1987. "Cognitive-Behavioral Strategies in the Prevention and Treatment of Antisocial Disorders in Children and Adolescents." In John D. Burchard and Sara N. Burchard (eds.), *Prevention of Delinquent Behavior.* Newbury Park, CA: Sage.

Moffitt, Terrie E. 1993. "'Life-Course-Persistent' and 'Adolescent-Limited' Antisocial Behavior: A Developmental Taxonomy. *Psychological Review* 100:674-701.

Morris, Edward K., and Curtis Braukmann, eds. 1987. *Behavioral Approaches to Crime and Delinquency: A Handbook of Application, Research, and Concepts.* New York: Plenum.

Morton, Teru. 1987. "Childhood Aggression in the Context of Family Interaction." In David, H. Crowell, Ian M. Evans, and Clifford R. O'Donnell (eds.), *Childhood Aggression and Violence: Sources of Influence, Prevention, and Control.* New York: Plenum.

Morton, Teru L. and Linda S. Ewald. 1987. "Family-Based Interventions for Crime and Delinquency." In Edward K. Morris and Curtis J. Braukmann (eds.), *Behavioral Approaches to Crime and Delinquency: A Handbook of Application, Research, and Concepts.* New York: Plenum.

Novaco, Raymond W. 1975. *Anger Control: The Development and Evaluation of an Experimental Treatment.* Lexington, MA: Lexington.

Olweus, Dan. 1991. "Bully/Victim Problems Among School Children: Basic Facts and Effects of a School Based Intervention Program." In Debra J. Pepler and Kenneth H. Rubin (eds.), *The Development and Treatment of Childhood Aggression.* Hills dale, NJ: Lawrence Erlbaum Associates.

Paternoster, Raymond, and Paul Mazerolle. 1994. "An Empirical Test of General Strain Theory." *Journal of Research in Crime and Delinquency* 31:235-263.

Patterson, Gerald R. 1982. *Social Learning Approach.* Vol. 3. Eugene, OR: Castalia.

Pepler, Debra J., Gillian King, and William Byrd. 1991. "A Social-Cognitively Based Social Skills Training Program for Aggressive Children." In Debra J. Pepler and Kenneth H. Rubin (eds.), *The Development and Treatment of Childhood Aggression.* Hillsdale, NJ: Lawrence Erlbaum Associates.

Pepler, Debra J. and Kenneth H. Rubin, eds. 1991. *The Development and Treatment of Childhood Aggression.* Hillsdale, NJ: Lawrence Erlbaum.

Platt, Jerome J., and Maurice F. Prout. 1987. "Cognitive-Behavioral Theory and Interventions for Crime and Delinquency." In Edward K. Morris and Curtis J. Braukmann (eds.), *Behavioral Approaches to Crime and Delinquency: A Handbook of Application, Research, and Concepts.* New York: Plenum.

Quay, Herbert C. 1987. *Handbook of Juvenile Delinquency.* New York: John Wiley.

Raine, Adrian. 1993. *The Psychopathology of Crime: Criminal Behavior as a Clinical Disorder.* San Diego: Academic Press.

Rankin, Joseph H., and L. Edward Wells. 1987. "The Preventive Effects of the Family on Delinquency." In Elmer H. Johnson (ed.), *Handbook on Crime and Delinquency Prevention.* New York: Greenwood.

Reiss, Albert J., and Jeffrey A. Roth. 1993. "Appendix A: The Development of an Individual Potential for Violence." In Albert J. Reiss and Jeffrey A. Roth (eds.), *Understanding and Preventing Violence.* Washington, D.C.: National Academy Press.

Roberts, Albert R., and Michael J. Camasso. 1991. "The Effect of Juvenile Offender Treatment Programs on Recidivism: A Meta-Analysis of 46 Studies." *Notre Dame Journal of Law, Ethics, and Public Policy* 5:421-441.

Rutter, Michael. 1985. "Resilience in the Face of Adversity." *British Journal of Psychiatry* 147:598-611.

Sampson, Robert J. 1992. "Family Management and Child Development. In Freda Alder and William S. Laufer (eds.), *Advances in Criminological Theory.* Vol. 3, *Facts, Frameworks, and Forecasts.* New Brunswick, NJ: Transaction.

Schweinhart, Lawrence J. 1987. "Can Preschool Programs Help Prevent Delinquen cy?" In James Q. Wilson (ed.), *From Children to Citizens.* Vol. III, *Families, Schools, and Delinquency Prevention.* New York: Springer-Verlag.

Spivack, George, J.J. Platt, and Myrna B. Shure. 1976. *The Problem-Solving Approach to Adjustment.* San Francisco: Jossey-Bass.

Stein, David M. 1987. "Companionship Factors and Treatment Effects in Children." *Journal of Clinical Child Psychology* 16:141-146. Stumphauzer, Jerome S. 1986. *Helping Delinquents Change: A Treatment Manual of Social Learning Approaches.* New York: Haworth.

Thornberry, Terrence P., Melanie Moore, and R. L. Christenson. 1985. "The Effect of Dropping Out of High School on Subsequent Criminal Behavior." *Criminology* 23: 3-18.

Toby, Jackson. 1983. "Crime in the Schools." In James Q. Wilson (ed.), *Crime and Public Policy.* San Francisco: ICS Press.

Vaux, Alan. 1988. *Social Support: Theory, Research, and Intervention.* New York: Praeger.

Wahler, Robert G. 1987. "Contingency Management with Oppositional Children: Some Critical Teaching Issues for Parents." In James Q. Wilson (ed.), *From Chil dren to Citizens.* Vol. III, *Families, Schools, and Delinquency Prevention.* New York: Springer-Verlag.

Warr, Mark. 1993. "Age, Peers, and Delinquency." *Criminology* 31:17-40.

Wilson, James Q. 1987. *From Children to Citizens.* Vol. III, *Families, Schools, and Delinquency Prevention.* New York: Springer-Verlag.

Zigler, Edward, and Nancy W. Hall. 1987. "The Implications of Early Intervention Efforts for the Primary Prevention of Juvenile Delinquency." In James Q. Wilson (ed.), *From Children to Citizens.* Vol. III, *Families, Schools, and Delinquency Prevention.* New York: Springer-Verlag.

5

The Notion of Control
and Criminology's Policy Implications

Jack P. Gibbs

Even apart from crime prevention, there are three reasons why control is a strategic notion for criminology and its policy implications. First, some theories actually describe the etiology of crime (unless indicated otherwise, always including juvenile delinquency) in control terms. Second, because social control is a major notion in most social sciences, sociology especially, *control* theories about crime forge links between criminology and those other sciences. Third, the notion of control should not be limited to social control or even control over human behavior, and expanding the notion extends criminology's policy implications beyond control theories to a criterion for assessing the policy relevance of all criminological work, including atheoretical (descriptive, exploratory) research.

Of course, the relevance of control for any field depends on the notion's definition. Attempted control is defined here as: *overt* behavior by an individual in the belief that (1) the behavior increases or deceases the probability of some subsequent condition and (2) the increase or decrease is desirable.[1] That definition differs from the counteraction-of-deviance conception of social control (for an extensive critique, see Gibbs, 1989:55-58) in two major respects. First, the definiendum is attempted control rather than social control, which permits recognition not only of the distinction between successful and unsuccessful control but also inanimate control, biotic control, and various types of *asocial* controls over human behavior (e.g., self-control, proximate control, and sequential control). Second, the definition recognizes the relevance of internal behavior, both cognitive and affective, but without limiting attempted control to intentional behavior in the narrow—conscious and deliberate—sense (e.g., an individual is attempting inanimate control when driving a car even though rarely aware of gripping the wheel).

71

Control Theories

Travis Hirschi (1969) is known for attempting to restate criminology's major question from "Why do humans commit crimes?" to "Why do humans not commit crimes?"[2] Neither question lessens the importance of this argument: No etiological theory about crime, whether pertaining to individual differences or variation in rates, will survive unless the theorist recognizes two types of conditions—those that generate criminal acts and those that inhibit them. Even if generative conditions could be ignored, inhibitory conditions can be equated with "control" only by leaving the latter term undefined. That defect haunts most versions of the control theory, and it reduces their policy implications.

Hirschi's Control Theory

This version (1969) reduces to the claim that the extent of a juvenile's delinquency varies inversely with the juvenile's attachment to persons, commitment to conformity, involvement in conventional activities, and belief in the moral validity of societal norms.[3] Unlike most well-known contending theories, Sutherland's and Merton's particularly, much can be said for the testability of Hirschi's theory, in large part because of his specification of the empirical referents of the four independent variables (attachment, commitment, involvement, and beliefs) and his introduction of an illustrative test procedure.[4] Moreover, even accepting purported tests of contending theories as defensible, the predictive accuracy of Hirschi's theory does not suffer in comparison; far from it.

The principal defect of Hirschi's theory becomes evident only when contemplating an attempt to improve its predictive accuracy by specifying other or additional empirical referents of the independent variables.[5] Hirschi's theory makes no stipulations as to such alterations or extensions; and the immediate reason is that he never set forth an explicit definition of control, let alone confronted conceptual issues and problems.[6] For that matter, as a consequence of leaving control undefined, Hirschi created the impression that a "control" variable is simply any variable that correlates negatively with delinquency. Be that as it may, the four independent variables in Hirschi's theory scarcely suggest any definition of control. Even granting that various kinds of attachments, commitments to conformity, involvements in conventional activities, and moral beliefs make an individual more vulnerable to control, none of those conditions are control in themselves by any extant definition. So it is hardly surprising that the theory is often referred to, even by Hirschi, as a "bond" theory rather than a "control" theory.

The foregoing criticism bears on the policy implications of Hirschi's theory. A theory about crime causation cannot be used to prevent crime unless the theory's independent variables can be manipulated, directly or indirectly but on a large scale in either case. Such manipulation is inconceivable without attempts to control someone's behavior (e.g., that of parents) as a means of controlling the behavior of potential offenders.[7] Although the point does not bear on validity, Hirschi has not identified means for manipulating his theory's independent variables, let alone feasible means.

The Gottfredson-Hirschi Version

The notion of control is clearly central in Gottfredson and Hirschi's (1990) general theory of crime.[8] Because the theory is stated discursively to an unprecedented extent, it cannot be summarized by quoting premises, all of which are left implicit. Space limitations preclude more than an introduction of three Gottfredson-Hirschi generalizations (all 1990) as suggestive: "We have defined crimes as acts of force or fraud undertaken in pursuit of self-interest" (p. 16), "People vary in their propensity to use force and fraud (criminality)" (p. 4), and "The level of self-control, or criminality, distinguishes offenders from nonoffenders" (p. 109).

Because Gottfredson and Hirschi do not explicitly and completely identify the manifestations of criminality (a propensity) other than crime itself, their assertion of a positive association between criminality and crime is unfalsifiable. For that matter, their frequent equating of self-control (see, e.g., the last quote) and criminality suggests a tautological relation. And that suggestion is reinforced by the failure to define self-control explicitly, let alone confront conceptual issues and problems. Indeed, Gottfredson and Hirschi never define the more inclusive notion—control or attempted control.[9] Consequently, they have contributed to criminology's stock of untestable theories, and readers of criminological journals are doomed to read many reports of the impossible—the falsification of still another unfalsifiable theory (see Barlow's commentary, 1991, especially pp. 241-242).

The criticism is not that Gottfredson and Hirschi stopped far short of a procedure for measuring either criminality or self-control. Although it may be that those two notions must be treated as constructs (i.e., they cannot be defined completely, let alone linked to an empirically applicable formula), a testable proposition could be deduced from the theory by linking either notion to some concept (essentially the opposite of a construct) *other than frequency of crime.* Gottfredson and Hirschi did move in that direction (1990:97): "The 'major' cause of low self-control thus appears to be ineffective child-rearing." But that statement would be a grossly incomplete step toward a testable theory even if "child-rearing effectiveness" were the only determinant of self-control. It is difficult to imagine anyone prescribing an empirically applicable procedure for measuring the effectiveness of child rearing, and the Gottfredson-Hirschi descriptions (especially 1990:97-100) of related parental techniques are only illustrative (e.g., prohibiting smoking), incomplete (e.g., the allusion to "minimum conditions"), and/or far too abstract (e.g., references to punishing children without any qualifications).

The Gottfredson-Hirschi theory is particularly instructive when it comes to policy implications. Had they identified the causes of ineffective child rearing in terms of mensurable antecedent correlates (i.e., *concepts* linked to empirically applicable formulas), their theory might well have been a major turning point in criminology. But the theory would not have had any particular policy implications, because currently there is no feasible and demonstrably efficacious way to alter child rearing, particularly on a large scale.

Deterrence Theories

Some twenty-five years after renewal of research on the deterrence doctrine, two conclusions appear indisputable. First, it is unrealistic to reduce the doctrine to one proposition (e.g., swift, certain, and severe legal punishments prevent crimes), if only because many more properties of legal punishments · could be relevant (see Gibbs, 1986). Second, because of two distinctions, general versus specific deterrence and absolute versus restrictive deterrence, it may prove necessary to state the doctrine as four distinct theories.

Space limitations preclude even further suggestions as to the prospective form of deterrence theories, a brief survey of deterrence research, or a commentary on the horrendous evidential problems. Important though they are, those three subjects need not be treated to make observations on the deterrence doctrine's policy implications and a few of the related research findings (for some key references, see Gibbs, 1986, and Chamlin, et al., 1992).

The deterrence doctrine is an instructive example of a criminological theory that has immediate policy implications. It is not just that the doctrine identifies possible determinants of offending (individual differences, including recidivism, and the crime rate); additionally, *some* properties of legal punishments can be manipulated by officials. Indeed, the doctrine pertains to two quite distinct but interrelated control attempts by legislators (or other "enactors") to control behavior—that of various legal officials (police, prosecutors, and judges particularly) and that of potential offenders. Both types of control attempt may appear obvious, but they reflect an instrumental quality of law that is alien to the perspective of Durkheim and advocates of the retributive doctrine. For that matter, it is commonly not recognized that legislators have effective control only over the presumptive severity of statutory penalties. Hence, it is hardly surprising that in recent decades legislators have virtually ignored a truly strategic finding of deterrence research: The certainty of legal punishments appears to have a far greater impact on the crime rate than does their severity. Indeed, insofar as deterrence researchers did aspire to influence criminal justice, their efforts were gross failures as control attempts. And it may be that special actions by professional associations (e.g., the American Society of Criminology) are essential for such research to have a real impact on penal policy.

Finally, the policy implications of deterrence research will be enhanced if all interested parties come to appreciate the distinction between two questions. First, how much do extant legal punishments deter crime? Second, how much could legal punishments deter crime? The second question touches on the *limits* of legal punishments, in particular, the objective certainty and presumptive severity of actual punishments, most of which can be described in terms of feasibility and cost-benefit.

The Potential Scope of a Control Theory

No advocate of the deterrence doctrine argues that the properties of legal punishments (prescribed and actual) are the sole determinants of the crime rate; hence, there is pressing need to take extralegal conditions, those that generate or inhibit crimes, into account when testing a deterrence proposition. That need has not been satisfied in any line of deterrence research. But not even solution of that horrendous evidential problem will overcome this objection: Insofar as the deterrence doctrine is limited to legal punishments, it can never be a general theory about crime.[10] The subject even bears on this question: Why have advocates of the control theory of crime left control undefined or defined it such as to implicitly deny the relevance of the controller's internal behavior (intention, beliefs, and so on)? They have done so, evidently, to permit recognition of myriad extralegal conditions that cannot be described as control in the conscious and deliberate sense.

Note again the objection to treating internal behavior as irrelevant when defining control or social control: Recognition of its relevance need not limit control to conscious and deliberate behavior. Moreover, a control theory about crime need not be restricted to actual or threatened punishments, extralegal or legal. The potential scope of a control theory will not be appreciated until social scientists, sociologists particularly, abandon their preoccupation with structural variables and come to recognize that in any social unit (groups, organizations, countries, and so on) virtually all members frequently attempt to control the behavior of other members by various means, punitive or impunitive. Moreover, control attempts may contribute to the inhibition or generation of criminality even though that consequence was not anticipated or recognized by those making the attempt. Thus, even if parents rarely supervise their children consciously with a view to preventing delinquency, obstinacy is required to deny that supervision is attempted control and may prevent delinquency (see, e.g., Larzelere and Patterson, 1990; Wells and Rankin, 1988; and Wilson, 1980).

The Relevance of Control
for Other Theories About Crime

The relevance of control for criminology is by no means limited to control theories about crime. Even if all versions of the control theory come to be abandoned, no alternative notion will be as important as is control in connection with criminology's policy implications.[11] Again, no criminological theory can be applied to realize a policy goal without manipulating the theory's independent variables, and such manipulation is bound to entail control attempts, probably on a massive scale. Furthermore, practical people notwithstanding, any attempt to realize a policy goal is guided by or implies a theory. And even when the distinction between pure and applied theory is accepted, the latter must be a control theory, though in a quite different sense than when criminologist use the term. For that matter, every applied theory or even an attempt to apply a theory (whatever the purpose) implies something about control's effectiveness and/or efficiency.

A Special Argument About Noncontrol Theories

Everything said about applying theories extends to any theory about crime, whether conventionally identified as a control theory or otherwise (i.e., a "noncontrol" theory). However, one consideration suggests that policy implications tend to be greater for control theories. Any genuine control theory about crime reduces to a generalization in this form: In some if not all types of social units, the crime rate would decline appreciably as a consequence of an increase or decrease in at least one particular kind of control. Such a theory is incomplete or ambiguous unless the description of the kind of control extends to an identification of control agents (e.g., possibly parents, employers, legal officials) and the targets of the attempts (e.g., possibly juveniles, employees). Yet not even the most complete description assures manipulability, and any attempt to increase or decrease some kind of control is an attempt at control in itself.

The foregoing can be clarified and made more plausible by briefly reconsidering control theories about crime. The deterrence doctrine has more immediate policy implications than other versions of the control theory because it clearly identifies the control agents and the kinds of control (punitive) that supposedly affect the crime rate. The corresponding identifications are obscure in Hirschi's theory and the Gottfredson-Hirschi theory, but even the relevance of control is obscure in noncontrol theories about crime. However, in examining the policy implications of the noncontrol theories, it is desirable to comment on how they might be restated so as to make control relevant. Such restatements are all the more justified because they would enrich the policy implications, and restatements should be entertained if only to further each theory's testability and predictive accuracy.

Differential Association Theory

Conventional interpretations of Sutherland's theory (Sutherland and Cressey, 1974) ignore a possible reason for his arcane terminology, especially "definitions favorable or unfavorable to law violations" and "differential association." Sutherland's terminology enabled him to avoid a less arcane but painfully obvious rendition: The greater the extent an individual's experiences have predisposed him or her to commit some particular type of crime, the greater the probability that he or she will commit at least one instance over an ensuing time period.[12] Should Sutherland's defenders object that "definitions" and "experiences" cannot be equated, Sutherland or his followers have not confronted the distinction, and drawing one will be difficult and controversial.

Rather than really work with "definitions favorable or unfavorable to crime," researchers have focused on the extent to which the research subjects (i.e., particular individuals) have associated with presumed criminals or delinquents. Sutherland himself emphasized such associations as being the primary source of definitions (read "experiences") favorable to crime, but he did not identify them as the exclusive source, and the "association focus" overlooks definitions unfavorable to crime. So why the focus on favorable associations rather than on experiences favorable *or* unfavorable to crime? Criminologists have ignored the question because the association focus makes it appear that purported tests of the theory are justifiable. But contemplate abandoning the association focus and then try to imagine someone purporting to measure the extent to which any individual's experiences have been on balance favorable to crime, whatever the type under consideration, or even claiming that only recent experiences are relevant.

Although there is vast difference between the testability of the "experiential" version and that of the "association" version, the contrast is far less in connection with policy implications. All too briefly, the policy implications of both versions are negligible. Surely there is little prospect of *controlling* behavior on a large scale so as to eliminate experiences favorable to crime.[13] For that matter, it is doubtful that independent observers can realize even appreciable agreement when identifying instances of the two types of experiences, and there is no procedure for assigning numerical weights to each instance. So, far from being essential, Sutherland's notions of "definitions" and "differential association" are obfuscations.

As for the future of Sutherland's theory, one particular line of expansion could enhance both testability and policy implications. Perhaps because Sutherland ostensibly doubted the preventive efficacy of legal punishments, he did not stress punishments as negative definitions (read "negative experiences") of crime and, conversely, impunitive reactions as positive definitions. The general point is, of course, that the notion of deterrence can be introduced into Sutherland's theory. Granted that the "definitional" impact of punishment of crime is extremely problematical at both levels, individual and aggregate, one policy implication of more stress on legal punishments (i.e., as "definitions") would be especially in keeping with the association version of Sutherland's theory. If individuals do acquire even a substantial share of their definitions favorable to crime through interpersonal interaction, there is rationale for *insulative* legal reactions to offenders, meaning those that reduce the interaction between offenders and their relatives or other close associates.

The Anomie Theory

After some fifty-five years (Merton, 1938, 1957) one generalization continues to summarize the theory: Among social units, the greater the disjunction between culturally approved (legal and institutionalized) goals and access to as well as emphasis on culturally approved means to those goals, the greater the rate of deviant behavior, including crime and delinquency. Over the years it has become fashionable to speak of "strain" theory rather than anomie theory. That label is less arcane, but it diverts attention from what should be an embarrassment for criminologists: After more than fifty years the theory is no more amenable to defensible tests than when first formulated. Specifically, no one has formulated an empirically applicable measure of any of the three independent variables—emphasis on goals, access to means, and emphasis on means—and Merton failed to stipulate a formula for combining the three values so as compute what would be a disjunction measure (see Gibbs, 1985:42-46, for extensive elaboration).

So how is it that numerous investigators have published reports of purported tests of the anomie theory? They have done so by examining the association between what is at most an indicator (not a measure) of only one of the three disjunction components and some variable pertaining to crime.[14] Thus, even if social class composition, class position, income inequality, or income were a defensible substitute for a measure of access to means (or differential access), the test would ignore emphasis on goals and emphasis on means.

The anomie theory is a good example of how neglect of some feature of a theory may drastically diminish both testability and policy implications. The most neglected feature in reported tests of the anomie theory is *emphasis on means*, a neglect encouraged by Merton's failure to maintain the distinction between that variable and access to means. Surely there is no basis for denying the relevance of emphasis on means, and just as surely legal punishments (actual and statutory) emphasize the consequences of pursuing certain culturally approved goals (material conditions, sexual experience) by illegal means. Accordingly, all deterrence research actually bears on the anomie theory.

The immediate caveat is not just that deterrence research is no more a complete test of the anomie theory than has been the case in conventional research; additionally, the efficacy of legal punishments (through deterrence or some other mechanism) cannot be assumed. Nonetheless, the connection between legal punishments and two major theories—differential association and anomie—is further justification for continuing deterrence research. As far as policy implications go, the immediate justification remains the manipulability of various properties of legal punishments. And a consideration of conventional research on the anomie theory is conducive to a greater appreciation of that justification. Briefly, it is pointless to presume that in the U.S. government, control of class composition or income inequality is technically or politically feasible, and there are even doubts about realizing truly substantial reductions of unemployment. Thus, any theory (anomie, Marxist, or what have you) that expressly or tacitly emphasizes economic determinism is virtually barren when it comes to policy implications; that is the foremost rationale for slighting such theories in this chapter. Lest some ideological bias be suspected, criminological theories that describe the etiology of crime in terms of biological factors, social integration, or social disorganization are also slighted and for the same reason (see brief surveys in Barlow, 1990:35-37, 46-49, 170-171; Bursik, 1988; Jensen and Rojek, 1992:180-194, 217-221, 340-341, 346; and Walters and White, 1989).

Opportunity Theory

The general idea is simple: Given an expansion of opportunities to commit some type of act, criminal or otherwise, its commission frequency increases (see Cohen and Felson, 1979; and the literature cited in Barlow, 1990:105-107, and Jensen and Rojek, 1992:346-348). To illustrate, researchers have reported a positive association between the number of automobiles presumably used in a territorial unit and that unit's auto theft rate, the number of commercial establishments and the territorial unit's robbery rate, and the residential burglary rate and the percentage of dwelling units temporarily unoccupied at some particular hour.

An etiological theory with impressive predictive accuracy is unlikely unless "opportunity conditions" are recognized, even if only when computing crime rates to test the theory. Nevertheless, when it comes to explaining variation in crime (individual differences or the rate), opportunity theory is subject to several objections, none of which are avoided in, to use the currently more fashionable label, "routine activities theory." The most obvious objection is that any version of the theory appears to identify at most only necessary conditions for a high crime rate or for a history of commission at the individual level. For that matter, it is commonly difficult to see how the condition in question (e.g., an unoccupied residence) is literally necessary for the crime (e.g., burglary), and resort to such expressions as "conducive to" or "increases the probability" is scarcely informative. Less obvious is that whatever the type of crime, the necessary conditions for its commission are seemingly infinite; consequently, even though myriad findings and empirical generalizations appear consistent with the theory, it is difficult to see how any test could falsify the theory. Any negative finding can be attributed to conditions, perhaps even identifiable conditions, not taken into account.

Despite reservations about opportunity theory, it may have more policy implications than does any contending theory. Perhaps most important, no criminological theory or proposed crime prevention measure is likely to be taken seriously by policymakers or their advisers unless there is some supporting evidence (though often far from systematic evidence; see, e.g., U.S. House of Representatives, 1991). In that connection, granted the previous caveat about opportunity theory's falsifiability, its testability is rivaled only by the deterrence doctrine. And when it comes to the predictive accuracy of constituent empirical generalizations, to date many research findings suggest that opportunity theory is superior. The deterrence doctrine is much more specific as to relevant independent variables, but the diversity of putative "opportunity conditions" has an advantage when it comes to crime prevention. If any condition is *necessary* for crime, its elimination is thus *sufficient* for crime prevention.

Unfortunately, opportunity theory's policy implications are far less than the foregoing suggests. Even if all of the putative constituent empirical generalizations were known to be both causal and valid, the theory offers little in the way of crime prevention, the reason being that the component specific independent variables cannot be manipulated readily, if at all. Consider, for example, evidence that participation of women in the labor force increases the rate of both residential burglary and forcible rape. Even if the two relations are truly causal, legislative action to reduce female employment is most unlikely.

Fortunately, opportunity theory's policy implications can be enhanced by integrating the theory and contenders, and the strategy is all the more attractive because many criminologists are unlikely (perhaps rightly so) to take policy considerations seriously unless they can at the same time further the pursuit of impressive theories, the goal of pure science. One integrative step lies in an answer to this question: Why is the residential burglary rate correlated with the amount of time that homes are temporarily unoccupied? It is plausible to presume that potential burglars perceive the condition as reducing apprehension risk, meaning that "timing" is attempted countercontrol by offenders. So the illustration points the way to an integration of a large component of opportunity theory and a large component of the deterrence doctrine. More important for present purposes, the integration would enhance opportunity theory's policy implications. For example, if temporarily unoccupied dwelling places increase the residential burglary rate through reduction of the apprehension risk as perceived by potential burglars, then governmental promotion of residential surveillance systems is an alternative to reducing the participation of women in the labor force.

Advocates of opportunity theory can claim that some of its variables (e.g., number of commercial establishments) are strictly opportunity conditions and have no connection with any consequence of legal punishments (e.g., deterrence, incapacitation). The claim is justified, but its import is diminished substantially on recognition that the ultimate goal is a general control theory about crime. The theory will treat legal punishments as relevant if only because law can be characterized as a vast organized attempt at control (backed by the threat of unlimited coercion) over attempts at control. Although that characterization is cumbersome, it directs attention to the fact that crimes in themselves are control attempts; hence, potential offenders are motivated to enhance the prospect of success. To illustrate, consider the strengthening of coin boxes in vending machines and public telephones, one of numerous tactics in "situational crime prevention" (see, e.g., Cornish and Clarke, 1987:934). Even assuming that the change does not further potential offenders' perception of apprehension risk, to describe the change as "reducing opportunity" is merely an allusion to a *decrease* in perceived inanimate control effectiveness. The more general point is that a control theory about crime could be such as to incorporate much of what commonly passes for rational choice theory.

Other Aspects of Control
and Criminology's Policy Implications

In light of all of the foregoing, extant criminological theories offer very little when it comes to crime prevention. That condition will prevail until theorists devote much more attention to the notion of control, including a conceptualization that emphasizes control's purposive quality. Even now, a greater emphasis on control will prompt recognition of the policy implications of criminological theories and promote research apart from any particular theory.

Secondary Deviance and Specific Deterrence

As conventionally interpreted, the theory of secondary deviance and the specific deterrence theory stand in stark opposition. Whereas the latter is conventionally interpreted as implying that severe punishments of offenders decrease recidivism, the former is conventionally interpreted as implying that such punishments increase recidivism. However, conventional versions of both theories fail to speak to a crucial question. In the case of the specific deterrence, the question is: What kinds of legal punishments for what types of offenses and offenders decrease recidivism? The question is the same for the secondary deviance theory except "decreases" becomes "increases" (for a more elaborate treatment, see Gibbs, 1985:35, 1986, 1987:826).

In the absence of a defensible answer to the questions, it is no wonder that neither theory has been supported substantially in tests; far from it. Indeed, defensible answers might make the theories complementary and are steps toward a theory about the effectiveness of attempts to prevent recidivism. Such a theory will not necessarily resurrect the rehabilitative ideal in U.S. penal policy, but it would offer a distinct alternative to more drift by default toward retribution and incapacitation. Given their sympathy for the underdog, advocates of the secondary deviance theory may balk at furthering the attempts of officials to control behavior, but from the outset the theory has been virtually an explicit negative critique of punitive penal policy and, hence, "available" for use by officials.

Societal Reaction Theory and the Deterrence Doctrine

Far from standing in clear opposition, societal reaction theory and the deterrence doctrine (for brief introductions, see Gibbs, 1985:34, 1986) seem unrelated, at least in that the validity of one has no bearing on the validity of the other. Their independence stems from the fact that whereas the deterrence doctrine takes properties of legal punishments as given, societal reaction theory could eventually extend to an identification of the determinants of variation in those properties.[15] Unfortunately, attention has been directed primarily toward explaining variation in the severity of reactions, legal or extralegal, and even more to identifying reaction contingencies (e.g., the accused's race or gender).

Should societal reaction theory and related research ever be extended to the determinants of variation in the objective certainty of legal punishments, at one and the same time it would contribute to a general theory of behavior control and have greater policy implications. The deterrence doctrine cannot be a recipe for crime prevention without an answer to this *control* question: How can the objective certainty of arrest for crime be increased? Should the answer (e.g., more police) appear obvious, any answer is bereft of policy implications unless feasibility and efficiency are taken into account.

An Especially Relevant Line of Atheoretical Research

When criminologists engage in research that bears on both a theory and policy issues, they are living in the best of all possible worlds. However, there is a place for descriptive or exploratory research, especially in connection with penal policy, and recent work on incapacitation is a good illustration. That work is based on the idea that legal punishment of an offender may make it difficult if not impossible for him or her to repeat the offense and perhaps any other (e.g., car thieves cannot practice their craft while incarcerated). To date, the research has focused on imprisonment's incapacitating effect, but it could be extended to executions, and the outcome might surprise advocates of capital punishment because the question is always: How much did this particular punishment reduce the crime rate through incapacitation?

The question has been pursued only in connection with imprisonment. It has proven extremely difficult to answer incontrovertibly (see, especially, Messinger and Berk, 1987), and it is unlikely that the investigators are satisfied with their methodology or confident in their conclusions.[16] However, although estimates of the incapacitating effects of imprisonment vary substantially (depending on the type of crime, the time period, the prison location, and methodology), all suggest that incapacitation is a prohibitively inefficient means of crime prevention. Thus, some findings indicate that a 1 percent decrease in the crime rate would require a 10 percent increase in the U.S. prison population (Messinger and Berk, 1987:774).

A Far Less Developed Line of Research

It is difficult to imagine any assessment of an attempt at crime prevention that is not plagued with a particular evidential problem—the need to take into account the possibility of a "displacement effect." Briefly, a change in legal reactions to a particular type of crime may decrease instances of that crime in some particular territorial unit but increase instances in nearby territorial units or increase instances of other types of crime (for a broader conception of displacement, see Cornish and Clarke, 1987:934).

Displacement research is not well developed, and a uniform methodology is not feasible. Thus, an escalation of police patrol activities in a particular city could decrease the total number of crimes in that city but increase the total in the city's suburbs. By contrast, an increase in the presumptive severity and/or objective certainty of legal punishments for robbery in a state may decrease the state's robbery rate but increase its burglary rate.

When testing a deterrence proposition, it may be defensible to ignore the possibility of displacement effects (i.e., for purely theoretical purposes the possibility is irrelevant). However, when criminological theories are applied to realize policy goals, the efficacy of control attempts becomes pivotal. The very idea of crime prevention surely means something more than a displacement of offenses. Indeed, one problem in incapacitation research is the need to take into account the extent that incarceration merely shifts crime from streets to prisons.

Although an assessment of a crime prevention program should consider the possibility of displacement effects, they need not be recognized in an etiological theory about crime. After all, were it not for changes in opportunities (with or without related changes in the objective and perceived certainty of apprehension) or changes in legal reactions to crime, there would be no displacement effects. For that matter, even if Cornish and Clarke (1987) have rightfully subsumed displacement effects under rational choice theory, there is nothing about the theory (or opportunity theory) that cannot be described and thought of in terms of attempted control, including countercontrol attempts by offenders.

A Narrow but Strategic Line of Research

Common sense notwithstanding, it has proven extremely difficult to make defensible estimates of the extent to which the availability of firearms influences the rate of violent crime, homicide in particular. Nonetheless, that line of research (see, especially, Kleck, 1991) is ripe with both policy implications and potential contributions to theoretical criminology.

Research on the availability of firearms and violent crime is virtually certain to bear on opportunity theory. Moreover, with or without encouragement by criminologists, legislators are likely to attempt furtherance of governmental control over the production, purchase, possession, and/or use of firearms. Each legislative action invites research on the efficacy of that control attempt, with . the evaluative research having both policy implications and a bearing on the deterrence doctrine.

Summary and Conclusion

Control could be criminology's central notion, meaning that the vast majority of criminologists can describe and think about their interests in terms of control. This chapter suggests at least two advantages along that line. First, such description and thinking promotes restatements of criminological theories and facilitates a synthesis of them. Second, the policy implications of criminological work can be both recognized and furthered more readily if examined in light of control, and that advantage is realized in assessing not only theories but also atheoretical lines of research.

The argument about policy implications extends to an even broader claim. Whatever the field, taking control as the central notion encourages an applied orientation in that field. That broader claim introduces the foremost danger: An exclusively applied orientation is conducive to sterility in any field. Taking control as criminology's central notion would increase that danger far less than it appears initially, because even from the perspective of pure science, control is a strategic notion for criminology. Specifically, criminologists can formulate theories about crime in which control is the central notion, and such theories will be richer in policy implications than are contenders. Moreover, because atheoretical research on crime prevention bears directly on the notion of control, it is always a possible contribution toward a general theory of control (i.e., one not limited to the efficacy of possible means of crime prevention). The most immediate danger is the possibility of an allocation of resources that favors applied research. That danger may be the primary reason why many criminologists appear wary of some lines of concern with policy implications of criminological work (see, e.g., Travis Hirschi's caustic commentary on "administrative criminology" in *Contemporary Sociology*, vol. 22, pp. 348-350). In any case, the danger could be reduced by abandoning peer reviews of isolated research proposals to agencies or foundations in preference for explicitly competitive reviews (i.e., each reviewer always ranks two or more proposals). Reviewers commonly recognize that from the perspective of pure science, two research proposals may have more or less the same merit; hence, favoring the proposal that has more policy implications would promote applied work in the field but without abandoning pure science. Of course, there are various criteria for assessing the policy implications of a research proposal but in criminology and the behavioral sciences generally there is this pivotal question: Would an attempt at large-scale manipulation of the independent variables be feasible?

Finally, numerous criminologists and perhaps even agency or foundation officials ostensibly have reservations about the notion of control that go beyond the sterility of an exclusively applied orientation in a scientific field. Briefly, although rarely expressed, there is a tendency to think of control as an evil. That tendency is no mystery. Try to find a citizen of a liberal democracy who either likes to be controlled or openly aspires to control others. Aversion to control is likely to be manifested in criticisms of criminologists who take the notion seriously, for they can be depicted readily as prospective architects of a real *1984*. Even so, it is foolish to think of crime prevention and control over human behavior as somehow separable. For that matter, it is a dangerous illusion to think that any social problem—unemployment, premature termination of education, poverty—can be eliminated without behavior control on a massive scale.

The subject takes on added significance because some astute commentators on the crime problem, such as Elliott Currie (1985), will decry the lack of emphasis here on such socioeconomic changes as major reductions in the unemployment rate, a much higher minimum wage, and a sharp increase in the school completion rate. Even if such changes could be expected to lower the crime rate (a very disputable expectation, unfortunately), the claim that such changes are technically and politically feasible is a control argument in itself. And whatever the rationale for expecting a decline in the crime, even if valid the claim is still another control argument.

Notes

1. For an elaborate conceptualization, including the identification of types and subtypes of attempted control, see Gibbs (1989:22-75).

2. Hirschi (especially 1969:3-15) does not phrase the two questions in exactly those terms; indeed, his terminology varies. However, no version of either question is likely to eliminate doubts about their logical independence.

3. There are several versions of the control theory of crime, but space limitation is not the only reason for focusing on Hirschi's version. Additionally, it is surely the best-known and most fully developed version.

4. Convention in sociology and criminology notwithstanding, reported tests of a theory are not sufficient evidence of testability. No reported test is defensible unless the theory is stated such that professionals in the field agree as to the *kinds* of falsifiable predictions that can be deduced from the theory. And no prediction is falsifiable without confidence that the prediction's constituent terms are empirically applicable, meaning that independent investigators report it is feasible to apply the terms (including formulas when the terms denote quantitative variables) and agree in reporting the results of their applications to the same event or things, including individuals or populations. Equally important, no prediction bears on a theory's validity unless it has been deduced from the theory by explicit rules. Accordingly, little can be said for the testability of the typical criminological theory because its constituent terms promise negligible empirical applicability. Neither the premises of the typical criminological theory nor the appropriate rules of deduction can be identified readily or without controversy. That condition will remain until criminologists replace the discursive mode of theory construction—merely the conventions of some natural language—for a formal mode (for elaboration, see Gibbs, 1985).

5. The specification of other empirical referents becomes imperative when attempting to test the theory through observations on adults or any population far removed socially or culturally from Richmond, California, circa 1964 or when endeavoring to enhance the theory's predictive accuracy through modification of prescribed measures of the independent variables. The latter possibility will become all the more relevant should criminologists ever come to recognize that the only way to avoid the current inconclusive if not contradictory assessments of contending theories is to judge them rigorously and exclusively in terms of seven dimensions of predictive power (for elaboration, see Gibbs, 1994).

6. Hirschi (see *American Journal of Sociology*, Vol. 96, p. 751) muddies the water by endorsing an emphasis on the purposive quality of control and yet not emphasizing that quality in what may be implicit or partial definitions of control in his two major theoretical works (Hirschi, 1969, and Gottfredson and Hirschi, 1990).

7. Lest the point appear all too obvious, extreme versions of labeling theory (according to which crimes are "social constructions") have only one implication for crime prevention: convince putative crime victims that they are deluded.

8. The notion's centrality in the theory is paradoxical in light of Hirschi's denial (*American Journal of Sociology*, Vol. 96, p. 751) that he can describe and think of criminology's subject matter in terms of control.

9. These failures to provide explicit definitions are all the more remarkable given Hirschi's rejection (*American Journal of Sociology*, Vol. 96, p. 750) of an elaborate

conceptualization of attempted control, including self-control, without so much as a hint of an alternative.

10. The objection is most commonly manifested in criticisms that depict the deterrence doctrine as being too narrow (for research on an expanded conception of deterrence, see Nagin and Paternoster, 1991). Such criticism would be more constructive if directed to this question: What extralegal conditions should be taken into account and how should they be considered when testing a deterrence proposition?

11. Consider two largely atheoretical lines of work by criminologists: first, proposals or evaluations of crime prevention programs (see, e.g., Rosenbaum, 1986); and, second, participation in debates over criminal law, as exemplified by recent literature on issues pertaining to drug control (see, e.g., Blumstein, 1993, and *Contemporary Sociology*, vol. 22, pp. 341-343). Although such lines of work may have greater policy relevance than does any extant theory about crime, this question makes "theory" always relevant: Given a clear-cut success or failure in crime prevention, why that outcome?

12. Lest the generalization appear tautological, it is a tacit rejection of genetic or biological determinism. Moreover, what has been said of Sutherlnd's theory largely applies also to "social learning theory" (especially Akers, 1985). Although the latter is much more testable, it is commonly characterized as being an extension of the former. Whatever the relation between the two theories, "learning" and "experience" are closely related notions.

13. Pessimism is even more justified in contemplating the policy implications of a "normative-attitudinal" version of Sutherland's theory that would include a premise something like this: Among individuals, the greater the ratio of criminally favorable experiences to criminally unfavorable experiences, the less the condemnation of crime. Given another premise that links the experience ratio to the frequency of offenses, it would be possible to deduce a theorem that asserts a negative association between the condemnation variable; and the frequency variable. However, both testability and predictive accuracy would depend appreciably on the measurement of the condemnation variable; and to date efforts along that line have not yielded impressive results (but see Burkett and Ward, 1993). Yet not even astonishing predictive accuracy would have policy implications, because there are really no reliable and feasible means to control attitudes and values, certainly not extensively.

14. In all tests the crime variable would be dubious even if based on absolutely reliable data. No investigator can claim that the variable is the *total* deviance rate or even the total crime rate. Rather, in all tests to date the variable has pertained to the rate for particular types of deviance, perhaps only one, and such tests require recognition of the direction of the imbalance between the disjunction components. (For example, a greater emphasis on goals than access to means is a condition quite different from a reversal of the two.) The second part of Merton's theory—his "modes of adaptation"—directs attention to types of deviance; but the logical connection between it and the first part (the summary generalization, supra) is obscure, and the second part has been virtually ignored in reported tests of the theory (for an extensive elaboration on this footnote, see Gibbs, 1985:42-46).

15. For that matter, what passes for societal reaction theory is more nearly a set of diverse arguments and research findings, some of which are inconsistent especially when it comes to identifying the paramount determinant of reactions to deviance and deviants (for elaboration, see Gibbs, 1987:826). Nonetheless, all of the arguments and findings

do reflect a concern with this question: What determines the character of reactions to deviance and deviants?

16. The research becomes all the more controversial and theoretical when considered in connection with the "criminal careers" model or paradigm (see *Criminology*, vol. 26, pp. 1-100).

References

Akers, Ronald L. 1985. *Deviant Behavior: A Social Learning Approach*, 3d ed. Belmont, CA: Wadsworth.

Barlow, Hugh D. 1990. *Introduction to Criminology*, 5th ed. Glenview, IL: Scott, Foresman.

———. 1991. "Explaining Crimes and Analogous Acts, or the Unrestrained Will Grab at Pleasure Whenever They Can". *Journal of Criminal Law and Criminology* 82:229-242.

Blumstein, Alfred. 1993. "Making Rationality Relevant—The American Society of Criminology Presidential Address." *Criminology* 31:1-16.

Burkett, Steven R,. and David A. Ward. 1993. "A Note on Perceptual Deterrence, Religiously Based Moral Condemnation, and Social Control." *Criminology* 31:119-134.

Bursik, Robert J., Jr. 1988. "Social Disorganization and Theories of Crime and Delinquency: Problems and Prospects." *Criminology* 26:519-551.

Chamlin, Mitchell B., Harold G. Grasmick, Robert J. Bursik, Jr.,and John K. Cochran. 1992. "Time Aggregation and Time Lag in Macro-Level Deterrence Research." *Criminology* 30:377-395.

Cohen, Lawrence E. and Marcus. Felson. 1979. "Social Change and Crime Rate Trends: A Routine Activity Approach." *American Sociological Review* 44:588-608.

Cornish, Derek B. and Ronald V. Clarke. 1987. "Understanding Crime Displacement: An Application of Rational Choice Theory." *Criminology* 25:933-947.

Currie, Elliott. 1985. *Confronting Crime*. New York: Pantheon Books.

Gibbs, Jack P. 1985. "The Methodology of Theory Construction." In Robert F. Meier (ed.), *Theoretical Methods in Criminology*. Beverly Hills, CA: Sage.

———. 1986. "Deterrence Theory and Research." In Gary B. Melton (ed.), *The Law as a Behavioral Instrument*. Lincoln: University of Nebraska Press.

———. 1987. "The State of Criminological Theory." *Criminology* 25:821-840.

———. 1989. *Control: Sociology's Central Notion*. Urbana: University of Illinois Press.

———. 1994 "Durkheim's Heavy Hand in the Sociological Study of Suicide." In David Lester (ed.), *Emile Durkheim: Le Suicide One Hundred Years Later*. Philadelphia: Charles Press.

Gottfredson, Michael, and Travis Hirschi. 1990. *A General Theory of Crime*. Stanford, CA: Stanford University Press.

Hirschi, Travis. 1969. *Causes of Delinquency*. Berkeley: University of California Press.

Jensen, Gary F. and Dean J. Rojek. 1992. *Delinquency and Youth Crime*, 2d ed. Prospect Heights, IL: Waveland Press.

Kleck, Gary. 1991. *Point Blank: Guns and Violence in America*. New York: Aldine de Gruyter.

Larzelere, Robert E. and Gerald R. Patterson. 1990. "Parental Management: Mediator of the Effect of Socioeconomic Status on Early Delinquency." *Criminology* 28:301-323.

Merton, Robert K. 1938. "Social Structure and Anomie. *American Sociological Review* 3:672-682.

———. 1957. *Social Theory and Social Structure*, Rev. ed. New York: Free Press.

Messinger, Sheldon L. and Richard A. Berk. 1987. "A Review Essay: Dangerous People." *Criminology* 25:767-781.

Nagin, Daniel S., and Raymond Paternoster. 1991. "The Preventive Effects of the Perceived Risk of Arrest: Testing an Expanded Conception of Deterrence." *Criminology* 29:561-587.

Rosenbaum, Dennis P., ed. 1986. *Community Crime Prevention: Does It Work?* Beverly Hills, CA: Sage.

Sutherland Edwin H., and Donald R. Cressey. 1974. *Criminology*. 9th ed. Philadelphia: Lippincott.

U.S. House of Representatives, Committee on the Judiciary, Subcommittee on Crime and Criminal Justice. 1991. *Selected Crime Issues: Prevention and Punishment*. Washington, DC: U.S. Government Printing Office.

Walters, Glenn D. and Thomas W. White. 1989. "Heredity and Crime: Bad Genes or Bad Research?" *Criminology* 27:455-485.

Wells, L. Edward, and Joseph H. Rankin. 1988. "Direct Parental Control and Delinquency." *Criminology*, 26:263-285.

Wilson, Harriet. 1980. "Parental Supervision." *British Journal of Criminology* 20:203-235.

6

The Public Policy Implications
of a Life-Course Perspective on Crime

John H. Laub, Robert J. Sampson, Ronald P. Corbett, Jr.,
and Jinney S. Smith

Current dialogue about crime policy in the United States is overwhelmingly biased toward punishment-based approaches, as demonstrated by harsher sentencing laws (e.g., "Three Strikes and You're Out") and expanded prison construction. Although deterrence, incapacitation, and retribution are important components of a comprehensive policy on crime, current public discourse on crime and its control has become rather predictable and uninspired.

If future policies are to lead to breakthroughs in reducing crime and delinquency, the current polarized debate over "tough" versus "soft" approaches must give way to a focus on "smart" versus "dumb" strategies. "Smart" policies are those that are supported by solid research. A commitment to "smart" policies means rejecting policies that are merely politically correct and in tune with the political values of the moment. Thus research rather than ideology and politics should govern the direction of crime control policies.

Using Sampson and Laub's (1993) age-graded theory of informal social control as our framework, we offer here a new perspective on crime and crime control that integrates a wide body of existing research on crime and antisocial behavior. We refer to this perspective as a life-course perspective on crime and crime control. In their recent book, *Crime in the Making: Pathways and Turning Points Through Life* (1993), Sampson and Laub argue that the causes of crime are rooted in three sources: weak social bonds to family, school, and work; disruption of relations between individuals and institutions that provide social capital; and the influence of structural disadvantage. Therefore, it would appear that current crime policies that focus solely on the deterrent and incapacitative effects of the criminal justice system are myopic and should be reconsidered in light of known facts about crime. In this chapter, we explore the implications of these ideas for public policies on crime.

Our paper is organized in the following fashion. First, we present a brief description of the life-course perspective. Second, we introduce the key elements of Sampson and Laub's age-graded theory of informal social control. Third, and most important, we identify at each stage of the life course—childhood, adolescence, and adulthood—the key policy implications of Sampson and Laub's age-graded theory of crime.

The Life-Course Perspective

The life course has been defined as "pathways through the age differentiated life span," where age differentiation "is manifested in expectations and options that impinge on decision processes and the course of events that give shape to life stages, transitions, and turning points" (Elder, 1985:17). Similarly, Caspi, Elder, and Herbener (1990:15) conceive of the life course as a "sequence of culturally defined age-graded roles and social transitions that are enacted over time." Age-graded transitions are embedded in social institutions and are subject to historical change (Elder, 1992).

Two central concepts underlie the analysis of life-course dynamics. A *trajectory* is a pathway or line of development over the life span, such as work life, marriage, parenthood, or criminal behavior. Trajectories refer to long-term patterns of behavior and are marked by a sequence of transitions. *Transitions* are marked by life events (such as first job or first marriage) that are embedded in trajectories and evolve over shorter time spans—"changes in state that are more or less abrupt" (Elder, 1985:31-32).

The interlocking nature of trajectories and transitions may generate *turning points*, or changes in the life course (Elder, 1985:32). Adaptation to life events is crucial because the same event or transition followed by different adaptations can lead to different trajectories (Elder, 1985:35). The long-term view embodied by the life-course focus on trajectories implies a strong connection between childhood events and experiences in adulthood. However, the simultaneous shorter-term view also implies that transitions or turning points can modify life trajectories—they can "redirect paths." Social institutions and triggering life events that may modify trajectories include school, work, marriage, and parenthood (see Rutter, Quinton, and Hill, 1990; Sampson and Laub, 1993).

We argue that a life-course perspective has much to offer to the study of crime. For example, adopting a life-course perspective forces one to look at crime and antisocial behavior in a developmental context and ask, What is the connection between antisocial behavior in childhood, delinquency in adolescence, and offending as an adult? In other words, can pathways to delinquency be explained? A life-course perspective also requires one to consider the possibility of change as individuals move through life-course trajectories. Thus, from a life-course perspective, several important questions emerge: Why are some juvenile delinquents able to turn their lives around and change their criminal behavior whereas others display a pattern of continuous antisocial behavior from childhood through adulthood? Once formed, can delinquent pathways be altered? In other words, are there turning points in life? These questions will be explored in more detail below.

An Age-Graded Theory of Informal Social Control

Since 1987, two of the authors of this chapter (Sampson and Laub) have been recoding, computerizing, and reanalyzing Sheldon and Eleanor Gluecks' longitudinal data on juvenile delinquency and adult crime.[1] The overriding goal of Sampson and Laub's project was to examine crime and deviance in childhood, adolescence, and adulthood in a way that recognized the significance of both continuity and change over the life course. To do so they synthesized and integrated the criminological literature on childhood antisocial behavior, adolescent delinquency, and adult crime with theory and research on the life course (see Sampson and Laub, 1992). By also rethinking the findings produced by longitudinal research, they were eventually led to develop an age-graded theory of informal social control to explain crime and deviance over the life span. Sampson and Laub then tested this theory on the longitudinal data reconstructed from the Gluecks' study (see Sampson and Laub, 1993; Laub and Sampson, 1993, for more details).[2]

The central idea of social control theory—that crime and deviance are more likely to occur when an individual's bond to society is weak or broken—is an organizing principle in Sampson and Laub's theory of social bonding over the life course. Following Elder (1985), Sampson and Laub differentiate the life course of individuals on the basis of age and argue that the important institutions of both formal and informal social control vary across the life span. However, they emphasize the role of age-graded *informal* social control as reflected in the structure of interpersonal bonds linking members of society to one another and to wider social institutions (e.g., work, family, school). Unlike formal sanctions, which originate in purposeful efforts to control crime, informal social controls "emerge as by-products of role relationships established for other purposes and are components of role reciprocities" (Kornhauser, 1978:24).

Sampson and Laub also examine social relations between individuals (e.g., parent-child, teacher-student, and employer-employee) at each stage of the life course as a form of social investment or *social capital* (Coleman, 1988, 1990). Specifically, they posit that the social capital derived from strong social relations (or strong social bonds), whether it be as a child in a family, as an adolescent in school, or as an adult in a job, dictates the salience of these relations at the individual level. If these relations are characterized by interdependency (Braithwaite, 1989), they represent social and psychological resources that individuals can draw on as they move through life transitions that traverse larger trajectories. Thus, Sampson and Laub see both social capital and informal social control as linked to social structure and they distinguish both concepts as important in understanding changes in behavior over time.

By uniting a developmental, life-course perspective with research on antisocial and criminal behavior, Sampson and Laub have developed a new theory of crime and delinquency over the life course. We present three key ideas from this theory and highlight some of the results of Sampson and Laub's study (see Sampson and Laub, 1993, for more details).[3]

Structure and Process in Adolescent Delinquency

The first building block in Sampson and Laub's theory is a focus on both structural and process variables. To illustrate, Sampson and Laub argue that informal social controls derived from the family (e.g., consistent use of discipline, monitoring, and attachment) mediate the effects of both individual and structural background variables. For instance, previous research on families and delinquency often fails to account for social structural disadvantage and how it influences family life. As Rutter and Giller (1983:185) have argued, socioeconomic disadvantage has potentially adverse effects on parents, such that parental difficulties are more likely to develop and good parenting is impeded. If true, one would expect poverty and disadvantage to have their effects on delinquency transmitted through parenting. Sampson and Laub's contention is that structural factors will strongly affect family and school social control mechanisms but that their influence will be largely indirect (but not unimportant) in the explanation of delinquency.

Overall, the results from Laub and Sampson's study support their integrated version of social control theory, which recognizes the importance of both structure and process. When the bonds linking youth to society—whether via family or school—are weakened, the probability of delinquency is increased. Negative structural conditions (e.g., poverty, family disruption) also affect delinquency, but largely through family and school process variables (see Sampson and Laub, 1993, chapters 4 and 5).

The Importance of Continuity Between Childhood and Adulthood

The second building block of Sampson and Laub's theory incorporates the idea of continuity in childhood and adolescent antisocial behavior over the life course. Drawing on a wide body of research (e.g., Loeber, 1982), Sampson and Laub contend that childhood and adolescent antisocial behavior (e.g., juvenile delinquency, conduct disorder, violent temper tantrums) extends throughout adulthood across a variety of life's domains (e.g., crime, alcohol abuse, divorce, unemployment). In other words, antisocial behavior in childhood predicts a wide range of troublesome adult outcomes. Further, they argue that childhood delinquency is linked to dimensions of adult social bonding, including economic dependency, educational attainment, attachment to the labor force, and quality of marital experiences.

In their study, Sampson and Laub found that independent of age, IQ, neighborhood socioeconomic status, and ethnicity, the original delinquents and nondelinquents in the Gluecks' study displayed behavioral consistency well into adulthood. Indeed, delinquency and other forms of antisocial conduct in childhood were strongly related to troublesome adult behavior across a variety of life's domains (e.g., crime, economic dependence, and marital discord) (see Sampson and Laub, 1993, chapter 6).

The Significance of Change in the Life Course

The third focus of Sampson and Laub's theory is on change in deviance and offending as individuals age. Having provided a role for continuity, Sampson and Laub nonetheless believe that salient life events and social ties in adulthood can counteract, at least to some extent, the trajectories of early child development. Hence a third thesis of Sampson and Laub's theory is that social bonds in adulthood —especially *attachment to the labor force* and *cohesive marriage*—explain criminal behavior regardless of prior differences in criminal propensity. In other words, pathways to both crime and conformity are modified by key institutions of social control in the transition to adulthood (e.g., employment and marriage). For instance, late onset of criminal behavior can be accounted for by weak social bonds in adulthood, despite a background of nondelinquent behavior. Conversely, desistance from criminal behavior in adulthood can be explained by strong social bonds in adulthood, despite a background of delinquent behavior.

In contrast to many life-course researchers, Sampson and Laub emphasize the quality or strength of social ties in these transitions more than the occurrence or timing of discrete life events (cf. Loeber and LeBlanc, 1990:430-432). For example, marriage *per se* may not increase social control, but close emotional ties and mutual investment increase the social bond between individuals and, all else equal, should lead to a reduction in criminal behavior. Employment by itself also does not necessarily increase social control. But employment coupled with job stability, commitment to work, and mutual ties binding workers and employers should increase social control and, all else equal, lead to a reduction in criminal behavior.

In their recent study, Sampson and Laub found that job stability and marital attachment in adulthood were significantly related to changes in adult crime: The stronger the adult ties to work and family, the less crime and deviance among both delinquents and controls. Despite differences in early childhood experiences, adult social bonds to work and family thus had similar consequences for the life trajectories of the 500 delinquents and 500 controls. Taken as a whole, then,

Sampson and Laub's findings suggest that social ties embedded in adult transitions (e.g., marital attachment, job stability) explain variations in crime unaccounted for by childhood propensities (see Sampson and Laub, 1993, chapters 7 and 8).

In sum, Sampson and Laub's theory attempts to unite continuity and change within the context of a sociological understanding of crime in the life course. By refocusing attention to the significance of both pathways and turning points in the life course, Sampson and Laub have the potential in their research agenda to unify divergent conceptions of stability and change in human development (see also Rutter, Quinton, and Hill, 1990).

Rethinking Crime Policy: A Life-Course Perspective

A life-course perspective on crime offers a new way of thinking about crime control policy. The central theme of crime policy should focus on developing and strengthening an individual's social bonds to society. The foundation of sound policy on crime is that strong social bonds provide informal social control, and this holds for each stage of the life course. In addition, the ideas of pathways and turning points, which stem from a life-course perspective, serve as useful metaphors in the development of crime policy. The concept of pathways suggests that some individuals are set on an often predictable and stable track toward delinquency and adult criminality through the combined negative influence of poor parenting and weak school and peer attachments. At the same time, the notion of turning points suggests that these pathways could be deflected or redirected by positive developments that strengthen social bonds to key institutions in society.

In the following section, social bonds, pathways, and turning points are emphasized in the context of the three phases of the life course—childhood, adolescence, and adulthood. For each phase, we illustrate the implications of recent research on crime in the life course for policy by highlighting specific strategies that we believe offer some promise for reducing criminal and antisocial behavior.

Childhood

A life-course perspective on crime urges us to seriously consider the role that families play in crime causation. Intervention programs that focus on enhancing the ability of parents to monitor, recognize, and discipline the misbehavior of their children appear to be most promising in reducing antisocial behavior and delinquency (Hirschi, 1995; Tremblay et al., 1992; Schorr, 1988; Patterson, DeBaryshe, and Ramsey, 1989).

We believe a starting point then is the development of parent training programs. Research has shown that early onset of delinquency is one of the best predictors of a future criminal career. Delinquency and other forms of misconduct—truancy, staying out late, and petty theft—are ignored or its effects are trivialized. Parents must learn parenting skills that are conducive to successful childrearing. These skills include "[to] (a) notice what the child is doing; (b) monitor it over long periods; (c) model social skill behavior; (d) clearly state house rules; (e) consistently provide sane punishments for transgressions; (f) provide reinforcement for conformity; and (g) negotiate disagreements so that conflicts and crises do not escalate" (Patterson, 1980:81). As Patterson argues, "parents who cannot or will not employ family management skills are the prime determining variables. ... Parents of stealers do not track; they do not punish; and they do not care" (1980:88-89).

Although the principle of all preventive efforts is to reach vulnerable populations as early as possible (see Yoshikawa, 1994), interventions that are not applied or prove ineffective in early childhood can be supplemented later. Young children who begin to manifest behavioral problems in the primary grades can be aided by schools that involve their parents in training programs promoting effective parenting. In this way, the unruliness of an eight-year-old can be constructively addressed before it manifests itself in an incident of serious delinquency.

At-risk children are most likely to become identified by health care professionals or schools staff, but the justice system can do its part for such children as well. The police should take seriously childhood and juvenile misconduct by enforcing truancy and curfew laws for all school-age children. When children come to court for childhood misconduct (i.e., status offenses), judges should make mandatory referrals to parent training programs for their parents. And probation officers should place greater emphasis on the family. Indeed, many young people on probation are parents themselves, and these individuals are often ill-equipped to carry out their parental responsibilities effectively. A justice system interested in preventing and reducing crime should address young probationers as parents and involve them in parent training programs as an element of their sentence.

Such an effort was recently begun in Massachusetts: Young men who have children and are placed on probation for unrelated offenses are enrolled in a "fatherhood" program (Office of the Commissioner of Probation, 1994). This program consists of a series of group sessions run jointly by probation officers and community volunteers. The purpose of the program is to inculcate responsible attitudes and behaviors in the young fathers by employing skillbuilding and training coupled with supportive counseling. Several aspects of fathering are addressed including demonstrating affection, imposing appropriate discipline, modeling positive behavior, and providing financial support.

Adolescence

Although the family is the most promising starting point, more complex and broad-based intervention strategies are needed to inhibit the developmental course of offending in adolescence. Whereas the emphasis for children at risk must be on strengthening their parents, adolescents on delinquent pathways may require interventions of a broader scope, including not only parental control and supervision but also strengthening social bonds to school, peers, and the community.

Parent Training Programs

Parent training programs are bound to be more effective the earlier they are introduced. Providing help and support to the parents of delinquent or antisocial youth is still worthwhile, however. As an example, a major district court in Massachusetts sponsored a program entitled "STEP" (Systematic Training for Effective Parenting of Teens) for families with young people before the court for delinquent offenses (Dinkmeyer and McKay, 1990). This program is led by specially trained probation officers and focuses on understanding and responding effectively to teen misbehavior.

High school students are increasingly becoming parents "prematurely," and these teenagers are among those at greatest risk for inadequate parenting. High school programs and curricula must expose young people to the perils of early pregnancies and then carefully educate, support, and coach those students who become parents while in high school. Young parents who cannot be helped through school are thus at least connected to a health care delivery system, which can be a second site for intervention. Each physician and clinic treating young people must accept its preventive and educational role with regard to potential and actual teenage parents. Whereas it is commonplace for new parents to attend a series of classes on childbearing and delivery, there is no equivalent emphasis on education for competent parenting. This is especially critical for young single parents.

Building School Ties

A key finding in Sampson and Laub's research is that attachment to school is a significant buffer against delinquent behavior. Accordingly, schools must work toward engaging youth in their education, making school relevant to their often fractured lives. Models exist for schools as multiservice centers, availing young people at risk and their families of the services not available elsewhere in the community. Teachers will understandably often bemoan the call on them to be social workers and parents as well as teachers. By seeing young people as members of families with problems that often undercut the children's commitment to school, the staff and teachers at 2 full-service school can ease access to support services through the "one-stop shopping" approach.

In *Full-Service Schools: A Revolution in Health and Social Services for Children, Youth, and Families* (1994), Dryfoos reports on the growing movement nationwide to bring services to where troubled teens and their families can most easily be found. By putting health, counseling, and recreational program's under one roof—and by keeping schools open into the evening so that the needy families can receive a "package of interventions" in one location—the conditions that make it difficult for troubled teens to commit to school can be more efficiently addressed.

Like the family, the school can be an important mechanism for bonding adolescent youth to conventional society. Schools represent an importance source of social capital. Social capital, as Coleman (1988) argues, lies in the structure of interpersonal relations and institutional linkages, and is created when these relations change in ways that facilitate action. Social capital is one of the mechanisms through which informal social control operates.

The concept of social capital is related to the colloquial phrase "connections," which signifies a pattern of affiliations with well-placed and influential people in the community, whose resources and influences could be tapped for help in "getting ahead." It is common wisdom that "connections" are what successful people often rely upon; constructive "connections" are precisely what most delinquents lack and what often alienate them from society and its institutions, including school.

Schools could help build social capital or "connections" so as to counteract delinquent tendencies. A mandatory requirement for community service in order to graduate would help ensure that each youth had a link to the wider social domain, with an opportunity to meet and work with responsible adults in joint projects for community betterment. In addition, community service would engage youth in various extracurricular activities, where they will be exposed to the salutary influence of positive peers and the discipline that comes with joint enterprise. The goal of this initiative would be to promote strong bonds with adult leaders, fellow classmates, and the community. For generations, this kind of volunteer work has created social networks, role models, and, ultimately, the social bonds that are the best hedge against future criminal behavior.

Building Community Ties

Courts also can lend support to this process of socialization and social bonding. In the earliest stages of a young person's difficulty with the law, juvenile courts might require the offender and his or her family to identify a mentor/advocate as an element of a probationary sentence (see Pearson, 1987). This mentor/advocate would be an adult member of the community who would supplement the work of the probation officer by overseeing the behavior of the youth and the actions of the family while also serving as a role model and a source of "connections" to the wider community. The particular mentor/advocate would, as much as possible, be drawn from the youth's neighborhood. Thus, a mentor would serve both as a caring, supportive individual and as a monitor, supervisor, and proxy parent.

If at-risk youth and those in trouble are to develop positive social bonds, neighborhoods must be reconceptualized as "villages" where responsible adults who live and work there fill the role of village "elders," taking responsibility for the well-being of the neighborhood and its residents by casting a particularly watchful eye on the neighborhoods's young people. The idea here is to foster *collective parenting* to encourage social networks of support that go beyond the immediate parent(s). But how does one establish a stronger sense of community in our cities? A group of Boston clergy have provided one possible answer.

In 1991, several Christian churches in Boston formed a coalition and took their ministries into the most disorganized and troubled neighborhoods of the city in an effort to reach out to the youth involved in serious gang and drug-related activities (Brown, et al., 1994). Among the ten points that served as the coalition's charter were commitments to "adopting" gangs that operated in the areas around their churches, to acting as advocates for court-involved youth, to offering (during) late-night walks educational and counseling services to street kids, to initiating neighborhood crime watches, to attracting economic development funds for the more impoverished parishes, and to having member churches serve as "drop-in centers providing sanctuary for troubled youth" (Brown, et al., 1994:13).

Since its founding, the coalition has grown in participation and achieved notable success. Among its most publicized successes were the establishment of a multimillion fund for low-cost mortgages and the sponsorship of a "Freedom Summer," which offered positive activities and job opportunities for inner-city youth and was widely believed to account for a period of diminished gang violence in Boston.

Adulthood

Sampson and Laub (1993) have argued that despite strong continuities between delinquency and adult antisocial behaviors, change is possible largely through adult attachments to the labor force and cohesive marital bonds. The key concept here is development of social capital in interpersonal relations in adulthood—social bonds to a spouse or to work. Thus, it is not enough to have a spouse or a job; more important is the quality of interpersonal ties. When an individual has cohesive ties in marriage or work, these ties involve investments made by their spouses and employers. Furthermore, they can bring about a reciprocal investment by the individual in his or her spouse or employer. Thus, it is the high strength and quality of these interdependent, reciprocal investments that brings about informal social control, deterring individuals from acting in ways that threaten such investments (e.g., committing a crime that may result in arrest or incarceration, which could weaken or break valuable social bonds).

The policy implications of these findings are, by necessity, indirect. There is little, within the realm of criminal justice or social policy, that can be done about finding the right spouse or job. These challenges, however, can be made less burdensome through changes in criminal justice and social policy. For example, in the correctional setting, counseling, education, and job training could be of assistance to those who sincerely participated in them. Another recommendation is the reduced use of incarceration and the greater use of community-based corrections. These may take the form of traditional or intensive-supervision probation, use of electronic monitoring, and greater use of furloughs and parole to assist the inmate in his or her reintegration into the normal world.

When these two options (fewer prisons and more rehabilitation in prisons) are considered, concerns of public safety are often raised, and there is skepticism about the efficacy of rehabilitative programs. However, greater use of intermediate sanctions (such as electronic monitoring, probation, and parole) does not necessarily mortgage public safety (LeClair and Guarino-Ghezzi, 1991; Geerken and Hayes, 1993). Furthermore, the research of the 1970s that fueled severe pessimism about rehabilitation has been shown to be overstated and inaccurate (see, e.g., Andrews et al., 1990).

Once an offender is released from prison, he or she is immediately faced with the challenge of reintegration. One critical means of improving the chances for rehabilitation is to do something about the job prospects of offenders. Many former offenders have severe educational and job skill deficits and require training to be marketable. The challenge of reintegration is heightened by the low availability of desirable low-skill jobs, particularly in urban areas. As a starting point any probationer or parolee who is not working should be required, as a condition of probation or parole, to obtain work or appropriate job training. Given that job stability is a powerful predictor of desisting from crime (Sampson and Laub, 1993), correctional programs must build strong ties to potential employers and to the world of adult education and job readiness. No offender should remain unconnected to one or the other.

Courts and correctional systems must also provide services involving the family of the offender. Community corrections has traditionally not seen the value of offering family services and support to probationers and parolees unless the underlying criminal offense was domestic in nature. Sampson and Laub's research makes clear that strong marital attachment helps to turn offenders away from a life of crime. Accordingly, it would be smart policy to assist offenders to become better spouses and help them through crises in their marriages by making appropriate counseling readily available. Helping offenders repair personal relationships, salvage marriages, or improve interpersonal skills so that permanent relationships are possible will all in the long run, contribute to law-abiding behavior.

Another means of enhancing social bonds to family after release from prison is to attempt to maintain bonds that existed before entering prison. Prisons can work harder at helping offenders build and sustain marital attachments. For those offenders who are married at the time of sentencing, visiting privileges should be liberalized in the service of saving the marriage and strengthening marital ties. Moreover, counseling should be offered to both offender and spouse regarding the difficulties involved in separation.

However, the success of individual attempts to reform and desist from crime can be greatly assisted or doomed to failure by society's responses. When an offender has completed the terms of his or her punishment, offenders should not be cut off from the most promising avenues for desistance from crime. And, though attitudes are difficult to change, Braithwaite's notion of "reintegrative shaming" is not a new idea. For example, note the following instructions given to New York City patrol officers in 1914:

> Do not hound or persecute ex-convicts. If a man has been convicted of a crime and has paid the penalty, he is entitled to start life anew and should receive assistance and co-operation from you in his endeavor to live a decent life. If he lives on your post do not tell his neighbors of his past; if he is seeking employment, or is employed, do not inform the employer for the sole purpose of having him discharged. Tell your superiors or members of the Detective Division so that they may keep a watch on him. If he is hounded by the police and prohibited from engaging in lawful vocation, there is only one door open to him, again to become a criminal. (New York City Police Department, 1914:12)

Does Incarceration Have Criminogenic Effects?

The life-course perspective has additional implications for specific crime policies in use today. The United States has embarked on an unprecedented incarceration policy concerning the use of incarceration (see, for example, Steffensmeier and Harer, 1993). From all appearances, the major thrust of current crime control policy—whether aimed at drugs or violence—is to lock up offenders regardless of age. For those offenders with extensive prior records, even longer sentences of incarceration are being called for. And, the most extreme formal sanction by the state—the death penalty—is being made available and is increasingly used. Such policies assume that either individual deterrence or incapacitation will reduce further violence. Yet rates of violence have recently risen in many of our nation's cities despite unprecedented rates of imprisonment and executions (Butterfield, 1992; Eckholm, 1993). How can this happen?

One clear possibility is that current policies are producing unintended "criminogenic" effects. Sampson and Laub's research offers some pointed findings on the deleterious effects of lengthy prison sentences. In their reanalysis of the Gluecks' data, Sampson and Laub have shown how long-term developmental effects of incarceration on crime and deviance may come about. Social bonds to employment were directly influenced by State sanctions. That is, incarceration as a juvenile and as an adult had negative effects on later job stability, and job stability was in turn negatively related to continued involvement in crime over the life course. Although we found little direct effect of incarceration on subsequent criminality, the indirect "criminogenic" effects appear substantively important in their developmental (see Sampson and Laub, 1993:162-168).

Simply put, lengthy prison terms severely damage the future job prospects of offenders. Two strategies for ameliorating this situation are required: First, we must seriously rethink our current overreliance on prison terms for property and drug offenders and examine the possibility that credible, strict punishments may be available in the community. Community-based sentences can satisfy the important principle of just deserts without the devastating impact on employability that comes with a prison sentence. Second, those who must be imprisoned should be able to update their education and participate in occupational programs in prison to align with current labor market realities so that the potential for postrelease employment is maximized. Sampson and Laub's analysis revealed that intraindividual change is possible, and therefore it is critical that individuals have the opportunity to reconnect to institutions such as family, school, and work *after* a period of incarceration (see also Cook, 1975; Braithwaite, 1989).

Conclusion

Although our thinking is currently unpopular, we believe that it is time to take a renewed look at social policies that focus on *prevention* as opposed to after-the-fact approaches that ignore the structural context of crime and neglect the basic institutions of society such as family, school, and work that provide informal social control via social bonds and social capital. We are not suggesting that imprisonment is unnecessary or undeserved or even that it has no deterrent effect on crime. Rather, our reservations about current crime policies reflect fears that such policies do not reduce crime and may in fact be counterproductive. Nor are we convinced that "old ideas in new slogans" are the answer. Witness the popularity of the "Three Strikes and You're Out" bandwagon.

Instead of cheap slogans, it is time for a broader crime policy that focuses on more than formal social control by the criminal justice system. Nongovernmental institutions such as families, schools, work settings, and neighborhoods must be the centerpiece of any crime reduction policy. The government can and should take the lead in strengthening these basic institutions of our society. As such, a more complex and long-term perspective that recognizes the linkages among crime policies, employment, family cohesion, and the social organization of inner-city communities is needed.

Reflecting these concerns, we have offered a theoretical and empirical framework from which to think in new ways about policies on crime. Public discourse about crime has been shortsighted and debates have largely centered on increasing punishment—getting tougher on crime. These debates have little connection to realistic policies for crime control. Much of this results from a failure of moral leadership on the part of politicians and government leaders when it comes to enunciating sound crime policy. Government can do only so much about crime, and whatever does work will take time. We have to invest over a generation to see lasting effects. We believe that most citizens realize and appreciate the complexity of the crime problem. Therefore, our aim is to reach those concerned about crime and who remain optimistic that social science research can inform effective crime control policy. We hope that our work can contribute to the development of "smart" policy on crime.

Notes

1. The Gluecks' *Unraveling Juvenile Delinquency* study involved a comparison of 500 boys from two Massachusetts reform schools for boys who were officially defined as delinquent and 500 nondelinquent boys as determined by official records and interviews with key informants. A unique aspect of this study was the matching design. Specifically, the 500 officially defined delinquents and 500 nondelinquents were matched *case-by-case* on age, race/ethnicity, measured intelligence, and neighborhood. The original sample in the *Unraveling* study was followed up at two different points in time—at the age of twenty-five and again at the age of thirty-two. (For more details see Glueck and Glueck, 1950, 1968, and Sampson and Laub, 1993).

2. All of the subjects in the Gluecks' *Unraveling Juvenile Delinquency* study were white males; thus, any analyses of these data are limited by the ethnic variation within this sample of white men. Nevertheless, our previous analyses suggest that crime in the Gluecks' era was not all that different from today in terms of its structural origins and underlying nature (Sampson and Laub, 1993). Therefore, we contend that the fact that sample members in the *Unraveling* study were drawn from settings of social and economic disadvantage yet were all white provides an important comparative base to assess current concerns of race, crime, and the underclass.

3. We argue that because the Glueck data are "old"—the subjects of the *Unraveling* study were born between 1924 and 1935—they provide an unusual opportunity to assess whether the causes of juvenile delinquency and adult crime are specific to a historical period. Thus, the "age" of the Glueck data becomes a strength, not a weakness. Indeed, a focus on data from the 1930-1960 time period leads to several interesting questions relevant to an understanding of current patterns of crime.

References

Andrews, D.A., Ivan Zinger, R.D. Hoge, James Bonta, Paul Gendreau, and Francis T. Cullen. 1990. "Does Correctional Treatment Work? A Clinically Relevant and Psychologically informed meta-analysis." *Criminology* 28: 369-404.

Braithwaite, John. 1989. *Crime, Shame, and Reintegration*. Cambridge: Cambridge University Press.

Brown, Jeffrey L., Ray A. Hammond, Eugene F. Rivers, Susie Thomas, Gilbert A. Thompson, Bruce H. Wall, and Samuel C. Wood. 1994. "10 Point Plan to Mobilize the Churches." *Sojourners* 23:13-15.

Butterfield, Fox. 1992. "Seeds of Murder Epidemic: Teen-Age Boys with Guns." *The New York Times*, October 19: 8.

Caspi, Avshalom, Glen H. Elder, Jr., and Ellen S. Herbener. 1990. "Childhood Personality and the Prediction of Life Course Patterns." In Lee Robins and Michael Rutter (eds.), *Straight and Devious Pathways from Childhood to Adulthood*. Cambridge: Cambridge University Press.

Coleman, James S. 1988. "Social Capital in the Creation of Human Capital." *American Journal of Sociology* 94: 95-120.

———. 1990. *Foundations of Social Theory*. Cambridge: Harvard University Press.

Cook, Philip J. 1975. "The Correctional Carrot: Better Jobs for Parolees." *Policy Analysis* . 1:11-54.

Dinkmeyer, Don, and Gary McKay. 1990. *Parenting Teenagers: Systematic Training for Effective Parenting of Teens*. Circle Pines, MN: American Guidance Services.

Dryfoos, Joy. 1994. *Full-Service Schools: A Revolution in Health and Social Services for Children, Youth, and Families*. San Francisco: Jossey-Bass.

Eckholm, Erik. 1993. "Teen-age Gangs are Inflicting Lethal Violence on Small Cities." *The New York Times*, January 31: 1, 26.

Elder, Glen H., Jr. 1985. "Perspectives on the Life Course." In Glen H. Elder, Jr. (ed.), *Life Course Dynamics*. Ithaca: Cornell University Press.

———. 1992. "The life course." In E. F. Borgatta and M. F. Borgatta (eds.), *The Encyclopedia of Sociology*. New York: Macmillan Publishing Company.

Geerken, Michael R., and Hennessey D. Hayes. 1993. "Probation and Parole: Public Risk and the Future of Incarceration Alternatives." *Criminology* 31:549-564.

Glueck, Sheldon, and Eleanor Glueck. 1950. *Unraveling Juvenile Delinquency*. New York: The Commonwealth Fund.

———. 1968. *Delinquents and Nondelinquents in Perspective*. Cambridge: Harvard University Press.

Hirschi, Travis. 1995. "The family." In James Q. Wilson and Joan Petersilia (eds.), *Crime*. San Francisco: ICS Press.

Kornhauser, Ruth. 1978. *Social Sources of Delinquency*. Chicago: University of Chicago Press.

Laub, John H. and Robert J. Sampson. 1993. "Turning Points in the Life Course: Why Change Matters to the Study of Crime." *Criminology*, 31:301-325.

LeClair, Daniel P., and Susan Guarino-Ghezzi. 1991. "Does Incapacitation Guarantee Public safety? Lessons from the Massachusetts Furlough and Prerelease Programs." *Justice Quarterly* 8: 9-36.

Loeber, Rolf. 1982. "The Stability of Anti-Social Child Behavior: A Review." *Child Development* 53: 1431-1446.

Loeber, Rolf and Marc LeBlanc. 1990. "Toward a Developmental Criminology." In Michael Tonry and Norval Morris (eds.), *Crime and Justice*. Chicago: University of Chicago Press.

New York City Police Department. 1914. *Police Practice and Procedure* New York: Police Department Bureau of Printing.

Office of the Commissioner of Probation. 1994. *Fatherhood Program*. Boston, MA.

Patterson, Gerald R. 1980. *Children Who Steal*. In Travis Hirschi and Michael Gottfredson (eds.), *Understanding Crime*. Beverly Hills, Ca: Sage Publications.

Patterson, Gerald R., B.D. DeBaryshe, and E. Ramsey. 1989. "A Developmental Perspective on Antisocial Behavior. *American Psychologist* 44: 329-335.

Pearson, Frank S. 1987. "Taking Quality Into Account: Assessing the Benefits and Costs of New Jersey's Intensive Supervision Program." In Belinda R. McCarthy (ed.), *Intermediate Punishments: Intensive Supervision, Home Confinement, and Electronic Surveillance*. Monsey, NY: Criminal Justice Press.

Rutter, Michael, and Henri Giller. 1983. *Juvenile Delinquency: Trends and Perspectives*. New York: Guilford Press.

Rutter, Michael, D. Quinton, and J. Hill. 1990. "Adult Outcomes of Institution-Reared Children: Males and Females Compared." In Lee Robins and Michael Rutter (eds.), *Straight and Devious Pathways from Childhood to Adulthood*. Cambridge: Cambridge University Press.

Sampson, Robert J. and John H. Laub. 1992. "Crime and deviance in the life course." *Annual Review of Sociology* 18: 63-84.

————. 1993. *Crime in the Making: Pathways and Turning Points Through Life*. Harvard University Press.

Schorr, Lisbeth B. 1988. *Within Our Reach*. New York: Doubleday.

Steffensmeier, Darrell J., and Miles D. Harer. 1993. "Bulging Prisons, an Aging U.S. Population, and the Nation's Violent Crime Rate." *Federal Probation* 57:3-10.

Tremblay, Richard E., Frank Vitaro, Lucie Bertrand, Marc LeBlanc, Helene Beauchesne, Helene Boileau, and Lucille David. 1992. "Parent and Child Training to Prevent Early Onset of Delinquency: The Montreal Longitudinal-Experimental Study." In Joan McCord and Richard Tremblay (eds.), *Preventing Antisocial Behavior: Interventions From Birth Through Adolescence*. New York: Guilford Press.

Yoshikawa, Hirokazu. 1994. "Prevention as Cumulative Protection: Effects of Early Family Support and Education on Chronic Delinquency and Its Risks." *Psychological Bulletin* 115: 28-54.

7

Neighborhood-Based Networks and the Control of Crime and Delinquency

Robert J. Bursik, Jr., and Harold G. Grasmick

One of the unifying themes that has characterized many contemporary crime control programs throughout the United States is the need for effective collaboration between neighborhood organizations and representatives of the criminal justice system. Although Skogan (1988) traces the rise of this current emphasis to the late 1970s and early 1980s, when shrinking municipal budgets forced many police departments to experiment with "off-budget" approaches to law enforcement, such programs have a long history, perhaps most notably reflected in the development of the Chicago Area Project in 1932 by Clifford Shaw and Henry McKay (Bursik and Grasmick, 1993b:160-166). In fact, many features of modern, neighborhood-based crime control efforts (such as the mobilization of local community leaders, the development of working arrangements between residents and the criminal justice system, and the utilization of former gang members) were central to the mission of the project.

The underlying principles of the Chicago Area Project were drawn in part from the social disorganization theory of urban crime that had been developed by Shaw and McKay (1931, 1942) and, as Skogan (1988:40) has observed, modern approaches continue to assume that "if disorganization is the root of the crime problem, organization is the solution." Yet, there is a mounting body of evidence that such crime control efforts may not be especially effective. Skogan (1988:71) suggests that although such failures may be due to the implementation of the programs, they also might reflect a deficiency in the underlying theory. This particularly may be the case when programs are grounded explicitly or implicitly within the social disorganization theory, for it has been criticized severely for a number of important deficiencies (see Bursik and Grasmick, 1993b:chapter 2). However, a growing body of recent research has attempted to address these issues by reframing the social disorganization framework as a systemic model that focuses on the regulatory capacities of relational networks that exist within and between neighborhoods. As such, the results of this newest wave of community-based crime and delinquency research have important implications for the development of crime control programs.

In this chapter, we first describe the basic social disorganization model and note the problems that have been highlighted in that approach. We then illustrate how the traditional model can be reformulated as a systemic theory that focuses on two levels of social control indigenous to a neighborhood. Finally, we argue that the traditional model is incompletely specified because of its neglect of extracommunity relational networks. However, we propose that these considerations can be easily addressed in a systemic framework.

The Traditional Social Disorganization Model

In one of the most ambitious data collection projects ever attempted in the United States, Shaw and his colleagues compiled a listing of all juvenile arrests and court referrals in the City of Chicago during selected intervals that spanned 1900 to 1933.[1] After they painstakingly mapped the residential addresses of all of these offenders on large maps of the city, two important patterns became clear. First, neighborhoods tended to maintain their "delinquency character" over extended periods of time in spite of changing racial and ethnic composi- tions. Thus, it became apparent to Shaw and McKay that ongoing neighborhood dynamics were associated with rates of delinquent behavior. Second, there was a general tendency for delinquency rates to decline with distance from the central business district.

Although extraordinarily labor-intensive, the mapping of the residential addresses of offenders was not especially novel in itself, for André Michel Guerry and Adolphe Quetelet each had published such studies in France during the Nineteenth century (see Morris, 1957). In fact, Shaw and McKay were not even the first to have plotted the addresses of juveniles referred to court in Chicago (see Breckinridge and Abbott, 1912).[2] Rather, the key innovative aspect of their research was the interpretation of the spatial patterns within the context of the human ecology and social disorganization theoretical frameworks that had been developed at the University of Chicago.

The negative association between delinquency rates and distance from the central business district suggested to Shaw and his colleagues that the distribu- tion of illegal behavior might be related to similar overall ecological processes that resulted in the positive correlation between distance and the socioeconomic composition of neighborhoods noted earlier by Burgess (1925) and Park and Burgess (1920). Park and Burgess argued that this pattern (called the biotic order) was the outcome of a struggle over the freedom to occupy and control desirable residential space. The clearest presentation of these processes occurs in Burgess (1925), in which he suggests that to minimize the costs of investment, real estate speculators who had purchased land surrounding the central business district in anticipation of its eventual expansion invested as little money as possible in the maintenance and upkeep of property in this area. Thus, the areas immediately surrounding the central business district were the least attractive in the city and, owing to the presence of inexpensive housing, functioned as the typical area of residence for immigrant ethnic groups. As these groups became assimilated into the local economic structure, they were assumed to move progressively outward into more attractive and more expensive housing, giving rise to the observed relationship between the socioeconomic composition of a neighborhood and its distance from the central business district.

Park and Burgess also argued that a second set of dynamics (called the moral order) pertaining to the accommodation of groups to one another was interdependent with these ecological processes. The social contact that initiated this accommodation was believed to create "sympathies, prejudices [and] personal and moral relations which modify, complicate, and control competition" (1926: 720) and which would be reflected in the norms, values, and beliefs of an area. Given these dynamics, neighborhoods were considered to be the result of the selective movement of populations into local communities associated with particular economic, cultural, or occupational groups (Burgess, 1925:54).

As shown by the introduction to their first major neighborhood monograph, the Shaw and McKay research was guided by this orientation from the very beginning (Shaw et al, 1929:4-5). However, again drawing from the work of Park and Burgess, they did not propose that the socioeconomic composition of a community had a simple, direct effect on its delinquency rate. Burgess (1925: 58-61) had argued that the rate of mobility that ensued from these urban dynamics was "perhaps the best index of the state of metabolism of the city" since the effects of primary group controls on behavior are likely to be the weakest and people are more likely to become confused concerning the local moral order where mobility is the greatest. Thus, the concept of mobility has two connotations in the Park and Burgess model. The first reflects the traditional notion of the spatial movement of the residential population, whereas the second refers to the degree to which neighborhood heterogeneity (especially in terms of the racial and ethnic composition) may give rise to competing moral orders (see Park, 1926).

Drawing from this intellectual context, Shaw and McKay proposed that the levels of residential mobility and heterogeneity in a community are a function of its economic composition. In turn, high levels of mobility and heterogeneity were expected to decrease the ability of the moral order and primary group controls to regulate the behavior of the residents in a neighborhood, resulting in higher rates of delinquency (see Figure 7.1). Therefore, the neighborhood feature most centrally related to the control of crime is its capacity to engage in such regulation. In this respect Shaw and McKay were influenced greatly by the

FIGURE 7.1. The Basic Shaw-McKay Model

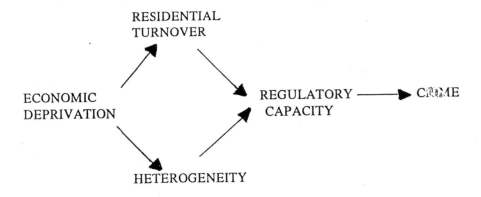

discussion of "social disorganization" presented by Thomas and Znaniecki (1920), whose work also had a major effect on Park and Burgess's conception of the moral order (see, for example, Park, 1926:57). For this reason, the Shaw and McKay model often has been referred to as the social disorganization theory of delinquency.[3]

Thomas and Znaniecki (1920:1128) defined social disorganization as the "decrease of the influence of existing social rules of behavior upon individual members of the group"; the primary indicator of this situation is the appearance of attitudes within a community that "impair the efficiency of existing rules of behavior" (1920:1131). As formulated by Thomas and Znaniecki, an organized community is one in which "social opinion concerns itself with all matters, outside happenings or individual acts, which possess a public interest, when its attitudes toward these matters are consistent and able to reach approximate unanimity, and when any common action considered necessary to solve the situation as defined by social opinion is carried on in harmonious cooperation" (1920:1171). This broad-based consensual orientation had a major influence on the framework developed by Shaw and McKay, leading to their emphasis on the customs, norms, goals, and values of a local community (see Shaw et al., 1929: 5). As a result, Shaw and McKay placed a special emphasis on the viability of local institutions (such as the family) that were assumed to socialize the residents into this cultural belief system.

However, Thomas and Znaniecki also gave careful consideration to the degree that the internal structure of relationships among local residents could facilitate the ability to take the "common action" necessary to solve a locally recognized problem. This is reflected in their concept of "social solidarity," which refers to the degree to which the need for individual success is less important than the need for the social recognition and approval of one's neighbors (Thomas and Znaniecki, 1920:1173-1174). Such recognition is allocated through a series of reciprocal networks that are assumed to bind members of the neighborhood to one another. To the degree that such solidarity does not exist, a community is considered to be disorganized. In more contemporary terms, the concept of social solidarity is identical to the dynamics of informal social control in which residents attempt to regulate the behaviors and attitudes of one another through the allocation of positive sentiment, approval, and esteem (see Hunter, 1985).

Although both normative and structural aspects of social disorganization are considered by Shaw and McKay even in their earliest work (see Shaw et al. 1929:204-206), the somewhat ambiguous presentation of their concepts led to a significant degree of conceptual confusion and logical inconsistency, as we shall discuss later in this chapter. However, the dual aspects of disorganization are clearly reflected in the philosophy and design of their Chicago Area Project. Shaw believed that crime prevention programs would.be successful only if they exploited the strengths of the existing system of social relationships (see Kobrin, 1959). Thus, the project in each neighborhood would be organized and directed by local community residents and would attempt to foster adult involvement in the everyday activities of youths in an attempt to increase a sense of neighborhood responsibility for delinquent activities. Presumably, the regulatory capacity of the neighborhood would increase with the development of such adult-youth networks. In addition, it was considered essential that the goals and programs of each individual project be developed and implemented by local residents, for otherwise there would be a danger of arbitrarily imposing middle-class values and beliefs on a group that might be characterized by an alternative cultural system (Pacyga, 1989).

Although the social disorganization framework was a central component of American criminology for a number of years, a number of important shortcomings led to its demise (see Bursik, 1988; Bursik and Grasmick, 1993b). For the purposes of crime control, the most important of these was the inability of the model to account for the existence of highly stable, well-organized neighborhoods that appear to have fairly uniform and consistent cultural systems yet have traditionally high rates of delinquency nonetheless (see, for example, Whyte, 1955).

Like Thomas and Znaniecki, Shaw and McKay presented a very broad conceptualization of normative consensus, including such considerations as the welfare of children, the desirability of education and constructive leisuretime activities, the need for a general health program, and the moral values symbolized by the family, church, and other local institutions (Shaw and McKay, 1942:170-172). Shaw and McKay argued that in areas of middle or high economic status, which tend to be characterized by relatively lower rates of delinquency, there is a "uniformity, consistency, and universality" of conventional values and attitudes (1942:170). In contrast, children from lower-class communities were assumed to be exposed to a diverse set of norms and standards of behavior, including those held by groups of residents whose moral values were in "direct opposition to conventionality as symbolized by the family, the church, and other institutions common to our general society. ... [Even] within the same community, theft may be defined as right and proper in some groups" (1942:171). Shaw and McKay proposed that out of this diversity would emerge a "delinquency tradition" that was transmitted to each of the various groups that would reside in any particular neighborhood over time, resulting in consistently high rates of illegal behavior despite changes in the racial and ethnic composition of the area.

As Kobrin (1971) has noted, the cultural elements of the Shaw and McKay model are not defined with any satisfactory degree of conceptual clarity or precision. Likewise, the empirical evidence that is provided in support of the "delinquency tradition" thesis is far from compelling. Shaw and McKay often illustrated their theoretical argument through a series of anecdotal and unsystematically selected passages drawn from Shaw's life history studies (see especially Shaw and McKay, 1931). In addition, their data indicated that the majority of offenses were committed in a group context.[4] Arguing that such groups exert pressure on their members to engage in illegal behavior (see Shaw and McKay 1942:174), Shaw and McKay occasionally used the proportion of delinquencies that were committed in association with companions as an indicator of the pervasiveness of cultural support for illegal behavior. Yet, as Kobrin points out (1971:126), such patterns in themselves do not provide any evidence that crime is legitimated by the residents of a neighborhood. In fact, Kobrin (1971:125) suggests that the term "delinquency tradition" may have been more figurative than literal for Shaw and McKay, used primarily to reflect the continuity within a neighborhood of a form of group behavior rather than the existence of an alternative cultural system.

As a result, their conclusions concerning the cultural components of the theory verged on the tautological. That is, some neighborhoods have high rates of delinquency (typically committed in groups) because they have an ongoing tradition of values and beliefs supportive of illegal behavior; the evidence for the existence of this tradition is high delinquency rates (typically committed in groups). The circularity of their cultural propositions led in part to the conclusion of some sociologists that Shaw and McKay defined social disorganization *as* delinquency (see Bursik, 1988).[5]

As a result of their theoretical logic, Shaw and McKay were forced to conclude that high-delinquency neighborhoods characterized by cultural systems that deviate from middle-class standards are disorganized by definition. However, strong counterevidence to this position has been presented in the literature. First, few studies have been able to document the existence of subcultures in the United States whose belief systems explicitly support involvement in serious forms of crime (see Sellin and Wolfgang, 1964, Rossi et al., 1974; Short and Strodtbeck, 1965; Wolfgang et al., 1985). Second, there are many highly stable, well-organized neighborhoods that appear to have fairly uniform and consistent cultural systems yet have long traditions of high rates of delinquency despite the fact that the residents "do not conduct their activities in a spirit of opposition to the culture of mainstream society" (Schwartz,1987:215).

When coupled with other trends in criminology that began to appear at the same time (see Bursik, 1988), these considerations led to an increasing disenchantment in the discipline with the Shaw and McKay framework. This orientation perhaps is best reflected in the sweeping statement of Unnever (1987:845) that "Shaw and McKay's theory of social disorganization...has been soundly dismissed." However, this proclamation is at best premature, for the social disorganization perspective has provided the intellectual heritage for a number of major contemporary theories of neighborhood dynamics and crime. Although these new approaches differ in important ways from the framework of Shaw and McKay, all maintain a human ecological orientation of some form and emphasize how these urban dynamics are related to the regulatory capacities of local communitiy.

The Systemic Reformulation of the Social Disorganization Model

Beginning in the early 1980s, research grounded in the heritage of Shaw and McKay quietly began to reappear in the literature (see Bursik and Webb, 1982; Bursik, 1986; Byrne and Sampson, 1986; Reiss and Tonry, 1986; Sampson, 1983, 1985; Taylor, Schumaker, and Gottfredson, 1985). Although a number of significant variations characterize this body of work, two important modifications of the Shaw and McKay model can consistently be noted. The first is that the only assumption concerning consensus that is necessary for the viability of the model is that citizens of American communities desire to live in residential communities that are relatively free from the threat of serious crime. Thus, most studies have focused on those crimes for which such consensus can be demonstrated, which roughly correspond to those referred to as "index crimes" in the Uniform Crime Reports (see Bursik and Grasmick, 1993b:21-22).[6]

Such a restriction is not necessarily a departure from the original Thomas and Znaniecki derivation of the social disorganization concept, for they did not assume that the communal sphere of public interest is rigid and unchanging over time. Rather, they noted that when alternative definitions of the situation (i.e. cultural systems) are introduced into a group, "the new tendencies are very often, after a period of struggle, simply left outside of the sphere controlled by public opinion...[and]...are treated as being of private concern" (p. 1173) as long as they are not socially destructive of existing relationships. Thus, it is not necessary to assume that organized neighborhoods are characterized by a fairly monolithic, homogenous set of cultural beliefs. Rather, it is only necessary to assume that consensus exists within the public sphere that crime is socially destructive. As a result, contemporary models within the Shaw and McKay tradition have been characterized by a very limited notion of cultural homogeneity. Since the cultural variation found in the traditional Shaw and McKay framework has been replaced by the assumption of cultural invariance in regard to this single goal, contemporary social disorganization theories tend to focus strictly on structural dynamics. That is, it is assumed that neighborhood crime and delinquency rates represent the effects of situational contingencies caused by the structure of the community and are not a reflection of a "semi-autonomous subculture" (Erlanger, 1979:235).

The second defining characteristic of contemporary social disorganization research is the assumption that neighborhoods represent patterned systems of interaction and association among the residents. Given this orientation, the reformulated model of social disorganization is sometimes referred to as the *systemic model of neighborhood crime*. Several key features of this model are worth noting.

1. *Systemic approaches emphasize ongoing patterns of information exchange as reflected in the networks and ties among the components of a system* (Buckley, 1967:43). Thus, the systemic approach to neighborhood crime assumes that the social structure of a community is represented in the totality of the complex sets of affiliations between members of local friendship groups, kinship groups, and associations (Berry and Kasarda, 1977:56). It is through these relational networks that the regulatory capacities of a neighborhood become actualized.

Most research has focused on two basic types of systemic control. The first, which has been called the *private level of control* (Hunter, 1985; Bursik and Grasmick, 1993b), focuses on the networks that integrate residents into the intimate informal primary groups of a neighborhood. It is through these associations that information is transmitted concerning expectations of appropriate behavior. If those expectations are violated, these networks are utilized to impose various informal sanctions on the offending member. Since analysts rarely have data pertaining to the precise nature of the communications that are transmitted through these networks, most work has focused on the potential capacity for private control in a neighborhood, especially as reflected in the number of friends or family living in close proximity to a given resident (see, for example, Sampson and Groves, 1989). In addition, systemic models have incorporated Shaw and McKay's emphasis on family structure and dynamics as an element of the private level of control (see, for example, Sampson, 1986).

The second or *parochial level of control* represents interpersonal networks in which communication among the members of the system does not have the same degree of intimacy as at the private level. For example, a resident may informally keep an eye on the public activities of local children or may alert fellow neighbors to the presence of outsiders who might be considered threatening. Therefore, this dimension of systemic control in part represents the supervisory capacities of a local community. In addition, it also represents residential participation in local institutions, such as churches, voluntary organizations, and schools. For example, through the relational networks that develop among members of community organizations concerned with crime prevention, information may be transmitted concerning desirable group actions and individual initiatives, such as target hardening, local surveillance, and crime reporting (Skogan, 1988:40).[7]

2. *Social organization is characterized by varying degrees of "systemness"* (Buckley, 1967:42). Recall that Shaw and McKay were criticized for not recognizing the many forms that social organization may take. Whyte (1955: 272), for example, observed that although the lower-class Cornerville neighborhood might appear to be disorganized to outside (presumably middle-class) observers, there actually was a fundamental "hierarchy of personal relations based upon a system of reciprocal obligations" out of which all Cornerville institutions were constructed. Therefore, systemic models of neighborhood crime recognize that an organized neighborhood may be reflected in a variety of social structures.

Although case studies of a small number of neighborhoods have successfully examined variations in social organization (such as Suttles, 1968), it is extremely costly to collect the relevant data in a large and representative sample of neighborhoods. As a result, only a few studies have examined the effect of variations in the nature of community networks on crime and delinquency rates. Nevertheless, it is generally recognized that the private and parochial networks found in urban communities will vary along several key dimensions. The first simply pertains to the *size* of the networks found in a neighborhood, that is, how many persons are bound together through formal or informal ties. Sampson and Groves (1989), for example, find that British neighborhoods in which respondents report relatively high average numbers of friends within a fifteen-minute walk of their homes have significantly lower rates of property crime (although this is not the case with personal violence). In addition, their research suggests that the private level may be a more relevant dimension of systemic control than the parochial.

A second dimension of systemic variation represents the degree to which the networks span the various groups residing in the area, or what has been referred to as *closure*. Greenberg, Rohe, and Williams (1985) report that residents are not likely to intercede in criminal events that involve strangers and are reluctant to assume responsibility for the welfare of property that belongs to people whom they barely know. Therefore, the social boundaries that may exist between groups in heterogeneous neighborhoods can decrease the breadth of supervisory activities because of the mutual distrust among groups in such areas.

Merry (1981), for example, describes a public housing project populated by Chinese, black, white, and Hispanic residents. Although over half of the families had lived in the project for more than ten years and there was substantial daily contact among members of these groups when using the project facilities, friendship networks rarely crossed racial and ethnic boundaries. In such a situation, the overall capacity of private networks to control the behavior of the residents is extremely limited (see Merry, 1981:96). More generally, Granovetter's (1973) discussion of urban networks suggests that when individuals are connected relationally to every other member of one network but to no one outside of that group, supervisory activities have to develop independently within each discrete network to ensure success in the control of crime throughout the community (Granovetter, 1973:1373-1374).

Again, the proposition concerning the closure of neighborhood networks is consistent with the traditional social disorganization assumption that heterogeneity may decrease the regulatory capacity of an area, thereby making it difficult to achieve the common goal of a relatively crime free community (see Kornhauser, 1978:75). However, this relationship is assumed to be strictly a function of the systemic structures that are more likely to characterize the relational networks found in heterogenous neighborhoods rather than a result of the presence of cultural variation. Similarly, the development of extensive private systemic networks is difficult when an area is characterized by high levels of residential instability (Kasarda and Janowitz, 1974; Berry and Kasarda, 1977), and local institutions may be difficult to maintain in a community characterized by rapid population changes.

As we have noted, it is difficult and expensive to collect sensitive network data on a large-scale basis. As a result, these two dimensions of systemic structure are the only ones that have been examined extensively. However, a full understanding of the sources of variation in "systemness" in the future will require a consideration of several other features of residential networks, such as *reachability* (the proportion of people in a network who can be contacted directly by all other persons in the group and the number of intermediaries who must be used to contact those members who cannot be contacted in this manner), *density* (the number of actual relationships, as opposed to people, represented in a network), *content* (the basis of the network tie, such as economic assistance, kinship allegiance, or friendship; this may be uni- or multidimensional), *directedness* (the extent to which network relationships are unidirectional or reciprocal), *durability* (the length of time the network has existed), *intensity* (the degree to which people feel obligated to honor obligations arising in the network), and *frequency* (the number of times in a given period of time that network members utilize the ties. For an excellent discussion of these dimensions, see Mitchell, 1969.) Only through a consideration of all of these elements will criminologists be able to derive a full sense of the nature of the "differential social organization" noted by Whyte and others.

3. *Aspects of a system's structure may change from time to time or even continuously without the dissolution of the system itself* (Buckley, 1967:43). In one respect this is an obvious characteristic of a model that has its roots in human ecology, for that perspective assumes that the key set of dynamics that gives rise to the structure of a city entails the spatial mobility of groups. Therefore, to varying degrees, all residential networks must face the potential addition and loss of members.

However, in another respect, this assumption differs dramatically from that reflected in Shaw and McKay's work, for contemporary systemic models assume that neighborhood relational networks are embedded in larger systems of relationships. That is, just as networks bind the residents of particular neighborhoods into a systemic structure, the individual neighborhoods also have ties among themselves that bind them into the broader ecological structure of the city. Therefore, the reformulation of the social disorganization approach has emphasized not only the degree to which neighborhoods may be functionally interdependent (see Hawley, 1950) but also the degree to which the nature of this interdependency has changed over time.

Shaw and McKay certainly did not consider neighborhoods to be isolated units. In fact, one of the central premises of the Park and Burgess model of human ecology was that neighborhoods are differentiated by their "characteristic function in the total economy and cultural complex of city life" (Wirth and Furez, 1938). However, Shaw and McKay *did* assume that the functional role of each community would stay relatively constant over time, noting the relative historical stability of neighborhood delinquency rates. This may have been true prior to 1940, but the ecological structure of many cities was significantly altered after World War II due to a variety of factors, such as the rise of suburbanization, the loss of certain industries, the elimination of restrictive covenants, and shrinking tax bases (see Bursik and Grasmick, 1993b:48-51).

The effects of such urban dynamics on the ecological structure of a city are reflected clearly in the development of what have been called "underclass" neighborhoods, that is, those predominantly populated by extremely poor, minority-status residents (see Wilson, 1987). In the traditional human ecology framework of Park and Burgess, the availability of unskilled jobs in manufacturing industries provided relatively open access to the occupational structure of urban areas. Unfortunately, as industries have moved into suburban and rural locations, those jobs that fostered the eventual ability to be residentially mobile have become decreasingly available to the residents of central city neighborhoods. At the same time, dramatic changes have occurred in the racial composition of some urban areas. For example, Wilson (1987:101) notes that the black population of the thirty-three largest central cities increased by more than 5,000,000 between 1950 and 1980, whereas the white population decreased by more than 9,000,000 during the same period. The coupling of such demographic shifts with the trends in urban economies has resulted in the concentration of extremely poor populations that are structurally prohibited from any significant degree of residential upgrading into central-city neighborhoods (see Wilson, 1987; Sampson and Wilson, 1991; Bursik and Grasmick, 1993a).

4. *A system is open. This means not only that it engages in interchanges with the environment, but that this interchange is an essential factor underlying the system's viability, its reproductive ability or continuity, and its ability to change* (Buckley, 1967: 52). This orientation represents the most important departure of contemporary systemic approaches from the traditional social disorganization model. There is no question that the private and parochial levels of control represent important regulatory mechanisms within a neighborhood. However, Spergel and Korbelik (1979) have shown that there are externally determined contingencies that mediate the ability of local networks and institutions to control the threat of crime. The role of external actors has been documented consistently in the resource mobilization literature, where it has been found that for a social movement to be successful (such as efforts to control crime in a neighborhood), it is necessary to develop effective linkages between the social movement and other groups in its environment that are outside the collectivity (see McCarthy and Zald, 1987). .

Likewise, Shaw and McKay have been criticized severely for failing to consider the political, social, and economic contexts in which local communities are embedded (see Snodgrass, 1976). As a result, their model implies that the dynamics that are related to delinquency rates most centrally are endogenous to the neighborhood. However, several studies have presented evidence that highlights the shortcomings of such an assumption. Heitgerd and Bursik (1987), for example, discuss a stable and homogenous working-class neighborhood in Chicago that was characterized by extremely high rates of delinquency. They note that these rates were significantly related to the degree of racial change occurring in adjacent areas and suggest that delinquent activities may have been used to "defend" the community from the in-migration of black populations. Likewise, Bursik (1989) has presented evidence that the political inefficacy of some of Chicago's neighborhoods led to the construction of public housing units within the area, which resulted in increases in residential mobility and delinquency.

Contemporary systemic approaches refer to the regulatory capacities that may develop as a result of the networks among neighborhoods and between neighborhoods and public/private agencies as the *public level of control* (a term again drawn from Hunter, 1985). Formally, this dimension refers to the ability to secure public and private goods and services that are allocated by groups and agencies located outside of the neighborhood. Since these goods are limited and are shrinking in many municipalities, local communities are engaged in a process of ongoing competition with other neighborhoods to acquire these resources. Therefore, systemic models must be sensitive to the effects that the allocation of and competition for external resources may have on the regulatory capacities of the affected areas.

Although very little empirical research has been conducted in this area vis-a-vis crime control, it should be noted that Whyte (1955:273) observed that "Cornerville's problem is not lack of organization but failure of its own social organization to mesh with the structure of the society around it." Therefore, the public level of control may be the missing theoretical link that would enable us to account for the presence of high rates of crime in areas in which that should not be the case. In the final section of this chapter, we examine the implications of these external systemic linkages for the local control of crime and delinquency.

The Public Level of Systemic Control

In a recent study, Bursik and Grasmick (1993a) show that after controlling for systemic factors, economically deprived neighborhoods of Chicago were still characterized by higher rates of delinquency than other areas. This is an important contradiction of the systemic approach, which predicts that the economic composition of a community should have only an indirect effect on the rates of illegal behavior (see Figure 7.1). Although they suggest that perhaps crime could be considered to be an alternative form of sustenance activity in impoverished neighborhoods (see Hawley, 1950), they also note that such patterns might reflect the failure of most systemic models to consider the ties of the neighborhood to the larger urban system in which it is embedded.

Cohen and Dawson (1993) document the degree to which residents living in the most economically deprived areas of Detroit (defined as those neighborhoods in which more than 30 percent of the population live at or below the poverty level) are structurally constrained in their political and economic opportunities, leading to a disengagement from the larger political system and a decrease in their feelings of political efficacy. For example, not only were these residents less likely to belong to formal and informal local groups than Detroit citizens living in nondeprived areas (as the systemic model would predict), but they also were less likely to know anyone influential, even second hand. Although the study by Hunter (1974) presents much stronger evidence of private and parochial systemic networks in primarily black neighborhoods of Chicago, this most likely is because his data were collected twenty years earlier than those of Cohen and Dawson; the more recent Chicago data discussed by Wacquant and Wilson (1989) are characterized by patterns very similar to those found in Detroit. Nevertheless, he too finds that black communities have a much more localized orientation, with few extracommunity ties to public and private agencies and institutions. Thus, as Logan and Molotch (1987:132) observe, the nature of systemic networks among black residents is not conducive to a linkage with external political and economic structures. That is, in terms of the arguments that we have presented in this chapter, the potential ability of the public level of control to serve as a source of residential regulation is very low.

This consideration also is suggested by Spergel and Curry's (1990) analysis of urban gang control strategies. The proportion of agencies in each of the cities in their sample that report community organization as a primary strategy is significantly related to the perceived effectiveness of those efforts in cities with a long history of gang-related problems as well as in cities in which the gang problem has only recently emerged (i.e., since 1980; see Spergel and Curry, 1990: Table 13.8). However, in those cities with chronic gang problems, the magnitude of this relationship is secondary to that associated with the proportion of agencies that emphasize the provision of opportunities as the primary strategy. Such opportunities reflect, in part, resources that are allocated by institutional structures that are not indigenous to the neighborhood, such as business, industry, and the municipal/federal government (p. Spergel and Curry 1990:297). Since the "chronic" cities tend to be larger and somewhat older than the "emerging" urban areas, we suspect that these are the locations in which stable low-income areas characterized by ongoing patterns of high crime rates are more likely to exist. To the extent that this is the case, the development of networks related to the public level of systemic control appears to be related to at least the perceived effectiveness of crime control programs.

The public dimension with the most obvious crime control implications is the networks that are developed between the local community and representatives of law enforcement agencies. In fact, although this factor is not considered in Shaw and McKay's theory of social disorganization, most communities involved in the Chicago Area Project appointed residents to act as liaisons between the neighborhood, the juvenile court, and the police department. Arrangements often were made in which these liaisons were notified if a local youth had been apprehended by the police and efforts were made to have such youth released into the custody of the liaison without the filing of an official arrest report.

Even the most rudimentary external relationship between neighborhood residents and law enforcement agencies—the reporting of crime or calls for service—appears to be at least partially related to relationships that have been developed between the community and the broader political structure. In their study of Champaign, Illinois, Nardulli and Stowe (1981:82-83) find that the level of citizen demands for police service is significantly related to the presence of civic or commercial elites on a residential block. They account for this pattern by proposing that people who are involved in civic or commercial activities on a regular basis have a good understanding of the scope of police capabilities, which they transmit to their neighbors through informal interactions or observation (Nardulli and Stowe, 1981: p. 86). Thus, the development of extracommunity networks for the purposes of crime control presupposes at least .

a minimal set of private, parochial, and public control structures that can familiarize local residents with the operations of public and private agencies and can represent the community to these constituencies so that a relationship can be developed (see Bursik and Grasmick, 1993b:154-157). Unfortunately, such structures are less likely to exist in the most economically deprived areas of a city, as shown by the research of Cohen and Dawson (1993) and Wacquant and Wilson (1989).

Even when fairly effective systems of private and parochial control exist in a neighborhood, such as was the case with Whyte's Cornerville, there may be a reluctance to form alliances with law enforcement agencies because of a general distrust of the police. As Whyte stated so succinctly (1955:126), the residents of Cornerville "look upon the officers as parasites and feel that the dregs of the department have been foisted upon them." This pattern cannot be attributed to a peculiarity of the area studied by Whyte, for a number of studies have documented the tendency for residents of low-income or African American communities to express much higher degrees of dissatisfaction with police services than those living in other neighborhoods (Lovrich and Taylor, 1976). For example, significant differences have been found in the ratings of police honesty and ethical standards by national samples of whites (43 percent rate these standards as high or very high) and blacks (29 percent) Maguire, Pastore, and Flanagan, 1993: Table 2.13).

Two factors may inhibit the development of effective network ties between neighborhoods and the police that could alleviate such dissatisfaction. Most research has found negligible evidence of neighborhood variation in the likelihood that the police will respond to a call for service (see, for example, Nardulli and Stowe, 1981, and the general discussion of Sherman, 1986). However, there also is broad documentation of great neighborhood variation in the dominant style of police work that characterizes police-citizen interactions (Black and Reiss, 1967). For example, after controlling for the nature of the offense, the demeanor of the suspect, and other related considerations, Smith (1986) finds that arrests are more likely to occur in neighborhoods of low socioeconomic status and that the use of coercive force is more likely in neighborhoods that are racially heterogeneous. As a result, the residents of such areas often are suspicious of the police because of their perception that they are being treated in an overly aggressive and antagonistic manner (McConville and Shepherd, 1992:38).

In many neighborhoods there is a perception of the police as "outsiders" who have little understanding of or sympathy for the residents of the communities they are patrolling (McConville and Shepherd, 1992). As a result, even when neighborhood programs have been established through the initiatives of the police, these efforts may face a significant degree of resentment from local residents who feel that law enforcement officers have a limited understanding of the problems they face on a daily basis (Podolefsky, 1983). In sum, although the existence of networks between neighborhoods and the police may be an important element in soliciting resources that can be used to control crime, they have been especially difficult to create and maintain in those impoverished areas of the city with high rates of crime.

Of course, the existence of a strong network between a neighborhood and law enforcement agencies is not a prerequisite for the establishment of a community-based crime control program. Relationships can be established with other social agencies concerned with crime or with neighborhood programs that already exist in other areas of the city. In fact, one of the more recent developments in the field of community policing has been an increasing emphasis on the development of networks between the police and other social institutions and agencies that serve the same area (see Weaver, 1993). However, a community can create these ties only if there are motivated local residents who already are aware of such sources of assistance and who are in a position to create such relationships or if they are helped in this enterprise. In systemic terms, the greater the degree of closure in the social structure of a neighborhood, the lower the probability that residents will have developed such ties to external agencies and associations (see Granovetter, 1973). Again, given the findings of Cohen and Dawson (1993) and of Wacquant and Wilson (1989), extremely impoverished communities have very little potential for the establishment of the necessary relationships. These structural considerations, in part, would account for the relationship between economic deprivation and crime observed by Bursik and Grasmick (1993a) without the necessity of incorporating nonsystemic elements into the model.

To this point the discussion has focused only on the solicitation of resources that are directly related to the control of crime. However, public networks can be utilized to solicit resources relevant to other aspects of community life that may indirectly increase the capacity of a neighborhood to control crime. Three other types of public systemic networks are worthy of note. The first represents the establishment of ties to local government. When cities experience severe financial strain (such as the threatened bankruptcy of New York City in the mid-1970s), cutbacks in services have a pronounced effect on the daily lives of the poor, who are much more dependent on publicly financed institutions such as schools and hospitals than the more well-to-do (Susser, 1982). In addition, many observers have discussed the recent changes in urban political economies that have led to the shift from manufacturing jobs to service industries in certain urban areas (see Wilson, 1987). Since these dynamics have been shown to be related to the systemic control structures of local communities (Bluestone and Harrison, 1982; Wacquant and Wilson, 1989), the ability of neighborhoods to successfully lobby local government (as well as industry) to maintain jobs and public services should be expected to indirectly lower the crime rate.

Likewise, in an effort to maximize the tax yield from community properties and minimize the public dollars necessary to service the neighborhood, many public agencies have been created to determine the allocation and use of land within cities through zoning regulations and construction incentives (Foley, 1973:111). Thus, residential areas are embedded in an urban system of competing neighborhood-based land interests (Castells, 1983; Logan and Molotch, 1987). Earlier in this chapter we noted the example of Chicago communities that were unable to prevent the construction of high-rise public housing within their boundaries (Bursik, 1989). Subsequently, those neighborhoods were characterized by increased rates of residential turnover, leading to increased rates of delinquency. The public level of systemic control would predict that if those neighborhoods had been able to successfully prevent this construction, the ensuing delinquency rates would not have been as high.

The second (and related) non-law enforcement source of public control represents ties to the local financial and mortgage establishment. It has often been noted that the level of residential stability found in poor urban neighborhoods is as much an outcome of conscious decisions made by the housing and lending industries as it is an outcome of the "natural" market mechanisms discussed by Park and Burgess (Hirsch, 1983). The degree to which this may affect the potential for effective private and parochial control is underscored strongly by the research of Taggart and Smith (1981), who show that between 1975 and 1977, Boston's financial institutions took significantly more money out of black neighborhoods in the form of savings deposits than they put back by way of mortgages. The core urban communities received only a 3 to 33 percent level of reinvestment of locally generated savings dollars in the form of mortgages, whereas the outermost suburbs were characterized by rates ranging from 108 to 543 percent. Such practices can have two important effects on the regulatory capacities of such neighborhoods. First, since it depresses the level of home ownership in the community, residents have less of a financial stake in community affairs than they would otherwise. In addition, it makes it more difficult for black inner-city residents to move into more desirable residential areas since they cannot "trade up" their homes (Logan and Molotch, 1987:129). Thus, because of their effects on the internal organization of residential communities, the actions of these industries may be at least partly responsible for the subsequent increases in crime and delinquency that have been observed (Bursik, 1986).

The final non-law enforcement base of public systemic control that should be noted represents networks that are developed with municipal agencies mandated to deliver other services to local communities, such as garbage collection, street and sewer repair, physical maintenance of local public facilities, the funding and staffing of educational institutions, safeguards on environmental quality, and so forth. As Lewis and Salem (1986:97) note, the quality of these services shape the "physical ambience" of neighborhoods and provide cues as to whether the community is a "good" or "bad" place to reside. Unfortunately, areas populated primarily by low-income and/or minority residents are likely to be limited in their ability to obtain the level of services or amenities found in other communities. Thus, it is no surprise that Lovrich and Taylor (1976) find that 53 percent of their black respondents felt that the services provided to their neighborhoods were not as good as the rest of the city, as opposed to only 4 percent of their white respondents.

The effects of weak neighborhood networks with municipal and social service agencies on the ability of communities to regulate themselves in terms of crime control have been explored most fully in the literature on incivilities and disorder. Wilson and Kelling (1982) note that once signs of neighborhood deterioration become widespread in a community, behaviors such as vandalism are much more likely because it is perceived that "no one cares." Skogan (1990:47) argues that these signs may also lead to a breakdown in the regulatory capacity of urban areas and presents evidence that high levels of disorder tend to be associated with lowered rates of mutual helping behavior among residents, satisfaction with the area, and stated plans to remain in the neighborhood. Thus, the inability of neighborhoods to bring external resources into the community to guard against such deterioration significantly decreases its systemic ability to control the behavior of its residents.

Conclusions

A systemic reformulation of social disorganization theory not only formalizes the dynamics that are implicit in that approach, but also significantly extends the perspective through a consideration of extracommunity dynamics and the competition for scarce resources within urban systems. Although our predictions concerning the regulatory capacities of the public level of control have yet to be tested empirically in a systematic manner, we have argued that the failure of neighborhoods to integrate themselves into the political, economic, and social systems in which they are embedded may account parsimoniously for the presence of apparently organized communities that have traditions of high crime and delinquency rates nonetheless.

The implications of the systemic approach to crime are not exclusively academic. As noted in the beginning of this chapter, evaluations of community-based crime control programs have found them to be relatively ineffective. Although a number of programmatic elements have been discussed in this regard, we are suggesting that it may be due in part to the fact that many of these programs are intellectually grounded in a particular theory of neighborhood crime. This theory does not consider whether local communities have developed networks with external constituencies that have the capacity to channel resources into the area, thereby affecting the ability of residents to regulate one another. We believe that three aspects of the reformulated systemic approach to neighborhood crime rates especially are relevant to contemporary crime control:

1. The potential of community-based programs to control crime becomes actualized through a neighborhood's system of formal and informal interactional systems. Where such networks are weak or essentially nonexistent, these programs can be expected to be only minimally effective. However, these often are the neighborhoods that could benefit most from such programs. Therefore, in extremely poor, unstable neighborhoods, it is necessary to foster much broader forms of intra-community linkages before the development of crime control programs per se.

2. The degree to which crime control efforts have community-wide effects depends on the degree to which relational networks span the various groups residing in an area. Therefore, special efforts must be made to foster such networks among the constituencies of heterogenous neighborhoods.

3. Effective crime control depends in part of the relationships that exist among the residents and local associations of an area and the primary public and private institutions of a metropolitan area that channel resources to urban neighborhoods.

Perhaps a final observation is in order. The development of intervention programs that are grounded in the social sciences often is characterized by a limited appreciation of the history of such efforts. Therefore, while the research of Shaw and McKay did not formally consider the dynamics of public control, they were essential components of their Chicago Area Project that appears to have been at least partially successful in the control of delinquency. That is, the development of successful contemporary community crime control may necessitate a reconsideration of a number of issues that were deemed to be centrally important over fifty years ago.

Notes

1. Although juveniles were the primary focus of the Shaw and McKay research, data also were collected pertaining to the placement of adults in Cook County Jail. McKay later updated the data collection through 1965; data pertaining to 1970 and 1980 were added by later researchers.

2. A similar study of Lawrence, Kansas had been published in 1915 by Blackmar and Burgess and one of Columbus, Ohio in 1923 by McKenzie.

3. Due to the influence of the work of Park and Burgess on their model, Shaw and McKay's framework sometimes is also referred to as the ecological theory of crime. This can be somewhat confusing, however, since there are other ecological theories of neighborhood crime (such as the routine activities model) which rely more on the ecological work of Hawley (1950) than Park and Burgess.

4. All Thomas and Znaniecki page citations are to Volume II of *The Polish Peasant in Europe and America.*

5. Malcolm Klein (1969) has criticized strongly the empirical basis which led Shaw and McKay to their conclusions concerning the group nature of delinquency.

6. Kornhauser (1978) has provided a very cogent response to this objection, conclusively showing that Shaw and McKay intended social disorganization to represent a set of dynamics that intervened between ecological change and delinquency.

7. Nevertheless, this assumption means that the reformulated social disorganization perspective is not appropriate when consensus over the perceived "badness" of an activity cannot be demonstrated. See Bursik and Grasmick (1993a).

8. Although it is limited to the regulation of illegal behavior, the private and parochial dimensions of systemic control are closely related to the defining features of "functional communities" as discussed by Coleman and Hoffer (1987) and Short (1990).

References

Berry, Brian J. L., and John D. Kasarda. 1977. *Contemporary Urban Ecology*. New York: Macmillan.

Black, Donald, and Albert J. Reiss, Jr. 1967. "Patterns of Behavior in Police and Citizen Transactions." *Studies of Crime and Law Enforcement in Major Metropolitan Areas*. Vol. 2, *Field Surveys III, Sec. I*. Washington, DC: President's Commission on Law Enforcement and the Administration of Justice.

Blackmar, F. W., and Ernest W. Burgess. 1917. *Lawrence Social Survey*. Lawrence: University of Kansas.

Bluestone, Barry, and Bennett Harrison. 1982. *The Deindustrialization of America: Plant Closings, Community Abandonment, and the Dismantling of Basic Industry*. New York: Basic Books.

Breckinridge, Sophonisba P., and Edith Abbott. 1912. *The Delinquent Child and the Home*. New York: Russell Sage Foundation.

Buckley, Walter. 1967. *Sociology and Modern Systems Theory*. Englewood Cliffs: NJ: Prentice-Hall.

Burgess, Ernest W. 1925. "The Growth of the City." In Robert E. Park, Ernest W. Burgess, and Roderick D. McKenzie (eds.), *The City*. Chicago: University of Chicago Press.

Bursik, Robert J., Jr. 1986. "Ecological Stability and the Dynamics of Delinquency" In Albert J. Reiss, Jr. and Michael Tonry, *Communities and Crime*. Chicago: University of Chicago Press.

———. 1988. "Social Disorganization and Theories of Crime and Delinquency: Problems and Prospects." *Criminology* 26:519-551.

———. 1989. "Political Decision-Making and Ecological Models of Delinquency: Conflict and Consensus." In Steven F. Messner, Marvin D. Krohn, and Allen E. Liska (eds), *Theoretical Integration in the Study of Deviance and Crime*. Albany: State University of New York Press.

———. 1993b. *Neighborhoods and Crime. The Dimensions of Effective Community Control*. New York: Lexington.

Bursik, Robert J., Jr. and Harold G. Grasmick. 1993a. "Economic Deprivation and Neighborhood Crime Rates, 1960-1980." *Law and Society Review* 27:263-283.

Bursik, Robert J., Jr., and Jim Webb. 1982. "Community Change and Patterns of Delinquency." *American Journal of Sociology* 88:24-42.

Byrne, James M., and Robert J. Sampson. 1986. *The Social Ecology of Crime.* New York: Springer-Verlag.

Castells, Manuel. 1983. *The City and the Grassroots: A Cross-Cultural Theory of Urban Social Movements.* Berkeley: University of California Press.

Cohen, Cathy J., and Michael C. Dawson. 1993. "Neighborhood Poverty and African-American Politics." *American Political Science Review* 87:286-302.

Coleman, James S., and Thomas Hoffer. 1987. *Public and Private High Schools: The Impact of Communities.* New York: Basic Books.

DuBow, Fred, Edward McCabe, and Gail Kaplan. 1979. *Reactions to Crime: A Critical Review of the Literature.* Washington, DC: U.S. Department of Justice, Law Enforcement Assistance Administration.

Erlanger, Howard S. 1979. "Estrangement, Machismo, and Gang Violence." *Social Science Quarterly* 60:235-249.

Foley, D. L. 1973. "Institutional and Contextual Factors Affecting the Housing Choice of Minority Residents." In Amos H. Hawley and Vincent P. Rock (eds.), *Segregation in Residential Areas.* Washington, DC: National Academy of Sciences.

Granovetter, Mark S. 1973. "The Strength of Weak Ties." *American Journal of Sociology* 78:1360-1380.

Greenberg, Stephanie W., William M. Rohe, and Jay R. Williams. 1985. *Informal Citizen Action and Crime Prevention at the Neighborhood Level.* Washington, DC: National Institute of Justice.

Hawley, Amos H. 1950. *Human Ecology: A Theory of Urban Structure.* New York: Ronald Press.

Heitgerd, Janet L., and Robert J. Bursik, Jr. 1987. "Extra-Community Dynamics and the Ecology of Delinquency." *American Journal of Sociology* 92: 775-787.

Hirsch, A. R. 1983. *Making the Second Ghetto: Race and Housing in Chicago, 1940-1960.* New York: Cambridge University Press.

Hunter, Albert J. 1974. *Symbolic Communities. The Persistence and Change of Chicago's Local Communities.* Chicago: University of Chicago Press.

———. 1985. "Private, Parochial and Public Orders: The Problem of Crime and Incivility in Urban Communities." In Gerald D. Suttles and Mayer N. Zald (eds.), *The Challenge of Social Control: Citizenship and Institution Building in Modern Society.* Norwood, NJ: Ablex.

Kasarda, John D., and Morris Janowitz. 1974. "Community Attachment in Mass Society." *American Sociological Review* 39:328-339.

Klein, Malcolm. 1969. "On Group Context of Delinquency." *Sociology and Social Research* 69:561-565.

Kobrin, Solomon. 1959. "The Chicago Area Project-A 25 Year Assessment." *Annals of the American Academy of Political and Social Science* 322:20-29.

———. 1971. "The Formal Logical Properties of the Shaw-McKay Delinquency Theory." In Harwin L. Voss and D. M. Peterson (eds.), *Ecology, Crime and Delinquency.* New York: Appleton-Century-Crofts.

Kornhauser, Ruth R. 1978. *Social Sources of Delinquency.* Chicago: University of Chicago Press.

Lewis, Dan A., and Greta Salem. 1986. *Fear of Crime: Incivility and the Production of a Social Problem*. New Brunswick, NJ: Transaction Books.

Logan, John R., and Harvey L. Molotch. 1987. *Urban Frontiers: The Political Economy of Place*. Berkeley: University of California Press.

Lovrich, Nicholas P., and G. Thomas Taylor. 1976. "Neighborhood Evaluation of Local Services: A Citizen Survey Approach." *Urban Affairs Quarterly* 12:97-222.

McCarthy, John D., and Mayer N. Zald. 1987. "Resource Mobilization and Social Movements: A Partial Theory." In Mayer N. Zald and John D. McCarthy (eds.), *Social Movements in an Organizational Society*. New Brunswick, NJ: Transaction.

McConville, Mike, and Dan Shepherd. 1992. *Watching Police Watching Communities*. London: Routledge.

Maguire, Kathleen, Ann L. Pastore, and Timothy J. Flanagan. 1993. *Sourcebook of Criminal Justice Statistics-1992*. Washington, DC: U.S. Department of Justice, Bureau of Justice Statistics.

McKenzie, Roderick D. 1923. *The Neighborhood: A Study of Local Life in the City of Columbus, Ohio*. Chicago: University of Chicago Press.

Merry, Sally E. 1981. *Urban Danger. Life in a Neighborhood of Strangers*. Philadelphia: Temple University Press.

Mitchell, J. Clyde. 1969. "The Concept and Use of Social Networks." In *Social Networks in Urban Situations: Analyses of Personal Relationships in Central African Towns*. Manchester, England: Institute for Social Research.

Morris, Terence. 1957. *The Criminal Area*. London: Routledge and Kegan Paul.

Nardulli, Peter F., and Jeffrey M. Stowe. 1981. *Politics, Professionalism, and Urban Services: The Police*. Cambridge, MA: Oelgeschlager, Guhn and Hain.

Pacyga, Dominic A. 1989. "The Russell Square Community Committee: An Ethnic Response to Urban Problems." *Journal of Urban History* 15:155-184.

Park, Robert E. 1926. "The Urban Community as a Special Pattern and a Moral Order." In Ernest W. Burgess, (ed.), *The Urban Community*. Chicago: University of Chicago Press.

Park, Robert E., and Ernest W. Burgess. 1920. *Introduction to the Science of Sociology*. Chicago: University of Chicago Press.

Podolefsky, Aaron M. 1983. "Community Response to Crime Prevention: The Mission District." *Journal of Community Action* 1:43-48.

Reiss, Albert J., Jr., and Michael Tonry, eds. 1986. *Communities and Crime*. Chicago: University of Chicago Press.

Rossi, Peter H., Emily Waite, Christine E. Bose, and Richard E. Berk. 1974. "The Seriousness of Crime: Normative Structure and Individual Differences." *American Sociological Review* 39: 224-237.

Sampson, Robert J. 1983. "Neighborhood Context of Criminal Victimization." Ph.D. dissertation, State University of New York at Albany.

———. 1985. "Neighborhood and Crime: The Structural Determinants of Personal Victimization." *Journal of Research in Crime and Delinquency* 22:7-40.

———. 1986. "Neighborhood Family Structure and the Risk of Personal Victimization." In James M. Byrne and Robert J. Sampson, (eds.), *The Social Ecology of Crime*. New York: Springer-Verlag.

Sampson, Robert J., and W. Byron Groves. 1989. "Community Structure and Crime: Testing Social Disorganization Theory." *American Journal of Sociology* 94:774-802.

Sampson, Robert J., and William J. Wilson. 1991. "Toward a Theory of Race, Crime, and Urban Inequality." Presented at the annual meeting of the American Society of Criminology, San Francisco.

Schwartz, Gary. 1987. *Beyond Conformity or Rebellion: Youth and Authority.* Chicago: University of Chicago Press.

Shaw, Clifford R., Frederick M. Zorbaugh, Henry D. McKay, and Leonard S. Cottrell. 1929. *Delinquency Areas.* Chicago: University of Chicago Press.

Shaw, Clifford R., and Henry D. McKay. 1931. *Social Factors in Juvenile Delinquency.* National Commission on Law Observation and Enforcement, no.13, *Report on the Causes of Crime,* Vol. 2. Washington, DC: U.S. Government Printing Office.

———. 1942. *Juvenile Delinquency and Urban Areas.* Chicago: University of Chicago Press.

———. 1969. *Juvenile Delinquency and Urban Areas.* 2d ed. Chicago: University of Chicago Press.

Sherman, Lawrence W. 1986. "Policing Communities: What Works?" In Albert J. Reiss, Jr. and Michael Tonry, (eds.), *Communities and Crime.* Chicago: University of Chicago Press.

Short, James F., 1990. "New Wine in Old Bottles? Change and Continuity in American Gangs." Pp. 223-239 in C. Ronald Huff (ed.), *Gangs in America.* Newbury Park, CA: Sage.

Short, James F., Jr., and Fred L. Strodtbeck. 1965. *Group Process and Gang Delinquency.* Chicago: University of Chicago Press.

Skogan, Wesley G. 1988. "Community Organization and Crime." In Michael Tonry and Norval Morris (ed.), *Crime and Justice: A Review of Research.* Vol. 10. Chicago: University of Chicago Press.

———. 1990. *Disorder and Decline: Crime and the Spiral of Decay in American Neighborhoods.* New York: Free Press.

Smith, Douglas A. 1986. "The Neighborhood Context of Police Behavior." In Albert J. Reiss, Jr. and Michael Tonry (eds.), *Communities and Crime.* Chicago: University of Chicago Press.

Snodgrass, Jon. 1976. "Clifford R. Shaw and Henry D. McKay: Chicago Criminologists." *British Journal of Criminology* 16:1-19.

Spergel, Irving A., and John Korbelik. 1979. *The Local Community Service System and ISOS: An Interorganizational Analysis.* Executive Report to the Illinois Law Enforcement Commission.

Spergel, Irving A., and G. David Curry. 1990. "Strategies and Perceived Agency Effectiveness in Dealing with the Youth Gang Problem." In C. Ronald Huff (ed.), *Gangs in America.* Newbury Park, CA: Sage.

Susser, Ida. 1982. *Norman Street: Poverty and Politics in an Urban Neighborhood.* New York: Oxford University Press.

Suttler, Gerald D. 1968. *The Social Order of the Slum.* Chicago: University of Chicago.

Taggart, Harriet Tee, and Kevin W. Smith. 1981. "Redlining: An Assessment of the Evidence of Disinvestment in Metropolitan Boston." *Urban Affairs Quarterly* 17:91-108.

Taylor, Ralph B., S. A. Schumaker, and Stephen D. Gottfredson. 1985. "Neighborhood Level Link Between Physical Features and Local Sentiments: Deterioration, Fear of Crime, and Confidence." *Journal of Architectural Planning and Research* 2:261-275.

Thomas, William I., and Florian Znaniecki. 1920. *The Polish Peasant in Europe and America*, Vol. 2. Boston: Gorham Press.

Unnever, James D. 1987. "Review of *The Social Ecology of Crime,* edited by James M. Byrne and Robert J. Sampson." *Contemporary Sociology* 16: 845-846.

Wacquant, Loic J.D., and William J. Wilson. 1989. "The Cost of Racial and Class Exclusion in the Inner City." *Annals of the American Academy of Political and Social Science* 501:8-25.

Weaver, Steven D. 1993. "Networking Systems Target Underlying Foundations of Crime." *Police Chief* 60:76-79.

Whyte, William F. 1955. *Street Corner Society*. 2nd ed. Chicago: University of Chicago Press.

Wilson, James Q., and George L. Kelling. 1982. "Broken Windows." *Atlantic Monthly* (March): 29-38.

Wilson, William J. 1987. *The Truly Disadvantaged: The Inner City, the Underclass, and Public Policy*. Chicago: University of Chicago Press.

Wirth, Louis, and Margaret Furez. 1938. *Local Community Fact Book*. Chicago: Chicago Recreation Commission.

Wolfgang, Marvin E., Robert M. Figlio, Paul E. Tracy, and Simon I. Singer. 1985. *The National Survey of Crime Severity*. Washington, DC: U.S. Department of Justice.

8

You Can Choose Your Friends, but Do
They Choose Your Crime?
Implications of Differential Association
Theories for Crime Prevention Policy

D. M. Gorman and Helene Raskin White

Several variations of associational theories have been proposed in the delinquency literature to account for the causes of delinquent behaviors. This chapter
explores these various theories and their implications for prevention programm-
ing. In the first two sections, we discuss the development of these theories and
their empirical support. Next, we describe existing prevention programs that
have incorporated concepts from associational theories in their models and
discuss the pitfalls and problems in designing these types of interventions. In the
final section, we outline the necessary components of an effective model for
crime prevention based upon differential association theory.

Associational Theories

Associational theories have their roots in Sutherland's (1947) differential
association theory (DA). Sutherland postulated nine statements to explain the
causes of all criminal behavior. Basically he stated that criminal behavior (like
all behavior), including its techniques and motives (both of which are necessary), is learned in interaction with other persons, primarily in intimate groups.
The crux of the theory is that an individual becomes delinquent if there is an
excess of definitions favorable to violation of the law over definitions unfavorable to violation within his or her groups. In other words, the groups provide
the individual with criminal and anticriminal patterns, techniques, motives, and
definitions of legal norms. The balance of definitions, which is determined by

frequency, duration, priority, and intensity of exposure to various groups, determines who will conform (Akers, 1985:40).

DA theory is generally considered to be part of a broader category of cultural deviance or subcultural theories. The basis of these theories is that a variety of subcultures exist in society with different norms regarding law violation. Persons are exposed to multiple groups and multiple definitions of what is "right" and "wrong." Through social interaction individuals are socialized into the ways of the group. Thus, there is differential access to both legitimate and illegitimate means and differential opportunities to learn various types of antisocial behavior, which, in part, explains the existence of multiple types of delinquent subcultures (Cohen, 1955; Cloward and Ohlin, 1960). (For a recent critical evaluation of DA theory, see Matsueda, 1988.)

Burgess and Akers (1966) reformulated DA theory in order to provide a more behaviorally oriented specification of the learning process. Their reformulation combined the principles of DA with Bandura's (1977) social learning model and was called "differential association-reinforcement theory." The emphasis of this theory was that deviant behavior is learned, like all behavior, according to the principles of conditioning and that behavior is a function of reinforcements (rewards and punishments). This learning can take place in both social and nonsocial situations (Akers, 1985:41).

Akers (1985) has advanced differential association-reinforcement theory and renamed it "social learning theory" (which is confusing given that Bandura's theory has the same name and is distinctively different). According to Akers, behavior is conditioned by social and nonsocial reinforcements and punishments. Behavior is learned in groups, which are the greatest source of reinforcement for the individual. Besides providing reinforcement, members of groups serve as models from whom behavior is imitated. Within groups, individuals also learn normative definitions concerning prosocial and antisocial behaviors. The individual incorporates these definitions, which serve as stimuli to engage in the behavior and expect certain reinforcements. Thus, *differential association* is the process of being exposed to different groups that provide the context in which learning takes place. *Differential reinforcement* is the process by which deviant behavior becomes dominant over conforming behavior. That is, given the choice of two alternative acts, the one that is positively reinforced with the greatest amount, frequency, and probability will be maintained. Considerable empirical evidence has been collected in support of Aker's theory (e.g., Akers et al., 1979; Johnson, 1988).

One interesting variant on DA theory is peer-cluster theory (Oetting et al., 1991). This theory was developed to explain drug use and postulates that among adolescents drug use takes place in peer clusters (small cohesive groups) that reinforce such use. Peers initiate youth into drugs, provide drugs, model drug use behavior, and shape drug use attitudes. According to this theory, exposure to these groups depends on psychosocial factors that make adolescents vulnerable to drug use, which include primarily anger, family strength and sanctions, religious identification, and school adjustment.

Johnson, Marcos and Bahr (1987) explain drug use in a similar vein. They found, as have many others (e.g., Warr and Stafford, 1991), that friends' behavior influences the delinquency of adolescents directly rather than by affecting adolescents' definitions (as Sutherland [1947] had posited). Johnson and his colleagues suggest that the associational influence of peers is not a result of peers influencing an adolescent's view of the behavior (as good or bad or right or wrong) but rather a result of associations with peers in situations that place immediate pressure on an adolescent to go along with the crowd and fear of rejection if he or she refuses. The theories of Oetting et al. (1991) and Johnson et al. (1987) relate to the social nature of drug use among adolescents (i.e., adolescents usually take drugs when they are with their friends rather than when they are alone and may have less relevance for other forms of delinquency that are not engaged in within a group context).

Recently, theorists have attempted to integrate concepts from DA theory with concepts from other delinquency theories, primarily social control theory (e.g., Elliott, Huizinga, and Ageton, 1985; Johnson et al., 1987; LaGrange and White, 1985). These integrated, or mixed, theories stress the notion of the importance of the interaction between type of peer group (delinquent versus nondelinquent) and extent of the bond to the group (high or low attachment and involvement). According to these theories, strong bonding to delinquent peers is a powerful predictor of delinquency and drug use (Agnew, 1991; Elliott, Huizinga, and Ageton, 1985). Thus, these theories support Sutherland's conception of the importance of frequency, duration, priority, and intensity of interactions for determining engagement in antisocial or prosocial activities (see also Warr, 1993).

In this section we have briefly examined the development of associational theories from DA, to social learning and other variations, to new integrated theories. All of these theories suggest that individuals learn deviant behavior in interaction with significant others who model or reinforce such behavior. During adolescence, the principal significant others who have influence on delinquent behavior are parents and peers.[1] In the following section we briefly review some of the empirical research on the influence of these significant others on adolescent delinquency.

Empirical Tests of Differential Association/Social Learning Theory

The Influence of Parents

Studies of adolescent drinking behavior stress the importance of parents as models (see White, Bates, and Johnson, 1991). Most research suggests that parents who drink teach their children to drink, but whether social learning occurs primarily through direct or indirect social reinforcement has not been adequately addressed. There are several plausible ways in which parents may differentially reinforce, either intentionally or unintentionally, their childrens' use of alcohol. One way is to forbid or punish use. Alternatively, youth may drink because they perceive that their parents expect them to drink. In fact, parents are generally the first ones to introduce alcohol to their children (Mandell, at al., 1963). Youth may also learn to drink because drinking on special occasions with their family is associated with positive consequences. (For greater detail on parental influences on drinking behavior, see White, Bates, and Johnson, 1991).

Research on drug use indicates that parental influence on children depends on the type of drug being studied. For example, Kandel, Kessler, and Margulies (1978) found that parental behavior is critical in initiation of adolescent alcohol use, that peer influence is most important in initiating marijuana use, and that both best friend's use and poor relations with parents are important in initiating use of other illicit drugs.

The delinquency literature stresses that modeling is not the basis for adolescents' learning of other forms of delinquent behavior from their parents; rather, parents influence their childrens' delinquent behavior through interactions in the family. Although a full discussion of the quality of the parent-child relationship as it relates to deviant behavior is beyond the scope of this chapter, it must be noted that this variable influences social learning processes because family members are the primary agents of socialization. They set up initial reinforcement contingencies and thus influence all stages of development. The quality of the interaction between the adolescent and his or her parents and the quality of the home environment have been shown to influence adolescents' drinking, drug use, and delinquent behavior regardless of what their parents' habits might be. Some of these variables include family relationships, attachment to family, communication, discipline, family conflict, parental love, parental control and monitoring, and family management techniques (Dishion and Loeber, 1985; Glynn, 1981; Hawkins, Catalano, and Miller, 1992; Loeber and Stouthamer-Loeber, 1986; Johnson and Pandina, 1991; Kandel, Kessler, and Margulies, 1978).

The Influence of Peers

The deviance-inducing effect of deviant peers as postulated by DA theory has been equally successful in explaining adolescent substance use (Akers et al., 1979; Johnson, Marcos, and Bahr, 1987; White, Johnson, and Horwitz, 1986) and delinquency (Elliott, Huizingar, and Ageton, 1985; Johnson, 1979; La-Grange and White, 1985; Matsueda, 1982). Virtually all studies that include peer delinquency find it to be one of the most, if not the most, powerful predictor of adolescent delinquency. Some research suggests, however, that peer influence is stronger for females than for males, possibly because females develop stronger friendships than males (Kandel, 1985). Similarly, Farrell and Danish (1993) suggest that peer influences are stronger for white than for African American adolescents.

According to an associational perspective, delinquent peers may influence an adolescent to engage in delinquency in three main ways: (1) by teaching definitions favorable to crime commission, (2) by rewarding deviant behavior, and (3) by modeling deviant behavior (Agnew, 1991). Although research has established that peers influence one another's deviant behavior, it is just as likely that the behavior is learned from the peer group as it is that adolescents select friends whose behaviors seem attractive. Some studies indicate that the causal path goes from delinquent peers to delinquency (e.g., Oetting et al., 1991); this is depicted in Figure 8.1A. Others indicate that the path goes from delinquency to delinquent peers (e.g., Brown et al., 1993); this is depicted in Figure 8.1B. It is currently acknowledged, however, that the relationship is reciprocal (Downs, 1987; Kandel, 1985; Thornberry 1990). That is, it appears that association with delinquent peers is just as much a consequence of delinquency as a cause of it. This relationship is depicted in Figure 8.1C. Adolescents originally select friends who are like themselves in terms of shared behaviors and attitudes. Then friends continue to influence one another as a result of continued associations (Kandel, Kessler, and Margulies, 1978). (For greater detail see Kandel, 1985.)

Research on the adolescent-peer delinquency relationship has been criticized because in most studies, the measures are based on adolescents' descriptions of their friends' behavior. Thus, the correlations are based on subjects' perceptions of friends' delinquency rather than on the actual delinquency of friends. However, when studies have matched data collected separately from subjects and their friends, they continue to find the strong associations in the adolescent-peer delinquency relationship (see Kandel, 1985).

Some theorists have argued that differences are likely to exist in the friendship bonds of delinquent versus nondelinquent adolescents (for a review see Giordano, Cernkovich, and Pugh, 1986). That is, it has been postulated that delinquents would not be as strongly attached to their peers as nondelinquents. Empirical research has not borne out this speculation. It appears that delinquents are just as close to their peers as are nondelinquents. In fact, Giordano et al. (1986) found that delinquents were more likely to influence each other, which suggests that delinquent peer groups may be more cohesive than conventional friendship groups. However, delinquent as compared to nondelinquent friendship groups were also more likely to experience conflict. Kandel and Davies (1991) also found that those young adults most involved in drug use tended to have more intimate friendships than other young adults. Thus, it is generally accepted that delinquents and nondelinquents have similar friendship

FIGURE 8.1. Four Models Depicting the Relationship Between Delinquency
and Peer Group Association

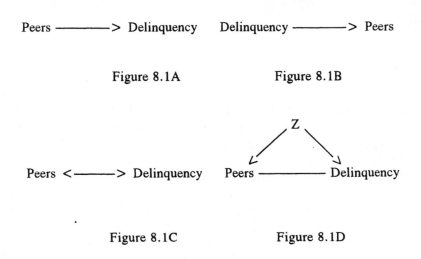

Peers ————> Delinquency   Delinquency ————> Peers

Figure 8.1A   Figure 8.1B

Peers <————> Delinquency   Peers ———— Delinquency

Figure 8.1C   Figure 8.1D

bonds. Those who are close to their friends and spend more time with them are
more likely to engage in behavior similar to their friends, whereas those who
are less attached and involved with peers are less likely to match their friends'
behavior regardless of whether it is prosocial or antisocial (Agnew, 1991;
Elliott, Huizinga, and Ageton, 1985).

Research into the nature of adolescent friendships consistently reveals the
existence of a few well-defined peer clusterings based on: (1) athletic and social
interests (the elite group—generally termed "populars" or "jocks" in the case
of males and "socies" in the case of females); (2) academic interests (generally
termed "hot-shots"); and (3) involvement in problem behaviors (generally
termed "dirts" or "burnouts") (Brown and Lohr, 1987; Brown et al. 1993;
Cohen, 1979; Mosbach and Leventhal, 1988). Nongroup members generally fall
into one of two categories, termed "normals" and "loners" (or "outcasts").
Delinquent behaviors have been found to be more common among members of
the "dirts" than among other peer groups (Brown et al., 1993; Downs and
Rose, 1991; Mosbach and Leventhal, 1988). Moreover, this high-risk group
differs from its low-risk counterpart in terms of factors such as self-esteem,
risktaking, definition of self, and type of parenting received (Brown et al.,
1993; Mosbach and Leventhal, 1988).

An interesting group of adolescents is the "loners," who are not affiliated with either delinquent or nondelinquent peer groups. One might speculate that such individuals would be more deviant than other adolescents. Yet research indicates that loners as compared to social adolescents are less likely to be involved in delinquent behavior (Tolone and Tieman, 1990).

Parents Versus Peers

Researchers with different theoretical orientations disagree about the relative influence of parents and peers during adolescence. In general, research indicates that peer influences increase with age during adolescence (LaGrange and White, 1985) and that peers exert a significantly stronger influence on adolescent drug use and delinquency than do parents (or other adults) (e.g., Hansen, et al. 1987; Huba and Bentler, 1980; White Johnson, and Horwitz, 1986). In studying drug use, Kandel and Andrews (1987), who collected data from best friends and parents, found that the socialization process varied depending upon the source of influence and the specific drug. Parental influence was most important prior to initiation, but peer imitation became most influential after initiation. Kandel (1985) notes that peer influences are more immediate and transitory than parental influences. Kandel also notes that parents are more important influences on future life plans whereas friends are more important influences on current life-styles.

Most of the research points to an interaction of parent and peer influences on adolescent delinquent behavior (for a review, see Glynn, 1981). For example, Fontane and Layne (1979) suggest that the peer culture reinforces drunkenness if parents display it and co-opts the parental influence of those parents who do not drink to drunkenness. Furthermore, peer influences can be ameliorated by protective family factors (Brook, et al., 1986; Brown et al., 1993). In addition, parents can influence their children's values and choice of friends and thus can make their children susceptible to the influence of either deviant or nondeviant friends (e.g., Hansen et al., 1987; Kline, Canter, and Robin, 1987; Simons, Conger, and Whitbeck, 1988). Hoffman (1993) found that peer influence on drug use was stronger than parental influence. He also found that parent-child relations had a direct effect on drug use and an indirect effect on choice of peers. Others have also found a strong association between parenting practices and later involvement with antisocial peers (Dishion, et al., 1991). At the very least, the family indirectly influences deviant behavior by defining the child's socioeconomic status, ethnic/cultural background, and environmental milieu (Zucker, 1976). Thus, as will be discussed later, intervening early with families might serve to prevent those most at risk of becoming deviant from later affiliating with similar deviant-prone peers.

In the above section, we discussed the effects of peers and parents on adolescent delinquency and drug use. We now describe prevention programs in each of these domains. The techniques presently used in each are essentially the same, no doubt because delinquent behavior and drug use so frequently occur in the same individuals (White, 1992). We focus on prevention programs since these are most germane to testing causal theories, such as differential association theory (Robins, 1992).

Peer-Led Interventions

The observation that youths who engage in delinquent acts tend to have friends who engage in similar acts has led to the development of peer group programs designed to reduce the risk of such behavior (Gottfredson, 1987). As noted above, this observation is open to at least two fundamentally opposed interpretations: first, that individuals with an already established pattern of delinquent behavior choose to associate with similarly delinquent peers (Figure 8.1B, above); second, that delinquent values and behavior are acquired through association with delinquent peers (Figure 8.1A, above). As will be discussed in greater detail below, peer group prevention programs are almost without exception premised upon the latter theoretical approach. That is, they assume that if affiliating with negative role models encourages the development of deviant behaviors, then sufficient exposure to positive role models might diminish the appeal of deviant friends and hence foster more conventional social ties and behaviors. Here we consider the evidence concerning the efficacy of such programs in two broad areas: juvenile delinquency prevention and drug use prevention.

Juvenile Delinquency Prevention Programs

Gottfredson (1987) reviewed a series of peer group prevention programs that employed, for the most part, positive peer culture (Vorrath and Brendtro, 1974) and peer culture development (PCD) techniques (National School Resource Network, 1980). Both of these approaches are derived from the guided group interaction (GGI) model of Bixby and McCorkle (1951) and can reasonably be considered as a single intervention strategy (Gottfredson, 1987). GGI is premised on the idea that "delinquents will learn to conform to conventional social rules by gaining more social rewards through conformity than through nonconformity" (Gottfredson and Gottfredson, 1992:315). Through free discussion in a group setting, it is anticipated that individuals will recognize problems with their own behavior and become aware of how their conduct is at odds with that of nondelinquent peers. Groups are composed of both "positive" and "negative" peers, with an adult leader providing some structure to the discussion through use of techniques such as posing questions to group members and summarizing important ideas (Gottfredson, 1987).

In his review of studies that had evaluated programs that were based directly on GGI or were derived from it, Gottfredson (1987) concluded that these all had inadequate research designs and methodologies and that therefore the results presented were open to numerous competing interpretations. Furthermore, in many cases the conclusions at which the authors had arrived (that the programs were effective in improving suspension rates, tardy rates, grades, attitudes toward school, and so on) were simply not supported by the data presented.

In addition, Gottfredson (1987) conducted an evaluation of a PCD program in Chicago public schools that was methodologically more sophisticated than earlier studies. Students who had previously been classified as (1) positive leaders, (2) negative leaders, (3) experiencing difficulties, or (4) not experiencing difficulties (conventional) were randomly assigned to either an experimental or control condition. The program took the form of a daily group meeting, run over the course of a fifteen-week school semester, and was designed to reduce the amount of negative peer association and influence experienced by group members. As Gottfredson and Gottfredson (1992) observe, it was thus fully in keeping with DA theory.

The program was implemented in both elementary school and high school settings, although the PCD staff considered it only appropriate to the latter. Among the high school students, the program was ineffective in preventing delinquent behavior. Indeed, where significant differences did emerge (e.g., in the case of drug use, serious delinquency, school suspensions, and police contacts), they favored the control group (i.e., students who did not receive the program had lower rates of drug use and serious delinquency). Among the elementary school children, the only positive program effect was in the area of enhanced internal control (although, as Gottfredson [1987] notes, one would expect two of the thirty-six experimental group-control group comparisons that were made to be statistically significant by chance alone).

In addition to not reducing delinquent acts among the experimental group, the PCD program also failed to change the targeted mediating variables through which it was intended to work, which were belief in conventional values and influence of positive peers. Thus, as Gottfredson and Gottfredson (1992) observe, the program evaluation does not allow rejection of the DA theory upon which it was premised. The program may simply have been inadequate to alter the peer group culture within an urban school setting. Indeed, Gottredson and Gottfredson (1992) conclude that this was almost certainly the case, arguing that the processes (such as early peer rejection) leading to the formation of deviant peer groups began to operate long before the program was implemented and were therefore unlikely to be affected by such a modest peer-led intervention.

This issue of whether other variables, such as early peer rejection, might be important in explaining both later group affiliation and delinquency will be returned to later. First, peer programs in the area of drug use prevention will be discussed.

Drug Use Prevention Programs

In recent years, drug use prevention programs have been dominated by the so-called social influence perspective. These programs conform to one of two basic types, one of which is focused principally on *resistance skills training* (RST) and one of which incorporates broader *personal and social skills training* through the inclusion of more "affective" components such as stress reduction, self-esteem enhancement, and decision making (Hansen, 1992). Central to both types of programs is the idea that initiation into drug use results principally from the adverse influence of negative peers and pressure from the media. Thus, adolescents are taught the skills necessary to identify such pressure and to resist it. In line with this, a number of large-scale prevention programs that purport to reduce the rate of initiation into drug use have been developed and evaluated (Gorman, 1992b). The delivery of many of these programs involves peer leaders as well as traditional adult educators.

The evaluation of Project ALERT (Ellickson and Bell, 1990) is among the most sophisticated in terms of research design and methodology. The program, delivered to 6,527 seventh-grade students from thirty junior high schools in Oregon and California, comprised eight sessions during the first year with three boosters during eighth grade. The sessions were concerned with examining the reasons why people do and do not use drugs, the consequences of use, identifying and countering prodrug pressures, developing ways of saying "no" to pressures, and identifying the benefits of resisting drug use. Schools were randomly allocated to one of three conditions: a teacher-led social influence program, a teacher-led/peer-assisted social influence program, and a no-intervention control group. The inclusion of peers in the delivery of the program was determined by the theoretical model upon which the intervention was premised, namely, social learning theory. In respect to this, Ellickson and her colleagues observe that

> Social learning theory posits that adolescents learn from others in two ways: (1) through direct modeling (imitation) of others' behavior; and (2) through reinforcement of adolescent beliefs, attitudes, and behavior by means of social approval or disapproval (Bandura, 1977). The use of teenage role models who do not use drugs and who disapprove of doing so is relevant to both ways of learning. (Ellickson, et al., 1988:11).

In addition, they cite the influence of communication theory, which stresses the need for the communicator to be a credible source of information to the target audience. Expertise and perceived similarity are factors that they consider to increase credibility.

Students in Project ALERT were followed up at three, twelve, and fifteen months. At the final follow-up, just 40 percent (3,852) of the subjects were interviewed. The effects of the program were assessed separately for use of alcohol, marijuana and cigarettes. Subjects were divided into one of three risk groups in terms of their baseline use of each substance: "nonusers," "experimenters", and "users". At each follow-up the effects of the program were assessed for a number of outcome variables—e.g., "ever used", "monthly use", "weekly use" and "quit"—not all of which were applicable to each risk group (e.g., "nonusers" could not "quit" at posttest).

The effectiveness of the program has been the subject of some debate. The authors conclude one report by stating: "These results indicate that the social influence model of prevention, as implemented in Project ALERT, works" (Ellickson and Bell, 1990:1303). Elsewhere, they state: "Project ALERT has provided rigorous, experimental evidence that the social influence approach can curb adolescent use of licit and illicit drugs" (Bell, Ellickson and Harrison, 1993: 463-464). In contrast to this, Gorman (1992b, 1994) has argued that the influence of the program is extremely variable across risk groups and across substances. Of the numerous comparisons made between the two groups who received the intervention program and the control group at follow-up, very few revealed a statistically significant difference. For example, just two of the thirty-five comparisons made between the peer-assisted group and control group in terms of marijuana use at follow-up were significantly difference (Gorman, 1994). The few differences that did emerge were mainly confined to the low-risk groups — that is, those who were nonusers or experimenters at baseline.

A recent report by the National Research Council (Gerstein and Green, 1993) also raises questions about the efficacy of Project Alert, noting that if the sample is regrouped and a comparison made between the two experimental conditions and the control condition *irrespective of baseline risk-group status*, there are no statistically significant differences in terms of use of alcohol or cigarettes at the final follow-up. In addition, although the effect of the program on marijuana use—a reduction of about one-sixth to one-fourth—is significant, the extremely high attrition rate (as much as 61 percent of baseline marijuana users) limits the interpretation that can be made of such a finding.

The World Health Organization (WHO) Collaborative Study (Perry, et al., 1989) also evaluated the effects of both an adult-led and a peer-led social influence program, the objective of which was to delay onset and minimize use of alcohol. The program entailed five sixty-minute sessions, which were concerned with identifying the consequences of alcohol use and nonuse, normative expectations about use, analyzing situations that involve use, identifying peer pressure, practicing refusal skills, analyzing advertisements, identifying nonalcohol places and situations, and an optional personal pledge not to drink until older. It was delivered to students aged eleven to eighteen years in three countries: Australia (n = 828), Chile (n = 195), and Norway (n = 1,306).

(The program was also delivered in Swaziland, but the control group initiated its own intervention in the course of the research and so could not be used for comparative purposes.) In assessing the effects of the program on alcohol use at a three-month follow-up, the sample was divided into baseline "nondrinkers" and "drinkers." Again, the authors report that the program was effective: "The data converge on the finding that peer-led education appears to be efficacious in reducing alcohol use across a variety of settings and cultures" (Perry et al., 1989:1146).

Once again, however, this interpretation of the data has been questioned (Gorman, 1992a, n.d.). The effects of the program were far from uniform across countries or risk groups, and, as with Project ALERT, it was not at all effective among those who had already initiated drug use. Among those who were nonusers at baseline, the results were statistically significant in just one of the three countries, Norway (see Gorman, 1992b, for a discussion of their practical or clinical significance).

Lest it be thought that Project ALERT and the WHO Collaborative Study are poor examples of this type of drug use prevention program, it should be noted that the results of other large scale social influence projects are, in general, no superior (Gorman, 1992b; Gerstein and Green, 1993). In addition, it has recently been observed that much of the literature on drug use prevention is marked by a tendency to "overinterpret" results concerning program effectiveness (Brown and Horowitz, 1993).

Theoretical Limitations of Peer-Led Programs

At a theoretical level, social influence programs display two fundamental weaknesses. Both of these relate to the way in which they conceptualize the relationship between peer group affiliation and delinquent behavior. First, they are premised on the idea that risk accruing from social influences such as peer pressure is broadly similar across all individuals and social groupings. As such they rely upon a *universal strategy* (Gordon, 1983) in which everyone in a given population (e.g., eighth-grade students) receives exactly the same program. Second, they assume that peer affiliation is always antecedent to delinquency.

With regard to the first of these issues, it has been shown that adolescent peer groups differ in their propensity to use drugs and engage in delinquent acts. The most obvious example of this is the "gang" common to large impoverished urban centers in the United States, the members of which have a greater propensity than nonmembers toward involvement in the illicit drug industry, violent behavior, and other activities that are disruptive and dysfunctional to their communities (Hagedorn, 1991). However, even among less disadvantaged and excluded segments of society, problem behaviors appear far more common among some adolescent peer groups than others. The peer group affiliation research, which was discussed above, has been conducted among predominantly white working- and middle-class adolescents and has consistently shown that deviant behaviors concentrate among members of the "dirts" as compared to other peer groups (Brown et al., 1993; Downs and Rose, 1991; Mosbach and Leventhal, 1988). Since this high-risk group differs from its low-risk counterparts in terms of factors such as risktaking and type of parenting received, program components other than resistance skills training are likely to be needed if interventions are to succeed with those who affiliate with this type of peer group.

With regard to peer-led interventions, it is instructive to contrast the description of the typical "dirt" with that of the typical peer leader. The former "is not only heavily involved in drug use and deviant activities but also inattentive to schoolwork and often hostile toward school adults; yet, group members seem to maintain a fairly strong self-image" (Brown et al., 1993:468). In contrast, the peer leaders are students that others "like, admire and would like to be like" and are generally "actively involved in other extracurricular school activities" (Klepp, Halper, and Perry, 1986:408). In drug prevention programs, peer leaders "serve as potent role models by demonstrating nonuse, by creating a norm that drug use is deviant rather than acceptable, and by providing alternatives to drug use" in addition to reinforcing "the importance of social responsibility" (Klepp, Halper, and Perry, 1986:407). It is hard to envisage any meaningful way in which these two types of students are peers, and it seems improbable that the peer leader will be a credible source of information about drug use to the average "dirt." The former's invitation to "think of some activities we can do to have fun that don't involve drinking alcohol" (part of a brain storming exercise suggested by Klepp, Halper, and Perry, 1986) is surely doomed to failure among those at most risk of becoming seriously involved in drug use.

In moving beyond broad-based peer-oriented programs in an attempt to prevent delinquent behavior among young people, it is necessary to base interventions on strategies other than the universal approach most frequently employed. This entails using theory to more precisely target or match an intervention to the needs of the intended audience (Gorman, 1992b). A recent study by Catalano and colleagues that examined drug use among African American and European American fifth-grade students found the latter to have higher rates of tobacco and alcohol initiation as well as several differences in the level of exposure to risk factors between the two groups (Catalano, et al., 1993). Although acknowledging the need for further replication, the authors observe that such findings suggest that it may be necessary to develop culturally appropriate prevention programs that take account of these differences. It should be noted that within the broad types of groupings analyzed by Catalano et al. (1993), substantial differences may also exist. For example, one study found that the relationship between socioeconomic status and drug abuse was stronger in the case of African American males than it was for white males or for females of either race (Barr et al., 1993). The authors explain the concentration of drug use among poor African American males in terms of Wilson's (1987) analysis of their marginal economic status that resulted from deindustrialization and they suggest that policy initiatives should attempt to increase educational and employment opportunities.

Thus, implicit in the targeting approach is the idea that the same problem (e.g., associating with delinquent peers and commission of delinquent acts) may be driven by fundamentally different factors in different populations (e.g., among poor inner-city minority youth as compared to among affluent white college students). A program may identify "at-risk" groups and attempt to effect change at three basic levels (Gordon, 198; Pillow, et al., 1991; Gorman, 1992b). First, programs can be developed that target a group in terms of some "marker" known to be associated with a greater risk of engaging in delinquent behavior (a *selected strategy*). Such markers can be identified at both the biological level (e.g., chemical imbalances) and the sociostructural level (e.g., residing in an impoverished urban environment), in the sense that both of these factors are known to be associated with elevated risk (of cocaine use in the 1990s, in the examples cited—see King, Curtis, and Knoblich, 1992, and Dunlap and Johnson, 1992, respectively). Second, programs can be targeted at youth exhibiting some early manifestation of problem behavior, such as extreme aggressiveness or anger (an *indicated strategy*). Third, programs can be targeted in terms of factors (e.g., parenting practices) that appear to link a more distant causal factor that might be resistant to change (e.g., a trait such as impulsivity) and later delinquent behaviors. All three approaches have advantages (e.g., increasing cost-effectiveness by delivering a program to those most in need) and disadvantages (e.g., potentially stigmatizing those targeted—see Pillow et al., 1991; Gorman, 1992b).

As to the second conceptual shortcoming of peer-led prevention programs—the relationship between group affiliation and deviant acts—these interventions are all premised on the idea that group affiliation precedes deviancy. As noted above, research indicates that similarity between adolescents and their friends in terms of their drug use and delinquency is a result of both socialization and prior selection (Kandel, 1985; Downs, 1987; Thornberry et al., 1990; Farrell and Danish, 1993). A number of intrapersonal, interpersonal, and broad sociocultural factors influence the causes of delinquency and drug abuse (Hawkins, Catalano, and Miller, 1992), and individuals may affiliate on the basis of these shared characteristics. This raises an additional possibility in explaining the relationship between peer affiliation and delinquency; namely, that some other variable or set of variables explains both an individual's choice of deviant peers and his or her involvement in deviant acts. This relationship is depicted in Figure 8.1D (above), with "Z" representing the third variable or set of variables that lead to increased risk. Such risk factors may operate at different levels, ranging from the genetic to the sociostructural.

In sum, intervention programs that attempt to teach skills to resist negative peer influences have not been very successful in preventing either delinquency or drug use. This may be due, in part, to their failure to match program content more appropriately to the needs of specific subsets of their target populations. Those at greatest risk appear to be particularly poorly served by these programs. In addition, given that there may be a set of factors occurring in early and middle childhood that predict both adolescent involvement in delinquent behavior and association with delinquent peers, resistance skills training programs may also have limited impact because of their failure to attend to these earlier influences. Delaying prevention initiatives until adolescence, and relying exclusively on resistance training, may be too little, too late.

Developing Effective Policy and Program Initiatives

With regard to the latter point, Hawkins, Catalano, and Miller (1992) recently presented a comprehensive review of risk factors for substance abuse. Of the seventeen factors they identify, one pertains to physiological vulnerability (i.e., biochemical and genetic risk factors), four pertain to contextual or socioeconomic factors (i.e., norms and laws regarding use and availability, extreme economic deprivation, and neighborhood disorganization), and twelve describe interpersonal or intrapersonal risk factors. The latter operate within four principal domains: the family (e.g., poor family management practices, low bonding, and family conflict); the school (e.g., low commitment to school and academic failure); the peer group (e.g., peer rejection and association with deviant peers); and attitudinal and behavioral factors(e.g., alienation, rebellion, and early and persistent manifestation of problem behaviors). Most of these same risk factors also predispose individuals toward delinquency (Hawkins et al., 1988).

As described in the *social development model* of Hawkins and his colleagues, risk factors for substance abuse and delinquency occur sequentially; that is, some are antecedent to others (Hawkins, Catalano, and Miller, 1992; Hawkins and Weis, 1985). For example, family risk factors are considered to precede both school-based and peer-related risk factors. As discussed above, this developmental sequence, in which parental behaviors and practices serve to either encourage or discourage children's drift into later high-risk activities such as affiliating with delinquent peers or engaging in antisocial acts, has been demonstrated in a number of studies (Brook et al., 1986; Brown et al., 1993; Kandel and Andrews, 1987).

In turn, there is evidence to suggest that both genetic risk factors and socioeconomic risk factors precede family influences. In addition, and of special relevance to the present discussion, both have also been shown to have an impact on peer affiliation among young people. With regard to the former, research suggests that certain character traits, such as impulsivity, poor inhibitory control, and emotional volatility, predispose individuals toward both delinquency and drug abuse and that these traits appear to have a large heritable component (Wilson and Herrnstein, 1985; Tarter, 1988). Children who display such traits and who are highly aggressive and disruptive tend to be rejected by their peers at a young age (Coie and Cillessen, 1993). For many, early rejection is maintained into adolescence, and this stability appears to be a function not only of the continued antisocial behavior of the child but also of the development of a consistently negative set of expectations and reactions on the part of the rejecting peers (Coie and Cillessen, 1993). Thus, by adolescence, an individual who at some time in the past has displayed poor impulse control and extreme excitability and aggressiveness, or who continues to display such behavior, may find himself or herself in the company of similarly impulsive, excitable, and aggressive peers, not so much because he or she has actively sought them out but rather because he or she has been excluded from other social groupings.

As for sociostructural risk factors, researchers using a range of research techniques have detailed the devastating impact of economic deprivation and social disorganization on family life, educational attainment, crime and delinquency, and drug use in the inner city (Anderson, 1990; Barr et al., 1993; Dunlap, 1992; Dunlap and Johnson, 1992; Wilson, 1987). Among the numerous consequences of concentrated urban poverty has been a change in the nature of peer group affiliations among adolescents who reside in such areas. For, although gangs have always been associated with poor inner-city neighborhoods, their role in the local economy, effects on community life, and composition of their membership have changed considerably in recent years (Hagedorn, 1991). Once considered as "functional" elements of African American neighborhoods, gangs are now essentially disruptive, principally because of their involvement in the illicit drug market. In addition, individuals now affiliate with gangs longer than in the past, simply because the economic opportunities for "maturing out" (i.e., good paying unskilled and semiskilled jobs) no longer exist.

Although not impossible, introducing policy initiatives designed to prevent delinquency and drug use at either the genetic or socioeconomic level is inherently difficult, involving, in the case of the former, major ethical and moral considerations and, in the case of the latter, expenditure of considerable resources and the political will to undertake such an enterprise. In the absence of policymakers being willing or able to substantially alter these distal influences, it makes sense to try to have a positive impact upon factors that occur early on in the sequence of events that lead to delinquency, that is, events that occur during a child's formative years. If this can be done, the research cited above would lead one to expect that individuals would then be more resilient when faced with later risk factors such as negative peer influence.

Such a view underlies the social development model of Hawkins and his colleagues (Hawkins, Catalano, and Miller, 1992; Hawkins et al., *Seattle* 1992; Hawkins and Weis, 1985). This model integrates elements of social learning theory (Akers, 1985; Bandura, 1977) and social control theory (Hirschi, 1969) and stresses the importance of children developing strong *bonds* to the principal institutions of socialization within modern society, the family and the school. Three conditions foster the development of strong social bonds: first, having opportunities for involvement in conventional and prosocial activities; second, having the necessary skills to participate in these activities; and, third, receiving reinforcement for participation. Hawkins and his associates (1992; *Seattle*, 1992) argue that those who establish such bonds in childhood will be less likely to be rejected by their peers and display early attitudinal and behavioral problems and will be more committed to school and more likely to succeed academically. This, in turn, will reduce the chances of them associating with deviant peers and hence their engaging in delinquent behavior and drug use.

Patterson and his colleagues (1989) have also developed a theoretical model that posits a developmental sequence leading to delinquent behavior in adolescence (Patterson, DeBaryshe, and Ramsey, 1989; Dishion et al., 1991). They too consider affiliation with deviant peers among adolescents to be just one point in an unfolding process involving, at early stages, rejection by conventional peers and academic failure in middle childhood and behavioral problems and poor parenting in early childhood. This work, and that of Hawkins, Catalano, and Miller (1992) and Coie and Cillessen (1993), indicate that the role of the peer group in the evolution of delinquent behavior is important developmentally much earlier than adolescence (Dishion et al., 1991), the point in the process at which most intervention programs come into play. In addition, Patterson et al. (1989), like Hawkins and his colleagues (Hawkins, Catalano, and Miller, 1992), recognize the role of distal causal influences in the development of delinquent behavior, such as low socioeconomic status and temperament traits, and suggest that the effects of such factors are mediated by family management practices.

Both the Hawkins and Patterson groups have developed and evaluated family-based interventions in accordance with their theoretical models (Hawkins et al., *Seattle*, 1992; Dishion, Patterson, and Kavanagh, 1992). These, along with other childhood interventions delivered in educational and family settings, suggest that programs can reduce the occurrence of early risk factors for delinquency and drug use, such as academic failure, peer rejection, and poor parenting (see Seitz, 1990, and Weiss, 1988 for reviews of these programs). Evidence is also emerging that indicates that early childhood interventions have long-term benefits, not only for those directly in receipt of them but also for society in general through, for example, reductions in crime (Barnett, 1993; Seitz, Rosenbaum, and Apfel, 1985). Thus, family-based programs represent a

potentially powerful form of intervention, especially if begun early and continued over a sustained period of time. There are, however, two fundamental
limitations evident in many of the family-based studies. First, even when
programs do work, it is often not clear from the evaluations why this is so
(Weiss, 1988; Seitz, 1990). Do such programs work through their effects on
family cohesion, bonding, communication and problem solving, or through
some other process? Answering this question would facilitate the development
of future programs. Second, the conclusions that can be drawn from evaluations
of most family-based programs are limited by sample bias resulting from
difficulties in recruiting parents to participate at the outset and high attrition
rates once the project is under way (Hawkins et al., *Seattle*, 1992). Sample bias
has been especially evident in those programs that have been established in
high-risk environments, despite considerable efforts on the part of program staff
to recruit and retain participants (e.g., Ruch-Ross, 1992). This raises the
question as to whether the most highly motivated and least vulnerable families
are self-selecting into programs, thereby making the programs appear more
effective than they actually are.

One potential way of improving participation is to make each individual
intervention strategy (e.g., family programs, school programs) part of broader
community-based initiatives. The most ambitious attempts at this are still in
progress and have yet to produce outcome data from which their effectiveness
can be assessed (e.g., Cook and Roehl, 1993). Again, the key issue here is
whether such programs can be effective where they are most needed—in
communities with high rates of crime, delinquency, and drug abuse. Community
anticrime initiatives have typically not flourished in socially disorganized
neighborhoods with high crime rates, although a recent study found that the
presence of drug problems appeared to stimulate "confrontational activism"
within communities (Skogan and Lurigio, 1992): That is, community members
actively engaged in patrols, rallies, evictions of drug dealers, and demolition of
the premises from which drugs were being sold. Clearly, prevention initiatives
in such communities need to have an impact on the supply and distribution of
drugs (whether this involves the sale of crack cocaine or malt liquor) rather than
simply relying on traditional demand strategies focused on educating the
potential drug user (e.g., peer-based resistance skills training programs).

Conclusion

This chapter began by tracing developments in associational theories of crime
and delinquency from the early writings of Sutherland (1947) to more integrative theories (e.g., Elliott, Huizinga, and Ageton, 1985; Johnson, Marcos, and
Bahr, 1987). We then examined empirical evidence in support of associational
theories, which showed that the relationship between peer group affiliation and

delinquency in adolescence tends to be reciprocal and that whether individuals are drawn into a deviant peer group is influenced by a number of factors, notably their relationship with their parents. Rather than affecting group affiliation directly, parents influence their children's behavior, which in turn affects their choice of peer group and whether others choose to associate with them. Some typical peer-based prevention programs in delinquency and drug use were then reviewed. These were shown to be of minimal effectiveness and conceptually limited in that they fail to address the complexity of the relationship between group associations and delinquency. Since the relationship between delinquency and peer affiliation is reciprocal, it is insufficient to intervene at the adolescent peer group level as these program do; rather, we must begin to identify and have an impact on the factors that lead adolescents to involvement with antisocial peers and to delinquent behavior.

In the final section of the chapter we used theory and research that shows that both delinquency and associating with antisocial peers are factors in a complex developmental sequence that begins to unfold in early childhood in order to suggest ways in which prevention programs might be made more effective. The limitations of the family-based and community programs developed along these lines, as well as the promise they hold, were discussed. Thus, these interventions were not presented as some universal panacea. Conceptually they appear to capture the nature of the relationship between individual delinquency and the associational influence of peers much better than school-based skills training programs. Nonetheless, their effectiveness remains to be demonstrated by a consistent body of empirical research.

Notes

Preparation of this chapter was supported in part from grants from the National Institute on Drug Abuse (#DA/AA 03395) and the Alcohol Education and Research Council and Portman Group of Great Britain.

1. Another potential agent of interpersonal influence on patterns of deviant behavior is the sibling. Limitations in space means that this literature is not reviewed here. However, see Brook et al. (1988) and Clayton and Lacy (1982) on the association between the illicit drug use of siblings, and see Lauritsen (1993) for sibling resemblance in delinquency.

References

Agnew, Robert. 1991. "The Interactive Effects of Peer Variables on Delinquency." *Criminology* 29:47-72.
———. n.d. "A Longitudinal Test of Social Control Theory and Delinquency." *Journal of Research on Crime and Delinquency*. Forthcoming.

Akers, Ronald L. 1985. *Deviant behavior: A Social Learning Approach*. Belmont, CA: Wadsworth.

Akers, Ronald L., Marvin D. Krohn, Lonn Lanza-Kaduce, and Maria Radosevich. 1979. "Social Learning and Deviant Behavior: A Specific Test of a General Theory." *American Sociological Review* 44:636-655.

Anderson, Elijah. 1990. *Streetwise: Race, Class, and Change in an Urban Community*. Chicago: University of Chicago Press.

Bandura, Albert. 1977. *Social Learning Theory*. Englewood Cliffs, NJ: Prentice-Hall.

Barnett, W. Steven. 1993. "Benefit-Cost Analysis of Preschool Education: Findings From a 25-year Follow-Up." *American Journal of Orthopsychiatry* 63:500-508.

Barr, Kellie E. M., Michael P. Farrell, Grace M. Barnes, and John W. Welte. 1993. Race, Class, and Gender Differences in Substance Abuse: Evidence of Middle-Class/ Underclass Polarization Among Black Males." *Social Problems* 40:314-327.

Bell, Robert M., Phyllis L. Ellickson and Ellen R. Harrison. 1993. "Do Drug Abuse Prevention Effects Persist into High School? How Project ALERT Did With Ninth Graders." *Preventive Medicine* 22:463-483.

Bixby, F. Lovell, and Lloyd W. McCorkle. 1951. "Guided Group Interaction and Correctional Work." *American Sociological Review* 16:455-459.

Brook, Judith S., Martin Whiteman, Ann Scovell Gordon, Carolyn Nomura, and David W. Brook. 1986. "Onset of Adolescent Drinking: A Longitudinal Study of Intrapersonal and Interpersonal Antecedents. *Advances in Alcohol and Substance Abuse* 5:91-110.

Brook, Judith S., Martin Whiteman, Carolyn Nomura, Ann Scovell Gordon, and Patricia Cohen. 1988. "Personality, Family and Ecological Influences on Adolescent Drug Use: A Developmental Analysis." *Journal of Chemical Dependency Treatment* 1:123-161.

Brown, B. Bradford, and Mary J. Lohr. 1987. "Peer-Group Affiliation and Adolescent Self-Esteem: An Integration of Ego-Identity and Symbolic-Interaction Theories." *Journal of Personality and Social Psychology* 52:47-55.

Brown, B. Bradford, Nina Mounts, Susie D. Lamborn, and Laurence Steinberg. 1993. Parenting Practices and Peer Group Affiliation." *Child Development* 64:467-482.

Brown, Joel H., and Jordan E. Horowitz. 1993. "Deviance and Deviants: Why Adolescent Adolescent Substance Use Prevention Programs Do Not Work." *Evaluation Review* 17:529-555.

Burgess, Robert L., and Ronald L. Akers. 1966. "A Differential Association-Reinforcement Theory of Criminal Behavior." *Social Problems* 14:128-147.

Catalano, Richard F., J. David Hawkins, Claudia Krenz, Mary Gillmore, Diane Morrison, Elizabeth Wells, and Robert Abbott. 1993. "Using Research to Guide Culturally Appropriate Drug Abuse Prevention." *Journal of Consulting and Clinical Psychology* 61:804-811.

Cernkovich, Stephen A., and Peggy C. Giordano. 1987. "Family Relationships and Delinquency." *Criminology* 25:295-321.

Clayton, Richard R., and William B. Lacy. 1982. "Interpersonal Influences on Male Drug Use and Drug Use Intentions." *International Journal of the Addictions* 17:655-666.

Cloward, Richard A., and Lloyd E. Ohlin. 1960. *Delinquency and Opportunity: A Theory of Delinquency Groups*. New York: Free Press.

Cohen, Albert K. 1955. *Delinquent Boys: The Culture of the Gang*. New York: Free Press.

Cohen, Jere. 1979. "High School Subcultures and the Adult World." *Adolescence* 14:491-502.

Coie, John D., and Antonius H.N. Cillessen. 1993. "Peer Rejection: Origins and Effects on Children's Development". *Current Directions in Psychological Science* 2:89-92.

Cook, Royer, F., and Janice A. Roehl. 1993. "National Evaluation of the Community Partnership Program. In Robert C. Davis, Arthur J. Lurigio and Dennis P. Rosenbaum (eds.), *Drugs and the Community: Involving Community Residents in Combatting the Sale of Illegal Drugs.* Springfield, IL: Charles C. Thomas.

Dishion, Thomas J., and Rolf Loeber. 1985. "Adolescent Marijuana and Alcohol Use: The Role of Parents and Peer Revisited." *American Journal of Drug Alcohol Abuse* 11:11-25.

Dishion, Thomas J., Gerald R. Patterson, and Kathryn A. Kavanagh. 1992. "An Experimental Test of the Coercion Model: Linking Theory, Measurement, and Intervention." In Joan McCord and Richard E. Tremblay (eds.), *Preventing Antisocial Behavior: Interventions from Birth through Adolescence.* New York: Guilford Press.

Dishion, Thomas.J., Gerald R. Patterson, M. Stoolmiller, and M.L. Skinner. 1991. Family, School, and Behavioral Antecedents to Early Adolescent Involvement with Antisocial Peers." *Developmental Psychology* 27:172-180.

Downs, William R. 1987. "A Panel Study of Normative Structure, Adolescent Alcohol Use and Peer Alcohol Use." *Journal of Studies on Alcohol* 48:167-175.

Downs, William R., and Steven R. Rose. 1991. "The Relationship of Adolescent Peer Groups to the Incidence of Psychosocial Problems." *Adolescence* 26:473-492.

Dunlap, Eloise. 1992. "The Impact of Drugs on Family Life and Kin Networks in the Inner-City African-American Single-Parent Household." In Adele V. Harrell and George E. Peterson (eds.), *Drugs, Crime and Social Isolation: Barriers to Urban Opportunity.* Washington, D.C.: Urban Institutute Press.

Dunlap, Eloise, and Bruce D. Johnson. 1992. "The Setting For the Crack Era: Macro Forces, Micro Consequences(1960-1992)." *Journal of Psychoactive Drugs* 24:307-321.

Ellickson, Phyllis L., and Robert M. Bell. 1990. "Drug Prevention in Junior High: A Multi-Site Longitudinal Test." *Science* 247:1299-1305.

Ellickson, Phyllis L., Robert M. Bell, Margaret A. Thomas, Abby E. Robyn, and Gail L. Zellman. 1988. *Designing and Implementing Project ALERT: A Smoking and Drug Prevention Experiment.* Santa Monica, CA: The RAND Corporation.

Elliott, Delbert S., David Huizinga, and Suzanne S. Ageton. 1985. *Explaining Delinquency and Drug Use.* Beverly Hills, CA: Sage.

Farrell, Albert D., and Steven J. Danish. 1993. "Peer Drug Associations and Emotional Restraint: Causes or Consequences of Adolescents' Drug Use." *Journal of Consulting and Clinical Psychology* 61:327-334.

Fontane, Patrick E., and Norman R. Layne, Jr. 1979. "The Family as a Context for Developing Youthful Drinking Patterns." *Journal of Alcohol and Drug Education* 24:19-29.

Gerstein, Dean R., and Lawrence W. Green, eds. 1993. *Preventing Drug Abuse: What Do We Know?* Washington, DC: National Academy Press.

Giordano, Peggy C., Stephen A. Cernkovich, and M. D. Pugh. 1986. "Friendships and Delinquency." *American Journal of Sociology* 91:1170-1202.

Glynn, Thomas J. 1981. "From Family to Peer: Transitions of Influence Among Drug-Using Youth." In Dan J. Lettieri and Jacqueline P. Lundford (eds.), *Drug Abuse and the American Adolescent* National Institute on Drug Abuse Research Monograph, Serial no. 38. Washington, DC: U.S. Government Printing Office.

Gordon, Robert S. 1983. "An Operational Classification of Disease Prevention." *Public Health Reports* 98:107-109.

Gorman, D.M. 1992a. Commentary on prevention. *Annual Review of Addictions Research and Treatment* 2: 505-507.

———. 1992b. "Using Theory and Basic Research to Target Primary Prevention Programs: Recent Developments and Future Prospects." *Alcohol and Alcoholism* 27:583-594.

———. 1994. "Preventing Adolescent Drug Use: The Effectiveness of Project ALERT." *American Journal of Public Health* 84:500.

———. n.d. Are School-Based Resistance Skills Training Programs Effective in Reducing Alcohol Misuse?" *Journal of Alcohol and Drug Education.* In press.

Gottfredson, Denise C., and Gary D. Gottfredson. 1992. "Theory-Guided Investigation: Three field experiments." In Joan McCord and Richard E. Tremblay (eds.), *Preventing Antisocial Behavior: Interventions from Birth Through Adolescence.* New York: Guilford Press.

Gottfredson, Gary D. 1987. "Peer Group Interventions to Reduce the Risk of Delin- quent Behavior: A Selective Review and New Evaluation." *Criminology* 25:671-714.

Hagedorn, John M. 1991. "Gangs, Neighborhoods, and Public Policy." *Social Problems* 38:529-542.

Hansen, William B. 1992. "School-Based Substance Abuse Prevention: A Review of the State of the Art in Curriculum, 1980-1990." *Health Education Research: Theory and Practice* 7:403-430.

Hansen, William B., John W. Graham, Judith L. Sobel, David R. Shelton, Brian R. Flay, and C. Anderson Johnson. 1987. "The Consistency of Peer and Parental Influences on Tobacco, Alcohol, and Marijuana Use Among Young Adolescents." *Journal of Behavioral Medicine* 10:559-579.

Hawkins, J. David, J. M. Jenson, Richard F. Catalano, and Denise M. Lishner. 1988. Delinquency and Drug Abuse: Implications for Social Services." *Social Service Review* 62:258-284.

Hawkins, J. David, Richard F. Catalano, and Janet Y. Miller. 1992. "Risk and Protective Factors for Alcohol and Other Drug Problems in Adolescence and Early Adulthood: Implications for Substance Abuse Prevention." *Psychological Bulletin* 112:64-105.

Hawkins, J. David, Richard F. Catalano, Diane M. Morrison, Julie O'Donnell, Robert D. Abbott, and L. Edward Day. 1992. "The Seattle Social Development Project: Effects of the First Four Years on Protective Factors and Problem Behaviors." In Joan McCord and Richard E. Tremblay (eds.), *Preventing Antisocial Behavior: Interventions From Birth through Adolescence.* New York: Guilford Press.

Hawkins, J.David, and Joseph G. Weis. 1985. "The Social Development Model: An Inte- grated Approach to Delinquency Prevention." *Journal of Primary Prevention* 6:73-97.

Hirschi, Travis. 1969. *Causes of Delinquency.* Berkeley: University of California Press.

Hoffman, John P. 1993. "Exploring the Direct and Indirect Family Effects on Adolescent Drug Use. *Journal of Drug Issues* 23:535-557.

Huba, George J., and Peter M. Bentler. 1980. "The Role of Peer and Adult Models for Drug Taking at Different Stages in Adolescence." *Journal of Youth and Adolescence* 9:449-465.

Johnson, Richard E. 1979. *Juvenile Delinquency and Its Origins: An Integrated Theoretical Approach.* Cambridge: Cambridge University Press.

Johnson, Richard E., Anastasios C. Marcos, and Stephen J. Bahr. 1987. "The Role of Peers in the Complex Etiology of Adolescent Drug Use." *Criminology* 25:323-339.

Johnson, Valerie. 1988. "Adolescent Alcohol and Marijuana Use: A Longitudinal Assessment of a Social Learning Perspective." *American Journal of Drug and Alcohol Abuse* 14:419-439.

Johnson, Valerie, and Robert J. Pandina. 1991. "Effects of the Family Environment on Adolescent Substance Use, Delinquency and Coping Styles." *American Journal of Drug and Alcohol Abuse* 17:71-88.

Kandel, Denise B. 1985. "On the Processes of Peer Influences in Adolescent Drug Use: A Developmental Perspective." *Advances in Alcohol and Substance Abuse* 4:139-163.

Kandel, Denise B., and Kenneth Andrews. 1987. "Process of Adolescent Socialization by Parents and Peers." *International Journal of the Addictions* 22:319-342.

Kandel, Denise B., and Mark Davies. 1991. "Friendship Networks, Intimacy, and Illicit Drug Use in Young Adulthood: A Comparison of Two Competing Theories." *Criminology* 29:441-467.

Kandel, Denise B., Ronald C. Kessler, and Rebecca Margulies. 1978. "Antecedents of Adolescent Initiation into Stages of Drug Use: A Developmental Analysis." *Journal of Youth and Adolescence* 7:13-39.

King, Roy, Deborah Curtis, and Guenther Knoblich. 1992. "Biological Factors in Sociopathy: Relationships to Drug Abuse Behaviors." In Meyer Glantz and Roy Pickens (eds.), *Vulnerability to Drug Abuse*. Washington, DC: American Psychological Association.

Kline, Rex B., William A. Canter, and Arthur Robin. 1987. "Parameters of Teenage Alcohol Use: A Path Analytic Conceptual Model." *Journal of Consulting and Clinical Psychology* 55: 521-528.

Klepp, Knut-Inge, Andrew Halper, and Cheryl Perry. 1986. "The Efficacy of Peer leaders in Drug Abuse Prevention." *Journal of School Health* 56:407-411.

LaGrange, Randy L., and Helene Raskin White. 1985. "Age Differences in Delinquency: A Test of Theory." *Criminology* 23:19-43.

Lauritsen, Janet L. 1993. "Sibling Resemblance in Juvenile Delinquency: Findings From the National Youth Survey." *Criminology* 31:387-410.

Loeber, Rolf, and M. Stouthamer-Loeber. 1986. "Family Factors as Correlates and Predictors of Juvenile Conduct Problems and Delinquency." In Michael Tonry and Norval Morris (Eds.), *Crime and Justice: An Annual Review of Research* Vol. 7. Chicago: University of Chicago Press.

Mandell, Wallace, Allan Cooper, Richard M. Silberstein, Jack Novick, and Emily Koloski. 1963. *Youthful Drinking: New York State, 1962*. Staten Island: NY: Wakoff Research Center.

Matsueda, Ross L. 1982. "Testing Control Theory and Differential Association: A Causal Modeling Approach." *American Sociological Review* 47:489-504.

———. 1988. "The Current State of Differential Association Theory." *Crime and Delinquency* 34:277-306.

Mosbach, Peter, and Howard Leventhal. 1988. "Peer Group Identification and Smoking: Implications for Intervention." *Journal of Abnormal Psychology* 97:238-245.

National School Resource Network. 1980. *Peer Culture Development* Technical Assistance Bulletin 28. Washington, DC: National School Resource Network.

Oetting, E. R., Susan Spooner, Fred Beauvais, and James Banning. 1991. "Prevention, Peer Clusters, and the Paths to Drug Abuse." In Lewis Donohew, Howard E. Sypher, and William J. Bukoski (eds.), *Persuasive Communication and Drug Abuse Prevention*. Hillsdale, NJ: Lawrence Erlbaum Associates.

Patterson, Gerald R., Barbara D. DeBaryshe, and Elizabeth Ramsey. 1989. "A Develop mental Perspective on Antisocial Behavior." *Psychological Medicine* 44:329-335.

Perry, Cheryl L., Marcus Grant, Gunilla Ernberg, Ramon U. Florenzano, M. Cecilia Langdon, Annie D. Myeni, Ragnar Waahlberg, Stein Berg, Karl Andersson, K. John Fisher, Debra Blaze-Temple, Donna Cross, Bill Saunders, David R. Jacobs, Jr., and Thomas Schmid. 1989. "WHO Collaborative Study on Alcohol Education and Young People: Outcomes of a Four-Country Pilot Study. *International Journal of the Addictions* 24:1145-1171.

Pillow, David R., Irwin N. Sandler, Sanford L. Braver, Sharlene A. Wolchik, and Joanne C. Gersten. 1991. "Theory-Based Screening for Prevention: Focusing on Mediating Processes in Children of Divorce. *American Journal of Community Psychology* 19:809-836.

Robins, Lee N. 1992. "The Role of Prevention Experiments in Discovering Causes of Children's Antisocial Behavior." In Joan McCord and Richard E. Tremblay (eds.), *Preventing Antisocial Behavior: Interventions from Birth through Adolescence.* New York: Guilford Press.

Ruch-Ross, Holly S. 1992. "The Child and Family Options Program: Primary Drug and Alcohol Prevention for Young Children." *Journal of Community Psychology,* (OSAP Special Issues):39-54.

Seitz, Victoria. 1990. "Intervention Programs for Impoverished Children: A Comparison of Educational and Family Support Model." *Annals of Child Development* 7:73-103.

Seitz, Victoria, Laurie K. Rosenbaum, and Nancy H. Apfel. 1985. "Effects of Family Support Intervention: A Ten-Year Follow-Up." *Child Development* 56:376-391.

Simons, Ronald L., Rand D. Conger, and Leslie B. Whitbeck. 1988. "A Multistage Social Learning Model of the Influence of Family and Peers upon Adolescent Substance Use." *Journal of Drug Issues* 18:293-316.

Skogan, Wesley G., and Arthur J. Lurigio. 1992. "The Correlates of Community Antidrug Activism." *Crime and Delinquency* 38:510-521.

Sutherland, Edwin H. 1947. *Principles of Criminology.* Philadelphia: Lippincott.

Tarter, Ralph E. 1988. "Are There Inherited Behavioral Traits that Predispose to Substance Abuse? *Journal of Consulting and Clinical Psychology* 56:189-196.

Thornberry, Terence P., Alan J. Lizotte, Marvin D. Krohn, and Margaret Farnsworth. 1990. "The Role of Delinquent Peers in the Initiation of Delinquent Behavior." Paper presented at the annual meeting of the American Sociological Association, Washington, DC.

Tolone, William L., and Cheryl R. Tieman. 1990. "Drugs, Delinquency and 'nerds': Are Loners Deviant?" *Journal of Drug Education* 20:153-162.

Vorrath, Harry, and Larry K. Brendtro. 1974. *Positive Peer Culture.* Chicago: Aldine.

Warr, Mark., 1993. "Age, Peers, and Delinquency." *Criminology* 31:17-40.

Warr, Mark and Mark Stafford. 1991. "The Influence of Delinquent Peers: What They Think or What They Do? *Criminology* 29:851-866.

Weiss, Heather B. 1988. "Family Support and Education Programs: Working Through Ecological Theories of Human Development." In Heather B. Weiss and Francine H. Jacobs (eds.), *Evaluating Family Programs.* New York: Aldine DeGruyter.

White, Helene R. 1992. "Early Problem Behavior and Later Drug Problems." *Journal of Research in Crime and Delinquency* 29(4):412-429.

White, Helene R., Marsha E. Bates, and Valerie Johnson. 1991. "Learning to Drink:

Familial, Peer, and Media Influences." In David J. Pittman and Helene R. White (eds.), *Society, Culture, and Drinking Patterns Reexamined.* New Brunswick, NJ: Rutgers Center of Alcohol Studies.

White, Helene R., Valerie Johnson, and Alan V. Horwitz. 1986. "An Application of Three Deviance Theories to Adolescent Substance Use." *International Journal of the Addictions* 21:347-366.

Wilson, James Q., and Richard J. Herrnstein. 1985. *Crime and Human Nature.* New York: Simon and Schuster.

Wilson, William Julius. 1987. *The Truly Disadvantaged: The Inner City, the Underclass, and Public Policy.* Chicago: University of Chicago Press.

Zucker, Robert A. 1976. "Parental Influence upon Drinking Patterns of Their Children." In Milton Greenblatt and Marc A. Schuckit (eds.), *Alcoholism Problems in Women and Children.* New York: Grune and Stratton.

9

Behavioral Strategy:
A Neglected Element
in Criminological Theory
and Crime Policy

Lawrence E. Cohen and Richard S. Machalek

Among the most common of crimes is a class of behaviors involving expropriation. Expropriation refers to a process whereby individuals or groups usurp material resources and services from others. Some but not all forms of expropriation entail the violation of criminal laws, and we call these expropriative crimes. Common examples include (but are not restricted to) robbery, burglary, larceny, auto theft, embezzlement, fraud, and confidence games. Recently, we proposed a general theory for explaining such crimes (Cohen and Machalek, 1988; Machalek and Cohen, 1991; Vila and Cohen, 1993; and Cohen and Machalek, 1994). Our thinking about expropriative behavior has been influenced strongly by studies of expropriation among nonhuman species. Behavioral biologists have observed various expropriative behaviors among numerous groups of animals including mammals, birds, and even insects. Biologists call such behavior "social parasitism," a term meant to denote a situation where at least two organisms interact and one benefits from the interaction at the expense of the other (Wilson 1975).

As it turns out, the incidence of social parasitism depends not only on the purely individual traits and characteristics possessed by animals (such as their size or strength) but on "sociological" factors as well. That is, whether some individuals engage in expropriative (social parasitic) activities depends, in large part, on what other individuals in the population are doing and the frequency and the competence with which they do it. Thus in many expropriative activities, the likely outcome or payoff derived from an act depends greatly on the particular strategy or combination of strategies selected by an individual and on how effective it is against the other strategies utilized by his or her competitors.

157

Although social parasitism among animals is a fascinating phenomenon in its own right, our interest in it stems from its sociological implications for human populations. High rates of expropriation can be a serious threat to any society, human or nonhuman. Sociologists have explained that expropriation violates two basic norms on which order in human society is based: the norms of reciprocity and fair exchange (Gouldner, 1960; Blau, 1964; Emerson, 1972). As a result, the study of expropriative behaviors in general, and expropriative crime in particular, should be of considerable interest to social scientists.

Although behavioral strategies have been routinely ignored by most criminological theorists, we have made them the primary focal point of our efforts to explain expropriative crime. If we interpret expropriative crimes as behavioral strategies and analyze them in a manner that is similar to the way in which biologists study behavioral strategies among animals, we not only gain new insights about the causes of expropriative crime, but we may also discover important clues for developing policies that can allow us to better cope with expropriative crime in human populations.

Strategy Dynamics

According to behavioral biologists, expropriative acts within populations are more or less likely to occur, in part, because of the *nature of the expropriative strategy itself* and the *context created by other strategies* present in a population. A *strategy* is conceived broadly as a behavioral policy, one of a set of possible alternative behaviors or programs that yield benefits to individuals or groups, whether these benefits are intended and consciously recognized or not (Axelrod, 1984). The most important point to remember about strategies in general is that they are behavioral patterns that proliferate (or decline) largely because of their consequences. Specifically, "successful" strategies, those that proliferate in populations, typically bestow some sort of benefit or advantage to the individuals who execute them. Such benefits come in various forms including an increased probability of survival and/or reproductive success (biological benefits), material gain (economic benefits), enhanced power, prestige or influence (social benefits), or an enhanced sense of personal fulfillment (psychological benefits). This list is only illustrative, not exhaustive, but it indicates the various types of benefits that can accrue from adopting certain behavioral strategies.

Although it is difficult to summarize adequately our theory in a very few pages, we locate the roots of expropriative crime in such ecological processes of social organization as routine patterns of human activity and the availability and distribution of resources and in modes of production and competition between interacting individuals within societies. Briefly, our central thesis with respect to the nature and proliferation of what we call expropriative crime is that the social organization of productive activity in societies creates an opportunity structure that often invites invasion by various strategies of "expropriation." Again, illegal *expropriation* describes a process whereby actors use coercion, deception, or stealth to usurp a valued resource from others. Alternatively, resources are often acquired by *production*, the process of employing techno- logy, energy, and raw materials to create goods and services. For example, the invention of the telephone and the technological advancements that have accompanied the development of this instrument have expanded greatly the productive activities of business and commerce within and across societies. At the same time, however, these technological advancements have also created opportunities for the evolution and spread of fraudulent telemarketing strategies as well as a host of other illegal activities that have bilked citizens out of billions of dollars. Hence, although individuals often benefit from mutual cooperation in productive activities, they may occasionally do as well, or even better, by exploiting the productive activities of others. When the expropriative act entails the violation of a criminal law, the behavior is described as an *expropriative crime*. Thus understood, expropriative crime is a predictable, *but not necessarily inevitable* by-product of normal patterns of social organization and conduct (for a complete description of our theory, see Cohen and Machalek, 1988).

As a strategy for acquiring resources, the effectiveness of expropriation depends on a number of factors, such as the number and productivity of producer strategists, the extent of competition among expropriators, the extent to which victims are experienced or naive in coping with criminal expropriators, and so on. We emphasize that the producer-expropriator dynamics explained through our theoretical perspective are explicitly sociological. We contend further that to better understand criminal expropriation within human popula- tions, we must expand the focus of crime analysis beyond the more traditional biological and psychological approaches that attempt to explain such behaviors *solely* on the basis of individual traits and social attributes of the persons most likely to engage in these acts. The crime analyst must also observe the manner in which a pattern of behavior can be shown to be influenced by other patterns of behavior. Therefore, we also deviate from many sociological theoretical approaches by arguing that in order to understand well the phenomenon of expropriative crime, it is wise to employ a dynamic theoretic model.

Our theory suggests that producer-expropriator relations typically involve dynamic changes in both the form and rate of expropriative strategies within and across populations. Strategies currently doing the best for their executors spread at the other's expense. By becoming more frequent, they may alter their own strategic environment and thereby affect the rate of their future success. The most successful strategies continuously adapt to compete against alternatives in the population. These dynamics are perhaps best illustrated when we identify the processes by which successful expropriative strategies provoke deterrent or protective counterstrategies from individuals and groups within societies. For example, the competitive ecological processes that give rise to expropriative crime over time frequently eventuate in defensive counterresponses executed by producers and law enforcement agents aimed at the control and prevention of crime. Increasing or improving protective countermeasures by producers could thus limit payoffs and/or increase the costs of crime for expropriators. Such anticrime strategies could in turn (at least temporarily), serve to decrease the rates of specific types of crime within communities. However, such measures, if effective, will serve also to encourage the development of new or modified illegal expropriative strategies by self-enhancing strategy innovators. Once these new or modified illegal strategies prove successful, they often spread quickly and stimulate further defensive counterresponses from producers and law enforcement agents, until a selfreinforcing dynamic system emerges that resembles an "arms race." This dynamic process eventually will yield one of two possible outcomes: (1) the expropriator/producer strategy ratio will oscillate indefinitely within the population at some nonzero level or (2) a stable population ratio of expropriative criminal to productive strategies will evolve. In either case, it is important to emphasize that the resulting ratio of criminal to noncriminal behaviors within populations reflects mainly the advantages of certain *strategy proportions* and not necessarily the traits and social characteristics of individuals within societies. This introduces an explicitly sociological dimension to the evolution of expropriative criminal strategies. It means that the population-level dynamics of social interaction among strategies (rather than just the different individual traits or social characteristics of actors, as maintained by Wilson and Herrnstein, 1985) become a crucial driving force shaping emergent patterns of behavioral diversity, including the relative incidence of criminal and noncriminal behaviors in populations.

Individuals, Strategies, and Expropriative Crime

We are not suggesting that the individual traits and social attributes of offenders are irrelevant to strategy evolution and hence the incidence of expropriative crime. To the contrary, we agree with many theorists who argue that within any particular social context, the probability that certain individuals will adopt and successfully execute a particular expropriative strategy can vary significantly with a wide range of sociocultural, physiological, psychological, economic, and developmental variables (that is, with individual traits and structural and historical conditions). Our point is that by confining one's analysis *solely* to such suspected individual or structural causal factors, the theorist fails to include important dynamic macro-level variables that have equally potent effects on the emergence and spread of expropriative crime within and across populations. We contend that by incorporating an analysis of expropriative strategies into a dynamic "theoretical equation," it is possible to explain, within a single general theory, the key individual- and macro-level forces that drive expropriative crime rates.

In fact, behavioral biologists have shown how one might incorporate both strategic factors and individual traits within a single theoretical framework by employing game theory models that view expropriation as a contest in which one party tries to obtain materials or services from the possession of another (see for example, Parker, 1974; Maynard Smith, 1974, 1979, 1982). Essentially, game theory is a mathematical technique concerned with analyzing relative benefits that accrue from various strategic choices. But it is also supposed in game theoretic models that assessments are made by contestants prior to and/or during the course of expropriative activities that determine largely their motivation to participate in and escalate such activities (for a detailed description of game theory, and an example of how it may be applied to our theory, see Vila and Cohen, 1993). Biologists, for example, have noted that strategy evolution is often guided by "assessments" of individual contestants on how they stack up against potential opponents on traits relevant to expropriative contest outcomes, such as being able to seize a resource from another by force. Such traits as relative size, strength, intelligence, experience, possession of weapons (e.g., claws, body armor, or other "technology") may be compared to those of one's opponent in a prospective expropriative contest. Biologists call the complete ensemble of traits possessed by an individual engaged in such expropriative contests the contestant's "resource holding potential" or RHP. In addition, RHP differences may be balanced or even offset in contests by the respective value that each competitor assigns to the contested resource—what biologists call its "resource value" or RV. That is, RHP deficiencies can sometimes be overcome in competitive encounters when the trait-deficient participant assigns a greater value to the contested resource than does his or her more RHP-advantaged opponent. In consciously or unconsciously deciding a course of action then, the "RHP superior" opponent may refuse to incur the cost required for acquiring or retaining a resource that he or she values less than his or her more highly motivated, but less advantaged, opponent.

No doubt asymmetries of individual ability and/or need are also important determinants of expropriative contest outcomes within human populations as well. Therefore, the concepts of RHP and RV should be equally relevant for explaining strategy evolution and motivation for human expropriative encounters. In our judgment, these two concepts can easily incorporate the traits and attributes identified by criminologists as the major determinants of crime. Again, we contend that if we borrow a similar model from the behavioral ecologists, we can produce a general theory that can identify both key individual and macro-level causal variables that drive expropriative crime rates in human populations (see Cohen and Machalek, 1988:481-488).

In sum, to be executed effectively, expropriator strategies require, on average, a motivated individual with RHP traits that are superior to its producer competition. In the absence of a capable executor, the expropriator may fail to overcome and thus succumb to the producer. Similarly, the social organization and cultural environment may inhibit or promote the success of a particular strategy. For example, among human groups, a repressive society with a large and well-trained police force and a culture that is intolerant of nonconformity may reduce the success rate of expropriator strategies. Finally, historical and material circumstance may also impinge on the success or failure of various strategies. Under certain environmental and historical conditions, for example, expropriative crime simply may not pay. The important point we wish to stress, however, is that with respect to determining patterns of expropriative behavior within populations, our position differs from many explanations of crime. We claim that it is not the individual characteristics of "contestants" that are most crucial in strategy selection, but rather the average payoff for alternative strategies employed within the population.

Within certain social contexts, then, expropriation can be a beneficial strategy that may yield more benefits than alternative, non-expropriative strategies. Thus, if we tally all the behaviors by means of which a population acquires goods and services, we may find a certain volume of expropriation in the population precisely because it is advantageous to those individuals who employ it. At this point, it is crucial to understand that we are *not* arguing that expropriator strategies spread throughout a population because individuals are always consciously aware of its benefits and decide to adopt it because of those benefits. In fact, individuals may acquire expropriator strategies in a variety of ways. For example, they may invent the strategy independently or they may acquire it incidentally by learning from or imitating others. The important point to remember is that individuals can, and do, acquire behavioral strategies (including expropriator strategies) without necessarily having to have a conscious awareness of the benefits accompanying a particular strategy. This is very important in realizing an advantage of our interpretation of expropriative crime when compared to certain other criminological approaches, such as the "rational choice" approach taken by many micro-economists. Our perspective allows us to assume that individuals may adopt and benefit from expropriative crime strategies without consciously realizing the strategic advantages of their behavior. That is, not all strategic actions taken by individuals are necessarily guided by rational choice in the narrow sense that strategists always pursue ends as effectively as possible or that they never err in ordering their preferences. Instead, it is our view that strategies are often selected on the basis incomplete and uncertain information. The result is that expropriative crime often represents a less than optimal choice made from a subjective and/or impulsive decision (for a similar view, see Cornish and Clarke, 1986). In short, people can act on behalf of their interests in an entirely unwitting manner (Cohen and Machalek, 1988).

Because our approach shifts attention from the individual to the behavioral strategy itself, it differs from many traditional criminological theories. Through our perspective we begin to think of competition as a process that occurs not among individuals but among alternative strategies. Thus, as a resource acquisition strategy, the expropriator may beat the producer, at least up to a point, in the ability to generate benefits for the individuals that execute it. As such, it may be more likely to be adopted by others. Notice the qualification, "up to a point." This phrase is important, because it directs our attention back to our notion that strategies may be more or less successful in relation to the frequency with which they are found in a population. If expropriation becomes extremely common, it may begin to yield, on average, fewer benefits than the producer has, even though the producer suffers occasional losses to the expropriator. Too many expropriators reduces the number of producers upon which they all depend, so competition among expropriators and the pressure they put on their victims may cause the balance to tip in favor of becoming a producer as the more beneficial strategy.

It is easy to imagine then that some strategies will be likely to become more common than others for a variety of reasons. First, some strategies may have characteristics that enable them to beat the competition. For example, to expropriate is often cheaper (in terms of time expended) than to produce (i.e., stealing a car is often a less costly way to acquire one than is working hard and trying to save enough money to buy one). Second, some strategies may do very well when they are present in small numbers but rapidly decline in success when they become more numerous. If too many individuals insist on expropriating items and only a few produce them, there could be more prospective thieves than items available to steal, and the average return of thievery would be almost nil. The success of such expropriative strategies is thus said to be "frequency dependent" (Fisher, 1930). Third, the composition of behavioral strategies within a population, called "strategy ecology" (Axelrod, 1984), may create opportunities for the proliferation of some strategies but, at the same time, may impose serious constraints on others. Finally, the success or failure of a particular strategy is influenced by the rate at which new strategies appear in the population. Axelrod (1984) refers to this influence as "strategy evolution."

Therefore, we can say that strategies are more or less likely to proliferate because of their characteristics and the strategy context within which they occur. More often than not, they are "successful" because of the advantages they bestow upon those who execute them, whether these benefits are recognized or not.

Having acknowledged the importance and influence of *strategy traits* and *strategy context* in our efforts to understand the proliferation and demise of expropriative crime, we now shift our attention to a critical question: What makes an expropriative strategy successful? Only by answering this question can we ever hope to devise strategies to cope successfully with expropriative crime.

Characteristics of Expropriative Crime Strategies

We have explained that patterns of expropriation within societies are influenced strongly, and perhaps decisively, by characteristics of expropriative strategies themselves. That is, some expropriative strategies have traits that, ceteris paribus, make them more likely to succeed. The idea of comparing strategies in terms of their probable success in face-to-face encounters is familiar to "contestants" of all sorts, whether such competition occurs in board games, athletic events, wars, among political parties, or between business organizations.

What sorts of characteristics might enhance the competitive success of strategies that are employed to expropriate resources from others? We offer a preliminary list of nine such strategy traits that we believe are most likely to enhance strategy success. Specifically, we contend that expropriative strategies are most likely to be successful to the extent that they are: (1) cryptic, (2) deceptive, (3) bold, (4) surprising, (5) evasive, (6) resistant, (7) stimulating, (8) mobile, and/or (9) mutable. Although it is possible for expropriative strategies to express two or more of these characteristics simultaneously, and in a few cases, it is possible for some of these traits to overlap, for the purpose of clarity we will discuss each trait individually.

Cryptic strategies are those that are undetected by their victims at the time the expropriative act takes place. One type of crime that usually fits this description is embezzlement. Although business officials are generally well aware that they are at risk to be victimized by employees and co-workers, illegally usurping funds over which one has some degree of control is most effective when the usurpation is not observed by victims or other guardians at the time it takes place. Hence, cryptic strategies, by definition, are among the most difficult types of expropriative crimes with which to cope because their very existence is unknown to victims at the time that they occur. They are then, in a sense, superior to many other expropriative strategies because they usually involve relatively minimal risk to their successful completion when they are executed.

Deception is another trait that can enhance the chances that an expropriative strategy will succeed. Deception misrepresents an expropriative strategy that is detected by the victim as being either benevolent or innocuous. An example of a deceptive strategy is a confidence game in which the victim is tricked into believing that the expropriator's activities are *mutually beneficial* to both the victim and the expropriator. Thus, the victim is deceived into misinterpreting the nature and consequence of his or her interaction with the expropriator in a supposed beneficial exchange relationship. Karl Marx, and various conflict theorists subsequently, have characterized the relationship between the capitalist and proletariat classes as a parasite-host relationship that is misrepresented by capitalists, via devices such as ideology, as a mutually beneficial relationship. Similarly, criminals who employ fraudulent expropriative strategies often misrepresent their illegal activity as a form of fair exchange. Thus, deceptive expropriative activities are often very effective because the victim is led to believe that he or she is the beneficiary of an especially "good deal," one that may prophetically appear to be "too good to be true."

Some expropriative strategies need not depend on being cryptic or deceptive. Instead, they are what we will call *bold*. A bold expropriative activity is highly visible to its victim, as the strategist who adopts this style of expropriation "makes no attempt" to conceal, disguise, or misrepresent herself. Instead, bold criminal strategies are those that generally attempt to overpower the victim and include illegal expropriative acts in which the strategy executor is able to exercise power over the victim. The victim is thus ordered to behave in a way dictated by the expropriator. Such expropriative crimes as robbery and high-jacking, as well as blackmail, extortion, and tribute paying are examples of strategies that we classify as bold. Bold strategies are most likely to be success-fully employed when there is significant RHP asymmetry between offender and victim, with the expropriator being RHP dominant on a characteristic (e.g., size and strength) or in possession of technological equipment (e.g. weapons) that significantly enhances the potential for "contest" success.

Deceptive and bold strategies are especially effective when combined with another quality of expropriative strategies, the element of *surprise*. All other things equal, the element of surprise is success-enhancing when its suddenness allows the expropriator to gain an immediate edge on the victim, before he or she is able to recognize the expropriative act or respond with evasive or defensive tactics.

Once executed, cryptic, deceptive, bold, and surprising strategies each have qualities that can affect the outcome of expropriative crime contests. Upon execution, however, expropriative strategies can encounter defensive reactive strategies from their intended victims. Accordingly, some expropriative strategies are more successful than others in coping effectively with such counterstrategy responses. One quality that is often useful in coping with counterstrategy tactics is the *evasiveness* of the expropriative strategy. Evasive expropriative strategies are those that succeed in avoiding retaliation by their victims. Imagine an expropriative strategy that minimizes the time that it spends exploiting a particular victim or a specific population of victims. For example, by expropriating resources only once (or perhaps only a very few times) and then targeting another victim or population of victims, a strategy is said to be behaving evasively. Evasive expropriative strategies are generally those that are able to stay ahead of their "reputations" by minimizing the time they spend among a particular population of victims. An example here would be "boiler rooms" that engage in telemarketing frauds. By continuously moving from location to location, operations that engage in telephone sales fraud are difficult targets to shut down for those charged with the job of protecting consumers.

Instead of depending on evasiveness, expropriative strategies may cope successfully with a victim's counterstrategy responses by possessing the quality of *resistance*. Whereas an evasive expropriative strategy avoids retaliation by the victim or law enforcement agents, a resistant strategy is impervious to the effects of such retaliation. As a quality that enhances expropriative strategy success, resistance complements bold expropriative strategies. Since bold strategies are transparent to their victims, they are likely to be recognized immediately and could thus activate quickly a defensive counterresponse from their intended targets. If a bold strategy is impervious to a particular counter-strategy, however, then its success is enhanced. "Resistance," then, is generally gained from a property or an RHP trait possessed by the expropriator herself. Extortion rackets employed against merchants by organized crime families and youth gangs have a long tradition in certain ethnic neighborhoods and are a good example of a resistant illegal expropriative strategy.

The six strategy traits discussed above all increase, on average, the probability that an expropriative strategy will, in fact, allow the offender to expropriate successfully a resource and escape immediate retaliation by a victim. The next strategy trait identified here pertains to the ability of an expropriative strategy to motivate its potential executor to adopt and deploy it as an overt behavior. We define expropriative strategies that are more likely to be adopted because their very enactment is intrinsically satisfying to their executors as *stimulating*. Stimulation is important because it can act as a powerful proximate motivator of activities, many of which involve risk-taking behaviors that constitute illegal expropriation. Armed robbery, burglary, and larceny are just a few examples of crimes that may be stimulating or "thrilling" to many of the expropriators that employ such strategies. Although our theory contends that strategies often proliferate because of their consequences, as we explained earlier, we need not assume that people are always motivated by a conscious awareness of potential beneficial consequences that result from the adoption and execution of a strategy, including expropriative crime. As a proximate motivator, the stimulation produced by committing an armed robbery or a theft may be more than sufficient to motivate such behavior, even independently of any material benefits that may derive from the criminal act itself. In fact, our theory leads us to suspect that stimulation can, in some instances, be an even more powerful intrinsic motivator of risk-taking expropriative behavior than is the rational assessment of potential extrinsic benefits (such as money) to be derived from committing an expropriative crime (Katz, 1988). By being "stimulating," an expropriative strategy can thus effectively "bypass" the potentially inhibiting effects of engaging in a conscious, a priori assessment of costs and material benefits that are likely to be associated with the execution of some expropriative crimes. Stimulation, then, can be an important psychological factor that would help explain the ability of an expropriative strategy to insinuate itself into the behavioral repertoire of criminals, because it allows us to account for the incidence and persistence of certain classes of expropriative crime that cannot be explained in terms of their extrinsic material yield, or "payoff."

Recall that at several points in our discussion we have emphasized that our theory shifts primary attention away from why particular individuals and groups may be likely to commit expropriative crimes and focuses instead on the population-level dynamics resulting from the types and proportional mix of expropriative strategies employed in societies. We prefer to focus primarily on the understanding of why one type of behavioral strategy rather than another proliferates within and across populations. In fact, we will go a bit further here by suggesting that an expropriative crime strategy that is sufficiently stimulating can "treat" the individuals who execute it as dispensable, provided that the strategy is sufficiently *mobile* or transmittible to insinuate itself into another executor after possibly having "caused" the former executor to become incarcerated or otherwise incapacitated. For this reason, the extent to which a particular expropriative strategy is more or less mobile also becomes a prime concern of crime analysts.

Mobility refers to the ease with which an expropriative strategy can be transmitted from one individual to another and thus the ease with which the strategy can migrate from population to population. Mobility and evasiveness are similar but not identical. Evasiveness refers to the ability of an expropriative strategy to avoid being neutralized by victim retaliation. Mobility, however, refers to the transmission of an expropriative strategy from executor to executor. The determinants of mobility are multiple. Some forms of expropriation are highly mobile because they are simple and easy to learn or imitate. Other expropriative strategies are mobile because they are distributed by a highly effective and efficient medium such as television (e.g., "copycat" crimes). Still other expropriative strategies are highly mobile because they are transmitted by people who are socially influential (i.e., peer and gang leaders, sports and entertainment celebrities, and community elites).

In addition, some expropriative crime strategies become more mobile when they enter the social interaction networks of well-established or "career" expropriators. For example, when a new expropriative strategy is adopted by an organized crime family, it is likely to pervade rapidly those social spheres that constitute the crime family's arena of operations. Expropriative strategies are also likely to become even more mobile when they appear in social contexts with high concentrations of experienced expropriators. For instance, this phenomenon has been captured by the modern lament that describes prisons as "graduate schools for criminals."

Highly mobile expropriative crimes thus represent one of the greatest existing threats to the development of effective policies for controlling crime. When contrasted to older, traditional societies, modern industrial societies represent near-optimal environments for the evolution of highly mobile expropriative crimes. For example, modern societies feature rapid and easily accessible transportation systems that are excellent conduits for expropriative crime. Similarly, the explosive development of sophisticated communications technologies virtually assures an increase in strategy mobility. Finally, advancements in transportation and communication technologies are complemented by the global trend toward increasing societal openness. For example, the dramatic decline in state restrictions over people's behavior in the former Soviet Union appears to have led to the rapid proliferation of expropriative "black market" criminal strategies, such as those that, according to national news reports, are now spreading in postcommunist Russia.

Mutability is the last strategy trait considered here as a crucial determinant of the potential success and proliferation of expropriative crimes. Mutability refers to the capacity of an expropriative strategy to change or adapt so as to accommodate changes in victim response and/or the social, cultural, or material environment. It is in this context that the phenomenon of the "arms race" between expropriators and the retaliation/defense of victims and law enforcement becomes relevant. Consider the expropriative crime of auto theft, for example. Auto theft strategies have inspired a series of defensive counterstrategies, each of which has contributed to the evolution of subsequent novel expropriative strategies to overcome such efforts. A rather long (and growing) list of novel defense strategies lends evidence to the case for the high mutability of auto theft strategies. We note specifically that auto theft strategies have evolved to overcome the increasingly complex theft protection devices of interior door locks without graspable door knobs, locking steering wheels, steering wheel bars, alarms, engine-disabling devices, electronic tracking units, and so on. Auto theft, then, is an excellent example of how strategy mutability enables expropriative success. Similar, but technologically more sophisticated examples can be found in the efforts of computer facilities to cope with the highly mutable expropriative strategies by means of which computer "hackers" can gain access to computer systems and the information they contain.

Before we close this section of the chapter, we wish to return to our distinction between *strategy evolution* and *strategy ecology* (Axelrod, 1984:51-54). Strategy evolution entails the process by which new "behavioral rules" that make up strategies are introduced into a population. Strategies evolve (1) as a result of mutations or alterations (intended or not) of an existing expropriative strategy, or (2) by the introduction of entirely new strategies into the population. New strategies may enter a population as a result of inventions or innovations within the existing population or as a result of diffusion from external populations. In any case, new or altered expropriative strategies represent new challenges to host populations by virtue of their novelty. Novelty, in general, makes expropriative strategies less detectable and less easily rebuffed by victims.

Strategy ecology, in contrast, refers to the distribution of given behavioral rules or strategies within a population. Here, the success of any given strategy depends, in part, on the context of other strategies within which it is located and executed. By "context" we mean the various types of strategies found in a population and their proportionate representation (e.g., frequency dependence). Again, a major implication of strategy ecology for our theory is that any finite population is likely to have a "saturation point" beyond which the advantages of expropriative crime diminish to a level such that the average member of the population would do better trying to earn a living from producing rather than expropriating.

Policy Implications

We now turn our attention to the policy implications that derive from our theory of expropriative crime. If our central premise is correct, then much expropriative crime is a normal by-product of the social organization of productive activity to the degree that it would be very difficult to eliminate a substantial amount of these crimes without modifying a way of life that, as citizens in a relatively open society, we take for granted. We should perhaps begin our policy analysis with a list of the aspects of the expropriative crime problem that are the *least* susceptible to amelioration, because they involve solutions that, in our judgment, (1) call for interventions without stipulating clearly defined goals that specify what the intended product of such processes should be, (2) fail to envision the possible negative unintended consequences that may result from the complex interactions among the forces and behaviors they are trying to affect, (3) are politically impractical, or (4) are cost-ineffective.

To be more specific, measures adopted to reduce the individual's desire to commit expropriative crime have generally involved attempts at *shaping preferences* so as to increase the costs of crime and enhance the taste for desired behavior (e.g., deterrence, diversion, and rehabilitation) or *shaping legitimate opportunities* in order to give economic incentives for desired behavior (e.g. training and employment programs). To date, most evaluations of these policies have not provided systematic empirical evidence to indicate that they have been effective in reducing crime, and there is little reason to expect that related policies will prove to be any more effective in the future. (For reviews of this literature, see Blumstein, Cohen, and Nagin, 1978; Sechrest, White, and Brown, 1979; Empey, 1982: 240-255; Bureau of Justice Statistics, 1985; Nagin and Paternoster, 1991.)

We suspect that there is considerable agreement among both laypersons and social control agents alike that criminals are in need of some kind of regenerative treatment—that they need to be educated, rehabilitated, and resocialized in some capacity (i.e., they indeed need their preferences shaped and/or to be given access to legitimate opportunities). Thus, many offenders are presently encouraged, or made to become involved in some type of change-oriented program. We note, however, that outside of trying to persuade criminals to refrain from engaging in illegal behavior, there is little general agreement on just precisely what it is that these offenders are to be turned into. Programs that have only the most vaguely and generally defined objectives of exactly what it is they are supposed to change offenders into are not good bets for succeeding at the difficult task of reducing crime.

In addition, many crime control policies in use are hopelessly static: They are not designed to appreciate the alternative possibilities for the criminal's subsequent behavior. Thus our theory suggests that many anticrime strategies can set off spirals of illegal counteractions and thus have severe but unintended negative consequences. The state's attempt to increase the security of its citizens can thus make them even less secure. The effort to contain an adversary engaged in illegal actions can create an even more committed criminal. The effort to reduce the criminal's illegal opportunities can have the unintended effect of greatly increasing his or her incentives to expand them.

Although examples of the above process are well known and described in the criminology literature, the conditions under which they are likely to occur are not well articulated. For example, many criminologists contend that prisons create environments that promote the reinforcement of criminal values and attitudes favorable to crime. More emphatically, some have suggested that prisons are seed beds for the transference of criminal skills, which, if true, would greatly accelerate expropriative strategy innovation and evolution among inmate populations. If prisons are indeed schools for crime, then according to our perspective, some of the recent developments in current incarceration policy have created even greater paradoxes for those who are charged with the control of crime. Not only are prisons and the custody they provide expensive and ineffective, but current incarceration policy is especially criminogenic because it has produced a record number of dense concentrations of potential executors among whom expropriative strategies can be shared. Put slightly differently, prisons today may represent near-optimal environments for the maximum mobility of expropriative crimes among potential strategy executors. To the extent that political leaders comply with current public demands for incarcerating even more criminals, we may obtain even higher mobility rates among expropriative strategies in the future. That is, current conditions of imprisonment may intensify the irony, inasmuch as prison overcrowding now creates court-induced pressures for the release of inmates after they have been incarcerated for relatively short periods of time. One might even say that the current trend toward incapacitating more people for shorter periods of time may represent an ideal social situation for maximizing the mobility of expropriative crime strategies. Not only can such a policy expose more people to opportunities for expanding their repertoires of expropriative strategies (in jails or prisons), but because of early release programs to cope with prison overcrowding, it may even allow expropriators to employ their newly acquired strategies much sooner than they otherwise would if they were incapacitated for longer periods of time.

In sum, policies that incarcerate more offenders for relatively short periods of time have been shown to be cost-ineffective because they are expensive and in general have failed to prevent recidivistic behavior. To the contrary, they may have the effect of actually *raising* the rate of expropriative crime by recidivists over that which would have resulted had they been incapacitated for the more customary periods of time. This situation represents a good example of a "social trap"—whereby decision-makers are drawn into patterns of behavior that produce results antithetic to their intentions. First, to satisfy the public, officials initiate a program that generates higher rates of incarceration. This causes prison overcrowding. Then, they have to utilize early prison-release programs to respond to court pressure to reduce prison overcrowding. This may in turn produce the very consequences that they initially attempted to avoid—higher crime rates.

In addition, it is difficult (if not impossible) for institutions seeking to eradicate self-interested illegal behavior by increasing the certainty, celerity, and severity of punishment to be successful within societies in which the social organization of productive activity provides relatively easy opportunities for certain, swift, and valuable rewards through these same illegal activities (Cohen and Felson, 1979). This paradox explains the difficulties inherent in crime policies suggested by those who believe that the only way to substantially reduce illegal behavior is to lessen social inequality through "legitimate opportunity shaping" (see, for example, Cloward and Ohlin, 1960; Walker, 1989:254-265). Previous attempts to reduce crime in this fashion (e.g. the "Mobilization for Youth" project and the "War on Poverty") have been fraught with difficulties in program implementation and with program failure (for the history and evaluation of such programs, see Moynihan, 1969; Marris and Rein, 1973; and Short, 1975). At best, such programs have provided only marginal opportunities to improve one's life chances, and they have also had difficulty succeeding in environments where the rewards for illegal behavior are often relatively much larger, more quickly obtained, and, in some cases, more stimulating than that which is provided through law-abiding behavior. At worst (as was the case in the 1960s, when both the number and the funding for such programs were at their peak), there is not now, nor has there ever been, the political will or the political constituencies necessary to allow for the effective implementation of such programs in this country, even if these programs were based on valid theoretical assumptions.

Our theory is thus pessimistic about the crime reduction potential of opportunity shaping policies in highly stratified societies such as ours. In fact, we believe that bold expropriative strategies in particular are most likely to proliferate in social situations in which there is appreciable social inequality. In fact, we may even go so far as to suggest that although the pressure to expropriate will be greatest at the bottom of the social ladder, the opportunities to engage in, and the ability to escape detection and/or avoid punishment for such behavior, will, in general, be greatest for those at the top of the status hierarchy. Hence, it is possible for the probability of bold expropriation to increase proportionately among *both* the economically disadvantaged *and* the economically advantaged as the degree of social inequality increases in a population. Bold expropriation thus presents another interesting paradox from our theoretical perspective. On the one hand, our theory clearly implies that any policy that could actually reduce RHP asymmetries (e.g., social inequality) in a population might also reduce the incidence of bold expropriation. On the other hand, as the crime reduction failure of the "War on Poverty" suggests, reducing socially structured inequality appears to be one of the greatest challenges faced by modern policymakers who are so inclined. Thus, we may expect that current patterns of social inequality will embolden people at both ends of the ladder of social inequality to expropriate from others. That is, in highly stratified capitalist countries, the "rich and powerful" will be emboldened to take advantage of their social dominance and power and expropriative resources from subordinates, whereas the "poor and powerless" will be emboldened by desperation to take the "better than nothing" course of action of trying to expropriate that which they do not have the legitimate opportunity to acquire by socially approved means. Our theory is therefore very clear about presenting a challenge to policymakers who would act against bold expropriative strategies: Reduce the degree of social inequality that motivates people to adopt bold strategies and contributes to the probable success of this type of expropriation. The implementation of this policy initiative, however, is largely a matter of political will. Such collective will was insufficient in the 1960s, and probably even less sufficiently available in the 1990s with the economy in relatively worse shape today than it was three decades earlier.

Finally, we are also not very optimistic about the long-term effectiveness of currently employed situational crime prevention strategies that attempt to reduce illegal opportunities through "target hardening," increased citizen surveillance, or by designing out crime environmentally. Although the contemporary evidence suggests that such strategies may provide some "modestly beneficial" short-term effects at crime reduction (see Roshier, 1989:118), our theory predicts that the long-term consequences of such strategies will be crime displacement and the stimulation of "arms races" that will lead to subsequent increases in illegal expropriative activities. For example, according to our theory, if criminal behavior were to become rarer due to effective situational crime control policies, realistically, society's investment in guardianship would soon decline. Because of the frequency-dependent dynamics inherent in expropriative crime, however, this very situation would again favor the rare criminal strategy and soon invite an increase in illegal expropriation.

Counterstrategies of Alerting and Educating

Granted that freedom and prosperity often give rise to the social and ecological conditions that favor the proliferation of expropriative crime strategies, is
there any conceivable basis for suggesting novel policies that might arrest the
expansion of such crimes at various levels of social organization in a heterogeneous society such as the United States? We suggest that such a goal could
perhaps be achieved by taking an approach modeled after that which is used by
public health officials to treat epidemics. Such an approach cannot change the
motivation for illegal self-interested behavior over the common good in social
systems or prevent the evolution of expropriative strategies from occurring in
systems of cooperative production. Nor could such a "public health" approach
allow us to anticipate the nature of novel expropriative strategies before they
appear. If implemented with sufficient intensity and duration, however, an
approach of this sort may achieve some long-term reductions in expropriative
crime by the following.

1. Developing sophisticated systems for collecting and disseminating
information on the specific social circumstances that favor the evolution
of different types of expropriative strategies. This could allow researchers
to identify specific strategies being used, and to isolate expropriation-
prone, susceptible, and vulnerable social and geographic areas.

2. Identifying those populations or subpopulations in terms of the extent
to which they are most at risk to a particular type of expropriative
strategy (e.g., minorities, recent immigrants, the elderly, particular
customer-client interactions).

3. Intensively teaching and informing the at-risk public how to detect, recognize, and report the specific forms of expropriative behavior for which
they are at greatest risk (i.e., give the particular strategy a "reputation"
among certain segments of the population).

4. Continually alerting the general public on how to avoid becoming victimized by expropriative strategies in general, and how to recognize them
before they can be successfully completed.

Again, such a program could obtain significant long-term benefits only if
delivered with great intensity and over a sustained period of time, and with the
same amount of effort as that which was employed in the 1950s and 1960s to
eliminate polio. Below we offer some preliminary but more specific suggestions
on how such a program might be able to reduce crime.

First, we suggest for consideration something like a "Center for the Prevention of Crime" modeled after the Centers for Disease Control in Atlanta. Such a center would have a permanent staff and budget and would continually receive reports from law enforcement agents, news media, and private citizens (perhaps via 1-800 phone numbers) on avoidable expropriative crimes. In particular, we would need complete and accurate "case history" information on the strategies employed to execute these crimes. Federal and state governments and the media would then expend great effort (and expense) to publicize and support the mission of this center. The center would thus be charged with performing a "crime assay" analogous to a "disease assay" employed by preventive medicine practitioners. Specifically, the focus here will be on diagnosing forms of expropriative behavior, and the populations at greatest risk, *not* the identification of criminally-predisposed individuals.

The center would be responsible for alerting potential victims and law enforcement agents by disseminating information through official channels and through the communication media. To reduce the chances that the at-risk population will be successfully victimized by a particular strategy, the potential victim population must be made "savvy." We note, however, that such a program should be balanced to the degree that such information does not promote undue suspicion and distrust among the general population.

For the moment, we leave the details of how to get political support for the creation of a crime center to others and concentrate instead on identifying some specific actions that could be useful in combating certain traits of expropriative strategies that make them more likely to be successful. For example, in coping with deceptive, cryptic, and evasive expropriative strategies, the basic problem lies in both detecting the illegal activity and in recognizing the act as an illegal form of expropriation. Our theory then, implies that the fundamental task to be faced in coping with such criminal strategies is identifying and disclosing their expropriative character. Potential victims of deceptive, cryptic, and evasive illegal behaviors could be educated about and alerted to expropriative behavior through the use of media devices such as the mailing and distribution of leaflets and posters, the publicizing of strategy-specific warnings on television and radio, the use of telephone chains among concerned citizens, the dissemination of information from schools, and other such communication and educational outlets. Recent developments in telecommunication systems also suggest new possibilities for educating the public about threats posed by these expropriative strategy traits. It seems reasonable to suggest that crime avoidance classes could be taught in public schools and that a public service, or even a special crime control cable channel, could be dedicated to issuing bulletins and alerts about the emergence or proliferation of particularly virulent new forms of deceptive expropriative strategies. With proper marketing and considerable community support, it is theoretically possible that the rapid and thorough dissemination of such information could inhibit significantly the proliferation of such expropriative strategies by transforming a naive, and thus vulnerable, population of potential victims into a less easily victimized population that is made "savvy" through these educational processes (see Machalek and Cohen, 1991). The population is thus made less vulnerable by giving these expropriative strategies a "reputation" (Axelrod, 1984). In fact, by gaining a reputation, an expropriative strategy may be less likely to be adopted and thus become less of a threat to potential victims. Some might fear that publicizing an "expropriative strategy alert" could have the unwanted effect of actually teaching the strategy to potential adopters. But since deceptive, cryptic, and evasive expropriative strategies depend on ignorance for their success and proliferation, learning how to execute such strategies would be of little value to a potential expropriator who acquired this information at the same time as did his or her prospective victim.

It should be recognized that the "alert and educate" counterstrategy defense discussed above is less effective against bold expropriative strategies. Since the effectiveness of bold strategies depends on RHP asymmetries, the prospective victim's problem usually is not in the recognition of the bold strategy for what it is but in trying to avoid it or deter its execution. Here, citizens would have to be educated to avoid certain situations in which bold strategies are most common (e.g., using ATM machines at night or when they are alone).

Our theory explains why it is likely to be frustrating, and even disturbing, to try to develop effective policies for coping with highly mobile expropriative strategies. Since expropriative strategies take advantage of modern communication and transportation technologies and a political climate that imposes minimal restrictions on the movements of populations, those who would control expropriative crime by limiting strategy mobility face an agonizing dilemma. The very sorts of actions that would regulate or restrict communication, transportation, and people's discretionary behavior are the sorts of restrictions that could inhibit mobility rates to expropriative crimes. Yet there is little evidence to suggest that people are willing to take such action to reduce the volume of expropriative crime. The freedom of association and movement enjoyed by people in modern democracies also enables the establishment and persistence of the sorts of social organizations and networks (e.g., crime syndicates) that function as highly effective conduits for the transmission of expropriative crimes across both geographic and social space.

Similarly, our theory leads us to somewhat vexing conclusions about the development of effective policies for coping with highly mutable expropriative crimes. The situation is rooted in the very nature of modern industrial social organization, which features extremely high rates of cultural innovation in general (Lenski, Lenski and Nolan, 1991:54-58). There is little evidence that would lead us to believe that the rate of cultural innovation, including the mutability rates of expropriative crime, is likely to decrease naturally. There is no more reason to believe that anything could be done, even if such a controversial decision were reached about inhibiting the sort of human creativity that yields novel forms of expropriation. Instead, our theoretical reasoning leads us to conclude that the only promising means for coping with mutable forms of expropriation would involve the following general principles: (1) Maximize detection and recognition efforts so as to be able to identify a novel form of expropriation as soon after it evolves as is possible, (2) disseminate information as rapidly as possible to prospective victim populations when a new expropriative strategy is discovered, (3) anticipate that new forms of production, often involving technological advance, will create occasions for the evolution of new or modified expropriative strategies and maximize the alertness and responsiveness of prospective victims, and (4) dedicate resources (human and material) to the rapid development of effective counterstrategies as soon as novel expropriative strategies are documented.

Again, our theory implies that we should expect the evolution of new and modified forms of expropriation as a normal and expected by-product of the dynamics of modern industrial life. Although there appears little reason to be hopeful about efforts to deter or inhibit the evolution of new or modified expropriative strategies, there is good reason to believe that we can cope more effectively with the mutability of expropriation by developing policies that promote "rapid-response" counterstrategies designed to inhibit the proliferation of expropriative crimes. Only through the sustained efforts to design novel crime counterstrategies and to modify existing ones is it possible to arrest the expansion of expropriative strategies in modern industrial populations.

Notes

We wish to thank Don C. Gibbons for his helpful comments on an earlier draft of this chapter.

References

Axelrod, Robert. 1984. *The Evolution of Cooperation.* New York: Basic Books.

Blau, Peter. 1964. *Exchange and Power in Social Life.* New York: John Wiley

Blumstein, Alfred., Jacqueline Cohen, and Daniel S. Nagin, eds. 1978. *Deterrence and Incapacitation: Estimating the Effects of Criminal Sanctions on Crime Rates.* Washington, DC: National Academy of Sciences.

Bureau of Justice Statistics. 1985. *Special Report: Examining Recidivism.* Washington, DC: U.S. Department of Justice.

Cloward, Richard A., and Lloyd E. Ohlin. 1960. *Delinquency and Opportunity.* New York: Free Press.

Cohen, Lawrence E., and Marcus Felson. 1979. "Social Change and Crime Rate Trends: A Routine Activity Approach." *American Sociological Review* 44:588-608.

Cohen, Lawrence E., and Richard Machalek. 1988. "A General Theory of Expropriative Crime: An Evolutionary Ecological Approach."*American Journal of Sociology* 94:465-501.

———. 1994. "The Normalcy of Crime: From Durkheim to Evolutionary Ecology."*Rationality and Society* 6:286-308.

Cornish, Derek B., and Ronald V. Clarke, eds. 1986. *The Reasoning Criminal: Rational Choice Perspectives on Offending.* New York: Springer-Verlag.

Emerson, Richard. 1972. "Exchange Relations and Network Structures." In Joseph Berger, Morris Zelditch, and B. Anderson (eds.), *Sociological Theories in Progress.* Boston: Houghton Mifflin.

Empey, LaMar T. 1982. *American Delinquency: Its Meaning and Construction.* Homewood, Il: Dorsey Press.

Fisher, R. A. 1930. *The Genetical Theory of Natural Selection.* Oxford: Clarendon Press

Gouldner, Alvin W. 1960. "The Norm of Reciprocity." *American Sociological Review.* 25:161-178.

Katz, Jack. 1988. *Seductions of Crime: Moral and Sensual Attractons in Doing Evil.* New York: Basic Books.

Lenski, Gerhard., Jean Lenski, and Patrick Nolan. 1991. *Human Societies: A Macrolevel Introduction to Sociology.* 5th ed. New York: McGraw-Hill.

Machalek, Richard. and Lawrence E. Cohen. 1991. "The Nature of Crime: Is Cheating Necessary For Cooperation?" *Human Nature* 2:215-233.

Marris, Peter., and Martin Rein. 1973. *Dilemmas of Social Reform.* 2nd ed. Chicago: Aldine.

Maynard Smith, John. 1974. "The Theory of Games and the Evolution of Animal Conflicts." *Journal of Theoretical Biology* 497:209-221.

———. 1979. "Game Theory and the Evolution of Behavior." *Proceedings of the Royal Society of London* B 205:475-488.

———. 1982. *Evolution and the Theory of Games.* Cambridge: Cambridge University Press.

Moynihan, Daniel Patrick. 1969. *Maximum Feasible Misunderstanding: Community Action in the War on Poverty.* New York: Free Press.

Nagin, Daniel S., and Raymond Paternoster. 1991. "The Preventive Effects of the Perceived Risk of Arrest: Testing an Expanded Conception of Deterrence." *Crimiminology* 29:561-587.

Parker, Geoff A. 1974. "Assessment Strategy and the Evolution of Animal Conflicts." *Journal of Theoretical Biology* 47:223-243.

Roshier, Bob. 1989. *Controlling Crime.* Chicago: Lyceum Books.

Sechrest, Lee, Susan O. White, and Elizabeth D. Brown, eds. 1979. *Rehabilitation of Criminal Offenders: Problems and Prospects.* Washington, DC.: National Academy of Sciences.

Short, James F. 1975. "The Natural History of an Applied Theory: Differential Opportunity and Mobilization for Youth. In Nicholas. J. Demerath, et al., (eds), *Social Policy and Sociology.* New York: Academic Press.

Vila, Bryan J., and Lawrence E. Cohen. 1993. "Crime as Strategy: Testing an Evolutionary Ecological Theory of Expropriative Crime." *American Journal of Sociology* 98:873-912.

Walker, Samuel. 1989. *Sense and Nonsense About Crime.* 2nd ed. Pacific Grove, CA: Brooks/Cole.

Wilson, Edward O. 1975. *Sociobiology: The New Synthesis.* Cambridge: Harvard University Press.

Wilson, James Q., and Richard J. Herrnstein. 1985. *Crime and Human Nature.* New York: Simon and Schuster.

10

Routine Precautions, Criminology, and Crime Prevention

Marcus Felson and Ronald V. Clarke

When reflecting on society's defenses against crime, criminologists and sociologists usually distinguish between two main systems of control, formal and informal. Formal social control has the purpose of defining, punishing and deterring crime and is exerted principally through the law and the criminal justice system. Informal social control attempts to induce conformity through people's routine supervision of each other's behavior, reinforced by rule making, admonition, and censure.

It is well understood that these two principal forms of social control are interdependent. The law and criminal justice system define and regulate the outer limits of unacceptable conduct, most of which is kept within bounds by the day-to-day exercise of informal controls. Without being backed up by the law and the criminal justice system, however, these informal controls would soon lose their force.

It is also widely recognized that as society evolves into more complex forms, informal control has to be increasingly supplemented by formal systems of control. This is because informal controls depend greatly on people in a community knowing one another and knowing who are each other's neighbors, relations and work mates. People may know each other this well in agrarian or rural societies, but they do not in urban and industrial societies. Consequently, these latter societies come to rely increasingly upon widely promulgated laws and a developed system of law enforcement.

Less well understood, however, is that informal and formal social controls are intertwined with and dependent upon a third important control system: routine precautions taken against crime by individuals and organizations.[1] Every day, we all do such things as lock our doors, secure our valuables, counsel our children, and guard our purses and wallets to reduce the risk of crime. To this end, we also buy houses in safe neighborhoods, invest in burglar alarms and firearms, and avoid dangerous places and people.[2] Similarly, schools, factories, offices, shops, and many other organizations and agencies routinely take a host of precautions to safeguard themselves, their employees and their clients from crime.[3]

Whole industries and sectors of employment exist whose sole purpose is to supply or service this need for personal and organizational security: manufacturers of alarms and surveillance systems, weapons makers, locksmiths, safe makers, guards and custodian services, security consultants, store detectives, guard dog handlers and ticket inspectors, to name but a few. Without this system of routine precautions, the task of informal social control would be immeasurably more difficult and the criminal justice system would be swamped by a flood of petty and more serious crimes.

Routine precautions will grow in importance with the decline of formal and informal controls, which is foreseen by some commentators.[4] Felson (1994) has listed some of the factors in the decline of informal control in modern society, including working mothers, larger schools, more casual employment, increased economic power of teenagers, and the separation of home and workplace. Many of the same factors have weakened the power of the criminal justice system. Offenders have become more anonymous and less detectable (most detections are the result of leads to the identity of perpetrators provided by victims and others). Their opportunities for theft and vandalism have greatly expanded with the growth in possessions. Their greater mobility has reduced the value of preventive patrol, which relies for much of its effect on the police knowing who should and who should not be present in particular places.

The job of the police has also been made more difficult by the increases in nighttime activity resulting from more transportation and more electricity. In addition, they have a wider range of behavior to regulate as more misconduct is brought within the purview of the criminal law. The criminal justice system is therefore deluged with offenses, many of a petty nature. It is increasingly ineffective as a deterrent and is becoming prohibitively costly. As the criminal justice system is less able to cope with the flood of crime, people turn increasingly to ways of protecting themselves. They become consumers of books and television programs purveying crime prevention advice. They learn self-defense and purchase car alarms and mace. In the same way, organizations adopt more sophisticated ways to screen employees and provide surveillance of their properties. They engage in background checks and drug screening. They install surveillance cameras and employ doormen. This demand for additional security is reflected in the tremendous growth of private policing, which in terms of numbers employed now outstrips the public police (Nalla and Newman, 1990).

The increased reliance on routine precautions is greatly assisted by technological development, which results in a proliferation of low-cost security devices and systems designed for particular offenses and particular settings. Harbingers of things to come are provided by the breathalyzer, by electronic PIN numbers, by Caller-ID, and by photo radar. Hardly dreamed of twenty years ago, these devices developed for use against specific crimes are now in routine use.

Routine Precautions and Criminology

Electronics may greatly expand the scope of routine precautions, but technology has always served to protect people from crime. Consider medieval times, when, long before the development of a recognizable criminal justice system, moats, drawbridges, and portcullises protected castles and cities. Swords were routinely worn by nobles and, in their absence, chastity belts by their ladies.

These routine precautions represented the technology of the day. They are integral to our conception of the Middle Ages and an important component of our cultural heritage. It is all the more remarkable, therefore, that only a few criminologists (e.g. Reiss, 1967; Suttles, 1972; Skogan and Maxfield, 1981; Marx, 1995) have paid any attention to routine precautions. Perhaps the causal link between precautions and reduced crime is too simple to attract the interest of sociological theorists. Or they may find distasteful the individual and collective preoccupation with protecting possessions, preferring to leave these matters to the security industry. According to Sherman (1993), many criminologists see police efforts to control crime as being reactionary and opposed to due process and they may see routine precautions in similarly negative terms. When discussed at all, these are generally treated not as an indispensable part of society's defenses against crime but as an undesirable response to fear, which, if unchecked, will lead to a fortress society.

The main reason, however, for the academic neglect of routine precautions is that, when thinking about the causes and the control of crime, criminologists have been too exclusively focused upon the offender and insufficiently focused upon the situation in which he or she operates. Thus it is no surprise that the focus of both formal and informal social control is the offender whereas for routine precautions, which have been generally ignored by criminologists, the focus is the situation.

A body of criminological theory is now beginning to develop, however, that gives due weight to the situation of crime, including "routine activity" theory (Cohen and Felson, 1979; Felson, 1994), the "life-style" theory of victimization (Hindelang, Gottfredson, and Garofaol, 1978), the "rational choice" perspective (Cornish and Clarke, 1986), Cusson's (1986) "strategic thinking," and Brantingham and Brantingham's (1993) "pattern theory." Despite their different points of departure, these all lead to a similar point of convergence: the need to explain crime by focusing on the immediate situation in which crime occurs (Clarke and Felson, 1993).

This can be illustrated by the two theories with which we are associated, routine activity theory and the rational choice perspective. The routine activity theory deals with the ebb and flow of human activities in time and space and how these interrelate to produce a physical convergence of the three minimal elements of crime: a likely offender, a suitable target, and the absence of a capable guardian. The focus of the theory is therefore the situation giving rise to crime. The rational choice perspective also focuses on the crime situation but concentrates on how it is perceived and evaluated by a potential offender who is seeking some benefit through illegal action.

Together with these advances in theory, developments in thinking about crime control have taken place that also focus upon the crime situation, including Crime Prevention Through Environmental Design (CPTED) (Jeffery, 1977), "defensible space" architecture (Newman, 1972), problem-oriented policing (Goldstein 1979, 1990), and designing out crime (Clarke and Mayhew, 1980). These approaches all focus on reducing opportunities for crime and are subsumed under the more general label of "situational prevention" (Clarke, 1983, 1992).

Routine Precautions and Situational Prevention

In one sense, situational prevention is the attempt to apply science to the routine taking of precautions. This does not simply mean improving the effectiveness of such things as locks, lights, and alarms through improved technology. That is the province of the security industry, whereas situational prevention falls clearly in the realm of criminology. It consists of three main components: the developed body of theory, referred to above, concerning the role of opportunity in crime; a standard approach to the analysis and solution of specific crime problems based upon the action research methodology (Lewin, 1947); and a set of distinct opportunity reducing techniques (Clarke 1992, 1995). It can be thought of as a systematic method of finding ways to reduce opportunities for highly specific categories of crime. This can be contrasted to our definition of routine precautions against crime as actions that the general populace applies in everyday life. Although some overlap between the two categories may occur, many routine precautions are not really situational prevention measures or at least are not among the more desirable of such measures.

Consider the following points:

1. Some routine precautions against crime do not in fact prevent crime for the people taking those precautions. For example, putting lights on when away from home probably will not fool potential burglars, who have plenty of other indicators of residential absence.

2. Some routine precautions against crime prevent crime for those taking the precautions but lead to so much displacement to others that the community is not well served by them. For example, steering wheel locks put only on some cars appear not to reduce auto theft but merely to displace it to nearby cars (but when such locks are universal, they produce significant reductions in overall car theft, (Webb, 1994).

3. Some routine precautions against crime, however well they may do the job, are costly to buy and install, are complicated or unreliable mechanically, or create problems for the user or others. For example, car alarms and home alarms can be very costly, often go out of kilter, and send out false alarms.

4. Some routine precautions may totally backfire, producing more crime rather than less. For example, walls around backyards in suburban areas may provide cover for burglars to enter. And guns bought for self-defense kill many more family members than intruders.

In each of these cases, routine precautions fail to represent the best of situational prevention. The reason is that situational crime prevention devotes itself to finding solutions that in fact produce overall reductions in crime are at minimal cost, emphasizing simplicity, and systematically reduce crime opportunities. Since ordinary citizens do not normally devote much time to thinking about these elements, they are likely to rely upon methods that they have heard about from others.

Substantive Concerns

The distinction between routine precautions and situational prevention is important for theory and practice, for it reminds us that our duty as experts is to obtain prevention information with some measure of independence. That may include listening to what citizens have to say and taking their routine precautions into account but not taking these as gospel. As new information is gathered about prevention, that information needs to be fed back to citizens, in hope of influencing their routine precautions in the future. (We shall return to this issue later.)

Why should we as criminologists do any better than ordinary citizens in devising crime prevention methods? Why should our methods be any better than routine precautions? The answer to this lies in crime theory and practice. If we know and understand more about crime than the average citizen, we ought to know more about how it occurs, and, just as important, we ought to be able to use our professional judgment when we do not have complete information. In other words, we should have many pieces of the crime puzzle from our empirical data, filling in other pieces of the puzzle from our theory. The combination should give a good enough image of criminal behavior that we can recommend situational prevention measures and adapt them to a variety of circumstances, thus offering citizens something significantly better than the routine precautions that they already follow. Here are some examples:

1. Citizens already know to lock their doors. But they think wrongly that the lock will by sheer strength prevent intrusion. Most locks are not that strong. Rather, they force intruders to make noise on entry. If the residents do not also trim their hedges, the neighbors will not hear the noise nor be able to see what is happening. Thus trimming hedges is an important cofactor in locking doors. This untested advice derives from crime theory and tangible thinking about crime—thinking not likely to be carried out by the average citizen, who does not think about crime in these terms. Indeed, most routine precautions do not consider the synergy of multiple factors in prevention.

2. Residents in high- crime neighborhoods often pay wrought iron companies to install bars on their windows. These companies generally put ironwork on all windows and doors. Yet our knowledge of burglary indicates that most entry is by rear or side windows or doors. The ironwork on the front is probably a waste of money. Moreover, building solid walls around yards helps defeat the purpose of the ironwork on the house itself. Residents would be better putting iron fences around yards, as opposed to solid walls, allowing neighbors to see through. Moreover, trimming hedges and getting to know neighbors could well do the work of the iron bars at virtually no cost.

3. Beavon, Brantingham, and Brantingham (1994) have shown that wide roads with many entering streets lead to more crime opportunities. Cul-de-sacs and other reductions in traffic flow serve to reduce local crime rates. Yet citizens often oppose slight increments in inconvenience from changing street patterns, not realizing that these will more than make up for that inconvenience in added safety. Criminologists can help citizens go beyond routine precautions and give them reasons for moderating some of their knee-jerk reactions.

4. Motorcyclists generally oppose helmet laws, which make their lives somewhat more inconvenient. They do not generally accept the safety enhancement arguments made by those in favor of helmet laws. What if motorcyclists were made aware of the crime prevention consequences of helmet laws, which have been shown in many countries to reduce the risk of theft. What if, in addition, the law enforcement community offered a general program to assist motorcyclists in preventing thefts, including helmet laws as a part of the program? Enlightening this segment of the population and helping it broaden its routine precautions against crime can produce greater general safety while reducing the unfortunate and widespread conflict over this issue.

5. When motocycle helmets are required, and that requirement is enforced, it becomes more difficult to steal a motorcycle on the spur of the moment with no helmet in hand. Thus thefts decline (See Mayhew, Clarke and Elliot, 1989).

In short, better substantive analysis helps situational prevention to supplement routine precautions, thus providing a better means for crime reduction.

Forgetting or Remembering Routine Precautions

Even when citizens have in mind effective routine precautions against crime, they do not necessarily follow their own precautions. Many people forget to lock doors, park in dangerous spots, walk down risky streets, stay out late and drink too much, and so forth.

How can society encourage people to follow their own best judgments? Several methods come to mind:

1. *Formal Social Control.* We have already mentioned the dangers of overburdening the criminal justice system but sometimes laws can be enacted that promote routine precautions. Juvenile curfews not only keep potential offenders in at late hours but also keep potential victims of crime inside and, presumably, safe. Closing hours for bars and liquor stores provide citizens with less to do out late, thus encouraging their compliance with routine precautions.

2. *Informal Supervision.* This is a specific kind of informal social control that occurs when family and friends keep an eye out and remind each other to lock the door, park under the light or closer to the destination, not stay out late, turn on the alarm, leave the jewelry in a safe place, and so on. This day-to-day supervisory control needs to be distinguished from socialization, which teaches people what they should do in hopes that they will do it later.

3. *Signage and Instructions.* Signs can be posted reminding people to lock office doors when leaving at night or to guard their purses on the subway. Hotels can remind guests to deposit valuables for safekeeping and provide them with information about safe areas to walk. In these and many other ways people are reminded of the need for precautions. These reminders should not be overdone, however, or they will lose their force.

4. *Product Design to Facilitate Routine Precautions.* Cars may buzz when keys are left in. Entrance doors to apartment blocks may be fitted with self-closing springs. Personal identification numbers (PINs) that include numbers chosen by the PIN holder are more easily remembered and thus more secure. All these design features encourage people toward safe behavior patterns.

5. *Design to Improve Natural Surveillance.* Public street lights, at least in theory, make a street safer, even if residents forget to turn on their private

lights. We have already mentioned some other ways, including trimming hedges and avoiding solid fences, to facilitate natural surveillance.

Broadening the Repertoire of Routine Precautions

We have noted the distinction between situational prevention and routine precautions. As our knowledge of both increases, we need to move citizens as far away as possible from the ineffective and counterproductive prevention methods toward those that work at minimal cost. This means broadening the public repertoire and finding simple ways to communicate knowledge. However, this does not mean ignoring everything the public thinks and does. Many people have good prevention ideas that are probably correct, from staying away from groups of young males drinking in the park to avoiding urban nooks and crannies. One of the main research challenges is to collect more detailed information from citizens on their repertoire of prevention ideas and experiences. Much research could then be to done verify the effectiveness of these techniques. Crime prevention research is essentially clinical research: It investigates the application of scientific principles toward solving crime problems. Such clinical research could be greatly enriched by drawing from citizens their various ideas about prevention. However, this could not be accomplished by taking only a handful of popular methods. Rather, one needs to derive from many observant people a more varied repertoire of ideas, even if most of those are employed by only a small proportion of the population.

As we learn more about what works, we need to feed back into practice information about crime prevention, thus helping to broaden the repertoire of good ideas and abandon the worst of routine precautions against crime. In the ideal world, routine precautions and situational prevention will begin to converge, with the general public drawing on better prevention ideas and putting them into action. One hopes that well before that ideal state would occur, criminologists in general would realize that situational crime prevention offers much more than locks and alarms and that the routine precautions taken by citizens in everyday life offer an important means for preventing crime. Perhaps then society would not have to turn either to draconian punishments or to utopian social philosophies.

Lessons from Medicine

In closing, it is illuminating to compare the history of criminology to the history of medicine. Criminology emerged largely from philosophy. Crime was seen as aberrant behavior and hence raised questions about human nature. These philosophical discussions then led to the examination of the philosophy of punishment and in time to treatments of crime as subfields of various social sciences.

Medicine, in contrast, derived largely from folk remedies. The latter consisted of a body of advice to people on how to avoid illness and to overcome it when it struck. Folk medicine ranged from learning various bits of information about herbs and diet as well as treatments which were highly intrusive. Although much folk medicine was administered by ordinary people to their family and themselves, some was administered by specialists (such as witch doctors or shamans) and was closely linked to religion.

One could easily dismiss all folk medicine as myth. Yet as human civilization proceeded to grow in its knowledge, some folk medicine proved to be correct or partly correct. Some herbs from the past are used today, albeit in purified forms and more careful dosages. Some falsehoods from the past led to some truths as more experience accrued. Most important, folk medicine kept theory and practice somehow linked. If folk medicine claimed to solve problems in the real world, there was always a chance to demonstrate such claims to be false or partly false. That possibility in time helped produce improvements in the science itself. Folk medicine was superseded mainly because modern medicine offered such improvements.

Most of modern criminology is far behind even folk medicine. It does not solve crime problems, and it does not even try to. Thus it avoids the opportunity for its own improvement. Most crime theories are so remote from real life that such evasion is built into their very structure. For example, the policy implication of strain theory is a complete restructuring of society, which in reality is not likely to occur anywhere. Biological theories do not at present identify genes or how to change them; nor is there any practical way to alter the gene pool. Rehabilitation theories could hardly be applied in practice on a large enough scale to succeed. Despite claims by some "practical policy" advocates, it is not practical to apprehend and punish or incapacitate a large enough share of the pool of offenders in a large modern society so as to reduce crime. Nor is it practical to abandon punishment to please labeling theorists, who never seem to think about protecting society and victims. In the end all of these theories become untestable in practice and thus unverifiable, leaving out for the moment the evidence and arguments against them in the first place.

Only by finding truly clinical criminology can we at last bring crime theory and crime prevention into the same world. By making promises of the latter we can also help verify or reject the former and thus develop criminology as a science. In doing so, we should not lose sight of a remarkable generality that emerges from the history of medicine: Public health measures have had far more impact upon morbidity and mortality than has treatment of individual patients. for example many public health measures have far surpassed surgery or other patient-centered methods in significance: Building sewers, treating water, modernizing plumbing, spraying swamps, inoculating children, inspecting food production and distribution This fact is well known in the fields of demography and public health, but not so well known to a population brought up to revere their individual physicians.

In the field of crime prevention we need to put this lesson into practice. It is very difficult to teach each citizen to take better routine precautions against crime. Although that effort should not be abandoned, it may be more efficient to apply situational prevention on a public health basis, "inoculating" a facility against burglary by removing its nooks and crannies, designing safer automated teller machines (ATMs), arranging convenience stores to reduce thefts and dangers to clerks and customers, and so forth. It is easier to change the minds of a few thousand organizations than to change the minds of 250 million individuals. By working with organizations rather than individuals, it may be possible to bring prevention to fruition more quickly while feeding back what is learned into improved criminology. That is the essence of science. And, perhaps the in time the lessons may filter to individuals as well.

Notes

1. The words "routine precautions" merit some definitional attention. The word *precaution* is itself interesting, for it implies that efforts can be made in advance to thwart danger. This does not include purely unplanned efforts to dig oneself out of trouble after having fallen into it. The word "routine" implies that such precautions require continued action, such as locking doors, trimming hedges, and avoiding dangerous places or excessive drinking. Thus buying an alarm or designing an environmnent will not succeed as one-time actions without follow-up activities.

2. Since precautions cannot interfere too much with basic sustenance activities, all persons face some limitations on what precautions they can routinely take. Thus those who work late cannot easily avoid coming home after dark, and those raising families have to go shopping where they can afford to buy.

3. Routine precautions are not identical to routine activities. Much of the security or danger produced by routine activities is anadvertent. By contrast, routine precautions constitue only conscious efforts to prevent crime.

4. Routine precautions are influenced by formal and informal control. Some jurisdictions fine people for leaving keys in cars or failing with other routine precautions. Families and friends exert informal social control to remind one another of their precautionary duties. However, these three aspects of crime control remain analytically distinct.

References

Beavon, Daniel J.K., Patricia L. Brantingham, and Paul J. Brantingham. 1994. "The Influence of Street Networks on the Patterning of Property Offenses." In *Crime Prevention Studies*, vol. 2, edited by Ronald V. Clarke. Monsey, NY: Criminal Justice Press.

Brantingham, Paul J., and Patricia L. Brantingham. 1993. "Environment, Routine, and Situation: Toward a Pattern Theory of Crime." In Ronald V. Clarke and Marcus Felson (eds.), *Routine Activity and Rational Choice*. Vol. 5, *Advances in Criminological Theory*. New Brunswick, NJ: Transaction Publishers.

Clarke, Ronald V. 1983. "Situational Crime Prevention: Its Theoretical Basis and Practical Scope." In Michael Tonry and Norval Morris (eds.), *Crime and Justice: A Review of Research*. Vol 4. Chicago: University of Chicago Press.

———. 1992. *Situational Crime Prevention: Successful Case Studies*. Albany, NY: Harrow and Heston.

———. 1995. "Situational Crime Prevention: Achievements and Challenges." In Michael Tonry and David Farrington (eds.), *Crime Prevention*. Vol. 19, *Crime and Justice: A Review of Research*. Chicago: University of Chicago Press.

Clarke, Ronald V., and Marcus Felson. 1993. "Introduction." In Ronald V. Clarke and Marcus Felson (eds.), *Routine Activity and Rational Choice: Advances in Criminological Theory*. Vol. 5. New Brunswick, NJ: Transaction Publishers.

Clarke, Ronald V., and Patricia M. Mayhew. 1980. *Designing out Crime*. London: HMSO.

Cohen, Lawrence E., and Marcus Felson. 1979. "Social Change and Crime Rate Trends: A Routine Activity Approach." *American Sociological Review* 44:588-608.

Cornish, Derek. B. and Ronald V. Clarke. 1986. *The Reasoning Criminal*. New York: Springer-Verlag.

Cusson, Maurice. 1986. "L'Analyse Strategique et Quelques Developpements Recente · en Criminologie." *Criminologie* 19:51-72.

Felson, Marcus. 1994. *Crime in Everyday Life: Insight and Implications for Society*. Thousand Oaks, CA: Pine Forge Press.

Goldstein, Herman. 1979. "Improving Policing: A Problem-oriented Approach." *Crime and Delinquency* April:234-258.

———. 1990. *Problem-Oriented Policing*. New York: McGraw Hill.

Hindelang, Michael J., Michael R. Gottfredson, and James Garofalo. 1978. *Victims of Personal Crime: An Empirical Foundation for a Theory of Personal Victimization*. Cambridge, Mass: Ballinger.

Jeffery, C. Ray. 1977. *Crime Prevention Through Environmental Design*. 2nd ed. Beverly Hills, CA: Sage.

Lewin, Kurt. 1947. "Group Decisions and Social Change." In T.M. Newcomb and E.L. Hartley (eds.), *Readings in Social Psychology*. New York: Atherton Press.

Marx, Gary T. 1995. "The Engineering of Social Control: The Search for the Silver Bullet." In John Hagan and Ruth D. Peterson (eds.), *Crime and Inequality*. Stanford: Stanford University Press.

Mayhew, Patricia, Ronald V. Clarke and David Elliot. 1989. "Motorcycle Theft, Helmet Legislation and Displacement." *Howard Journal of Criminal Justice* 28:1-8.

Nalla, Mahesh, and Graeme Newman. 1990. *A Primer in Private Security*. Albany, NY: Harrow and Heston.

Newman, Oscar. 1972. *Defensible Space: Crime Prevention Through Urban Design*. New York: MacMillan.

Reiss, Albert J. Jr. 1967. "Public Perceptions and Recollections about Crime, Law Enforcement, and Criminal Justice." In vol. 1, Section 2, *Studies in Crime and Law Enforcement in Major Metropolitan Areas*. Washington, DC: Government Printing Office.

Sherman, Lawrence W. 1993. "Why Crime Control is Not Reactionary." In David Weisburd and Craig Uchida (with Lorraine Green) (eds.), *Police Innovation and Control of the Police*. New York: Springer-Verlag.

Skogan, Wesley G. and Michael Maxfield. 1981. *Coping with Crime. Individual and Neighborhood Reactions*. Beverly Hills, CA: Sage Publications.

Suttles, Graham D. 1972. *The Social Construction of Communities*. Chicago: University of Chicago Press.

Webb, Barry. 1994. "Steering Column Locks and Motor Vehicle Theft: Evaluations from Three Countries." In Ronald V. Clarke (ed.), *Crime Prevention Studies* Vol. 2, Monsey, NY: Criminal Justice Press.

11

Reintegrative Shaming, Republicanism, and Policy

John Braithwaite

This chapter summarizes the explanation of crime in the theory of reintegrative shaming. It then shows how republican political theory instructs us in how to apply the explanatory theory in a decent way. The theory motivates communitarian rather than statist solutions to our crime problems. The communitarianism advocated is not neighborhood communitarianism, the participatory democracy of the eighteenth-century New England town meeting. In the twentieth century, struggles for such local direct democracy have dissipated idealism because they attempt too much. I will argue that forms of communitarianism that can focus moral energies and reduce crime in the automobile age are social movement politics and the individual-centered communitarianism of the New Zealand Maori idea of family group conferences.

The Explanatory Theory

The key idea of the theory of reintegrative shaming (Braithwaite, 1989) is that some societies have higher crime rates than others because their citizens less effectively shame criminal behavior. The societies with low crime rates are not those that punish crime most effectively, but those that are most effectively intolerant of crime. Shaming in the theory means all social processes of expressing disapproval that have the intention or effect of involving remorse in the person being shamed and/or condemnation by others who become aware of the shaming. The forms that shaming take are culturally specific, ranging from highly formal ceremonies such as criminal trials to subtle informalities such as the raising of an eyebrow.

It is not just that shaming is a more effective deterrent than punishment, though there is reason to believe that the fear of disapproval by others has more effect on crime than the fear of formal punishment (Tittle, 1980; Nagin and Paternoster, 1991). Shaming also contributes to the internalization of the wrongfulness of crime. Through being shamed ourselves, but, more important, from observing the shaming of others who break the law, we are educated to believe that crime is wrong. Once cultural practices of shaming have accomplished this internalization, punishment by pangs of conscience becomes a much more powerful deterrent than fear of disapproval by others. The disapproval of our own conscience is delivered with more certainty than disapproval by others, who may not find out about our misdeeds. Self-disapproval is also delivered in a more timely way because it *precedes* the actual commission of the crime, as well as immediately following it, whereas social disapproval may lag long after the act.

So shaming accomplishes moral education about the wrongfulness of crime as well as deterrence through both social disapproval and self-disapproval. The most important effects of shaming, however, are not mediated by deterrence at all. Most readers of this chapter will have had some person give them trouble during the past month. One of the ways you might have sought to solve that problem was by murdering the troublesome person. Ask yourself why you did not solve your problem by murdering the person causing it. Most of us will reach the conclusion that we did *not* weigh up the benefits of murder against the possible costs of getting caught, being punished, being disapproved by others, and suffering the pangs of our own conscience. Rather, we conclude that murder never crossed our minds as a way of solving our problem. Somehow murder had been rendered unthinkable as a mode of problem solving. It is not that we calculated the costs and benefits of murder or struggled with our conscience; murder was right off our deliberative agenda. Most of us refrain from committing murder most of the time because murder is simply unthinkable to us. The key to crime prevention is grasping an understanding of how this unthinkableness is accomplished. According to the theory of reintegrative shaming, cultural practices of shaming make a crime unthinkable.

In cultures where shaming works well, shaming ceremonies give a salience to community deliberation about the wrongfulness of crime. Crime is not something left to professionals such as judges and social workers to clean up (or sweep under the carpet); it is something citizens talk about. Through participating in disapproval of the harm done by specific criminal acts in their experience, citizens educate each other about why certain kinds of acts, called crime, are simply wrong. Understanding that something is a crime then triggers a process of well-socialized citizens convincing themselves that this kind of conduct is unthinkable so that in the future they will not deliberate over its costs and benefits.

Someone who accepts this theory must therefore reject radical abolitionist prescriptions that we would be better off if we had no such concept as crime in our ways of thinking about problems of living. On the contrary, the theory of reintegrative shaming suggests that the concept of crime is a powerful cognitive resource in enabling voluntary, democratic-participatory, nonpunitive forms of social control. For example, if citizens in a democracy decide that a new technology is so dangerous that it must never be exploited (e.g., a new biological weapon), it is important to criminalize the conduct of corporations that produce the technology. In one symbolic swoop, this lets all companies know that it is morally unacceptable to weigh up the costs and benefits of production: It is simply a crime and should be unthinkable. The democratic process of legislating for criminalization is a more efficient and decent mechanism of social control here than any alternative. One alternative would be to say to corporate America: "You can calculate the costs and benefits of producing this technology, but if you allow it to do harm, you will have to pay for the costs of this harm." This alternative runs a variety of risks: companies may miscalculate; detecting and estimating the costs of the harm may be difficult, and so on. We are better off for the symbolic resource of being able to say that this is a crime—something the legislature and most citizens believe to be morally wrong in any circumstance.

So far, so good. But there is a big problem with shaming criminal conduct. Labeling theory (e.g. Becker, 1963) highlights this problem. According to labeling theory, one of the effects of labeling persons as criminal is that they can become more likely to be criminal. Labeling a safecracker, for example, risks the possibility that they will have a self-identify as a safecracker affirmed by the labeling. We see the dynamics of labeling daily in the interactions of parents and teachers with young children: "You call me bad and I'll show you how bad I can be," the labeled child implicitly, and sometimes explicitly, says.

The theory of reintegrative shaming takes the labeling perspective more seriously than other criminological theories. It does this by partitioning shaming into two types—reintegrative shaming and stigmatization. When shaming is reintegrative, crime is reduced. When shaming is stigmatizing, the predictions of labeling theory apply and crime may be increased. The crucial theoretical move is this partitioning of shaming into a type that has a counterproductive effect on crime and a type that has a productive effect. Actually, practices of shaming are conceived as lying along a continuum ranging from highly reintegrative forms of shaming to highly stigmatizing forms. All cultures are complex mixes of reintegrative and stigmatizing shaming practices. But to the extent that reintegrative shaming is more dominant than stigmatization in a culture, the culture will have less crime.

How then does the theory distinguish reintegrative shaming from stigmatization? Stigmatization is disrespectful shaming whereas reintegrative shaming communicates respect for the person as well as disapproval of that person's deed. Prisons are the best places to see stigmatization at work; loving families are the best places to see reintegrative shaming. The parent reproaches the child for a serious misdeed and sends him to his room. Later, however, the parent goes to the room, hugs the child, letting him know through word and gesture that, although his deed is disapproved, he is approved, indeed loved, as a person.

Reintegrative shaming involves

- Disapproval while sustaining a relationship of respect
- Ceremonies to certify deviance (sent to room) terminated by ceremonies to decertify deviance (forgiving hug)
- Disapproval of the evil of the deed without labeling the persons as evil
- Deviance not being allowed to become a master status trait (e.g. junkie, bully)

Stigmatization involves

- Disrespectful disapproval, humiliation
- Ceremonies to certify deviance but no ceremonies to decertify deviance
- Labeling the person, not just the deed, as evil
- Deviance allowed to become a master status trait

At its worst, stigmatization drives offenders into criminal subcultures: The drug user labeled a junkie finds a subculture of drug use where junkies are able to reject their rejectors, mutually affirm drug-using identities, and learn practical things like where to buy and how to sell drugs.

The Normative Theory

Like deterrence theory and any other explanatory theory of social control, the theory of reintegrative shaming is likely to be politically dangerous unless it is combined with a normative theory of when it is morally right to apply it. Because shaming is a powerful form of social control, it can be oppressive. When we shame young girls for being assertive while shaming gentle boys for not being manly, this is a patriarchal patterning of shaming that reproduces the subordination of women and the domination of men. It is a patterning of shaming that seems oppressive and morally wrong. Yet when we shame boys for violence against girls and shame adults who forbid girls from being assertive, we have a patterning of shaming that seems liberating and morally right.

Is there a general account we can give of the conditions for when shaming is right and when it is wrong? One such account is provided by Braithwaite and Pettit's (1990) republican theory of criminal justice. According to republican theory, shaming (like criminalization) is wrong when the consequence of shaming is to reduce liberty (where liberty is conceived in a republican way). We call republican liberty *dominion.*

The core claim of Braithwaite and Petit's normative theory is that criminal justice policies should be designed so as to maximize dominion. There is not space in this chapter for a full exposition of how a republican conception of freedom differs from a liberal conception. It is called republican because of its grounding in the thought of thinkers such as Montesquieu (1977) and eighteenth-century political reformers like Jefferson. One of the ironies of American history is that the republican political movement that Jefferson led ultimately became the Democratic Party, not the Republican Party.

Dominion is a social, relational conception of liberty as opposed to liberty as the status of simply being left alone by others. You only enjoy republican liberty—dominion—when you live in a social world that provides you with a set of subjective assurances of liberty. Dominion is a citizenship status of assurance against falling into the status of slavery, falling under the power of others. Being a social, relational conception of liberty, by definition it also has a comparative dimension. To fully enjoy liberty, you must have equality of liberty prospects with other persons. If this is difficult to grasp, think of dominion as a conception of freedom that by definition incorporates the notions in the republican slogan: liberté, égalité, and fraternité—or sororité according to feminist reinterpretation (Karstedt, et al. 1997).

Braithwaite and Pettit (1990) argue that their republican normative theory offers advice on what kinds of conduct should be criminalized and what should be decriminalized. It also offers guidance on when it is right and wrong to shame deviant conduct (Braithwaite, 1994). The theory says that we should shame conduct when doing so will increase dominion. When shaming will reduce dominion (as in shaming a young girl for being assertive), then the shaming is wrong. It is wrong because it threatens freedom as liberté-égalité-sororité. Moreover, it is right to shame those who do such shaming. It is right to shame oppressors for engaging in a type of shaming that threatens dominion.

Implications

Communitarianism I: Social Movement Politics

The most important implications for crime prevention of a republican interpretation of the theory of reintegrative shaming are not about government policy. As Sunstein (1988) has argued, civic republicans believe in active citizenship—community participation in public life—as fundamental to republican ideology. It follows that republicans must take seriously social movements of citizens, organized influence from below, as vehicles for progressive change. Such social movements are precisely the vehicles that can deliver changes that can lower the crime rate.

I will now sketch very briefly an argument to this end outlined in more detail elsewhere (Braithwaite, 1994). This is that republican criminology enables a decisively changed, and more optimistic, way of thinking about the crime problem. The theory enables us to see that (1) the most serious crime problems in contemporary societies are precisely the crime problems we are in the best position to reduce, and (2) the changes needed to effect these reductions have gathered considerable momentum in societies such as Australia during the past two decades.

In my own country, Australia, the crimes that cause greatest harm to persons are domestic violence (Scutt, 1983; Hopkins and McGregor, 1991), corporate crimes of violence such as occupational health and safety offenses (Braithwaite and Grabosky, 1985:1-41), and drunk driving (Homel, 1988). The property offenders that cause the overwhelming majority of criminal losses are white-collar criminals (Grabosky and Sutton, 1989).

There is a common structural reason why these particular offense types are Australia's greatest crime problems. These are offender types that have all enjoyed a historical immunity from public disapproval of their crimes, and they have enjoyed this immunity because of the structural realities of power. The worst of Australia's white-collar criminals have been unusually respectable men, and they are men who have been hailed as our greatest entrepreneurial heroes. Violent men have enjoyed historical immunity even from the disapproval of the police when they have engaged in acts of domestic assault (Scutt, 1983: chapter 9; Hatty and Sutton, 1986; Wearing, 1990). This has been because of considerable sharing of common values between the offenders and the police about the prerogatives of men to engage in violence in the personal kingdoms of their homes. Since police who answer calls about domestic violence are the main window through which public disapproval might enter the domestic domain, this patriarchal collusion has been effective until very recently in preventing domestic violence from becoming a public issue.

Australian patriarchy takes the culturally specific form of a male mateship culture in which gender-segregated drinking is important (Sergeant, 1973). Women were not to be found in public bars in Australia until the 1970s. Pub and club drinking followed by driving is something that most Australian males have done many times, something that they regard as important to sustaining patterns of mateship and find difficult to regard as shameful. As a consequence of the strong support that drunk driving has enjoyed in such a patriarchal collusion, informal disapproval by mates and formal disapproval by the courts has been historically muted.

These then are the bases for my claim that the particular crime problems that do the most harm in Australia have been allowed to continue because of the muted or ambivalent disapproval they elicit, where this limited disapproval arose because of patterns of power. However, since the mid-1970s all of these forms of crime have been targeted by social movements concerned to engender community disapproval of them. The most important of these was the women's movement. Domestic violence was an important issue for the Australian women's movement of the late Nineteenth century (Allen, 1986). At first the resurgent women's movement of the early 1970s did not give any significant priority to domestic violence (Hopkins and McGregor, 1991). By the mid-1970s, this was changing. Major conferences, including rather important conferences organized by feminists at the Australian Institute of Criminology, drew attention to the issue, as did subsequent criminological research (O'Donnell and Craney, 1982; Scutt, 1983; Hatty, 1985; Stubbs and Wallace, 1988). The most important momentum, however, came from the feminist refuge movement, strategically supported by femocrats working within the state (Hopkins and McGregor, 1991).

This social movement has had a considerable impact. Current affairs programs in the media now carry a regular fare of stories exposing the evils of domestic violence. Police education curricula, responding to feminist critiques (Hatty and Sutton, 1986; Scutt, 1982), have begun to push the line that domestic violence is a crime and a priority concern for Australian police services (McDonald et al., 1990; see also Stubbs and Wallace, 1988). Domestic violence is now much more out in the open in Australia. Although private condoning of domestic violence continues, the public voices that are heard today are the voices of condemnation. And this is progress.

In a longer chapter of mine in another book (Braithwaite, 1994), I attempt to show that Australian social movements against white-collar crime and the consumer and environmental movements, though weaker than their American counterparts, have had effects on business and community attitudes on the shamefulness of problems like illicit pollution. And I suggest that the social movement against drunk driving has had a substantial effect in reducing death on the roads. Thus it is precisely with respect to our most serious crime problems in Australia—crimes against women, white-collar crime, and drunk driving—that social movements have been making greatest progress over the past two decades. I do not suggest that the progress has been decisive or overwhelming—patriarchy is not about to breathe its last gasp, the environment continues to collapse, and drunk driving is still a major killer.

Yet if some progress has been made in the places that count most, mainstream criminological methods are likely to leave us blind to any accomplishment. Crime statistics suggest that domestic violence is getting worse, because some accomplishments of the social movement against domestic violence have been to make the police more sensitive to the problem and to provide support to women who wish to lodge complaints against violent spouses (Hopkins and McGregor, 1991).

This is true of white-collar crime and is true generally: When a form of crime becomes more shameful, the community and the police discover more instances of that form of crime. So if bank robbery is shameful and insider trading is not, the community and the police will have the impression that bank robbery is the more common and more serious of these two problems. This is so even when we know that "the best way to rob a bank is to own it."

Communitarianism II: Community Accountability Conferences

Contemporary republicans cannot long nostalgically for the communitarianism of the Eigtheenth century New England town meeting. Social movement politics is one form of communitarianism that can affect crime and that can work in the Twenty-First century (Soltan, 1993). Now I consider another more micro form of communitarianism that can also work in the age of the automobile and into the future: community accountability conferences.

Although the idea of community accountability conferences was deduced from the theory of reintegrative shaming, I discovered that such conferences (and the theory of reintegrative shaming, for that matter) had been invented by Maori tribes hundreds of years ago. The New Zealand state has adapted and institutionalized Maori thinking through the Children, Young Persons and their Families Act of 1989. This statute enables both white and Maori juvenile offenses to be dealt with through "family group conferences" instead of juvenile courts. A youth justice coordinator convenes a conference to which are invited the offender, the offender's family (extending often to aunts, grandparents, and cousins), other citizens who are key supports in the offender's life (perhaps this might be a football coach he particularly respects), the victim, the victims supporters (often family members), the police, and in some contexts a youth justice advocate.

This kind of conference, which often accommodates twenty or more participants, is more radically communitarian than Northern Hemisphere models of victim-offender reconciliation, which tend to be more dyadic encounters mediated by a mediation professional who sits between the parties. More important, the community accountability conferences, particularly as adapted from New Zealand in New South Wales and Canberra, have a different theoretical rationale from Northern victim-offender reconciliation. The *selection principle* with conference invitations is designed to structure two ingredients into the conference. Inviting the victim and victim supporters to confront the offender with the harm they suffered is designed to structure shaming into the conference. Inviting as offender supporters the people who care most about (and are respected most by) the offender structures reintegration into the conference.

The *agenda* of the conference is also structured around these two ingredients. First, the offender is empowered to describe the incident in his or her own terms. Then, the victim, victim supporters, and the offender's family have the opportunity to describe the harm the incident caused them. Offenders are often very good at erecting barriers to protect themselves from the shame over the consequences of what they have done. Making them face the people who have suffered those consequences often breaks through these barriers—often not. Sometimes a shaft of shame from the victim will be deflected by the offender, only to spear like a stake through the heart of the offender's mother, sitting beside the offender, causing her to sob. Then it can be the tears of the mother —her disappointment, her shame, her public ordeal—that pierce the offenders' defenses against shame.

When the offender does confront the consequences of what he or she has done, the citizens present invariably implicitly or explicitly invite him to take responsibility for it. In every conference I have observed, this has evoked an apology to the victim. Most victims then reciprocate with some gesture or utterance of forgiveness. It is in fact rather hard for human beings who receive a face-to-face apology in public not to respond with some sort of gesture of forgiveness. Hence, the agenda also structures reintegration into the conference through the simple device of being victim-centered. The job of the conference is to come up with a solution to the problems the victim has suffered. This will often involve the payment of restitution. The conference also seeks to avoid stigmatization through being problem-centered rather than offender-centered. The conference also seeks agreement on a plan of action to ensure that the problem does not recur. Usually, the offender will take responsibility for important parts of this plan, but typically the responsibility will be shared with other participants.

Hence, we have an uncomplicated procedure that structures both shame and reintegration into a community conference through both simple selection principles for conference invitations and a victim-centered agenda that conduces to a sequence of confrontation-remorse-apology-forgiveness-help. Of course, it is an empirical question whether reintegrative shaming occurs at these conferences and whether that particular version reduces crime. Preliminary qualitative studies are to varying degrees encouraging on the first question but silent on the second (Alder and Wundersitz, 1994; Braithwaite and Mugford, 1994; Maxwell and Morris, 1993; O'Connell and Moore, 1992). One nonexperimental study suggests that reintegrative shaming increases compliance with the law (Makkai and Braithwaite, 1994), and more definitive experimental evaluations of conferencing are planned (Sherman, Braithwaite, and Strang, 1994).

I have shown that the policy implications of the theory are clear, but no one has shown that they are right. I have tried to suggest at least that they are practical. Many versions of communitarianism and community policing amount to a utopian yearning for lost geographical community that is not to be found in the contemporary metropolis. Even simple programs such as Neighborhood Watch do not work very well because most people are not interested in making the minimal commitment to their neighborhood that it requires. Most people in Australian and New Zealand cities do, in contrast, respond to invitations to participate in community accountability conferences. We are flattered when a young person in trouble nominates us as one of the people in the neighborhood, the school, or the extended family whom she respects most and we respond by coming along to support her. Equally, we are flattered when a victim nominates us as someone he would like to have support him, so we come. When participants fail to show up, it is more through administrative incompetence than failure of community. In the modern metropolis, community has not been lost so much as transformed from a geographical basis to a multitude of interest-based communities (Sampson, 1987). So the conference is a practical sort of communitarianism designed to tap these diffuse and multiplex bases of community; it is an individual-centered communitarianism. Community is constructed on the basis of a practical appeal to bonds of care toward a particular individual. The theory assumes that if citizens cannot be found who care about a particular individual—the aunt who lives in another city, the respected football coach, the one teacher who gave the kid an even break, the friend on the street—then we have an incompetent conference coordinator, not an individual totally devoid of social bonds.

Finally, the model is attractive for multicultural cities like Auckland and Sydney because it rejects the court-based notion of a single right way of doing justice that must be transacted consistently according to this correct model. Aboriginal or Croatian citizens can run conferences in ways that seem culturally appropriate to them as Aborigines or Croatians (see Braithwaite and Mugford, 1994).

Like all models grounded in criminological theory, this one will fail for many types of cases. This is inherent in the application of criminological theories that will ever be only partial in their explanatory power. The challenge of institutional design is to cover the weaknesses of one intervention with the strengths of another. Hence, we need to design criminal justice institutions such that when reintegrative shaming fails, we can give deterrence a chance to succeed and when deterrence fails, it is possible to try an incapacitation strategy (e.g., imprisonment, license cancellation) in the most intransigent cases (see Braithwaite, 1993, 1994, for a republican analysis of how to maximize dominion with such a dynamic strategy).

Can It Work in America?

As a criminological theorist, I seek to write things of some interest to criminologists from many countries. As a policy analyst, however, I try to limit my prescriptive writing to Australia, leaving it to Russians to think about whether the theories have any application to Russia. In this chapter I will break this rule to make a few remarks to American readers who constantly ask if these ideas can work in America. Of course, we will never truly know if they would work until someone does some empirical work to find out.

It can be said that the United States is no less multicultural a society than Australia and New Zealand, so that the pluralist analysis of the abject failure of the univocal justice of courtrooms in multicultural societies seems no less apposite. The foundational empirical claims of the theory of reintegrative shaming are probably no less true. Indeed, the body of empirical findings about the patterning of crime that the theory sets out to explain are mainly American empirical findings, not Australian ones. For example, the findings from perceptual deterrence studies that informal disapproval has more effect in reducing crime than formal sanctions are almost entirely American (Tittle, 1980; Nagin and Paternoster, 1991).

Although the loss of geographical community is obviously more profound in America than in Japan or Wagga Wagga, the prescription of Communitarianism I, social movement politics, surely has more, not less, force in America than in such places. I can think of no country that has a social movement politics as vital as the United States. The problem with American social movement politics, from my theoretical perspective, is that it can be so stigmatizing. Many in the consumer movement want to lock up corporate criminals and throw away the key; many in the women's movement want to fight men's violence with the violence of a criminal justice system that degrades misogynists in the way they "deserve." Equally, many in American social movement politics reject strategies based on the degradation of adversaries. Increasingly we do see practices of respectful negotiation with the enemy by the American environmental movement, for example.

With regard to Communitarianism II, it seems reasonable to expect community accountability conferences to work better in Wagga Wagga than in South Central Los Angeles. Yet it seems reasonable to expect almost any strategy to fail more often in South Central Los Angeles. But that is not the crucial prediction of the theory. The theoretical effect is about the size of the gap (in crime) between stigmatizing and reintegrative strategies. My prediction would be that a randomized controlled trial of conferencing versus court processing in South Central Los Angeles would produce a bigger difference in reoffending rates than in Wagga Wagga. Why? Because the negative effects of traditional stigmatic criminal justice processing are likely to be dramatically greater in Los Angeles than in the comparatively caring criminal justice system of Wagga Wagga.

The theoretical logic here is the same as that which predicts that the gap in domestic violence reoffending rates between processing by stigmatizing arrest versus nonarrest will be greater for black, unmarried, unemployed men than for respectable, well-bonded (married, employed) white men. This is because we should predict that the effects of stigmatic processing in increasing crime to be much worse for black, unemployed men who are deeply resentful of the racism they believe have suffered at the hands of an alien system. Broadly, this prediction is supported by the results of American experiments on the effect of arrest on domestic violence (Sherman, 1992). Hence the prediction that the comparative advantage of conferencing over court will be greater in a multicultural metropolis suffering high unemployment than in a homogeneous white town with little unemployment. The counterproductive effects of criminal justice degradation ceremonies in escalating defiance and anger should be so much greater in communities with oppressed minorities. Thus, the increased capacity to do good. These are predictions that can be, and should be, tested empirically.

Neither Communitarianism I nor Communitarianism II seems contemporarily impractical in the way that a Jeffersonian rural republicanism does. Although Jefferson deserves his status as a civic republican icon, in this respect Madison's republicanism is more contemporarily relevant than Jefferson's. Madison argued in the Federalist Papers against nostalgic small-town communitarianism because of the way liberty is at threat from an engulfing tyranny of the majority in a tight rural community (Madison, Hamilton, and Jay, 1987). Liberty would be enhanced by enlarging the republic, enabling the tyrannies of local majorities over nonconformists to be contested in wider communities.

Madison's worry about American civic republicanism was not so much about citizens not being active enough to make it work but about them being overactive in oppressing and stigmatizing nonconformists. If there is a distinctive worry about making republican ideas work in America compared with other nations, it still seems to be Madison's worry. America does not seem to have less active citizens than other democracies—quite the contrary. Tocqueville, foreshadowing the posse/Batman/Terminator as the leitmotif of America's greatest cultural export, at the same time saw America as having an usually active citizenry on matters of crime control and an unusually stigmatizing one:

> In America the means available to the authorities for the discovery of crimes and arrest are few.
> There is no administrative police force, and passports are unknown. The criminal police in the United States cannot be compared to that of France; the officers of the public prosecutor's office are few, and the initiative in prosecutions is not always theirs; and the examination of prisoners is rapid and oral. Nevertheless, I doubt whether in any other country crime so seldom escapes punishment.
> The reason is that everyone thinks he has an interest in furnishing proofs of an offense and in arresting the guilty man.
> During my stay in the United States I have seen the inhabitants of a county where a serious crime had been committed spontaneously forming committees with the object of catching the criminal and handing him over to the courts. In

Europe the criminal is a luckless man fighting to save his head from the authorities; in a sense the population are mere spectators of the struggle. In America he is an enemy of the human race and every human being is against him. (Tocqueville, 1969:96).

Tocqueville concludes that the outcome of participatory justice against these "enemies of the human race" was a tyranny of the majority:

When a man or a party suffers an injustice in the United States, to whom can he turn? To public opinion? That is what forms the majority. To the legislative body? It represents the majority and obeys it blindly. To the executive power? It is appointed by the majority and serves as its passive instrument. To the police? They are nothing but the majority under arms. A jury? The jury is the majority vested with the right to pronounce judgement; even the judges in certain states are elected by the majority (Tocqueville, 1969:252)

Although Tocqueville's account of nineteenth century America is doubtless exaggerated here, I suspect it is still true that American citizens are both more agitatable and more stigmatizing about crime than West Europeans, who continue to show no signs of joining either posses or social movements for the reintroduction of capital punishment. If this is true, then policies to direct institutional practices away from stigmatizing agitation toward more reintegrative citizen participation should have comparatively more payoff in America than elsewhere in the West.

References

Alder, Christine, and Joy Wundersitz. 1994. *Family Conferencing and Juvenile Justice: The Way Forward or Misplaced Optimism?* Canberra: Australian Institute of Criminology.

Allen, Judith. 1986. "Desperately Seeking Solutions: Changing Battered Women's Options Since 1880" in Suzanne E. Hatty (ed.), *National Conference on Domestic Violence,* vol. 1, Australian Institute of Criminology Seminar Proceeding no.12. Canberra.

Becker, Howard S. 1963. *Outsiders: Studies in the Sociology of Deviane.* New York: Free Press.

Braithwaite, John. 1989. *Crime, Shame and Reintegration.* Cambridge: Cambridge University Press.

Braithwaite, John. 1993. Beyond Positivism: Learning from Contextual, Integrated Strategies. *Journal of Research in Crime and Delinquency* 30:383-399.

———. 1994 "Inequality and Republican Criminology." In John Hagan and Ruth Peterson (eds.), *Inequality and Crime.* Palo Alto, CA: Stanford University Press.

Braithwaite, John, and Peter Grabosky. 1985. *Occupational Health and Safety Enforcement in Australia.* Canberra: Australian Institute of Criminology.

Braithwaite, John and Stephen Mugford. 1994. "Conditions of Successful Reintegration Ceremonies." *British Journal of Criminology* 34:2.

Braithwaite, John, and Philip Pettit 1990. *Not Just Deserts: A Republican Theory of Criminal Justice.* Oxford: Oxford University.

Grabosky, Peter, and Adam Sutton eds. 1989. *Stains on a White Collar.* Sydney: Federation Press.

Hatty, Suzanne. 1985. *National Conference on Domestic Violence.* Canberra: Australian Institute of Criminology.

Hatty, Suzanne, and Jeanne Sutton. 1986. "Policing Violence Against Women" in Suzanne E. Hatty (ed), *National Conference on Domestic Violence,* Vol. 2, Australian Institute of Criminology Seminar Proceeding no.12. Canberra.

Homel, Ross. 1988. *Policing and Punishing the Drinking Driver: A Study of General and Specific Deterrence.* New York: Springer-Verlag.

Hopkins, Andrew, and Heather McGregor. 1991. *Working for Change: The Movement Against Domestic Violence.* Sydney: Allen and Unwin.

Karstedt, Susanne. 1992. "Liberté, Égalité, Sororité: Quelques Reflexions sur la Politique Criminelle Feministe." *Deviance et Societé* 16:287-296.

Karstedt, Suzanne, Madison, James, Alexander Hamilton, and John Jay. 1987. *The Federalist Papers.* London: Penguin.

McDonald, B., et al. 1990. *The New South Wales Police Recruit Education Programme: An Independent Evaluation.* Sydney: NSW Police Department.

Madison, James, Alexander Hamilton, and John Jay. 1987. *The Federalist Papers.* London: Penguin.

Makkai, Toni, and John Braithwaite. 1994. "Reintegrative Shaming and Compliance with Regulatory Standards." *Criminology* 32:361-385.

Montesquieu, Baron de. 1977. *The Spirit of Laws.* abridged and edited by D. W. Carrithers. University of California Press.

Maxwell, Gabrielle, and A. Morris. 1993. *Family Victims and Youth Justice in New Zealand Wellington.* Wellington: Institute of Criminology, University of Victoria.

Moore, David, B. 1993. "Facing the Consequences: Conference and Juvenile Justice." Paper presented at the National Conference on Juvenile Justice of the Australian Institute of Criminology, Canberra.

Morris, A., and G. Maxwell. 1992. "Juvenile Justice in New Zealand: A New Paradigm." *Australian and New Zealand Journal of Criminology.*

Morris, Norval. 1966. "Impediments to Penal Reform." *University of Chicago Law Review* 33:627-656.

Nagin, Daniel S., and Raymond Paternoster. 1991. "The Preventive Effects of Perceived Risk of Arrest: Testing and Expanding a Conception of Deterrence." *Criminology* 29:561-587.

O'Connell, Terrence. 1993. "It May Be the Way to Go." Paper presented at the National Conference on Juvenile Justice of the Australian Institute of Criminology, Canberra.

O'Connell, Terrence, and David Moore. 1992. "Wagga Juvenile Cautioning Process: The General Applicability of Family Group Conferences for Juvenile Offenders and their Victims." *Rural Society* 2:16-19.

O'Donnell, J., and J. Craney, eds. 1982. *Family Violence in Australia.* Melbourne: Longman Cheshire.

Sampson, Robert J. 1987. "Communities and Crime." In Michael R. Gottfredson and Travis Hirschi (eds.), *Positive Criminology.* Newbury Park, CA: Sage.

———. 1983. *Even in the Best of Homes.* Melbourne: Penguin.

Sergeant, Margaret. 1973 *Alcoholism as a Social Problem,* Brisbane: University of Queensland Press: Brisbane.

Sherman, Lawrence W. 1992. *Policing Domestic Violence.* New York: Free Press.

Sherman, Lawrence W., John Braithwaite, and Heather Strang. 1994. "Reintegrative Shaming of Violence, Drink Driving and Property Crime: A Randomised Controlled Trial." Unpublished grant proposal. Australian National University, Canberra.

Soltan, Karol Edward. 1993. "Generic Constitutionalism." In Stephen L. Elkin and Karol Edward Soltan (eds.), *A New Constitutionalism.* Chicago: University of Chicago Press.

Stubbs, Julie, and D. Wallace. 1988. *Domestic Violence: Impact of Legal Reform in NSW Sydney.* New South Wales Bureau of Crime Statistics and Research.

Sunstein, Cass. 1988. "Beyond the Republican Revival." *Yale Law Journal* 97:1539-1590.

Tittle, Charles R. 1980. *Sanctions and Social Deviance.* New York: Praeger.

Tocqueville, Alexis de. 1969. *Democracy in America.* New York: Anchor Books.

Wearing, Rosemary. 1990 "A Longitudinal Analysis of the 1987 Crimes (Family Violence) Act in Victoria." Report to Criminology Research Council, Canberra.

12

Gendered Criminological Policies: Femininity, Masculinity, and Violence

Elizabeth A. Stanko

The sensational news coverage of the Lorena and John Wayne Bobbitt cases resulted in the acquittal of both parties. Neither the husband's long-term physical and sexual abuse of her, nor her inflicting grievous bodily harm on him, was officially acknowledged as criminal violence. Clearly *something happened* that resulted in serious charges being laid by police and prosecutors. But juries acquitted each of them, characterizing their alleged crimes as individual, pathological acts. (Indeed, Lorena Bobbitt, not John Wayne Bobbitt, was committed to a mental hospital immediately following the trial; her defense accepted by the jury was that she was temporarily insane.) As a result, neither party was held criminally responsible for his or her violence. What, after all, is criminal violence? How can we theorize about it and its prevention?

The inability to understand violence and its wider implications is exacerbated by ignoring the lens of gender. Public policy in particular fails to develop a comprehensive picture of the damaging effects of violence because it continues to separate *normal* violence (violence is most likely to involve family, friends, and acquaintances) from so-called *public* violence (violence that strikes unexpectedly in public places). Although there has been a wider recognition of domestic violence, fear and loathing continue to focus on young men running amok in public while ignoring the high proportions of young men's violence to each other. This private-public divide has blinkered social policy and added to our confusion of how we understand violence, its location in our mundane lives, and its often prevailing support within a wider cultural and political context.

People themselves largely decrimininalize acts of violence, either by failing to report the event to authorities in the first place or by refusing to cooperate when they or others do report. This individual process differs from the job of criminal justice agents, which is to select those violent acts charged and prosecuted as criminal violence. The process of criminalization is itself selective:

Only a small proportion of criminal violence, reported to police, actually results in public prosecution. Both processes favor the decriminalization of violence, in effect, *normalizing* it. Both processes are heavily dependent on victims' silence and others' assessments of their worthiness as good, competent complainants as grounds for excluding violent events from adjudication in various justice systems (Stanko, 1977; Frohmann, 1991; Bumgarden, 1992). Both processes seem to have complex relationships with the dominant imagery of violence that looms everlarge in our daily newspapers, local television news, and movie screens (Daly, 1994). And, finally, both processes support, reinforce, and legitimate a social order that is structured through a gendered, racist, and economic order largely unfettered by legal statute (see also Keith, 1994; MacKinnon, 1989; Matoesian, 1993; Simon, 1988; Smart, 1989; Stanko, 1985).

Yet the moral panic about violence in the United States and the United Kingdom is not in reference to the kind of violence so graphically described during the Bobbitt trials. It is the random, unpredictable violence of young men (often associated with young black men [Katz, 1988]) that apparently continues to cause the greatest anxiety. When policymakers speak of violence getting out of hand, they are not usually speaking about the significant amount of violence that occur's between known others. Even when they do highlight the high proportions of men's confrontational violence (some of which may result in lethal consequences (Daly and Wilson, 1988; Polk, 1994), policymakers worry about the "innocent" by- bystanders. We seem to worry and theorize about the impact of violence on those presumedly law-abiding citizenry, as if to dismiss the possibility of detrimental impact of violence on those living with it daily, such as the homeless or the poor and addicted. Such myopia, heightened by racism, has led, I believe, to the delay in spotlighting the devastating impact of violence within Afro-American communities in the United States (see also Davis, 1990; Gibbs and Merighi, 1994). I am suggesting that our inability to *see* the violence of everyday life has stultified our theorizing and consequently our policy to minimize it.

This chapter explores the theoretical and research contributions of feminist-inspired inquiry on men's violence against women and children, and, most recently, on men's violence against men, with an eye to developing public policy around violence prevention. I suggest that crime prevention should be addressed to both specific and general aspects of how women and men experience, avoid, and minimize violence within their everyday lives. Such policy speculation is influenced by my own theoretical training in critical criminology and ethnomethodology which treats the mundane world as problematical and as providing the clues to a way forward grounded in how people actually experience violence in everyday life. Finally, I will set out a challenging agenda, with practical and theoretical relevance to the minimization of violence in women's and men's lives.

What Is Violence?

Broadly speaking, violence involves inflicting emotional, psychological, sexual, physical, and/or material damage. I include emotional and psych- ological harm because threat and intimidation have consequences for how safe individuals feel. Anxiety about criminal violence is often fueled by fear, which is focused on the diffuse threat people feel from its potential. Whether physical or psychological, the harm felt by the recipient varies, as does the long-term impact on his or her everyday life. A recent experience of violence, or its threat, may have significant effects, altering an individual's routines and personal life-style, or it may have little noticeable influence on daily life. Living within "climates of unsafety" (Stanko, 1990), where people feel especially vulnerable to verbal or physical aggression, also takes its toll on people's well-being and quality of life.

We usually associate violence and its use with individuals (Stanko, 1994), and this association limits our thinking. The violence of institutions, such as within prisons, or that of state-sanctioned agencies, such as the use of deadly force by police, is rarely treated as problematical[1] and subject to the detailed scrutiny or condemnation we save for those violent men (usually) and women (sometimes) we demonize as "inhuman." So too do we rarely include deaths at work, unless, as in the UK, police or prison officers are killed (Levi, 1994). In a recent review article, Levi suggests that the exclusion of workrelated deaths, as well as deaths due to negligent or reckless driving, is a commentary about how violence is defined as the individual action of individual offenders. In our desire to distance ourselves from the incivility of war—another form of collective violence—such as that which took place in Vietnam or more recently in Bosnia-Herzegovina,[2] we assume that present-day Western society is safe. If danger does arise, we locate our fear of danger onto young male hooligans (Pearson, 1983).

In using a legal framework to define criminal violence, criminologists opt for a perspective on violence that individualizes it. This perspective has been heavily influenced by the demands of criminal statutes for evidence in a criminal trial. Criminology, as a discipline, concentrates on legally-defined crime, documenting the causes of violence of individuals (or groups of individuals such as gangs). It has turned to biological, psychological and sociological reasons to explain violence (mostly men's). Violence, in the context of these explanations is generally assumed to be gratuitous, meaningless, unwarranted. Katz (1988) assails criminologists for such a narrow-minded approach. He reminds us throughout the detailed descriptions of the minutiae of traditionally defined criminal violence that "the use of violence beyond its clear materialist justification is a powerful strategy for *constructing* purposiveness." (emphasis in original (1988:322). But it is difficult to understand many of Katz's subjects without the powerful contribution of masculinity in shaping the form of confrontational violent crime used, for which defending men's honor or reputation is paramount (Daly and Wilson, 1988; Polk, 1994).

Theorizing Violence, Theorizing Gender

Understanding why some men who live in urban wastelands (see Davis, 1990) cast themselves as dangerous *toughs* is to place the development of identity and sense of self within its historical and cultural evolution (see also Connell, 1991) and, more important to me, to take the contribution of gender and gender order seriously. Undeniably, patterns of violence affect women and men differently. Violence and its threat is an acute reality for women: Fear of violence, especially sexual assault, has resulted in restrictions on life-style and mobility more so for women than men (Gordon and Riger, 1988; Stanko, 1995). The impact of domestic sexual terrorism on women has been acknowledged. Clearly, domestic violence and sexual assault are interwoven within women's heterosexual relationships with men (Kelly 1988; Stanko, 1985). Women are also targets for sexual harassment and pestering on the street and homophobic attack. Gay men too are clearly targets for homophobic attack. Men overall are killed and physically assaulted at rates far higher than are women: They are killed and assaulted by other men in contests over status, in competition for control over women, over territory or other material goods, and in rage over perceived or experienced social and psychological humiliation.

Gender becomes a crucial lens. For example, because violence is too often interpreted as male behavior, women's violence is typically explained as a hormonal abnormality. In other words, explanations for women's violence suggest that women who commit violent acts are not *normal* women. Research on women's violence (at least those few women who end up criminally liable for their violence), though, suggests that many of the features evident in studies of violent men who are imprisoned also feature prominently in these women's lives: poverty, histories of violent victimization, drug addiction, and participation in the underground economy. But the contribution of women to violent crime is still very low, and when women are characterized as violent, they still live within a social and political context where men largely control the economy, the street's (see also Maher and Curtis, 1992), the workplaces, the institutions, and the governments. We are quick to overlook structural explanations for violence—especially the violence that is so pervasive in the lives of the so-called underclass or of those who make a living from disorganized drug dealing, robbery, or other forms of illegal, predatory activity.

Where gender has become most salient is in feminist theorizing about domestic violence. Feminist research has emphasized the instrumental impact of serial, intentional, and directed violence by men on women (Dobash and Dobash, 1979; Hoff, 1990). Women are most likely to be injured, raped, and to receive medical attention as a result of assaults by known assailants. Strong evidence suggests that men do not sustain the same level of serious injuries at the hands of intimates (unless they are killed, often in self-defense, by women they batter). The 1992 British Crime Survey suggests that men report "domestic" incidents to police twice as often as do women (Mayhew, Maung, and Mirrlees-Black, 1993). Yet research indicates that it is women (or those acting on behalf of women) who ask police for help in 90 to 95 percent of requests for assistance in domestic violence. Nor do men seek emergency and secure accommodation such as in refuges for battered women (the one refuge in the UK for so-called battered husbands is closed for lack of need). So although there may be men who report experiencing violence at the hands of their wives/part- ners (Straus and Gelles, 1990), the meaning and intent of this violence does not have the overall *collective* impact on men's lives as such violence does for women.

Much of the evidence in studies of violence between intimates (or former intimates) suggests that gender structures men's sense of entitlement to women's services in that "the sources of conflict leading to violent events reveal a great deal about the nature of relations between men and women, demands and expectations of wives, the prerogatives and power of husbands and cultural beliefs that support individuals' attitudes of marital inequality" (Dobash and Dobash, 1992:4). In other words, the meaning of intimate violence lies within the individual, collective, and cultural understanding of being male or female. Using a theoretical perspective that takes gender seriously, policy and practice must be sensitive to the contribution of gendered power in situations of heterosexual domestic violence. Men use violence against women in domestic situations, as observed most notably by Dobash and Dobash (1992) and Daly and Wilson (1988), as

1. a result of men's possessiveness and jealously
2. an expectation concerning women's domestic work
3. a punishment for women for perceived wrongdoing
4. a prop to men's authority

The frame of gender, and the context of women's subordination, would be lost in a "gender-neutral" explanation of violence within heterosexual rela- tionships. The debate continues between those who propose the "symmetry" of violence in relationships (Straus and Gelles, 1990) and those who argue that the effect of domestic is asymmetrical, with the greatest burden of the violence directed by men to women. Ellis (1994), for instance, in a study of separating couples found that both women and men reported various forms of violence in about one-third of the separations but that during the separation process, husbands are most likely to use violence to control their wives. Intentional hurting of wives by husbands increased during the last six months prior to separation, reports Ellis, but is not a unique phenomenon to estrangement. Although some women may slap their husbands, there is little evidence that it *means* the same thing to both partners (see Dobash and Dobash, 1992).

But we do know that "among married couples, estrangement is associated with markedly elevated rates of violence, lethal and sub-lethal" (Ellis 1994). Straus and Gelles (1990) propose that women's violence "equally" contributes to its perpetuation and go so far as to suggest that women stop using violence in order to stop men using violence. Schwartz and DeKeseredy, in a recent article criticizing Straus and Gelles, suggest that this distorts our understanding of gender. They say that "by characterising women as being as violent as men, reporters and academic writers develop and reinforce negative images of those women who are struggling to end violent situations" (Schwartz and DeKeseredy, 1993:258).

Strong evidence suggests that women's subordination is reflected in patterns of domestic abuse, in women's escape plans, and in the widespread denial of the existence of such violence within presumably happy marriages. The significant contribution of feminist scholarship is that we finally see the ordinariness of violence within the home and within the ritual of courting. We also see that these private experiences of violence have had a significant impact upon women's lives and have had devastating consequences for women who flee violence. It is essential that we understand the meaning of violence for men who use it as social control (some of which is currently being gathered through "offender" treatment programs). Additionally, if there are men who experience violence at the hands of their wives, what does this mean in the context of masculinities? Surely, all the evidence suggests that, by and large, men do not live in constant terror after they have separated, that men are rarely killed by women pursuing them, and that men do not live within a climate of sexual terrorism that women report living in.

Any discussion therefore of the meaning of violence must include the wider context of gender, the institutionalization of subordination (in various forms) and people's individual and cultural resources to live free of violence. So far, the movement to halt violence in women's lives has no equivalent in the demand for a halt to the violence in men's lives. Why would this be the case when all the official data indicate that men are far more likely to encounter violence than are women? Why have we overlooked the violence in men's relationships with each other?

The gendered context within which acts of violence occur is one key to review how violence works in everyday life, often outside the attention of the criminal justice system, to sustain and to reinforce a social order that privileges displays of power over another person, be that person male or female. Let's take a look at violence from a gendered lens to see what contribution a feminist, structurally grounded perspective has on our understanding of violence and its meaning in women's and men's lives. Without this perspective, I suggest, we will be unable to move forward to devise strategies to minimize the impact of violence on all our lives.

Men, Crime, and Violence

By all accounts, young men are the most at risk to personal violence. Consistently confirmed through crime surveys (Hindelang, Gottfredson, and Garofalo, 1978; Hough and Mayhew, 1983; 1985; Mayhew, Dowds and Elliot 1989; Mayhew, Maung, and Mirrlees-Black, 1993) and emergency medical records (Shepherd, 1990), men's experiences of violence include a wide variety of situations: racist attacks, homophobic abuse, random robbery, intragang and intergang rivalry, pub brawls, unprovoked attack, police (state-sanctioned) violence, and domestic abuse (most commonly perpetrated by other men). According to the 1992 British Crime Survey, for instance, men reported violent assault occurring in the following situations (in order of frequency): the street, closely followed by the pub, "other," a work-related environment, the home, in a mugging, and domestic.

Routine activities and lifestyle theories, often the most advanced in explanations of exposure to violence, suggest that features of men's lives— notably their time out of the home, away from suitable guardianship, and in contact with willing offenders—influence their risk of encountering violence (Cohen and Felson, 1979; Hindelang, Gottfredson, and Garofalo, 1978). Although these theories note the powerful predictors of victimization that rest in demographic factors, such as age, race, sex, and marital status, they do not treat these factors as problematical.

Although life-style/routine activities theories are used to explain greater vulnerability to crime of certain categories of men, these theories fail to address the thorny issues of how power and powerlessness, mediated by class, race/ethnicity, age, gender, physical ability, and so forth, influence the risk of victimization and of offending. Nor do they say anything about what exposure to violence *means* to men. Life-style theories are devoid of critical commentary about how the structure of men's lives influences their negotiations of masculinities, which, as some have observed (notably Connell, 1987, and Stanko, 1990), typically revolve around violence and its avoidance. What we are left with, in the analysis of victimization, is the now classic finding that young men who go out drinking three times or more a week are more likely to be victimized. Why would men's leisure lead to violence? Is violence men's leisure? How is some of this leisure defined as criminal violence? What this says about men's experiences of violence is very little: We must rely on *hard men* stereotypes to distance ourselves from the impact of violence on men's lives. We assume that negotiating violence does not worry men, for they report feeling safe to crime survey researchers (see Stanko and Hobdell, 1993).

We must turn to the literature on masculinity to give us some insight into men's actual or potential experiences of violence, whether it be criminally defined or not. Although in the sociological literature there has been a debate on why some men get involved in certain sorts of violence, we have a tendency to categorize men as *either victims or offenders*. For the purpose of this discussion, it is necessary to explore this particular conflation of categories carefully.

My suspicion is that we have failed to examine the impact of victimization on men because we have assumed that male victims are willing partners in their harm. That is, for young men, there is an assumption that men provoke violence. In some respects, as Polk (1994) argues in his exploration of confrontational homicide, this is indeed the case. In an examination of male-on-male homicides in Victoria, Australia, Polk found that 22 percent of these homicides were a result of confrontations over seemingly trivial events. Name-calling, flirtations with assailants' girlfriends, racist or homophobic slurs, or even "dirty looks" may be cited as the start of an altercation. Polk suggests that these provocations make sense within men's lives as negotiations of status, power, and marginality. Others, notably Katz (1988) and Luckenbill (1977), have observed that lethal violence is a dynamic process, where both victim and offender are actively engaged. But the data suggest that confrontational homicide is "definitely (though not exclusively) masculine" (see also Daly and Wilson, 1988). Men in the United States lead the world in lethal violence: For young men, aged fifteen to twenty-four, homicide rates are the highest of nonwarring countries. Moreover, black men are seven times more likely than white men in the United States to be killed. In the United States homicide ranks twelfth as a cause of death and sixth as a cause of premature mortality (Centers for Disease Control, 1992:164).

But to assume that all male-on-male assault is participatory (that is, it is difficult to distinguish between the "guilty" and the "innocent" participant) is surely mistaken. Although men report more incidents of assault to crime survey researchers than do women, and also seek medical attention for their wounds at rates higher than those of women (Shepherd, 1990), they are reticent to speak about their experiences, perhaps because they are portrayed as asking for their assault or because they "should have been man enough to fend it off." In a study of men's reactions to physical assault, Stanko and Hobdell (1993) found that when men were assaulted, others, including family, co-workers, and police, reacted in mixed ways to so-called unprovoked attacks. Moreover, the men themselves measured the violence they met and judged it to be "fair" or "unwarranted." We suggest that

> part of men's knowledge involves anticipating and/or avoiding masculine character contests, even if they choose actively to initiate them. Vulnerability to attack stem[med] from situations where the (later) victim did not start the fight himself or where the "rules" changed; for example, with the opponent pulling out a knife. Violence may be "justified" when the other man or men initiate the fight. (Stanko and Hobdell, 1993:405)

We further argue that being male has a profound impact on how men interpret and react to physical confrontation. Our study suggests that men view their victimization from "a male frame," "the essence of which sees victimization as 'weak and helpless'" (1993:413). I suspect this is true for many cases of sublethal confrontational assault.

Katz's (1988) "hardmen" construct their toughness out of avoidance of weakness: Rage flows from humiliation as one form of denying vulnerability. Katz suggests that violence is one way of transcending disadvantage. Yet Katz goes a step further, positing that criminally violent men's identities are synonymous with their willingness to use brutality. "Hardness" is not only used to confirm identities of "badass" men, but also works to control others.

Violence and its threat are instrumental in enforcing working agreements within the informal economy: Violence is a necessary ingredient for keeping business going (Hobbs, 1994). As Hobbs observes, the "craft skills and traditional trades" have changed in the entrepreneurial market of the underground economy. The drugs trade, for instance, operates on fear; violence polices participants, assuring their trustworthiness. Disputes over territories for goods and services, violations of agreements, betrayals, and the failure to repay loans are a few of the justifications for the use of violence within the illegal economy. People who do not pay expect retaliation, and "teaching one a lesson" in timely accounting commonly involves the use of violence.

Thus in the informal economy the salience of violence as the preserve of order makes sense. The use of violence to police the drug, gun, and untaxed goods markets, for instance, is essential. But very little of the violence used as contract assurance in the informal economy comes to the attention of the police (although police do worry about the sophisticated weapons used), and even less of it ends up before the courts. Violence, within the structure of criminal justice, must be committed, it seems, unprovoked, except if such violence results in lethal consequences. But a quick study of sentencing patterns, no doubt, would illustrate that certain killings are taken more seriously than others (for an in-depth study, see Myers, 1994). So, too would certain robberies, assaults, thefts, and so forth (Stanko, 1977).

As Cretney et al. have observed, violence is not usually considered a "harm done to 'the fabric of society'" (1994:15). Judging whether physical and sexual harm has been done and is worthy of societal condemnation is steeped within a *gendered, structural viewing*: The meaning of the violence is assessed within the wider context of race, class, legality, and so forth. Harm done by criminal associates to each other is not considered harmful to the community as a whole, unless someone dies. Few subjected to the sanctions of the informal economic network would lodge complaints to police. Without the aid of a gendered lens to widen the understanding of what violence *means* to those who experience and commit it, debates and discussions about the use of, and reactions to, violence are subsumed under men's discourses about weakness and survival techniques, which themselves have significantly influenced how *criminal* violence is understood. Although Katz has contributed to the development of the understanding of some men in the United States, he has neglected a wider view about how violence works in the lives of men who are not the "hardmen" but nonetheless rape, beat, and abuse others (Dobash and Dobash, 1992; Godenzi 1994; Messerschmidt, 1993; Connell, 1987; Hearn, 1993). Although it is the case that not all men are violent (and it is here, I suggest, where research should be conducted), violence and its avoidance pervade men's maturation from childhood through adolescence and not unusually into adulthood (Stanko, 1990). Moreover, the violence used by men outside the informal economy to control the domestic and sexual services of women results in few criminal cases.

Therefore, it is essential to explore the meaning of violence for men *as men*, regardless of whether they be victims *or* offenders (or both). No doubt, men who commit violence, as well as men who are on the receiving end, are often one and the same men. This fact is rarely explored, only surfacing, for instance, in critiques of imprisonment. Sim's (1994) powerful essay on men in prison challenges criminologists to examine what it means for men to experience imprisonment. The fact that we tacitly accept the violence of prison glosses over the potential damage this does to the men who spend time within its walls. Says Sim: "Violence and domination in prison can therefore be understood not as a pathological manifestation of abnormal otherness but as part of the normal routine which is sustained and legitimated by the wider culture of masculinity: that culture condemns some acts of male violence but condones the majority of others" (Sim 1994:105). Assaults in prison have long been associated with prison life. Staff and inmates alike are targets and offenders. According to recent figures on assault within English and Welsh jails, both attacks on staff and inmates have increased significantly.[3] Threat and intimidation, though, have long been recognized as essential in controlling prisoners, especially male prisoners.

Yet our thinking about violence prevention must not exclude the effect of living within a regime of legitimate state violence. Do we really expect men, subjected to inhuman treatment at the hands of guards and inmates alike, to emerge as gentle, socialized, respected, and respectful members of the wider community? How could we even think that the experience of state violence would not spill outside the prison walls (see, for instance, Stevens, 1994)? Violence, and especially its threat, is itself a powerful and successful mechanism of social control supposedly used to frighten young people out of crime. In programs allegedly promoting crime prevention, prisoners menacingly tell of bullying, exploitation, and harm that befall other prisoners. "Scared straight" merely normalizes state violence. As long as there is "good order and discipline" inside, easing the work of the guards, few questions are asked about prison's internal operations of intimidation. The inmate who refuses to cooperate may be labeled, as Sim points out, the "ballbuster",—the prisoner who refuses to buckle to the control of either inmate or guard routines. Thus, the lens of gender can assist in unpicking institutional dynamics of legitimate violence which, I suggest, contributes to reproducing some men's violence outside the prisons.

Finally, the anomaly—that men report fear of crime three times less often than do women—should be a curiosity for criminologists. Here too is an occasion where gendered explanations for men's responses shed light on criminological phenomenon that have such popular salience. But to date this has largely been ignored as a topic of interest. Why do men say they do not fear violence, especially since all the official data feature young men as its prominent victims? After all, if the evidence on men's lives suggest's anything, it describes the prominence that the negotiation of violence has in men's lives (Seidler, 1991; Connell, 1987; Segal, 1990). Surely violence avoidance is something each boy learns when growing up (Stanko 1990), with some, as Katz observes, *choosing* an image of violence, because of the attraction to particular forms of masculinity.

Why then have we ignored masculinity when we discuss violence? Why do we assume that men do not fear violence? Why do we assume that if we fail to intervene in the violence men use on each other that it will not affect all our lives? And how could we possibly explain women's fear of sexual terrorism without including the strong and persistent cultural support for men's rationalizations of violence to women? Why then has the concern for crime prevention spotlighted women and children? It is, I believe, because we have taken for granted men's violence toward each other.

Women, Crime, and Violence

Feminist research and theorizing about the prevalence of violence directed toward women places men's violent behavior in the center frame. Overwhelmingly, women's contact with the criminal justice system is as victims; only one in ten people arrested for violence is a woman.

Women report fearing crime at levels three times that of men. Consistent over time and among jurisdictions, women's fear of crime has been explained by criminologists as reflections of vulnerability (social and physical) (Skogan and Maxfield, 1981); as largely a reflection of fear of sexual assault (Warr, 1985), termed "the female fear" (Gordon and Riger, 1988); and as a "fear of men" (Stanko, 1987, 1990). Yet women are considered at low risk to violent victimization (Felson 1994). Felson, in a recent treatise on crime, concludes that "time spent in family and household settings is less risky than time away from those settings" (Felson, 1994:39). Because the home features more prominently in women's routine activities, especially for those with child-care responsibilities, the home, not the street, poses the greatest threat. The detail of the Canadian survey on violence against women (Statistics Canada, 1993), however, found that almost one-half of women reported violence by men known to them and one-quarter reported violence by a stranger. Moreover, one-half of women with previous marriages reported violence by a previous spouse and one in six currently married women reported violence by their spouses. Additionally, domestic threat and crime are least likely to be reported to official agencies whose data are used to calculate risk.

Violent victimization, for women, is most likely to occur in and around the home, rarely coming to the attention of police and survey researchers. In many respects, vulnerability to violence at home is distinctively female. Women's typical assailants are their intimate and former partners. Male friends, acquaintances, co-workers, neighbors, and clients are the most likely to threaten and to be violent to women. According to the 1992 British Crime Survey, for example, women reported the occurrence of violence in the following situations: the home, domestic, in a mugging, the street, the pub/club, "other" assaults, and the work-based environment. What kinds of clues does this list provide for the meaning of situations women report as violent to survey researchers? With the exception of "mugging" and "street", all of the other locations are familiar ones to the victims: homes, leisure facilities, work spaces. In eight of ten domestic violence incidents reported to the crime survey, women were attacked by men (Mayhew et al. 1993). The U.S. surgeon general found that the battering of women is the "single largest cause of injury to women in the United States," accounting for one-fifth of all hospital emergency room cases (cited in Zorza, 1992:46). Violence, for women, arises largely from familiarity.

Suggests Pain (1993:65), "Particularly in the context of women's experiences of male violence and threatening behaviour, fear of crime, for women, ought to be taken to refer to more a pervading state of alertness than a momentary terror." Women's fear of crime, often characterized as "out of proportion" to our potential risk of violence, may be analyzed as a diffuse sense of the danger of *the familiar*. This state of alertness, I have argued, applies to women's relationships to men known and to strangers (Stanko, 1990, 1987).

As virtually all acknowledge, women's experiences of physical and sexual abuse go largely unreported to criminal justice agencies. The FBI recognizes that many sexual assaults fail to come to their attention: Their estimates suggest that one in four rapes are reported. Feminist research, however, indicates that even this is an underestimate: Russell's (1982) ground-breaking work documented the risk of rape and attempted rape to be 46 percent. (This particular study has come under recent attack by Neil Gilbert, who suggest's that feminists are exaggerating women's experiences of sexual assault. His retort consists of analyzing the official UCR data—data that even the FBI believes are seriously flawed when it comes to counting sexual assault.)

Canadian studies are far more sophisticated than those in the United States or Britain. As part of a national commitment to minimizing the impact of violence upon women's lives, the Canadian government undertook a national survey of violence against women. Highlights of the Violence Against Women Survey (Canada, 1994) are worth summarizing:

- One-half of all Canadian women have experienced at least one incident of violence since the age of sixteen.
- Almost one-half of women reported violence by men known to them and one-quarter reported violence by a stranger.
- One-quarter of all women have experienced violence at the hands of current or past marital partner (including common-law unions).
- As noted earlier, one in six currently married women reported violence by their spouses; one-half of women with previous marriages reported violence by previous spouses.

Canadian women reported to researchers incidents that rarely came to the attention of the police: Only 6 percent of sexual assault and 28 percent of physical assault incidents were reported to police (Statistics Canada, 1994).

Thus feminist researchers, and state research informed by feminist thinking, explain women's fear of crime as a realistic appraisal of endemic abuse (Kelly, 1988; Hanmer and Saunders, 1984; Russell, 1984; Stanko, 1985). More important, feminists have located women's experiences of violence within a continuum of unsafety (Stanko, 1990). This has resulted in women's restricted use of public space (Valentine, 1989; Pain, 1993) and in creative strategies women use to protect themselves in public (Gardener, 1980, 1988, 1990). Pain terms the psychological impact of women's fear of crime as the "sharp end of patriarchal control" (1993:117).

The frame of femininity contextualizes women's lives as enveloped by men's violence. Thus, as MacKinnon (1982) has suggested, to be a woman means "to be rapable." Using the frame of gender, women's lives and their experiences of violence reflect the context of their subordinate position to men. The reality of women's experience of violence is profoundly affected by their experiences of violence at the hands of men. For women the meaning of violence is interwoven with their experiences of *being women.* Any violence prevention work must address the issue of women's subordination as key to understanding why and how women view sexual integrity at risk in Western societies. Institutional reforms must be examined for the subtle ways subordination of women is maintained through the practice of law, through the discretionary decisions of its employees, and through social policies that purport to be "gender-neutral" (see, for example, Matoesian, 1993).

This does not mean, though, that women do not commit violence. Indeed there is a strong need to understand why women use violence themselves and what this use of violence means. When women are violent, the targets of their actions are often their violent spouses, the children under their care, and other women (the confrontational type of violence so characteristic of men's relationships to other men). Explanations for women's violence emphasize the biological (often characterized as hormonal) or the psychological roots of women's aberrant behaviour. Violence, according to these perspectives, is just not "feminine". As Heidensohn (1985) observes, the social control of women is largely successful, but when women are violent, they somehow are imperfectly feminine. (In contrast, "hardmen" and "badasses" are part of the continuum of "normal" masculinities.)

As suggested earlier, "criminal" men use violence as part of the inner workings of the informal economy. Although some women survive within the informal economy, such as acting as drug dealers or prostitutes, they are by no means equal participants (Hobbs, 1994; Maher and Curtis, 1992); nor are they liberated women. Nowhere has the vilification of women as violent offenders been stronger than in the public debate about "crack mothers" in the United States. In a challenging and illuminating article, Maher and Curtis (1992) place women within systems of subordination of gender, the informal economy, and the labor market. The influx of women into prison under convictions for violence and/or drugs has led policymakers to wonder about women's increasing criminality. In an analysis of the crack trade in Brooklyn, of public sites of the "clean-up campaign" in New York City's war on drugs, the authors demonstrate how so-called crack moms endure poverty, racism, lack of access to adequate health care and housing are barely surviving via the informal economy. Curtis and Maher conclude that policymakers have been hunting women drug users/sellers as a ploy to demonstrate the seriousness of government's "war on drugs". The authors say:

> The connection between either emancipation or crack cocaine and women's "criminality" and violence is revealed as simplistic and a contextual. ...To assume that the complexity of women's [or men's] lives—including their crimes, violence, and drug taking—exists in a singular monocausal relationship to biology, psychology or pharmacology that can be "read off" aggregate indices is simply to miss the point. (Maher and Curtis, 1992:250)

No doubt some women are violent—dangerous to themselves and others. Yet women's dangerousness is most likely to be directed to those closest to them, and as all the evidence indicates, when women are fighting for their own lives, it is hardly surprising that sometimes they kill their abusers. What is amazing is that they do not kill more of them.

Normal Violence, Criminal Violence

By all accounts, violence is largely normalized as a routine part of many people's life histories. We have even given names to specific kinds of violence: domestic violence, bullying, hate crime, homophobic violence, racial violence, religious intolerance, random attack, "drive-by" shootings, and many others. A few random killers even proclaim that murder serves to signify the "right to life." We seek "to reduce violence," as if, by a wave of the magic wand, we can devise a strategic plan that will erase hatred, subordination, and vulnerability. We like to characterize violence and the fear of violence as a problem of vulner-able groups (see also Pain, 1993).

My theoretical perspective combines an interrogation of the everyday, often hidden (yet very apparent), features of the experiences of violence with structural parameters of gender power. Complexities of hegemonic masculinity (see Connell, 1987) impinge on the lives of both women and men, and a study of violence helps make the impact of patriarchal power and structures visible.

Despite the high pitch of angst and concern about the decline of the West indicative in fear of criminal violence, public policy continues to overlook the major structural contributors to unsafety: economic uncertainty and exploitation and social and gender subordination. We overlook the violence of the informal economy because we assume that "those people" deserve what they get. So drug dealers, prostitutes, marginally employed illegal immigrants, protection racketeers, and gang members may well use violence with impunity against each other. But as soon as it "gets out of line", moral panic about the rise in violence skyrockets. Normal citizens buy guns, only to find that these weapons are most dangerous for the family members the gun was allegedly meant to protect (Kellerman and Mercy, 1992). Others buy guard dogs, who also pose the most danger to family and neighbors. Still others may use personal alarms or other protective devices to ward off danger. Even if this type of technology works, it does so by displacing the danger onto others more vulnerable.

Our characterization of violence, and its meaning for women and for men, is faulty. We distance ourselves from the greatest harm—abuse and violence from known others—preferring to wax lyrical about the importance of traditional values to restore civility into what appears to be the jungles of the street. As I have suggested elsewhere, we choose to locate our anxieties away from ourselves:

> We gather our knowledge of danger and of violence in private, yet it is in the public domain that the thinking about crime and violence takes place. The public debate about crime, in too many respects, wrongly silences our private understandings abou personal danger. And the way in which anxiety about safety is publicly expressed serves to separate the fear of crime from our private knowledge about danger. For despite the clear evidence that the risk of inter-personal violence is overwhelmingly from those near and dear to us, we all seem to worry about threats from strangers. (Stanko 1990:145).

So how are we to inform public policy in order that we might begin to minimize the violence within our midst?

The Challenge of Change: Policy to Practice

To understand the meaning of ordinary violence and to explore how the definitions of criminal violence are distorted versions of *normal* violence, we must use the lens of gender. Women and men are significantly affected by the way they, and others, envision appropriately feminine and correspondingly masculine behavior. Any public policy to reduce violence must be acutely sensitive to the way gender articulates the meaning and the experience of committing and/or experiencing violence.

To focus on the reduction of criminal violence is to surely miss most of what happens to people and how, people understand where, how and why violence occurs. Feminists broke the silence about how women experience sexual and physical assault as an extension of heterosexuality: the "sharp end of patriarchy" (Pain, 1993). For men, the sharp end is killing them as well, for the adaptation of masculinities within exploited economic conditions leads to very dangerous conditions indeed. While we continue to distance ourselves (the alleged middle-class "respectability"), the emergence of "hardmen" is having devastating consequences, particularly in inner-city America. The strength of the drug economy and informal, often illegal, employment create conditions where negotiating business includes negotiating violence. In the home, we have plenty of evidence that microsocial gender power is achieved through directed violence toward wives/partners.

Moreover, as Davis (1990) so eloquently describes in his rich description of the development of Los Angeles as a city of fear, the participation of the police in the provision of safety is constantly diminished. Violence minimization, Davis so argues, cannot be achieved by a police force that itself fears violence. As a result, poor communities are left to "police" themselves, as women are left to fend off men's violence in private. Indeed, the police are active participants in keeping some young men, and in particular young African-American (in the United States) and African-Caribbean (in Britain) men, under surveillance as a form of social control. The failure to recognize structural features that support and legitimate violence, such as the ideologies of dominance found in asymmetrical relations of power molded through hierarchies of gender, race, class, and so forth, allows micropolitics of domination to continue unimpeded.

Violence minimization must begin with a recognition of the typical forms of violence, previously masked by theory blind to the impact of gender and structural exploitation. Violence has many uses: to control women, to police the informal economy, to cordon off the poor from middle-class America, to attain a sense of manliness that eschews vulnerability.

Violence and intimidation work because as a society we do not take collective responsibility for it—we blame it on individuals. At least the feminist communities, with their networks of shelters and rape crisis centers, attempt to intervene on collective bases in the daily devastation of men's violence to women. Locking men up in prison individualizes the problem and the solution. But I see no other collective strategies being devised. All the policies are directed to individually devised, individually executed negotiations of violence, assisted by technology and private investment. For example, some may purchase a mobile telephone to make contact with help in the event of encountering danger; some may move to "safer" neighbourhoods to avoid encountering the drug sellers or the violence that spills over from the informal economy and the tensions of negotiating the street. Some alter their movements in public to avoid notice. Battered women change their domestic habits to minimize the ire of their husbands/partners.

Until there is recognition of the collective nature of individual events of violence, we will not move forward on minimizing it. Doing so means using a multiple-front, collective response that takes seriously how violence is interpreted and understood by women and men alike. But it also means adopting a theoretical perspective that treats gender as a master status and advocates using a methodological approach that interrogates the everyday meaning of violence as it is produced, interpreted, codified, and resisted by women and men throughout their daily lives. In effect, criminology's view of violence has for too long been blinded by moral, patriarchal, racist, and economic ideologies that have privileged a particular view about what is criminal violence—unprovoked violence that happens between strangers. As feminist research has illustrated, such a view misses the majority of what threatens and harms women. And as I and others (Polk 1994) argue, much of what harms men is sorely missed as well.

Notes

1. When such violence is the target of commentary or resarch it is often dismissed as the complaints of "radicals" and not those who uphold the legitimacy of the state.

2. Many of the acts of systematic torture and rape are examples of unspeakable pain. Whether there will be criminal trials for war crimes remains to be seen.

3. Assaults on staff have risen from 1,750 in 1989/1990 to 2,887 in 1993/1994. Attacks on inmates are up from 1,932 to 2,236. One in nine prison officers were assaulted in 1993 (*The Guardian*, March 14, 1994).

References

Bumgarden, M. P. 1992. "The Myth of Discretion" In K. Hawkins (ed.), *The Uses of Discretion* Oxford: Clarendon Press.

Centers for Disease Control. 1992. "The Prevention of Violence: Position Paper From the Third National Injury Control Conference." H.S. Department of Health and Human Services. Atlanta, Georgia, April.

Cohen, Lawrence., and Marcus Felson. 1979. "Social Change and Crime Rate Trends: A Routine Activity Approach." *American Sociological Review* 44:588-608.

Connell, Robert. 1987. *Gender and Power.* Palo Alto, CA: Stanford University Press.

———. 1991. "Live Fast and Die Young: The Construction of Masculinity Among Young Working-Class Men on the Margin of the Labour Market." *Australian and New Zealand Journal of Sociology* 27(2):141-171.

Cretney, Antonia, Gsyan Davis, C. Clarkson, and Jon Shepherd. 1994. "Criminalizing Assault: The Failure of the 'Offence Against Society' Model."' *British Journal of Criminology* 34(1):15-30.

Daly, Kathleen. 1994. "Celebrated Crime Cases and the Public's Imagination: From Bad Press to Bad Policy.", Paper delivered to the Australian and New Zealand Society of Criminology, Sydney, September.

Daly, Martin, and Margo Wilson. 1988. *Homicide.* New York: Aldine de Gruyter.

Davis, Mike. 1990. *City of Quartz.* London: Vintage.

Dobash, R. E., and R. P. Dobash. 1979. *Violence Against Wives.* New York: Free Press.

———. 1992. *Women, Violence and Social Change.* London: Routledge.

Ellis, Desmond. 1994. "Marital Violence: Sexual Symmetry and Asymmetry Among Separating Couples." Unpublished paper, LaMarsh Centre on the Study of Violence, University of Toronto.

Felson, Marcus. 1994. *Crime and Everyday Life.* Thousand Oaks, CA: Pine Forge Press.

Frohmann, Lisa. 1991. "Discrediting Victims' Allegations of Sexual Assault." *Social Problems* 38(2):213-226.

Gardener, Carol Brooks. 1980. "Passing-By: Street Remarks, Address Rights and the Urban Female." *Sociological Inquiry* 50(3-4):328-356.

———. 1988. "Access Information: Public Lies and Private Peril." *Social Problems* 35(4):384-397.

———. 1990. "Safe Conduct: Women, Crime and Self in Public Places." *Social Problems* 37(3):311-328.

Gibbs, Jewelle T., and Josheph Merighi. 1994. "Young Black Males: Marginality, Masculinity and Criminality." In Tim Newburn and Elizabeth Stanko (eds.), *Just Boys Doing Business?* London: Routledge.

Godenzi, Alberto. 1994. "What's the Big Deal: We Are Men and They Are Women."In Tim Newburn and Elizabeth Stanko (eds.), *Just Boys Doing Business?* London: Routledge.

Gordon, Margaret, and Stephanie Riger. 1988. *The Female Fear.* New York: Free Press.

Hanmer, John, and Shelia Saunders. 1984. *Well-Founded Fear.* London: Hutchinson.

Hearn, Jeff. 1993. "How Men Talk About Men's Violence to Known Women." Paper presented to the Masculinities and Crime Conference, Brunel University.

Heidensohn, Francis. 1985. *Women and Crime.* London: Macmillan.

Hindelang, Michael, Michael Gottfredson, and James Garofalo. 1978. *Victims of Personal Crime.* Cambridge, MA: Ballinger.

Hobbs, Dick. 1994. "Mannish Boys: Danny, Chris, Crime, Masculinity and Business. In Tim Newburn and Elizabeth Stanko eds.), *Just Boys Doing Business?* London: Routledge.

Hoff, Lee A. 1990. *Battered Women as Survivors.* London: Routledge.

Hough, Mike, and Pat Mayhew. 1983. *The British Crime Survey*. London: HMSO.

———. 1985. *Taking Account of Crime: Key Findings from the 1984 British Crime Survey*. London: HMSO.

Katz, Jack. 1988. *Seductions of Crime: Moral and Sensual Attractions in Doing Evil*. New York: Basic Books.

Keith, Michael. 1994. *Race, Riots, and Policing*. London: University of London Press.

Kellerman, A.L. and James A. Mercy. 1992. "Men, Women, and Murder: Gender Specific Differences in Rates of Fatal Violence and Victimization."*The Journal of Trauma* 33:1-5.

Kelly, Liz. 1988. *Surviving Sexual Violence*. Oxford: Polity.

Levi, Mike. 1994. "Violent Crime."in M. Maguire, R. Morgan and R. Reiner (eds.), *The Oxford Handbook of Criminology*. Oxford: Oxford University Press.

Luckenbill, David. F. 1977. "Criminal Homicide as a Situated Transaction." *Social Problems* 26:176-186.

MacKinnon, Catherine. 1982. "Feminism, Marxism, Method and the State: Toward a Feminist Jurisprudence." *Signs: Journal of Women in Culture and Society* 84:635-658.

———. 1989. *Toward a Feminist Theory of the State*. Cambridge: Cambridge University Press.

Maher, Lisa, and Robert Curtis. 1992 "Women on the Edge of Crime: Crack Cocaine and the Changing Contexts of Street-Level Sex Work in New York City." *Crime, Law, and Social Change* 18:221-258.

Matoesian, Greg. 1993. *Reproducing Rape:Domination through Talk in the Courtroom*. Cambridge: Polity.

Mayhew, Pat, Lizanne Dowds, and David Elliot. 1989. *The 1988 British Crime Survey* London: HMSO.

Mayhew, Pat, Natalie Maung, and Catriona Mirrlees-Black. 1993. *The 1992 British Crime Survey*. London: HMSO.

Messerschmidt, James. 1993. *Masculinities and Crime*. Lanham, MD:Rowman & Littlefield.

Myers, Melanie. 1994. "Felony Killings and Prosecutions for Murder Exploring the Tension Between Culpability and Consequences in the Criminal law." *Social & Legal Studies* 31:149-179.

Pain, Rachel. 1993. "Crime, Social Control and Spatial Constraint: A Study of Women's fear of sexual violence." Ph.D. thesis, University of Edinburgh.

Pearson, Geoffrey. 1983. *Hooligans*. London: Macmillan.

Polk, Kenneth. 1994. "Masculinity, Honour and Confrontational Homicide."in Tim Newburn and Elizabeth Stanko (eds.), *Just Boys Doing Business?* London: Routledge.

Russell, Diana E. H. 1982. *Rape in Marriage*. New York: Free Press.

———. 1984. *Sexual Exploitation*. Beverly Hills, CA: Sage.

Schwartz, Martin D., and Walter S. DeKeseredy. 1993. "The Return of the 'Battered Husband Syndrome' Through the Typification of Women as Violent." *Crime, Law, and Social Change* 20:249-265.

Segal, Lynn. 1990. *Slow Motion*. London: Virago.

Seidler, V. 1991. *Recreating Sexual Politics*. London: Routledge.

Shepherd, Jon. 1990 "Violent Crime in Bristol:An Accident and Emergency Department Perspective." *British Journal of Criminology* 303:289-305.

Sim, Joe. 1994 "Tougher than the Rest." in Tim Newburn and Elizabeth Stanko (eds.), *Just Boys Doing Business?* London: Routledge.

Simon, Jonathan. 1988. "The Ideological Effect of Actuarial Practices." *Law & Society Review* 22:771-800.

Skogan, Wesley, and Michael Maxfield. 1982. *Coping with Crime.* London: Sage.

Smart, Carol. 1989. *Feminism and the Power of Law.* London: Routledge.

Stanko, Elizabeth. 1977. *These Are The Cases That Try Themselves.* Ph.D. thesis, City University of New York Graduate School.

———. 1985. *Intimate Intrusions.* London: Routledge.

———. 1987. "Typical Violence, Normal Precaution: Men, Women, and Interpersonal Violence in England, Wales, Scotland, and the USA." In John Hanmer and Sheila Maynard (eds.), *Women, Violence, and Social Change.* London: Macmillan.

———. 1990. *Everyday Violence.* New York: Pandora.

———. 1994. "Challenging the Problem of Individual Men's Violence." In Tim Newburn and Elizabeth Stanko (eds.), *Just Boys Doing Business?* London:Routledge.

———. 1995 "Women, crime and fear." *Annals of the American Society of Political and Social Science.* In press.

Stanko, Elizabeth, and K. Hobdell. 1993. "Assault on Men." *British Journal of Criminology* 333:400-415.

Statistics Canada. 1994. "Wife Assault: The Findings of a National Survey." *Juristat Service Bulletin* 14.

Stevens, David J. 1994. "The Depth of Imprisonment and Prisonization: Levels of Security and Prisoners' Anticipation of Future Violence." *The Howard Journal of Criminal Justice* 332:137-157.

Straus, Murray A. and Richard J. Gelles. 1990. *Physical Violence in American Families.* New Brunswick, NJ: Transaction.

Valentine, Gill. 1989. "The Geography of Women's Fear." *Area* 214:385-390.

Warr, Mark. 1985. "Fear of Rape among Urban Women." *Social Problems* 323:238-250.

Zorza, Joan. 1992. "The Criminal Law of Misdemeanor Domestic Violence, 1970-1990." *The Journal of Criminal Law and Criminology* 83:46-72.

13

Repressive Crime Control and Male Persistent Thieves

Neal Shover and Belinda Henderson

The 1970s were marked by dramatic changes in the way political leaders and elite academicians interpreted and talked about crime. One indication of this was declining support for labeling theory as the dominant theoretical interpretation of criminal behavior. Labeling theory placed squarely on the shoulders of the state and its social control apparatus part of the responsibility for individual persistence in deviance and criminality. Formal processing by agencies such as the police and courts, it predicted, exacerbates the problems offenders encounter when they try to make a clean break with their past. For this and other reasons as well, official intervention in miscreants' lives may increase the odds of further criminal behavior.

Labeling theory's loss of favor was followed by the reappearance of explanations for crime originally advanced by classical criminological theorists. Economists and cognitive psychologists along with many in the criminological mainstream advanced an interpretation of crime as *choice*, offering models of criminal decisionmaking grounded in the assumption that the decision to commit a criminal act springs from the offender's assessment of available options and their net payoffs (e.g., Becker, 1968; Heineke, 1978; Carroll, 1978; Reynolds, 1985; Roshier, 1989). Empirically, crime-as-choice interpretations of offending focus attention on offenders' perceptions of threats, their estimates of rewards and risks associated with their behavioral options, and how they decide to commit crime or to select specific targets.

One result of the crime-as-choice movement is growing empirical interest in offender decision-making, particularly by *persistent thieves*. These offenders commit robberies, burglaries, and acts of theft, the crimes that invariably and immediately come to mind when the subject of crime is raised in conversation or is featured in the media. Persistent thieves are those who despite having at least one adult conviction for robbery, burglary, or theft return to further crime commission. Many of them commit crime over several years and serve multiple jail or prison terms in the process. This chapter begins with a review of research on persistent thieves' crime-commission decisionmaking. Then we describe some social psychological impacts of imprisonment, including both an increase in offenders' rationality and, paradoxically, a tendency in the short run to see arrest and reckoning as minimal threats. We conclude, first, by noting the policy initiatives that were spawned by the crime-as-choice ideology and, second, by suggesting that manipulating the schedule of prison years threatened for designated crimes probably is a crude and clumsy tool for fighting persistent thieves. We suggest that less attention be focused on increasing the risk of crime and more on raising estimates of the payoffs from conforming behavior.

Decisionmaking and Life-Style

A growing and methodologically diverse corpus of research on crime-commission decisionmaking by persistent thieves has produced a clear and uncontested description of it. In 1983, investigators from the University of Massachusetts conducted a ten-state survey of prison inmates. In self-administered confidential surveys, the prisoners were asked how often they "personally thought about" the possibility "that [they] might get caught when [they] were getting ready to do a crime." Of the 1,038 men who were serving a prison sentence for armed robbery, burglary, auto theft, theft, or any combination of these offenses, 47 percent answered "seldom" or "never" (Wright and Rossi, 1985:96). When they were questioned specifically about the crime for which they were serving time, 72 percent said they were not worried about getting caught at the time they committed it (Wright and Rossi, 1985:55). Data collected from 83 imprisoned burglars revealed that 49 percent did not think about the chances of getting caught for any particular offense during their last period of offending. Although 37 percent of them did think about it, most thought there was little or no chance it would happen (Bennett and Wright, 1984a:Table A14). Interviews with 113 men convicted of robbery or an offense related to robbery revealed that "over 60 percent...said they had not even thought about getting caught." Another 17 percent said that they had thought about the possibility but "did not believe it to be a problem" (Feeney, 1986:59-60). Prison interviews with 77 robbers and 45 burglars likewise revealed their "general obliviousness toward the consequences [of their crimes] and no thought of being caught" (Walsh, 1986:157). An informant who was interviewed for the University of Tennessee Desistance Project[1] commented that "you don't think about getting caught, you think about how in hell you're going to do it *not* to get caught, you know." His comments were echoed by another informant who said, "The only thing you're thinking about is looking and acting and trying *not* to get caught."

None of this means that offenders are indifferent to the possibility of arrest: "I wasn't afraid of getting caught, but I was cautious, you know. Like I said, I was thinking only in the way to prevent me from getting caught." Another informant, interviewed following his release from prison, was questioned about a crime he committed years earlier:

Q: Were you thinking about bad things that might happen to you?
A: None whatsoever.
Q: No?
A: I wasn't worried about getting caught or anything, you know. I was a positive thinker through everything, you know. I didn't have no negative thoughts about it whatsoever.

Even on the occasions when they do reflect beforehand on the possibility of arrest, persistent thieves usually manage to dismiss legal threats easily and carry through with their plans. Data from interviews with thieves and former thieves are consistent:

Q: Did you worry much about getting caught? On a scale of one to ten, how would you rank your degree of worry that day?
A: [T]he worry was probably a one. You know what I mean? The worry was probably one. I didn't think about the consequences, you know. I know it's stupidity, but it didn't—that [I] might go to jail, I mean—it crossed my mind but it didn't make much difference.

Clearly, one of the most striking aspects of decisionmaking by persistent thieves is that nearly one-half or more give little or no thought to the possibility of arrest and confinement when deciding whether to commit criminal acts. Indeed, many are remarkably casual in weighing the formal risks of arrest and imprisonment. As an informant put it, "You think about going to prison about like you think about dying, you know."

One reason so little attention is paid to the risk of arrest is that many offenders determine deliberately and consciously to put out of mind all thoughts of it. Interview and observational data collected on 105 active residential burglars showed that they consciously employed decisionmaking techniques that allowed them to neutralize fear of sanctions. "The most common involved a steadfast refusal to dwell on the possibility of being apprehended" (Wright and Decker, 1994:127). Ethnographic interview data collected on formerly imprisoned persistent thieves paint a similar picture:

Q: Did you think about [the possibility of getting caught] very much that night?
A: I didn't think about it that much, you know....[I]t comes but, you know,

you can wipe it away.

Q: How do you wipe it away?

A: You just blank it out. You blank it out.

Another informant told us simply, "I try to put that [thought of arrest] the farthest thing from my mind that I can."

In 1978, the Rand Corporation conducted a three-state survey of 2,190 jail and prison inmates. Subjects were questioned about how they committed crimes in the period before their arrest and confinement. Forty-seven percent of the 1,199 men accused or convicted of robbery, burglary, theft, or auto theft said they "never" or only "sometimes" "worked out a plan" before they went out to do crimes (Peterson, Chaiken, and Ebener, 1984:105). Asked how much time they "usually" spent planning their crimes, 47 percent of the thieves in the University of Massachusetts survey responded they usually did not plan "at all" (Wright and Rossi, 1985:95). This suggests, and interviews confirm, that even on the occasions when they successfully avoid arrest, the criminal planning and follow-through of most persistent thieves have a distinct improvisational quality.

One of the most important reasons persistent thieves do not think about or plan their crimes carefully is because a high proportion of them are under the influence of alcohol or other drugs at the time. University of Massachusetts investigators found that 55 percent of the 1,038 inmates serving time for robbery, burglary, automobile theft, or theft were "drunk" or "high on drugs" when they committed the crime for which they were serving time (Wright and Rossi, 1985). Alcohol and other drugs affect offenders' decisionmaking, typically by simplifying both deliberation of options and the weighing of alternatives (Bennett and Wright, 1984b; Cordilia, 1985).

Drug use by persistent thieves typically occurs in a social context with the result that group dynamics also can affect decisionmaking (Cordilia, 1986). The experience is encapsulating in the sense that it pushes members' extrasituational identities and concerns to the background of attention (Lemert, 1967). After a few hours together consuming alcohol or smoking marijuana, men who scarcely know one another may come to feel they are the best of friends and be willing to do nearly anything to ensure that the camaraderie and good feelings do not end prematurely. This can cause them "to focus on the proximate reward of group cohesion and to be less aware of the longer-term negative consequences" of their actions (Cordilia, 1985:170). The effects of drugs and the social psychological effects of group identity and participation not only diminish offenders' reasoning ability but also erode their willingness to decline participation in group projects, criminal though they be.

Instead of paying close attention to the potential negative consequences of their actions and planning carefully so as to improve their odds as much as possible, persistent thieves generally focus their thoughts on the money that committing a crime may yield and how they plan to use it when the crime is behind them. In 1976, the Rand Corporation surveyed 624 prisoners in five California prisons to identify factors that explain their rate of offending prior to imprisonment (i.e., the number of crimes per month). After analyzing data on prisoners' perceptions of the likely costs and rewards of criminal participation, the investigators concluded: "[R]espondents who were most certain in reporting that they would be arrested or otherwise suffer for crime did not report committing fewer crimes. Rather,...individual offense rates are related only to offenders' perceptions of the benefits to be derived from crime" (Peterson, Braiker, and Polich, 1981:xxvi). The results from studies of decisionmaking in which other methodologies were used are consistent. And in a study in which subjects were asked to rank the importance in decisionmaking of four dimensions of potential targets, the amount of gain offenders expected to receive was "the most important dimension" whereas the certainty of punishment was ranked as least important (Carroll, 1982). Evidence from offenders' first-person accounts is consistent also:

I didn't think about nothing but what I was going to do when I got that money, how I was going to spend it, what I was going to do with it, you know.

See, you're not thinking about those things [possibility of being arrested]. You're thinking about that big pay check at the end of thirty to forty-five minutes worth of work.

At the time [that you commit crime], you throw all your instincts out the window. ...Because you're just thinking about money, and money only. That's all that's on your mind, because you want that money. And you throw, you block everything off until you get the money.

Although no one disputes that persistent thieves engage in some process of calculation before committing crime, it is obvious they are a long way from being patient and thorough decisionmakers. Further, they weigh utilities different from the ones assumed by many policy promoters who look to crime-as-choice for ideological support. As Dermot Walsh (1980:141) points out, offenders' "definitions of costs and rewards seem to be at variance with society's estimates of them."

Life as Party

An enhanced understanding of criminal decisionmaking can be gained if we examine it in the context of the lifestyle characteristic of many persistent thieves: *life as party*. The hallmark of this life-style is enjoyment of "good times" with minimal concern for obligations and commitments that are external to the person's immediate social setting. It is distinguished in many cases by two repetitively cyclical phases and correspondingly distinctive approaches to crime. When offenders' efforts to maintain the life-style (i.e., their party pursuits) are largely successful, crimes are committed in order to sustain circumstances or a pattern of activities they experience as pleasurable. As Walsh (1986:15) puts it, crimes committed under these circumstances are "part of a continuing satisfactory way of life." By contrast, when offenders are less successful at party pursuits, their crimes are committed in order to forestall or avoid circumstances experienced as threatening, unpleasant, or precarious. Corresponding to each of these two phases of party pursuits is a distinctive set of utilities and stance toward legal risk.

Persistent thieves spend much of their criminal gains on alcohol and other drugs (Petersilia, Greenwood, and Lavin, 1978; Maguire, 1982; Gibbs and Shelley, 1982; Figgie International, 1988; Cromwell, Olson, and Avery, 1991). Their criminal proceeds, as Walsh has noted (1986:72), "typically [are] used for personal, non-essential consumption (e.g., 'nights out'), rather than, for example, to be given to family or used for basic needs." Interviews with 30 active Texas burglars revealed, for example, that they "stressed need for money to fulfill expressive needs as the primary motivation for their criminal behavior. Only one informant reported a primary need for money to purchase something other than alcohol or drugs or for partying" (Cromwell et al., 1991:21). Thieves spend much of their leisure hours enjoying good times.

Because it is enjoyed in the company of others, life as party generally includes shared consumption of alcohol or other drugs in bars and lounges, on street corners, or while cruising in automobiles. In these venues, party pursuers celebrate and affirm values of spontaneity, independence, and resourcefulness. Spontaneity means that rationality and long-range planning are eschewed in favor of enjoying the moment and permitting the day's activities and pleasures to develop in an unconstrained fashion. This may mean, for example, getting up late, usually after a night of partying, and then setting out to contact and enjoy the company of friends and associates who are known to be predisposed to partying.

Party pursuits also appeal to offenders because they permit conspicuous display of independence (Persson, 1981). This generally means avoidance of the world of routine work and freedom from being "under someone's thumb." It also may include being free to avoid or to escape from restrictive routines: "I just wanted to be doing something. Instead of being at home, or something like that. I wanted to be running, I wanted to be going to clubs, and picking up women, and shooting pool. And I liked to go to [a nearby resort community] and just drive around over there. A lot of things like that. ...I was drinking two pints or more a day. ...I was doing Valiums and I was doing Demerol. ...I didn't want to work."

The proper pursuit and enjoyment of life as party is expensive, largely because of the cost of drugs. As one subject remarked: "We was doing a lot of cocaine, so cash didn't last long, you know. If we made $3,000, two thousand of it almost instantly went for cocaine." A portion of their income may be used for ostentatious display and enjoyment of luxury items or activities that probably would be unattainable on the returns from blue-collar employment.

Given the expenses involved, life as party requires continuous infusions of money and no single method of generating funds allows enjoyment of it for more than a few days. Consequently, the emphasis on spontaneity and independence is matched by the importance attached to financial resourcefulness. This is evidenced by the ability to sustain the life-style over a period of time. Doing so earns for offenders a measure of respect from peers for their demonstrated ability to "get over," and it translates into "self-esteem...as a folk hero beating the bureaucratic system of routinized dependence" (Walsh, 1986:16). The value of and respect for those who demonstrate resourcefulness means that criminal acts, as a means of sustaining life as party, generally are not condemned by the offender's peers.

The risks of employing criminal solutions to the need for funds are approached blithely but confidently in the same spontaneous and playful manner as are the rewards of life as party. The interaction that precedes criminal incidents is distinguished by circumspection and the use of linguistic devices that relegate risk and fear to the background of attention. The act of stealing, for example, is referred to obliquely but knowingly as "doing something" or as "making money":

Q: Okay. So, then you and this fellow met up in the bar...Tell me about the conversation?

A: Well, there wasn't much of a conversation to it, really...I asked him if he was ready to go, if he wanted to go do something, you know. And he knew what I meant. He wanted to go make some money somehow, any way it took.

To the external observer, inattention to risk at the moment when it would seem most appropriate may seem to border on irrationality. For the offender engaged in party pursuits, however, it is but one aspect of behaviors that are rational in other respects. It opens up opportunities to enjoy life as party and to demonstrate commitment to values shared by peers. Resourcefulness and disdain for conventional rationality also affirm individual character and style, both of which are important in the world of party pursuits.

Party Pursuits and Eroding Resources

Paradoxically, the pursuit of life as party can be appreciated and enjoyed to the fullest extent only if participants moderate their involvement in it while maintaining identities and routines in the straight world. Doing so maintains its "escape value" but it also requires an uncommon measure of discipline and forbearance. Extended and enthusiastic enjoyment of life as party threatens constantly to deplete irrevocably the resources needed to sustain enjoyment of its pleasures. Some offenders become ensnared increasingly by the chemical substances and drug-using routines that are common there. In doing so, the meaning of drug consumption changes. Once the party pursuer's physical or psychological tolerance increases significantly, drugs are consumed not for the high they once produced but instead to maintain á sense of normality by avoiding sickness or withdrawal.

Party pursuits also erode legitimate fiscal and social capital. They cannot be sustained by legitimate employment and they may in fact undermine both one's ability and inclination to hold a job. Even if offenders are willing to work at the kinds of employment available to them, and evidence suggests that many are not, the physical demands of work and party pursuits conflict (Cromwell, Olson, and Avery, 1991). Few men can spend their nights drinking and playing in bars and routinely and predictably arise early the next morning for work. The best times of the day for committing many property crimes also are the times the offender would be at work; days spent searching for suitable businesses to rob or homes to burglarize cannot be spent at work. It is nearly impossible to do both consistently and well. For those who pursue life as party, legitimate employment often is foregone or sacrificed (Rengert and Wasilchick, 1985). The absence of income from noncriminal sources thus reinforces the need to find other sources of money.

Determined pursuit of life as party also may affect participants' relationships with legitimate significant others. Many offenders manage to enjoy the life-style successfully only by exploiting the concern and largesse of family and friends. This may take the form of repeated requests for and receipt of personal loans that go unreturned, occasional thefts, or other forms of exploitation. Eventually, friends and even family members may come to believe that they have been exploited or that continued assistance will only prolong a process that must be terminated. As one subject told us, "Oh, I tried to borrow money, and borrow money and, you know, nobody would loan it to me. Because they knew what I was doing." After first refusing further assistance, acquaintances, friends, and even family members may avoid social contacts with the party pursuer or sever ties altogether.

Finally, when party pursuits are not going well, feelings of shame and self-disgust are not uncommon (Frazier and Meisenhelder, 1985). As a result, unsuccessful party pursuers may take steps to reduce these feelings by distancing themselves voluntarily from conventional others. When party pursuers sustain severe losses of legitimate income and social resources, regardless of how it occurs, they grow increasingly isolated from conventional significant others. By reducing interpersonal constraints on their behavior, this simplifies and facilitates criminal decisionmaking.

As their pursuit of life as party increasingly assumes qualities of difficulty and struggle, offenders' utilities and risk perceptions also change. Increasingly, crimes are committed not to enhance or sustain the life-style so much as to forestall unpleasant circumstances. Those addicted to alcohol or other drugs, for example, must devote increasing time and energy to the quest for monies to purchase their chemicals of choice. Both their drug consumption and the frequency of their criminal acts increase (Ball, Schaffer, and Nurco, 1983; Johnson et al., 1985). For them, as for others, the inability to draw on legitimate or low risk resources eventually may precipitate a crisis. An informant told of a time when, facing a court appearance on a burglary charge, he needed funds to hire an attorney:

> I needed some money bad or if I didn't, if I went to court the following day,...the judge was going to lock me up. Because I didn't have no lawyer. And I had went and talked to several lawyers and they told me...they wanted a thousand dollars, that if I couldn't come up with no thousand dollars, they couldn't come to court with me. ...So I went to my sister. I asked my sister, I said, "look here, what about letting me have seven or eight hundred dol-lars ."...And she said, "well, if I give you the money you won't do the right thing with it." And I was telling her, "no, no, I need a lawyer." But I couldn't convince her to let me have the money. So I left. ...I said, shit, I'm fixin' to go back to jail. ...So as I left her house and was walking—I was going to catch the bus—the [convenience store] and bus stop was right there by each other. So, I said I'm going to buy me some gum. ...And in the process of me buying the chewing gum, I seen two ladies, they was counting money. So I figured sooner or later one of them was going to come out with the money. ...I waited on them until...one came out with the money, and I got it.

Confronted by crisis and preoccupied increasingly with relieving immediate distress, offenders eventually may define themselves and their experiences as propelled by forces beyond their control. Behavioral options become dichotomized into those that hold out some possibility of relief, however risky, and those that promise little but continued pain. Legitimate options are few and are seen as unlikely solutions, whereas a criminal act may offer some hope of relief, however temporary. Acts that once were the result of blithe unconcern with risk can over time come to be based on a personal determination to master or reverse what is experienced as desperately unpleasant circumstances. As a result, inattention to risk in the offender's decisionmaking may give way to the perception that he has *nothing to lose*: "It...gets to the point that you get into such a desperation. You're not working, you can't work. You're drunk as hell, been that way two or three weeks. You're no good to yourself, and you're no good to anybody else. Self-esteem is gone [and] spiritually, mentally, physically, financially bankrupt. You ain't got nothing to lose." Desperate to maintain or reestablish a sense of normality, he pursues emotional relief with a decision to act decisively, albeit in the face of legal odds recognized as narrowing.

The threat posed by possible arrest and imprisonment, however, may not seem severe to some desperate offenders. As compared to their marginal and precarious existence, it may even be seen as offering a form of relief: "When I [got] caught—and they caught me right at the house—it's kind of like, you feel good, because you're glad it's over, you know. I mean, a weight being lifted off your head. And you say, well, I don't have to worry about this shit no more, because they've caught me. And it's over, you know."

In sum, because of offenders' eroding access to legitimately secured funds, their diminishing contact with and support from conventional significant others, and their efforts to maintain drug consumption habits, crimes that once were committed for recreational purposes increasingly become desperate attempts to forestall or reverse uncomfortable or frustrating situations. When the offender is pursuing the short term goal of maximizing enjoyment of life, legal threats can appear either as remote and improbable contingencies when party pursuits fulfill their recreational purposes or as an acceptable risk in the face of continued isolation, penury, and desperation.

The Prison Experience

Imprisonment and its potential as a crime-control strategy occupy a key place in most interpretations of crime as choice. It is argued that when the general population witnesses from afar what happens to those who are convicted and confined, the threat of incarceration deters them from offending. And for those who fail to heed the warning, a taste of "the joint" presumably deters recidivism.

Rationalization of Crime

Prison has this deterrent effect in large part because exposure to a measured dose of confinement as a response to specific criminal acts supposedly nurtures the *rationalization of crime*. This is the process by which persons develop and bring to bear in decisionmaking a more precise calculus and metric of crime and punishment. By contributing to this process, imprisonment replaces an emotion-laden and impulsive decisionmaking process with a more careful and prudent one.

Juveniles generally use minimal deliberation before committing crime. They often become involved in stealing without having developed an autonomous and rationalized set of criminal motives. Questioned retrospectively about their criminal motives when they were juveniles, forty-nine imprisoned armed robbers reported using little or no sophistication in planning the offenses they committed Juveniles often commit offenses for "expressive" reasons such as hostility, revenge, thrills, or peer influence (Petersilia, Greenwood, and Lavin,

1978:60-65, and 76). The result is that the potential repercussions of crime to some extent are blunted. Juveniles neither possess nor bring to bear a precise, consistent metric for assessing the potential consequences of delinquent episodes. They fail to see or to calculate carefully their potential losses if apprehended. For many youth, crime is a risk-taking activity in which the risks are only dimly appreciated or calculated.

Imprisonment is one of the most important accelerants of the rationalization of crime, the process by which it is transformed into a somewhat more calculated affair than it is for most juveniles. Imprisonment promotes criminal rationalization because, in clarifying previously inestimable variables in offender's criminal calculus, it also transforms it. In causing offenders to see more clearly that criminal definitions and crime control are rational matters, it improves their ability to calculate before acting. By familiarizing them with the definitions and penalty tables at the heart of the criminal code, imprisonment promotes a keener awareness of the potential costs of criminal behavior and a more clearly articulated understanding of the price of crime. Generally this process begins in jail and then continues in prison:

Q: Did you know of the penalties [for crime]?
A: Well once you get to prison you learn. ...You learn a lot of things in prison. What other people was doing and got caught at and stuff like that.
Q: How did you come to know about [the] penalties?
A: [From] a combination of friends being arrested...and then by me being arrested, you know. When you're in jail you learn a lot of things, you know. You've got guys—everybody has got their own problems and everybody is trying to tell you, you know, "you've got your problems, but I'm trying to tell you how I got busted and why I got busted" and what, you know, I should do. And we're exchanging views. You're tell[ing] me, "well man, here's all they can do to you is this, that and the other. Here's what they did to me on the same thing."

In the recounted experiences of fellow prisoners, they learn the range of sentences and the "going rate" for common crimes. They learn to think of the criminal code as a table of specific threats to which specific, calculable punishments are attached. Never mind that the entire criminal justice apparatus is clumsy and seemingly nonrational in *operation*, the claim of rationality that underpins and justifies it is not lost on the prisoner.

Another way that imprisonment promotes the rationalization of crime is by helping elevate *money*, the most calculable of payoffs, to the forefront of criminal motives. Prison conversations are laced with depictions of criminal acts as a means of acquiring money, perhaps even "big money." This talk is not without effect. Money increasingly assumes more importance as a criminal objective. After serving a term in the National Training School, an informant and his friends began robbing gamblers and bootleggers. I asked him,

Q: Did the desire for excitement play any part in those crimes?
A: No, I think the desire for excitement had left. It was, we recognized that it was a dangerous mission then because we knew that gamblers and bootleggers carried guns and things like that. And it was for, you know, just for the money.

And an ex-thief has written: "When I first began stealing I had but a dim realization of its wrong. I accepted it as the thing to do because it was done by the people I was with; besides, it was adventurous and thrilling. Later it became an everyday, cold-blooded business, and while I went about it methodically...I was fully aware of the gravity of my offenses" (Black, 1926:254). Young prisoners learn the importance of assessing and committing crimes on the basis of an increasingly narrow and precise metric of potential benefits and costs. In the words of one informant, "Whatever started me in crime is one thing, but at some point I know that I'm in crime for the money. There's no emotional reason for me being into crime."

The prison world is filled with talk of crime as a rational pursuit, some of it pushed by administrators and some of it by prisoners' peers. Men who are abject failures at crime talk as if they were successful and well-informed professionals. To those who do not know better, prison conversation makes criminal success seem easily attainable so long as offenders plan and execute better. Friends and other inmates generally admonish them to use their head and commit crime in ways that tip the odds in their favor—in short, to be rational about it.

One of the consequences of this is that some young prisoners come to believe crime can be both a lucrative and a low-risk enterprise so long as one is "careful." The prison experience seduces them into believing that they can avoid arrest. Those who return to stealing often do so with confidence because they now plan marginally better than in their adolescent years:

I didn't worry too much about getting caught because, like I said, I put a lot of planning and forethought into it. ...The potential gain that I saw increased substantially. The risk diminished because I was a lot more aware of my capabilities.

I was aware of what could happen now, if I got busted again, how much time that I could receive in prison by me being locked up and incarcerated that first time. ...I learned about different type crimes that would get you the most time. ...I'd always weigh my chances of being captured, being caught, and I'd always have an escape plan.

Forty-nine imprisoned armed robbers said that during their young adult years they developed a new confidence in their ability to avoid arrest for their crimes;

their concern about it declined significantly (Petersilia, Greenwood, and Lavin, 1978:69-70).

In fact as in the fantasies of prisoners, the odds of being arrested for any specific criminal act are not great (Felson, 1994). These men analyze past offenses to develop more perfect criminal techniques and success as if there is a finite, manageable number of ways a criminal act can fail. An interview with a British thief reveals this reasoning process:

Q: When you're arrested, what are your reactions at that moment
A: I think the first thing's annoyance—with myself. How could I be so stupid as to get nicked? What's gone wrong, what have I forgotten, where have I made the mistake (Parker and Allerton, 1962:149)?

Like him, some former prisoners confidently assume that once the full array of errors and "mistakes" is learned prison is a thing of the past: "Every person who ever did time can tell you what he did wrong to get caught. Every one feels that all he has to do is rectify that one mental error and he's on his way. I knew what had gone wrong in the McDonald's stickup. We hadn't planned carefully. I knew I could do it right this time" (McCall, 1994:22). Those who continue to commit crimes after their first incarceration do think about the possibility of legal sanction more than in the past and show marginally improved planning in crime commission (Petersilia, Greenwood, and Lavin, 1978:60).

If the rationalization of crime was the only consequence of imprisonment, it could be considered successful. The experiential consequences of imprisonment, however, go beyond those envisioned by most advocates of crime as choice. Given life in state programs and entrusted to bureaucracies, crime control policies often produce unplanned or unintended consequences that diminish their effectiveness. That is the case with imprisonment; Even though it makes offenders more rational about crime, it causes some to believe either that the odds of being captured may not be great or that the pain of penalty is not excessive in any case. How does this happen?

Reassurance

Despite the fact that many have previous experience with confinement as juveniles or as jail inmates, nearly all men approach with trepidation their first prison sentence. Their image of the world they are about to enter has been formed from old movies, sensationalized media reports, and jail conversations with inmates who have prison experience under their belt. Those on their way to prison for the first time see it as a test of their mettle, one they understand must be endured "like a man." Although many are confident, others fear involuntary segregation from the outside world and the violence and exploitation related in jail stories. Impending imprisonment is never experienced with greater anxiety than by the uninitiated.

Penitentiary confinement tends to polarize prisoners. Some recoil from it and resolve never again to do anything that would put them back in a similar situation. Those who can count on strong interpersonal support and respectable, well-paid employment may avoid returning to it, particularly if they lack identification with crime as a way of life. For other prisoners, however, the reaction is different. They adapt and grow acclimated to their surroundings as they learn about prison sentences, prison life-styles and the ins and outs of the correctional system (e.g., sentence reduction for "good and honor time"). Many are reassured by learning they will not have to serve their maximum sentence:

> Q: When I asked you how much time you did, you said, "Nothing, 18 months." Did that not seem like much time to you?
>
> A: I always thought it wasn't nothing because I went and did it and come on back here. But it really wasn't eighteen months, it was thirteen months and something. See, they give me eighteen months...[and] they give me so much off for good behavior. Just like this time I'm doing now. To you fifteen years would be a lot of time because you don't quite understand it. But after you get into the system here, then they give you so many points for this and so many points for that...and when you get through looking at that you really don't have to stay as long as you might think.

John Irwin (1985) has described how inmates new to the jail environment undergo several forms of adaptation that effectively decrease the shock and suffering they experience if they should be confined to jail again. Specifically, jail confinement erodes their conventional sensibilities, teaches them how to cope successfully with a depriving and dangerous environment, and acclimates them to deviant norms, adaptations, and others. What is true of the jail and its impact is true of the prison as well. Experience with it may undermine its value as a deterrent to future criminal conduct.

Conservative commentators and political leaders are quick to say that imprisonment is not meant to be a pleasant experience. And it is not, at least for the overwhelming majority of those who suffer it. Even for those who have spent more than one stint in prison, "it's a terrible thing to have to put up with" (Crookston, 1967:96). But those who discover that they can survive satisfactorily or even thrive in the prison world are changed by this realization. Surviving the prison experience teaches the important lesson that one can "handle it" (Martin and Sussman, 1994:23). Coping successfully with confinement reassures its survivors by allaying doubts and uncertainties. They now know that they can "handle" one of the harshest penalties that the state can impose on anyone. The new reassurance can lessen the perceived threat of prison life:

Q: Prison must not be much of a threat to you.

A: It's not. Prison wasn't what I thought it was.

Q: What do you mean by that?

A: When I went in,...well, at that point in time it was kind of an awful thing to go to prison. That's what I had always heard. But when I got there and then found out that "Well hell, look who is here"..."I didn't know he was here or they was here"...Then I seen that I'm a man just like they are and I can make it.

Q: What kind of effect did that first time you were incarcerated have on you?

A: I was 17 years old, and they sent me to a men's prison, you know. And I went down there, and I made it, you know. I survived it. And I come out, I thought, a man. ...It just showed me that what, you know, what I had been afraid of happening wasn't nothing to be afraid of.

The harshness of prison is diminished not only by the realization that they can do time but also by the presence in prison of friends from the streets or acquaintances from other institutions. For too many of those who pass through it once, the prison experience will leave them less fearful of and better prepared for a second trip if that should happen:

Q: Did you, did you actually think at [the time you passed forged checks] that, "hey, I could go to jail for this?"

A: I think I thought about it, but I didn't care if I went to jail. Jail was just, I was used to jail. Jail wasn't a threat to me.

Q: Before you went to prison the first time in your life, was it a threat to you?

A: Yeah, it was, the first time was. It was a change.

Q: Was prison something that you were kind of scared of?

A: *Scared of!* I was even scared for the first year that I was in prison. Because I knew nothing about the life-style. But now I do know about the life-style, and it doesn't scare me. I would rather not be locked up. I'd rather get out and get my head screwed on right, and stay away from alcohol where I didn't do anymore crime, but I'm not able to do that.

Implications

The ascendant popularity of crime-as-choice interpretations of offending in the past two decades was matched by dramatic changes in American criminal justice. Crime control policies justified by theories of rehabilitation were supplanted or joined by new ones based on notions of deterrence and incapacitation. Political figures seized upon growing citizen anxiety over economic and life-quality issues to cast an array of offenders as domestic enemies and adversaries in a "war on crime." The crime-control apparatus now provides increased punishment across its operating spectrum, including jail, training school, and prison populations that have soared to historically unprecedented levels (Kreisberg, DeComo, and Herrara, 1992; Bureau of Justice Statistics, 1992; Irwin and Austin, 1994).

Our increasingly repressive efforts have been directed particularly at so-called career criminals, those who commit crime at high rate and generally persist at doing so. Measures such as the "Three-Strikes-And-You're-Out" legislation are predicated on the belief that the threat of imprisonment will deter them and others from committing crime and, once caught and imprisoned, will deter them from recidivism. Many of the sentencing reforms that swept the United States after 1975, for example, explicitly threaten harsher penalties for these offenders.

The research on persistent thieves' decisionmaking reviewed in this chapter proceeded from the premise that "there can be no more critical element in understanding and ultimately preventing crime than understanding the criminal's perceptions of the opportunities and risks associated with [criminal activities]" (Rengert and Wasilchick, 1989:1). The policy significance of the foregoing description and the interpretation of crime-commission decisionmaking are not easy to formulate, however. They are based almost entirely on studies of known offenders and there is no way of knowing how widely their experiences can be generalized. It could be argued that lessons about crime control drawn from their experiences are of limited generalizability precisely because of their demonstrated propensity and willingness to commit property crimes previously. Nor is it possible to determine how much their decisionmaking and response to imprisonment reflect innate differences or *experiential effects*, that is, the effects on risk perception of past success in committing crime and avoiding arrest (Gottfredson and Hirschi, 1990; Paternoster et al., 1983). Given these problems, we must be cautious in sketching the theoretical and crime control implications of our observations.

Current official constructions of deterrence-based policies and strategies take insufficient account of factors and conditions that constrain their decisionmaking and limit substantially the rationality they employ when doing so. Offenders do calculate to some degree and in some manner, but the process is constrained severely by the life-styles they pursue. Our review shows unequivocally, for example, that when they make a decision to commit crime, persistent thieves are not attuned to nuances of criminal penalties. Research on active residential burglars reports, for example, that the research subjects "made hurried, almost haphazard, decisions to offend while in a state of emotional turmoil" (Wright and Decker, 1994:211). The prison experience, moreover, erodes perceptions of harshness and reassures because of knowledge that it can be endured. Persistent thieves rationalize crime and believe they can perfect criminal techniques and become successful. This suggests we should be extremely wary of crime control proposals that promise significant reductions in street crime for marginal increases in threat and repression. It is past time for greater modesty in crime-control claims that are made justified by theories of crime as choice.

The theory of crime as choice highlights offenders' assessments of the legitimate and illegitimate opportunities and the risks of each. Crime control policies that build on this model generally confine their attention almost exclusively to altering risk. In doing so, they ignore entirely the theoretically obvious: Offenders' behavior can be changed not only by increasing threat but also by increasing *legitimate opportunities*. It is important to make this point if for no reason other than the fact that increased legitimate opportunities extend the choices available to offenders and increase the risk of criminal decisions. Our review of research on decisionmaking by persistent thieves shows that risk is hardly a consideration in their calculus, but profits and opportunities are. It is possible that an increase in legitimate opportunities would influence the outcome of their decisionmaking; offenders may be more likely to choose profitable legitimate opportunities than criminal opportunities.

Crime control policies grounded in an interpretation of crime as choice generally are premised on the assumption that legal threats have a constant meaning across all contexts and situations. This is not the case, if for no other reason than because men who commit common-law crimes are affected by moods such as desperation or arrogance. At other times their decisionmaking process is distorted by the influence of drugs, by co-offenders, or by a combination of the two. Nothing said here is meant to imply that legal threats do not have *some* deterrent effect, only that tinkering with them on the assumption offenders are aware of and behaviorally sensitive to the changes is naive or even disingenuous.

Notes

The analysis in this chapter is based on research supported by grants #80-IJ-CX-0047 and #86-IJ-CX-0068 from the U.S. Department of Justice, National Institute of Justice (Neal Shover, principal investigator. Points of view or opinions expressed here do not necessarily reflect the official position or policies of the Department of Justice.

1. Supported by the National Institute of Justice, the principal research objective was an enhanced understanding of crime desistence by male persistent thieves. A detailed description of the research objectives and methodologies are presented in Shover and Honaker (1992).

References

Ball, John C., John W. Schaffer, and David N. Nurco. 1983. "The Day-to-Day Criminality of Heroin Addicts in Baltimore: A Study in the Continuity of Offense Rates." *Drug and Alcohol Dependence* 12:119-142.

Becker, Gary. 1968. "Crime and Punishment: An Economic Approach." *Journal of Political Economy* 76:169-217.

Bennett, Trevor, and Richard Wright. 1984a. *Burglars on Burglary*. Hampshire: Gower.

———. 1984b. "The Relationship Between Alcohol Use and Burglary." *British Journal of Addiction* 79:431-437.

Black, Jack. 1926. *You Can't Win*. New York: A. L. Burt.

Braly, Malcolm. 1976. *False Starts*. New York: Penguin.

Bureau of Justice Statistics. 1992. *Correctional Populations in the United States, 1990*. Washington, D.C.: U.S. Department of Justice.

Carroll, John S. 1978. "A psychological Approach to Deterrence: The Evaluation of Crime Opportunities." *Journal of Personality and Social Psychology* 36:1512-1520.

———. 1982. "Committing a Crime: The Offender's Decision." In J. Konecni and E.B. Ebbesen (eds.), *The Criminal Justice System: A Social-Psychological Analysis*. San Francisco: W. H. Freeman.

Cordilia, Ann T. 1985. "Alcohol and Property Crime: Exploring the Causal Nexus." *Journal of Studies on Alcohol* 46:161-171.

———. 1986. "Robbery Arising Out of a Group Drinking-Context." In Anne Campbell and John J. Gibbs (eds.), *Violent Transactions*. New York: Blackwell.

Cromwell, Paul F., James N. Olson, and D'Aunn W. Avary. 1991. *Breaking and Entering: An Ethnographic Analysis of Burglary*. Newbury Park, CA.: Sage.

Crookston, Peter. 1967. *Villain*. London: Jonathan Cape.

Feeney, Floyd. 1986. "Robbers as Decision-Makers." In Derek B. Cornish and Ronald V. Clarke (eds.), *The Reasoning Criminal: Rational Choice Perspectives on Offending*. New York: Springer-Verlag.

Felson, Marcus. 1994. *Crime and Everyday Life*. Thousand Oaks, CA: Pine Forge.

Figgie International. 1988. *The Figgie Report Part VI--The Business of Crime: The Criminal Perspective*. Richmond, Va.: Figgie International Inc.

Frazier, Charles E., and Thomas Meisenhelder. 1985. "Criminality and Emotional Ambivalence: Exploratory Notes on an Overlooked Dimension." *Qualitative Sociology* 8: 266-284.

Gibbs, John J., and Peggy L. Shelly. 1982. "Life in the Fast Lane: A Retrospective View by Commercial Thieves." *Journal of Research in Crime and Delinquency* 19:299-330.

Gottfredson, Michael, and Travis Hirschi. 1990. *A General Theory of Crime*. Stanford: Stanford University Press.

Heineke, J. M., ed. 1978. *Economic Models of Criminal Behavior*. Amsterdam: North-Holland.

Irwin, John. 1985. *The Jail*. Berkeley: University of California Press.

Irwin, John, and James Austin. 1994. *It's about Time: America's Imprisonment Binge*. Belmont, Calif.: Wadsworth.

Johnson, Bruce D., Paul J. Goldstein, Edward Preble, James Schmeidler, Douglas S. Lipton, Barry Spunt and Thomas Miller. 1985. *Taking Care of Business: The Economics of Crime by Heroin Abusers.* Lexington, MA: D. C. Heath.

Kreisberg, Barry, Robert DeComo, and Norma C. Herrera. 1992. *National Juvenile Custody Trends 1978-1989.* Washington, DC: U.S. Department of Justice, Office of Juvenile Justice and Delinquency Prevention.

Lemert, Edwin. 1967. "An Isolation and Closure Theory of Naive Check Forgery." In Marshall B. Clinard, and Richard Quinney (eds.), *Criminal Behavior Systems: A Typology.* New York: Holt, Rinehart and Winston.

McCall, Nathan. 1994. *Makes Me Wanna Holler.* New York: Random House.

Maguire, Mike, in collaboration with Trevor Bennett. 1982. *Burglary in a Dwelling.* London: Heinemann.

Martin, Dannie M., and Peter Y. Sussman. 1994. *Committing Journalism: The Prison Writings of Red Hog.* New York: W. W. Norton.

Nagin, Daniel S., and Raymond Paternoster. 1991. "On the Relationship of Past to Future Participation in Delinquency." *Criminology* 29:163-189.

Parker, Tony, and Robert Allerton. 1962. *The Courage of His Convictions.* London: Hutchinson.

Paternoster, Raymond, Linda E. Saltzman, Gordon P. Waldo, and Theodore G. Chiricos. 1983. "Estimating Perceptual Stability and Deterrent Effects: The Role of Perceived Punishment in the Inhibition of Criminal Involvement." *Journal of Criminal Law and Criminology* 74:270-297.

Persson, M. 1981. "Time-Perspectives Amongst Criminals." *Acta Sociologica* 24:149-165.

Petersilia, Joan, Peter W. Greenwood and Michael Lavin. 1978. *Criminal Careers of Habitual Felons.* Washington, DC: U. S. Department of Justice, National Institute of Law Enforcement and Criminal Justice.

Peterson, Mark A., and Harriet B. Braiker, with Suzanne M. Polich. 1981. *Who Commits Crime? A Survey of Prison Inmates.* Cambridge, Mass.: Oelgeschlager, Gunn & Hain, 1981.

Peterson, Mark, Jan Chaiken and Patricia Ebener. 1984. *Survey of Jail and Prison Inmates, 1978: California, Michigan, Texas.* Ann Arbor: Inter-university Consortium for Political and Social Research.

Rengert, George F., and John Wasilchick. 1985. *Suburban Burglary.* Springfield, IL.: Charles C. Thomas.

———. 1989. "Space, Time and Crime: Ethnographic Insights into Residential Burglary." Final Report Submitted to the National Institute of Justice, U. S. Department of Justice.

Reynolds, M. O. 1985. *Crime by Choice: An Economic Analysis.* Dallas: Fisher Institute.

Roshier, Bob. 1989. *Controlling Crime: The Classical Perspective in Criminology.* Chicago: Lyceum.

Shover, Neal, and David Honaker. 1992. "The Socially Bounded Decision Making of Persistent Property Offenders." *Howard Journal of Criminal Justice* 31:276-293.

Walsh, Dermot. 1980. *Break-Ins: Burglary from Private Houses.* London: Constable.

———. 1986. *Heavy Business.* London: Routledge & Kegan Paul.

Wright, James D., and Peter H. Rossi. 1985. *Armed Criminals in America: A Survey of Incarcerated Felons, 1983.* Ann Arbor: Inter-university Consortium for Political and Social Research.

Wright, Richard T., and Scott Decker. 1994. *Burglars on the Job.* Boston: Northeastern University Press.

14

White-Collar Crimes and Other Crimes of Deception: Connecting Policy to Theory

Michael Levi

In the introduction to their edited book *Crime*, Wilson and Petersilia (1995) observe that "By 'crime' we mean what the average person thinks of as predatory or street crime—muggings, murders, assaults, rapes, robberies, burglaries, and other thefts. This is not a book about white-collar or organized crime or about political or commercial corruption. These are all important subjects, but they are beyond the scope of this volume. An entire book could be produced on any one of these other topics, and we hope that many will be."

This statement does not seek to explain or justify *why* these subjects "are beyond the scope," a judgment set out as if it were a product of some inherent qualities of the phenomena rather than an editorial decision. Nor does the book state anywhere the seriousness with which certain forms of white-collar crime and corruption are viewed by the general public—surely one criterion for inclusion in a book whose cover proclaims it as a look "at the most pressing problem of our time" To many people in Alaska, or in the sites of environmental disaster whose plight has not been remedied by the Superfund (Barnett, 1993), white-collar crime is a great deal more palpable than are metropolitan street gangs. Furthermore, though only possible regulatory offenses are under investigation by the U.S. Securities and Exchange Commission in December, 1994, as I write this, some of the residents of newly bankrupted Orange County, California, may feel that allegedly reckless gambling with their taxes on the advice of (and to the profit of) Merrill Lynch has harmed them more than have the nearby Los Angeles gangs. But despite these critical observations, Wilson and Petersilia's choice of omissions reflect one populist view about the kind of crimes that are debated around election time and feature most frequently as representations of evil in the newspapers and on the television screens in the United States and, for that matter, in other Anglo-Saxon countries. (I make that distinction because in many former communist and Third World countries and in Italy, the crime debate may be less about street crime but more about political corruption and white-collar crime.)

Concern about at least some forms of white-collar crime is not in principle the exclusive preserve of the political left. Although some large corporations and wealthy individuals commit white-collar crimes, many are also the victims of it. And because of some forms of it (savings and loan frauds, for example, which reportedly cost the equivalent of 3 percent of the U.S. gross national product), many middle-class as well as poor people have to pay more in taxes than they would otherwise. Moreover, antitrust and other forms of producer misconduct, as well as market manipulation and some other forms of financial services malpractice, distort ideal pricing mechanisms. So although the labeling of particular acts as "white-collar crime" remains highly contested ideological terrain and although nearly all who do research on it are politically left of center, one can be a "conservative" or free marketeer and still be concerned with reducing at least some forms of white-collar crime.

One way out of the terminological dilemma that still bedevils white-collar crime (Geis, 1992) is to differentiate between frauds for gain and corporate crimes that deliberately or inadvertently hurt people or the environment. However, though the individual harms caused by many in the latter category may not be directly intended, it is normally more profitable—especially in the short run, or even in the long run if no severe civil or regulatory action ensues—for such crimes to occur than not to occur, so financial motives are often implicated in decisions not to prevent them (or in thoughtlessness which may remain thoughtless precisely because the downside risk of unsafety has not been high enough to make decision-makers conscious of its human significance). Nevertheless, partly to avoid writing a textbook and partly because Fisse and Braithwaite (1993) have recently reviewed so well the issues involved in regulating corporate crime, I have decided to focus here on the causes and control of financial crime involving the manipulation of trust, though I shall occasionally refer to other forms of white-collar crime.

The Socio-Economic Dimensions of White-Collar Crime and Criminality

White-collar crime was originally envisioned, inter alia, as a forum through which a mirror could be held up to the influence of social prestige and power upon law enforcement and punishment. Many writers have preferred to focus upon the resources and values entailed in its control (especially compared with the control of street and household crime) rather than upon its causes. Because of the systematic conscious and unconscious biases that are believed to enter into its processing as early as the stages of recording and investigation, data sets of officially processed offenders are an even more unreliable guide to its incidence than they are to street and household crime. And because of the absence of victimization surveys in this arena (Levi and Pithouse, n.d.), studies that go one stage further back tend to be anecdotal rather than systematic. However, studies that reflect the decisions of regulatory agencies such as health and safety at work may include acts that are unintended and/or that do not meet all the "normal" criteria of criminal culpability. (This may not be relevant, though, and empirical research on regulation suggests that most corporations are processed administratively or criminally only after several informal warnings, giving them de facto the status of intended or reckless acts.)

In an attempt to focus on the characteristics of the crime rather than the status of offenders, Shapiro (1990) suggests that we begin sampling from settings of trust and examine how fiduciaries define and enforce trust norms, the structural opportunities for abuse, the patterns of misconduct that ensue, and the social control processes that respond. However, trust violation can place behaviors such as check and credit card fraud squarely in the frame, and since so many more people—most of whom have modest social backgrounds—commit such acts than, for example, defraud pension funds or run fraudulent savings and loan corporations, the result is to make the set of white-collar criminals much more like other property offenders and much less like "the powerful" than many authors such as Sutherland (1983) intended. We are left with what one might term "blue-white collar crime" (Hagan, 1988; Weisburd et al., 1991; Levi, 1992; Levi and Pithouse, n.d.). Consequently, when reviewing the adequacy (or heuristic value) of explanations of white-collar crime, it is even more important than usual to consider what sort of data criminologists are using as the baseline for their theories.

Explaining White-Collar Crime

Opportunities for Crime:
Forms of Social Organization as Criminogenic Factors

There are a number of possible avenues that one might travel along in accounting for white-collar crime. One is to take some data set on offenders—convicted or not—and to try to see what explanatory accounts best fit the data. Another might be to examine in a more abstract way what dimensions of contemporary social organization appear to contribute to white-collar crime opportunities. I will begin with the latter perspective and then discuss the former.

What factors influence the development of abuse of trust? Shapiro (1990) notes that agents end up with a great deal of power because they hold information that cannot readily be assessed or verified by their principals—information about profitability and risks, for example, and information about how they have disbursed funds—what insurers term "moral hazard." Agents, such as banks, can engage in non-arm's length loans to their friends, using collateral which is fictitious, forged, stolen, or grossly overvalued by supposedly independent professionals such as real estate valuers. To reduce such risks, principals seek out as their agents people of "good reputation": This sometimes is ascertained by their being members of recognized professional bodies with vetting procedures (and, perhaps, compensation funds for those who lose their money through fraud), but it may also be attained (not only in less developed countries) by picking people who are part of their social and business circle and who have (or are believed to have) a mutual stake in society—schoolfriends, for example, or members of the same religious group, golf club or masonic lodge. Such judgments are not always reliable. In the words of one of my bankruptcy fraudster informants (Levi, 1981), when asked what the code of the professional fraudster was: "Do your friends first; they're easier." Principals can seldom physically see what their agents are doing but rely instead upon contracts that may require (in law) prior permission for particular sorts of transactions (e.g., futures contracts) beyond a particular sum of money and upon the face validity of paperwork such as share certificates or contract notes or bank deposit certification. Particularly if the principals are looking at faxes, but also if they are viewing original documents with which they are unfamiliar, all of these can be forged with the use of recent technologies.

In modern society, there is a whole spectrum of control that we exercise over others. Our bankers, for example, are pure agents in current account transactions: They undertake only the transactions that we instruct (though as with BCCI, if they have embezzled enough, we may find that there are no funds left to transfer). Other relationships are "fiduciary" or "trust" relationships in which principals give trustees much greater discretion. Pension funds are the most important example, where knowledge of losses may arise decades after the fraud.

Fraudsters make use of the modalities of normal life to conceal their crimes, and they have the advantage that (normally, except in the case of some classic "cons" such as in the film *The Sting*) they have legitimate business and thus are not trespassers, as burglars and robbers commonly are. It is consequently harder to conduct an audit trail of their activities as a simple test of whether they have legitimate business doing what they are doing in the place where it is being done. One can extend Shapiro's suggestion about examining trust settings beyond the area of fiduciaries, who, in law, are persons with a legal responsibility for the faithful handling of trust funds, to others in society who are trusted. In *The Phantom Capitalists*, I revealed how because of rules of company formation aimed at maximizing the ease with which people could start up business, it was easy for firms to be set up to obtain on credit large quantities of goods without intending to pay for them, which were readily resold for cash as the company owners absconded (Levi, 1981, 1984).

Although there are some organizations that are dedicated to the pursuit of fraud or other malpractice, for the most part, it appears that malpractice grows out of, first, salesperson dependence on individual commission payments, which distort seller behavior and give a major financial disincentive to honest representations: From 1994, to avoid the risk of further abuses in the selling of unsuitable pension and other products (and to avoid large fines from regulators for continuing abuses), major British life insurance companies are paying their sales staff fixed salaries with very little commission element. (It remains to be seen what effect this will have on level of sales and corporate profitability.) Second is the classic Mertonian anomie approach: the setting of high organizational profit targets with relatively little attention to be paid as to how those targets are to be achieved. Jenkins and Braithwaite (1993) show how nursing home fraud is made easy by loose regulation—which is aimed at encouraging people to set up private nursing homes. And fraud is made more likely in the profit sector because nursing home owners—often large corporations—put pressure on senior managers to attain particular profit goals, which can be attained only by cutting corners on patient care and facilities. This does *not* mean that some types of abuse cannot occur equally in the public sector: Patient abuse and torture by nurses, neglect, and exploitation are examples that are common under public ownership. But these tend to take the form of unregulated brutality rather than the desperate search to meet organizational targets.

Motives for White-Collar Crime

I have explored above the concept of crime as opportunity in a more abstract way than is normally found. But opportunities do not themselves "cause" crime: There have to be elements of personality and/or culture that give people the vision and motivation to exploit such abstract opportunities. Braithwaite's absorbing review essay on *Crimes of the Middle Classes* by Weisburd et al. (1991) asserts that "[c]rime can be motivated by (a) a desire for goods for use; (b) a fear of losing goods for use; (c) a desire for goods for exchange; and (d) a fear of losing goods for exchange. My proposition is that (a) and (b) are more relevant to motivating the crimes of poor people; (c) and (d) are more relevant to motivating the crimes of wealthy people and organizations" (Braithwaite, 1993b:223).

Although—whether dealing with white-collar or violent crime—it is illuminating to focus upon fear of loss (symbolic and material) as well as the more conventional criminological orientation of prospect of gain, having more than one can use is almost a necessary condition for the label "wealthy." However, "use-value" is a more elastic concept than Braithwaite implies: the desire to retain one's fleet of Rolls Royces, Lear jets and helicopters *for use* may motivate many white-collar crimes, though their "usefulness" can include symbolic display in creating envy, attracting women for sex, and status competition. (These motivations also apply to many apparently law-abiding chief executives, who carry on working long hours even though they are very wealthy.)

An alternative commonplace way of expressing the principle is that white-collar crimes are committed out of greed, not need. Marginal utility of income may fall as income rises (Braithwaite, 1992; Wheeler, 1992), but the perceived sufficiency of disposable income is affected by what are deemed in their reference group to be "necessities", as well as by "addictions" to displays of conspicuous consumption (such as flying friends around the world for parties), to drugs, to gambling, and so on. Their absolute income levels may vary considerably, but high levels of personal indebtedness are a common feature of male white-collar offenders compared with garden-variety offenders and with citizens generally. Cressey (1953) found that embezzlers had generally lived well beyond their means for some time before deciding to embezzle (or, as they saw it, to "borrow"). Many of those defined by Levi (1981, 1984) as "slippery slope" fraudsters simply continue to behave (and spend) as if their businesses are highly profitable long after they have become incapable of repaying their debts. Bear in mind that the gendered dimensions of "the fast life," combined with blocked opportunities for females in gaining access to posts such as corporate finance director that give them opportunities to defraud, help to explain gender differences in white-collar crime (Daly, 1989; Levi, 1994).

Braithwaite (1989) has written evocatively about the superior regulatory power of shame, in particular reintegrative shaming, compared with retributive punishment. However, shame levels depend significantly upon the reference group values of those who contemplate crime: The narrower the reference group and the more tolerant it is of particular forms of crime in particular circumstances, the less that shame will operate. Thus Japan, which regulates street and household crime very effectively, has an almost unrivaled appetite for financing political parties (principally the Liberal Democratic Party) out of "donations" from those who wish to be awarded government building contracts or issue their shares on the stock market. Although many Japanese political leaders—all of them male—have been forced to resign when exposed, they remain powerful behind the scenes thereafter. The explanation for crime then shifts to how particular "rationalizations" develop, to the visibility of the crimes to others inside and outside the reference group (and the time lags involved in this visibility), and to cultural transmission theories of how tolerance and/or stigma are perpetuated.

The absence of upper-world ethnographies or even surveys makes separating the culture(s) of business crime from the culture(s) of business deeply problematical. For if we take seriously Veblen's observation (1967:237) that "the ideal pecuniary man is like the ideal delinquent in his unscrupulous conversion of goods and persons to his own ends, and in a callous disregard of (i.e. freedom from) the feelings of others or remoter effects of his actions," it is hard to see how the cultural values of a criminal capitalist can differ greatly from a law-abiding one, at least in terms of constructs such as an obsession with power and control (Hagan, 1988). Survival—a flexible concept—in a competitive local or global market becomes an over-riding value or "technique of neutralization" that can justify white-collar law-breaking and may be reinforced by business school. That aspect of masculinity that emphasizes individual striving and achievement may account for breaking the rules, while the other aspect which stresses group loyalty and support may account for covering up the misconduct (Levi, 1994). Many white-collar offenders with lawful jobs both have and covet current social respectability, and those operating in an organizational setting evade responsibility by appealing to the necessity of obedience to corporate objectives and/or of supporting their families. Nevertheless, seeming trustworthy and socially respectable—especially if one's selling and deal-making roles involve *repeat* relationships—is an important economic as well as social attribute for both legitimate and illegitimate businesspeople. And there are marked variations within and between cultures in levels of white-collar crime, suggesting that culture mediates masculinity. So what constitutes rational choice may depend not only on the risks of detection and of formal action but also on broader cultural values and personality dimensions such as how long one's planning horizons are.

Control Theory and White-Collar Crime

Allied to some of the discussion earlier in this chapter is the work of Gottfredson and Hirschi (1990: 190-191), who claim that white-collar offenders are not specialized or different in any particular way. Rather, given opportunities to commit offenses, like other criminals whose behavior is purportedly explained by their general theory, white-collar criminals "too are people of low self-control, people inclined to follow momentary influence without consideration of the long-term costs of such behavior." To the extent that this is not tautological, that is, that poor self-control is derived from continued offending, it is amenable to falsification, and both Benson and Moore (1992) and Green (1993) have sought (in my view, successfully) to falsify the theory, at least as it applies to white-collar offending.

Benson and Moore (1992:252) observe: "Contrary to the claims of Gottfredson and Hirschi, we find that those who commit even run-of-the-mill, garden-variety white-collar offenses can, as a group, be clearly distinguished from those who commit ordinary street offenses. ...[Their] rejection of motives as important causal forces is misguided. Because motives are generated by macro social and organizational processes, a fully developed theory of white-collar crime must take these processes into account."

There are significant differences between white-collar and other offenders with respect to stability of work record and general antisocial undisciplined behavior that, I would predict, would be even greater for employee than for outsider fraud, since—except for those inheriting wealth and social position—personal discipline may be a prerequisite of the opportunity to become a well-established insider who later turns to fraud. Thus, higher rates of social deviance are found among recidivist (who presumably are defrauding mainly from outside the victim organizations rather than as employees or executives) than among non-recidivist fraudsters (Benson and Moore, 1992:264). Green's (1993) data from Georgia indicate that just over half the convicted embezzlers had a previous theft record, and there is some limited support to the "poor self-control" thesis as applied to some persistent fraudsters. However, one must look also at the period of the life cycle at which problem drinking and drug use appeared, for they may reflect value disruption precipitated, for example, by marital or mental breakdown or the loss of perceived job security. (Cutbacks in the financial services industry, for example, may reduce employee loyalty by making them feel that their employers do not care for them.) There are parallels with some of the symptoms that Gottfredson and Hirschi (1990) associated with low self-control: Some corporate buccaneers who become involved in major frauds may be self-centered persons who (like war heroes) indulge in risktaking and have low frustration tolerances, but most substantial frauds do require some patient build-up and self-control beyond that of the typical burglar and car thief.

So rather than homogenize white-collar offenders, one should note the broad empirical support in the data for a four-fold typology of fraudsters, which I would term *preplanned (i and ii), intermediate,* and *slippery-slope* fraudsters (see also Levi, 1981, 1988). The first set have high offending rates with little offense specialization and high involvement in other forms of deviance (Benson and Moore, 1992:268), and fit well with the Gottfredson and Hirschi model. The second set are the more disciplined planners of offenses, who may build up their plots with considerable patience and skill over a long period of time and may steal millions of dollars from each scam, making it unnecessary for them to commit large volumes of offenses. The third set, intermediates, are people who turn to fraud out of resentment, thwarted ambition, and/or the late development of a taste for the high life, perhaps under persuasion from career criminals. The final, "slippery-slope" set are those who just carry on trading while insolvent, recklessly persuading themselves that they can repay their debts or even suppressing consciousness that they are insolvent. The latter two categories can be affected by downturns in the economy, making them suddenly less prosperous than they were previously (Levi, 1981; Simpson, 1987; Barlow, 1993). Indeed, supporting my point, the downturn in fortunes of many British lawyers since the late 1980s, due to increased competition and reduced turnover in the property market, has led to an explosion of frauds by them.

To this analysis, I would add that it is misleading to think of "criminal opportunities" as a simple construct. Some white-collar (and other) offenders, like business entrepreneurs generally, may be people of vision who can see possibilities of exploitation in their environment that do not occur to the rest of us. In a sense, they integrate objective features of their environments in special ways, though at a more routine level they may learn techniques (in the Sutherland sense) from their peer groups in executive suites or in the "Club Fed" (luxurious) prisons to which they are normally sent if convicted. Whether one can actually predict those potential white-collar offenders whose self-control will crumble when faced by stress is currently unproven (though some psychologists get money for performing pesonality tests that *claim* they can do so).

In summary, I share the view of Braithwaite, who observes:

> Positivism produces an avalanche of nonsignificant findings, even in a system of scientific production that is biased in favour of highlighting significant effects, because specificity of context is overwhelmingly important in deciding whether a crime will occur or a war will break out. Even positivist theories that are empirically robust in terms of certain kinds of static tests will generally fail to predict effective intervention because they will not be sufficiently dynamic to cope with the way context unfolds in specific circumstances." (Braithwaite, 1993a:384).

The Control of White-Collar Crime

White-collar crime—particularly the part that relates to health and safety issues—is one of the few areas of criminology where serious attention has been paid to cross-cultural issues. Undoubtedly, this complicates matters, at more than just a political level, because regulatory recipes can seldom have the same ingredients even within the first world, let alone throughout the whole world. "What works" will depend on the particular histories and cultures of different countries or even regions within countries, but what is actually practiced is subjected to fluctuations depending upon political and media pressures. Reisman (1979:106) observes that there is a pattern in America of "crusades" over commercial bribery, in which periods of "sound and fury" are followed by "business as usual." This is by no means unique to America, though as with its tendency towards prohibitionist crusades generally (from alcohol to insider trading and money laundering), there does appear to be a streak of puritanism in American culture that does internal cultural battle with the dynamics of profitability and global economic domination. Braithwaite (1993a:387) makes the following proposition: "The art (rather than the science) of applied criminology is the gift of being able to perceive multiple theoretical significances in a practical problem, thus bringing the practitioner to a nuanced understanding of the problem. This nuanced understanding, seeing the problem in many ways at once, seeing it through different theoretical prisms, enables an integrated strategy of problem solving."

However, his is not an empirical description of the actual process of how crime control policies have developed in the past: Rather, it is a normative perspective on how they *should* develop and be integrated with theories of the middle range that make dynamic sense of the data. Following on from the theoretical approaches discussed earlier, it would appear that the routes through which white-collar crimes may be tackled are (1) rational choice theory, operating both on increasing the risks of detection and salient sanctions, and on reducing opportunities; (2) altering perceptions of harmfulness, reducing the cultural availability of techniques of neutralization; and (3) working creatively on ways in which people and corporations can prosper without breaking the law. The third is too large a topic for this chapter, so I shall focus on a variety of dimensions of (1) and (2).

Criminal Justice Responses to Financial Crime

Criminal justice policies are both a reflection and a cause of perceptions of harm, and they generally are determined by what the political market will bear (and has become habituated to). In the United States, this reflects populist pressures (including the media) and political lobbying. In white-collar crimes (particularly in the regulation of health and safety issues), many potential defendants with an ongoing corporate identity have a normally positive image in the eyes of lawmakers and law enforcers (as contrasted with "unproductive" members of the "underclass"), and most corporate crime control is conducted by *forward-looking* compliance orientation rather than by *backward-looking* (and retributive) enforcement orientation. Thus, to varying degrees, but in almost every sphere of white-collar crime from fraud to regulatory offenses, arrest and prosecution are viewed as a subordinate method of behavioral regulation. This applies even to those white-collar crimes that victimize corporations. For example, credit card companies' awareness of police disinterest in their victimization (and forensic difficulties in connecting offenders to crimes) means that even though almost all credit card fraudsters are blue collar, their focus is on prevention rather than deterrence through criminal law sanctions (Levi, Bissell, and Richardson, 1991).

Insofar as etiological theory of white-collar crime guides this "policy" on white-collar crime at all (which it must do at an unconscious level), the underlying *motif* is that unlike the "dangerous classes," most of those who commit or might commit white-collar crime can be trusted to have a "fundamentally" law-abiding orientation because they have sufficient stake in society not to require deterrence by punishment. In the punishment sphere, despite some pressures towards tougher sentences on the grounds of social fairness, sentencers often assume that white-collar offenders have suffered enough by the mere fact of exposure and/or that conviction or even a well-publicized administrative sanction will take them out of circulation by warning the public of the risk they represent (Wheeler, Mann, and Sarat, 1988; Levi, 1987, 1989). This is sometimes tied in with a caveat emptor (buyer beware) approach to the role of the State according to which, since frauds require voluntary contracts, putting potential contractors on their guard is sufficient adherence to the principles of laissez faire: If individuals or institutions such as banks subsequently want to lend money to fraudsters, that is their prerogative, and they must stand the loss. Nevertheless, most systems do have a paternalist element in them. In some specific fields such as legal practice and the provision of investment and banking services, risk to the public is reduced by preventing known offenders from accessing particular jobs—what I have termed "incapacitation without custody" (Levi, 1987).

Nevertheless, despite the superior political and ideological claims of the "war on drugs," considerable resources—especially at a federal level—have been devoted to the investigation of crimes of deception, partly via the use of interstate communications that give federal jurisdiction (Marx, 1988; Poveda, 1992). Furthermore, money-laundering regulations developed to deal with organized crime can also, at least in principle, assist in *proactive* monitoring of the known activities of white-collar criminals and, more plausibly, in *reactive* examination of financial audit trails after the exposure of the crime (Alabama Law Review, 1992; Gold and Levi, 1994). But unlike with street crimes, it is harder to predict in advance "hot spots" where sophisticated fraud takes place (or even to conceptualize what this might mean spatially), and there are fewer high-rate offenders against whom to mount surveillance operations (which, anyway, might have to take place for a long time before they detected any criminal plots, making them relatively expensive compared with street crime).

Consequently, there are two strategic directions in which policing major fraud might go. First, both reactively and proactively, there is the development of long-term expertise and motivation among investigators and prosecutors, though this is inhibited by the relatively low ratio of prosecutions per officer hour and by the greater organizational prestige of drugs investigation, even within the FBI. (In Britain and many European countries, the situation is far more difficult due to performance indicator pressure; to the near universality of the principle of "tenure" under which no officers can stay in the same post for longer than four years; and to the fact that small squad size leaves few promotion opportunities for ambitious officers who wish to stay in fraud investigation.) Second, more controversially, there is the development of more proactive policing strategies: (1) such as are practiced by the U.S. Postal Inspectorate in placing fake get-rich-quick scheme advertisements in the newspapers and then sending warning letters to those who reply, to be on their guard against such schemes, and (2) such as ABSCAM and other infiltration schemes where federal agents work undercover to expose corruption, money laundering, and other financial crimes (Marx, 1988; Levi, 1993, n.d.). One danger in the latter, however, is not only the up-front cost but also the risk to civil liberties in all proactive policing: How are targets determined, and how does one ensure that their selection is "reasonable" and is not politically motivated? Former president Nixon's use of the Internal Revenue Service as an instrument of damage to his political opponents is a case in point (Block, 1991), as was his attempts to control the investigation of the Watergate break-in, which led ultimately to his resignation (Emery, 1994).

This generates a major dilemma: The balance between ensuring independence from political interference, on the one hand, and preserving political and financial accountability, on the other. Quite apart from the financial expense of guarding the guardians, which drains the Exchequer of funds that can be deployed for other purposes—seen most wastefully in the low-yield rituals of many Police Complaints Systems, which fail to satisfy complainants, the public, or the police (Goldsmith, 1993), the process of reinvestigating white-collar scandals (such as Whitewatergate in 1994-1995) is itself part of the politicized process. The risk is that people retreat into a postmodern epistemological nihilism in which "the truth" is entirely a subjective artifact of the "show trial" process. In the United States, political complexities and overlapping federal and state jurisdictions may make it difficult for stable corrupt relationships to be sustained over time, but the device of the "independent" special prosecutor—though valuable—does not guarantee the fair distribution of investigative resources or the conscientious pursuit of investigations. The important issues of accountability raised by serious fraud prosecutions are unlike most faced in other arenas and arise principally because of the combination of (1) lack of transparency of decision-taking (at case acceptance, investigative resource allocation, use of search and interview powers, and prosecution decision levels) with (2) the political (with a small or large "p") ramifications of particular cases. (As far as we know, adult high-status persons are seldom involved in any property crimes other than fraud or corruption.) Given the restricted access to the information (including the judgments of witness credibility) upon which such decisions—including the decision not to accept a case for detailed investigation—are made, it is almost impossible to objectively disentangle whether the non-prosecution of senior industry or governmental persons is due to direct influence, to the cultural homogeneity of the governing class, or merely to the well-attested fact that remoteness from actual decisions makes it hard to convict people for corporate crime. A requirement to give reasons for decisions to complainants and/or to other governmental departments who refer a case for prosecution may go some of the way. However, although the Freedom of Information Act and congressional oversight make decisionmaking more open to review and criticism in the United States than in most European countries (especially Britain), there is no perfect solution to the risk of political interference, seen most dramatically in conflicts during 1994 between the Milan magistrates investigating the *tangentopoli* scandals of corrupt relationships between businesspeople, Mafia, Camorra, and many leading Italian politicians and the then Italian prime minister Berlusconi, whose own family and business interests were among the many targets of the investigation. In December 1994, the leading investigating magistrate, di Pietro, resigned his post in protest at the way in which the minister of justice had organized inspections of his own department, allegedly to ensure its propriety.

Criminal prosecution has a considerable symbolic significance, and the redrawing of boundaries of acceptability by public degradation ceremonies such as prosecution can have a considerable impact on elites, to the extent that for many white-collar defendants, the process is the punishment, irrespective of conviction outcomes (Levi, 1993; Fisse and Braithwaite, 1983). Apart from these grand issues, the American criminal justice system appears to have fewer difficulties in convicting white-collar accused than do its common-law counterparts in England and Australia or even in Canada. This may be partly because the relatively lengthy sentences (compared with England and Australia) imposed by the federal and some state sentencing guidelines, combined with plea bargaining, generate sufficient incentive for those. in the United States to cooperate with the prosecutors (Levi, 1993), incriminating their colleagues in the process. There remains scope for heated arguments about how fair such sanctions are compared with sentences for other offences—as Reiman's (1994) title puts it, the rich get richer and the poor get prison—but when interpreting the data ideologically, one should bear in mind that (1) many of the *victims* of such frauds are wealthy individuals and/or corporations and (2) it arguably is legitimate (on "rational choice" deterrent and on retributive grounds) to take into account the secondary impact on offenders' occupational prospects and social position, even if this does look like "double punishment" for those members of the underclass who have no initial grace from which to fall (see Levi, 1987, 1989). From a principled reformative perspective, it is arguable that in the case of crimes committed for the corporation (and where the corporation still remains alive, because many "slippery-slope" offenses are committed to postpone the date of liquidation or to steal funds from companies going bust), far greater emphasis than at present should be placed upon the use of corporate probation and other "public interest" sanctions: The aim is to disenfranchise the existing beneficiaries of crime without making employees or the public suffer from the imposition of a corporate death penalty (Etzioni, 1993; Fisse and Braithwaite, 1993; Lofquist, 1993).

Fraud Prevention

This brings me to consider the final element in this chapter: the prevention of fraud. This can be taken at several levels, for example, opportunity reduction, rationalization stripping, and motivation reduction (though rationalizations and motivation are connected). The field is capable of substantial differentiation: There are financial crimes where organizations themselves can be left to regulate in their own interests, and others where the state can (and/or should) play a role in ensuring protection for those incapable of looking after themselves (for example, in consumer fraud where no outsider can readily tell if impurities or if food content differs from that described on the label). As regards external regulation, at a *normative* level, following the "selfish gene" principle that it makes better utilitarian sense for social survival and resource optimization to begin by seeing if cooperation "works" than to assume that one will not get voluntary displays of civic virtue, one possibility is to aim for a system of regulation based on trust, with regular inspections and graduated punitive sanctions for those who show themselves to be unwilling to "play the game". Illustrating their theme with data from their study of nursing home compliance, Braithwaite and Makkai (1994) observe that nursing home misconduct can be picked out by inspectors, using subtle contextual knowledge as well as quantitative predictors, but that when managers perceive that they are not trusted, their behavior deteriorates. They recommend enhancing civic responsibility by creating dialogue between corporate managers and their staff and community groups. (See also Fisse and Braithwaite, 1993, for a development of these themes.) This trust approach contrasts with the "amoral calculator" perspective implicit in the work of Shapiro (1990) and by some of the corporations (particularly U.S.-headquartered) I have interviewed, under which one assumes that people and companies will defraud unless the probability and consequences of sanctions are high enough to deter them (given their own circumstances, which may vary considerably).

The choice of "appropriate" regulatory strategy depends also on where the sources of harm are—from within the corporation or from outside it—and on whether violators see that they are doing wrong or even are breaking the law at all. For example, if embezzlers truly believe that they are "just borrowing", this may require a different control strategy from that if they are "just stealing but reckon they won't be detected or prosecuted."

It is important to clarify one's target population for crime prevention measures. *Anyone* who has money or is able to borrow it is capable of being victimized by fraud: "Popular capitalism" has spread securities ownership to the middle classes (particularly following privatization in Europe) and if we add in people who have an interest in investments via life insurance, personal pension schemes, and mortgages, the majority of the population are susceptible to being defrauded directly or indirectly. Only *some* of these victims are in a position to take evasive action. Savers and investors can put pressure on the people they entrust with their money to take greater care of it (and upon compensation schemes that underwrite the conduct of the fraudulent and the reckless). But except for large institutional investors who have often proved reluctant to intervene, they cannot *dictate* the fraud prevention strategies of their management.

In some cases, for example, mail order and telemarketing frauds, it may be rational to impose third-party liability on media advertising the activity, to ensure that they check that the firms exist and are properly set up for the kind of business that they advertise.

In the case of frauds *against* companies, prevention ideas must reach individuals at *all* levels of organizations, for although the credit manager or the head of security in a large company may be concerned about fraud, the managing director may be more concerned about corporate image and sales. So if organizational policy is to be changed, it is the *senior* managerial personnel who have to be convinced about the desirability of or necessity for this. Fraud, in other words, should be part of the strategic plan of loss control within any organization (Levi, 1988; Levi, Bissell, and Richardson, 1991; Burrows, 1991).

Preventing Frauds on Individuals

Many investment frauds succeed by convincing members of the public that they have an opportunity to get in on the ground floor of a surefire winner and that if they do not invest, they will bitterly regret their overcautiousness. They exert considerable psychological pressure to achieve this goal. Rationally, and after the event, participation in such schemes often seems absurd, and victims feel humiliated by their gullibility, making them feel guilty (as do some rape victims} and reluctant to report (Levi and Pithouse, n.d.). For example, mathematically, any chain letter or pyramid/multilevel selling scheme will have exhausted the entire country's population within six months, so the simple rule is *don't subscribe*. The first step towards protecting against investment fraud is the following. If an investment seems too good to be true, it probably is. Always ask why, if it such a certain winner, the borrower needs *your* capital at rates higher than he could get from a bank. Never subscribe to a "make your fortune" or real estate time-share scheme on the spot. Always take it to an independent individual and if that person is skeptical, heed his or her advise rather than dream of success.

Another method that fraudsters use—particularly since the initiation of compulsory registration and competence/integrity testing of those selling financial services—is to build up an aura of respectability by claiming impressive qualifications or membership of a professional body that is approved by the government and/or that has a compensation scheme. Such false claims are often a criminal offense in themselves, irrespective of proof of fraud, but this will not worry the fraudster very much, since he or she hopes not to be around the area or even the country if victims ever get around to complaining to the police or self-regulatory organization, making it unlikely that the case will be followed up. So the second major preventative measure is to check that the qualification or membership of the approved body is genuine. If a broker is not a member, no compensation will be paid. Be particularly wary of offers that come from overseas, because it is very expensive and troublesome to sue or even to expect prosecutors to pursue matters successfully abroad.

Preventing Fraud on Business

The aim of crime prevention is to keep the criminal out. Normally, this is conceived of in terms of steering columns, locks, and bolts: better physical protection. However, in the case of fraud, a different set of preventative methods must be employed. There are some physical measures that are relevant—access controls to reduce the risk of illicit entry to computers or computer areas and random checks to ensure password change and difficult password availability—but the major threat comes from people with whom the defrauded party has a contractual relationship of some kind. In this sense, fraud prevention is closer to family violence prevention than to burglary prevention: The danger is already within, but what businesspeople need to do is to take avoiding action and change the nature of the relationship.

Entry Control. The first line of defense against fraud is entry control, which may be applied to both employees and outside contractors. For *internal* frauds, entry controls may take the form of vetting employees or members of professional associations to ensure that they are "fit and proper persons." However, the absence of criminal convictions is by no means a guarantee of probity. In the past, the low rate of reporting and prosecution of fraud meant that fraudsters were unlikely to be convicted—many people suspected of dishonesty are allowed simply to resign rather than being prosecuted. But the absence of any real references on employees is commonplace in fraud cases.

Postentry Control. Many of the largest frauds have been committed by people whose personal backgrounds are such that they would have satisfied the prima facie integrity and competence checks implicit in the Gottredson and Hirschi (1990) model of generic antisociality and poor self-discipline. Disciplined preplanned fraudsters and both intermediate and slippery-slope fraudsters will therefore readily pass this Maginot line. The focus then shifts to internal management systems and compliance monitoring (for internal frauds) and creditworthiness checking (for external ones). Here, organizational tone is important. It is impossible to state whether there is any displacement effect whereby intending fraudsters choose to work for organizations that have a lax reputation, but "sucker lists" are passed around by *external* fraudsters, and this may be true of internal ones too. Alhough there will always be people whose ability to rationalize verges on the magical, clear policies that set out the acceptability and unacceptability of particular practices will diminish the scope for self-deception, particularly if they are applied consistently and fairly.

More generally, fraud prevention measures might involve educating colleagues and internal security to watch out for and enquire into the circumstances of employees who are living in a style far in excess of their salaries. Several defrauded firms had allowed employees on modest salaries to go on driving new Porsches and taking expensive holidays without conducting any enquiry or a more than superficial one into how they could afford this. Where the person enjoying the high life is a member of senior management, however, as many postscandal reports have noted, there are serious difficulties in knowing to whom one should report. Here, nonexecutive directors can play a vital role as impartial insiders, but since they tend to be selected by the existing senior executives, mechanisms should exist to enhance the independence in reality by having public interest directors. The underlying theory is that employees and the public are all stakeholders directly and indirectly and that they (along with minority shareholders) should be able to influence fraud prevention as well as other areas of potential misconduct by the corporation or its senior personnel.

Clear rules on own-account dealing by employees of financial institutions are vital. The mere existence of clear rules tells us nothing about whether they are followed. The use of nominee shareholdings—preferably in companies controlled from Panama, Liechtenstein, the Netherlands Antilles, or any of the morass of Third World islands who offer banking secrecy as their principal trading asset—and suspense accounts, from which one can load profitable deals into one's own account and unprofitable ones into the trust's accounts, are examples of activities that are difficult to monitor successfully unless the individual is very greedy or unless there is some reason why stock exchanges mount special investigations, for example, insider dealing suspicions arising from sudden market price movements prior to company announcements.

The role of ethical statements is a controversial one in business schools and practice. One American-based transnational I interviewed had a code of ethics that is expressed strongly and is applied vigorously. This company sends annual letters to suppliers drawing their attention to the code of business ethics and in particular to the requirements not to make gifts or take other actions toward employees that would contravene this. All senior employees have to sign an annual representation to say that they are not aware of and have not during the year contravened the code of business ethics. There is a limit as to how much private sector monitoring can occur, but the important thing is to have lines of accountability that can lead subsequently to individually attributable blame.

Much more difficult to prevent are frauds that involve collusion, and they can occur in any area of business. These fraudsters are the people in the cashier's department (perhaps in league with computer assistants) who pay phony invoices against goods that have not been received, the people in the purchasing department (or, perhaps, more senior than that) who get a rake-off from the supplier, or the manager who extends loans or credit terms to doubtful enterprises in which he or she has a covert interest. The main prevention method is to require standard devices such as double signing of checks, counter-signing of records of checks, and careful controls over purchasing and contracting in public and private sectors, with *prompt* checks to verify claims about how the money was spent. However, where there is collusion (and/or hostility to management and poor internal communications, often as a result of authoritarian management styles), the checks do not operate, and this increases the length of time that the fraud can continue undetected.

Crime prevention in the business world has to be seen in its economic, political, and social contexts (see Levi, 1987, 1988). Theoretically, private-sector judgments should differ from public-sector concerns, because it may not—in narrow terms—be rational for private sector organizations to take into account the externalities (i.e., the costs and benefits accruing to society at large) of their crime prevention decisions in the way that it would be rational for public-sector organizations to do. (Thus, if opportunities to use stolen credit cards lead to street robberies and burglaries, this is not part of the private-sector cost-benefit analysis.) In practice, of course, many public-sector organizations behave as if they were private ones: They have their own organizational agendas, unless benefits to other public-sector units can somehow be built into their own performance indicators. Even then, *personal* "glory factors" often intervene to frustrate bureaucratic harmonization. However, the classical theory of the corporation as profit-maximizer would suggest that in the private-sector, the *organizational* financial bottom line reigns supreme, though the social and political advantages of being seen as a "good corporate citizen" means that it is not easy to predict precisely what a rational corporation would do.

Conclusions

I have tried to indicate the interconnectedness between the causes and control of white-collar crime, not just in the tautological sense that opportunities are part of causes but also in the sense that a cultural climate can be created (or inhibited) in which financial crimes of various kinds become commonplace. Rationality of both individuals and organizations, let alone of society as a whole, is a more difficult concept to operationalize than is commonly assumed, for it depends partly on value choices and risk orientations that can properly vary. However, in the Reaganite and Thatcherite obsession with "private-sector good, public-sector bad," the role of public regulation has been subjected to considerable strain, as the savings and loan debacle illustrates (Calavita and Pontell, 1990; Pontell and Calavita, 1992). Simultaneously, with the devaluation of civic responsibility in the rush for personal advancement as the engine of the enterprise culture, in the enhanced climate of job insecurity with which even the middle classes in the "culture of contentment" have been plagued in the 1990s, the motivation to be honest has been submerged in the politics of envy. The ambivalent tension between laissez-faire ideology and the risk that in practice is entailed for liberty to be "done" is clear. And particularly given the imperfect informational market necessitated by the growth of agency and organizational complexity, not everyone is a good judge of their own interests, especially when they are being actively deceived.

What is required is not just some modicum of initial vetting of the competence and integrity of those who hold funds in trust, but also a more continuous flow of monitoring that ensures that even if—as is inevitable—people are able to defraud, their gains will not be allowed to continue for long without detection, so the total losses will be diminished. (Similar issues of transparency arise in corruption. See Grabosky, 1989.) The values of those in power may also have to be modified by reducing the amount of social distance—and thereby the subculturally reinforced sociopathy—between themselves and other stakeholders in society: workers, consumers, and citizenry in general. This may go against the grain of history, but even though the collapse of communism has left people bereft of international alternative models, the authoritarian populist right has the opportunity to gain from the collapse of confidence in capitalism and in its abilities to handle the complexities of an interdependent global economy.

In the aftermath of BCCI, banking regulators have moved toward a more integrated approach to global regulation, with clearer lines of responsibility for institutions operating in more than one market. Furthermore, in many First World countries—though not in the former communist countries that remain vulnerable to fraudulent dream-sellers—national regulators such as the U.S. Securities and Exchange Commission impose informational requirements upon those who wish to do business in their country. Nevertheless, unless businesspeople learn to share information to reduce their exposure to multiple victimization and unless we have the self-confidence to build up a more communitarian trust culture of regulation backed by sanctions, the anomic nightmare of a de-centered universe of unregulatable institutions remains just around the corner, as countries vie with each other to underbid regulation in order to attract providers of employment. As Oscar Wilde observed, "all of us are in the gutter, but some of us are looking at the stars."

References

Alabama Law Review. 1992. Special Issue on Money Laundering.

Barlow, Hugh D. 1993. "From Fiddle Factors to Networks of Collusion: Charting the Waters of Small Business Crime." *Crime, Law and Social Change,* 20:319-338.

Barnett, Harold. 1993. "Crimes Against the Environment: Superfund Enforcement at Last." *The Annals of the American Academy of Political and Social Science*, January: 119-133.

Benson, Michael. 1985. "Denying the Guilty Mind: Accounting for Involvement in White-Collar Crime." *Criminology.* 23:583-607.

Benson, Michael, and E. Moore. 1992. "Are White-Collar and Common Offenders the Same? An Empirical and Theoretical Critique of a Recently Proposed General Theory of Crime." *Journal of Research in Crime and Delinquency.* 15: 251-272.

Block, Alan. 1991. *Masters of Paradise: Organized Crime and the Internal Revenue Service in the Bahamas.* New Brunswick: Transaction.

Braithwaite, John. 1989. *Crime, Shame, and Reintegration.* Cambridge: Cambridge University Press.

———. 1992. "Poverty, Power, and White-Collar Crime: Sutherland and the Paradoxes of Criminological Theory." in Kip Schlegel and David Weisburd (eds.), *White-Collar Crime Reconsidered.* Boston: Northeastern University Press.

———. 1993a. "Beyond Positivism: Learning from Contextual Integrated Strategies." *Journal of Research in Crime and Delinquency* 30:383-399.

———. 1993b. "Crime and the Average American." *Law and Society Review* 27:215-231.

Braithwaite, John, and Tony Makkai. 1994. "Trust and Compliance." *Policing and Society* 4:1-12.

Burrows, John. 1991. *Making Crime Prevention Pay: Initiatives from Business.* Crime Prevention Unit Paper 27. London: Home Office.

Calavita, Kitty, and Henry Pontell. 1990. "'Heads I Win; Tails You Lose': Deregulation, Crime and Crisis in the Savings & Loan Industry." *Crime and Delinquency* 36:309-341.

Coleman, James. 1987. "Towards an Integrated Theory of White-Collar Crime." *American Journal of Sociology* 93:406-439.

Cressey. Donald. 1953. *Other People's Money.* New York: Free Press.

Daly, Kathleen. 1989. "Gender and Varieties of White-Collar Crime." *Criminology* 27:769-794.

Emery, Fred. 1994. *Watergate.* London: Chatto and Windus.

Etzioni, Amitai. 1993. "The U.S. Sentencing Commission on Corporate Crime: A Critique." *The Annals of the American Academy of Political and Social Science* January: 147-156.

Fisse, Brent and John Braithwaite. 1983. *The Impact of Publicity on White-Collar Crime.* Albany: SUNY Press.

Fisse, Brent and John Braithwaite. 1993. *Corporations, Crime, and Accountability.* Cambridge: Cambridge University Press.

Geis, Gil. 1992. "White-Collar Crime: What Is It?." In Kip Schlegel and David Weisburd (eds.), *White-Collar Crime Reconsidered.* Boston: Northeastern University Press.

Gold, Michael, and Michael Levi. 1994. *Money Laundering in the UK: The Impact of Suspicion-Based Reporting.* London: Police Foundation.

Goldsmith, Andrew, ed. 1993. *Complaints Against the Police in International Perspective.* Oxford: Oxford University Press.

Gottfredson, Michael R., and Travis Hirschi. 1990. *A General Theory of Crime.* Stanford: Stanford University Press.

Grabosky, Peter. 1989. *Wayward Governance: Illegality and its Control in the Public-sector.* Canberra: Australian Institute of Criminology.

Green Gary S. 1993. "White-Collar Crime and the Study of Embezzlement." *The Annals of the American Academy of Political and Social Science.* January:95-106.

Hagan, John. 1988. *Structural Criminology.* Cambridge: Polity Press.

Hirschi, Travis, and Michael R. Gottfredson. 1987. "Causes of White-Collar Crime." *Criminology* 25:949-974.

Jenkins, Anne, and John Braithwaite. 1993. "Profits, Pressure and Corporate Lawbreaking." *Crime, Law and Social Change* 20:221-232.

Katz, Jack. 1980. "The Social Movement Against White-Collar Crime." In Egon Bittner and Shelden Messenger (eds.), *Criminology Review Yearbook*, vol 2. Beverly Hills, CA: Sage.

Katz, Jack. 1988. *Seductions of Crime: Moral and Sensual Attractions in Doing Evil.* New York: Basic Books.

Levi, Michael. 1981. *The Phantom Capitalists.* Aldershot: Gower.

———. 1984. "Giving Creditors the Business: The Criminal Law in Inaction." *International Journal of the Sociology of Law* 12:321-333.

———. 1987. *Regulating Fraud: White-Collar Crime and the Criminal Process.* London: Routledge.

———. 1988. *The Prevention of Fraud.* Crime Prevention Unit Paper 17. London: Home Office.

———. 1989. "Fraudulent Justice? Sentencing the Business Criminal" In Pat Carlen and D. Cook (eds.), *Paying for Crime.* Milton Keynes: Open University Press.

———. 1991. "Sentencing White-Collar Crime in the Dark: The Case of the Guinness Four." *Howard Journal of Criminal Justice* 28:257-279.

———. 1992. "White-Collar Victimization." In Kip Schlegel and David Weisburd (eds.), *White-Collar Crime Reconsidered.* Boston: Northeastern University Press.

———. 1993. *The Investigation, Prosecution, and Trial of Serious Fraud.* Royal Commission on Criminal Justice Research, Study No.14. London: HMSO.

———. 1994. "Masculinities and White-Collar Crime." In Tim Newburn and Elizabeth Stanko (eds.), *Just Boys Doing Business,* London: Routledge.

———. n.d. "Covert Operations and White-Collar Crime." in Gary Marx and C. Fijnaut (eds.), *Undercover: Police Surveillance in Comparative Perspective.* Daventer: Kluwer.

Levi, Michael, Paul Bissell, and Tony Richardson. 1991. *The Prevention of Cheque and Credit Card Fraud.* Crime Prevention Paper 26. London: Home Office.

Levi, Michael, and Andrew Pithousen. n.d. *Victims of Fraud.* Oxford: Oxford University Press.

Lofquist, William. 1993. "Organizational Probation and the U.S. Sentencing Commission." *The Annals of the American Academy of Political and Social Science* January: 157-169.

Marx, Gary, 1988. *Undercover.* Berkeley: University of California Press.

Pontell, Henry, and Kitty Calavita. 1992. "Bilking Bankers and Bad Debts: White-Collar Crime and the Savings and Loan Crisis." In Kip Schlegel and David Weisburd (eds.), *White-Collar Crime Reconsidered.* Boston: Northeastern University Press.

Poveda, Tony. 1992. "White-Collar Crime and the Justice Department: The Institutionalization of a Concept." *Crime, Law and Social Change.* 17:235-252.

Nettler, Gwynn. 1974. "Embezzlement Without Problems." *British Journal of Criminology* 14:70-77.

Reiman, Jeffrey. 1994. *The Rich Get Richer and the Poor Get Prison.* 4th ed. Englewood Cliffs, NJ: Prentice-Hall.

Riesman, Martin. 1979. *Folded Lies.* New Haven: Yale University Press.

Shapiro, Susan 1990. "Collaring The Crime, Not the Criminal: Liberating the Concept of White-Collar Crime." *American Sociological Review* 55:346-364.

Simpson, Sally S. 1987. "Cycles of Illegality: Antitrust Violations in Corporate Anerica." *Social Forces* 65:943-63.

Sutherland, Edwin. 1983. *White-Collar Crime: The Uncut Version.* New Haven: Yale University Press.

Vaughan, Diane. 1992. "The Macro-Micro Connection in White-Collar Crime Theory." In Kip Schlegel and David Weisburd (eds.), *White-Collar Crime Reconsidered.* Boston: Northeastern University Press.

Veblen, Thorsten. 1967. *The Theory of the Leisure Class.* New York: Viking Press.

Weisburd, David, Stanton Wheeler, Elaine Waring, and Nancy Bode. 1991. *Crimes of the Middle Classes.* New Haven: Yale University Press.

Wheeler, Stanton. 1992. "The Problem of White-Collar Crime Motivation." In Kip Schlegel and David Weisburd (eds.), *White-Collar Crime Reconsidered.* Boston: Northeastern University Press.

Wheeler, Stanton, Kenneth Mann, and Austin Sarat. 1988. *Sitting in Judgment.* New Haven: Yale University Press.

Wilson, James, Q., and Joan Petersilia. 1995. *Crime.* San Francisco: Institute for Contemporary Studies Press.

Wolfe, Tom. 1987. *Bonfire of the Vanities.* London: Paladin.

Zeitz, Dorothy. 1981. *Women Who Embezzle or Defraud: A Study of Women Convicted Felons.* New York: Praeger.

15

A Public Policy Agenda for Combating Organized Crime

Darrell J. Steffensmeier

No other area in the field of criminal justice is as difficult to define, describe, operationally deal with, evaluate, conduct research on, and develop policy recommendations for as organized crime. Indeed, there is no agreement on a definition of organized crime in either the law enforcement or the academic communities, except that it must relate to groups of people engaged together in criminal enterprises. For example, federal and state RICO (Racketeering Influenced and Corrupt Organizations) statutes are aimed at organized crime, but nowhere do they define organized crime. Rather, by their titles and their definitions they address "racketeering" in terms so general that in their civil aspects they provide remedies for the most conventional of white-collar crimes.

This chapter explores the nature of organized crime, identifies the four major forms having the greatest impact on the United States, and concludes with proposals for an effective public policy that is driven by accumulated theory and research. Note at the onset that I do not devote much space to the many drug groups and networks that have emerged in the past couple of decades and that constitute the core of what is usually referred to as "nontraditional organized crime." These groups typically are ephemeral and short-lived, and the scope of their crime activities is limited (they usually are involved only in the drug trade). I also do not address other forms of financial and economic crime that powerfully affect in adverse ways whole areas of productive, social, and institutional life. For instance, corporate conspiracies, such as the Milken-led Drexel-Burnham "insider trading" scheme, are not dealt with—even though they may be as or even more threatening to the social frabric and in many respects also fit standard definitions of "organized crime."

Key Elements of Organized Crime. Most analysts of organized crime would agree that the essential elements designating organized crime involve the following:

- Those involved associate for the purpose of engaging in criminal activity on a sustained basis; there is considerable continuity in the "life" of the organization or network.
- They engage in enterprise crime, namely, (1) illegally providing goods or services, and (2) seeking to maintain and extend market share.
- Like any business, these activities require a fair amount of cooperation and organization. The more sophisticated organizations are hierarchical (i.e., three or more levels of power differentiation) and also have an overarching structure that involves mechanisms for leadership succession, membership recruitment, and dispute resolution.
- They use violence and corruption to facilitate their economic activities— for self-protection, settlement of disputes, and the carrying out of illicit activities.
- They have a reputation (e.g., based on violence, trust) of "being able to deliver" and of "getting things done" (e.g., providing protection from other crime groups, the law, and so on).

Fundamentally, organized crime is about the exploitation of business or market opportunities. In many instances, the organized crime groups can be treated as if they were business firms with material, organizational, and managerial assets that make it possible to maintain their extraordinary staying power (Moore, 1987). Analysts disagree, however, about issues such as size, structure, and cohesion of criminal organizations. At one end of the spectrum, organized crime is described in terms of large hierarchical organizations that are structured rather like traditional corporations. At the other end, organized crime is described in terms of small, fluid networks that are rather amorphous in structure and are characterized by considerable opportunism.

This is a bogus dichotomy, however. Criminal organizations fall along a continuum from large to small and from formal hierarchical (even bureaucratic) structure to fluid network organizations. Criminal organizations falling at either end of the continuum may be equally adaptable to the exigencies of the illicit marketplace. The Colombian cartels and the Sicilian Mafia, for example, have demonstrated remarkable adaptability in spite of their large size and organizational sophistication.

In addition to *size* and *degree of formal structure*, criminal organizations can be identified and compared relative to their *scope of criminal activities*. Some groups are highly specialized and focus on one kind of activity such as prostitution or drugs. Other groups engage in a broader range of criminal activities such as gambling, extortion, drug trafficking, and various financial scams.

Criminal organizations or networks also vary in terms of their *geographic scope*—local, national, or transnational. A powerful transformation is occurring whereby organized crime increasingly is becoming transnational in character. Less and less are the criminal activities of criminal organizations constrained by national borders. Further, organized crime groups that are still predominantly domestic in scope can be expected in the future to increase their exploitation of global opportunities.

A final dimension concerns the *scale of impact on the citizenry and on the political and economic structure of a nation or nations.* The American Mafia and the major transnational crime organizations represent what Arlacchi has termed *large-scale organized crime* to refer to those powerful criminal groups "able to engage in political and economic activity both through legitimate official structures and by illegal means, and which can adversely affect whole areas of productive, social and institutional life" (Arlacchi, 1986:213). Large-scale organized crime is not limited to the United States but has recently emerged as a real and pressing problem on a global scale.

Dimensions of the Organized Crime Problem in America

The American Mafia

Italians are but one in a long succession of immigrant groups to become involved in organized crime in the United States. The Irish were the first group to become involved on a large scale, followed by East European Jews and then by Italian and Sicilian immigrants. In recent years Hispanic and Chinese immigrants have made a place for themselves in organized crime. But Italian-American organized crime, of which La Cosa Nostra (LCN) is the archetype, has achieved broader dominance over a wider range of criminal activities than that of any other ethnic group, and for a longer period of time. And it has become the standard to which all other organized crime groups are compared.

Other criminal groups have succeeded in establishing syndicates that coordinate criminal activity within limited territories or for certain populations, particular forms of crime, or short periods of time, but none has matched LCN in longevity, nationwide span of control, and versatility of criminal pursuits. LCN has been and is involved in almost every kind of scam imaginable, from truck hijackings to bankruptcy fraud; in supplying illegal goods and services; in extortion; in political corruption; in labor racketeering; and in infiltration and control of legitimate businesses. It has been and continues to be a major player in the drug trade. LCN is by far the dominant player in illegal gambling and loan-sharking in U.S. cities where there is a sizable Italian population. Finally, its capacity to extort from other illegal operators and legitimate businesses, to illegally monopolize legitimate businesses (e.g., waste hauling), and to engage in labor racketeering is virtually unique among U.S. crime groups.

Today, about two dozen LCN "families" are centered in urban areas with relatively large Italian-American populations, such as New York and Chicago. The networks of these families are expansive, moreover, so that localized Mafia groups and Mafia-connected criminal activities exist in a substantial number of U.S. cities. Legislation made to counter organized crime, notably the Racketeer Influenced Corrupt Organizations (RICO) Act, was designed with LCN in mind. Indeed, until recently, "LCN" and "organized crime" were considered to be synonymous terms by many law enforcement authorities.

More is now known about LCN than about other organized crime groups. During the 1980s, in particular, a wealth of information became available through numerous mob trials and the testimony of LCN informants. This information both confirmed and refined the picture provided by earlier sources, including the "government version" of the Mafia that was articulated in 1967 by the President's Crime Commission and in a subsequent monograph written by Donald Cressey (1969), a consultant to the commission.

This newer evidence confirms that LCN exists; that it is structured and possesses a hierarchical chain of command; that it is self-perpetuating; and that becoming a "made" member involves initiation rites and pledges of loyalty, secrecy, and violence. The LCN family operates autonomously in many U.S. cities, but individual groups are joined together in a crime confederation in which a limited amount of authority has been ceded to a governing National Commission. The Commission regulates interfamily conflicts but does not attempt to run the day-to-day operations of the syndicates.

Moreover, events have not borne out the prediction of "ethnic succession." Italian groups continue to constitute the most enduring and stable organized crime network, contradicting the view that criminal ethnic groups, once they became well-established in America, would yield the underworld to newer immigrants farther down the social ladder of assimilation and success. New immigrant groups have entered the world of organized crime (and continue to do so), but none has ever approached the ongoing reach and stability of La Cosa Nostra.

The bureaucratic analogy sometimes applied to La Cosa Nostra, however, appears to have been overstated (and perhaps misdirected). Its structure is looser and more decentralized than the organizational charts imply. Day-to-day operations of organized crime are often quite haphazard, both because of inadequate managerial skills on the part of most participants and because of the need for secrecy—which sets limits on managerial control. Relationships between family hierarchy and members—as well as associations with other family groups—are flexible and fluid. Individual members have sufficient autonomy to build their own power bases and connections. They make their own deals with other criminals, businesses, labor leaders, and government officials based on potential profits or services required.

There are differing views on the American Mafia's current status and its future. Clearly, the activity level of a number of La Cosa Nostra families is less today than it was a decade ago. Several factors have contributed to this decline: changing illicit markets (especially drugs); advancing age and attrition in membership: the decline of ethnic communities in urban areas; the shift of political power from cities to the federal government, including the decline in the local "political machine;" the decline of unions; the development of overlapping enforcement jurisdictions; and the increased effectiveness of federal enforcement efforts. These together have reduced three main historical assets of the Mafia—centralized corruption of police and local officials, a disciplined work-force, and reputation.

The most important factor appears to be the more intense and effective law enforcement activity directed at the Mafia. The "war against the mob" of the past two decades is unprecedented, particularly that directed at the New York families. Principal was the adoption in the early 1980s of a long-term strategy using RICO to develop cases against the Mafia families as criminal enterprises. Many law enforcement officials believe that if the "war" continues to be strongly waged, "it is possible to remove La Cosa Nostra as a significant threat to American society" (Sessions, 1988).

The optimistic prediction of the Mafia's demise, however, is contradicted by FBI field reports noting that the prosecutions have had a tremendous impact on the hierarchy of the families but little effect on Mafia-related activity (Pennsylvania Crime Commission, 1990). Joseph Pistone, a former FBI agent who spent six years working undercover as "Donnie Brasco" and infiltrated the NY Colombo and Bonanno LCN Families, has concluded that it is the *subculture* of neighborhoods with roots in southern Italy that explains LCN's long-term survival. Breaking up the Mafia requires breaking down this subculture. He states that "there is a large pool of potential members and leaders just waiting to take over from those we convict" (Pennsylvania Crime Commission, 1990:188).

Emerging or Previously Ignored Crime Groups

Today, besides traditional Italian organized crime, it is widely recognized that there exists in every metropolitan area of this nation a collage of ethnic groups-- Asians, blacks, Colombians, Dominicans, Jamaicans, Mexicans, Syrians, Lebanese and Russians—involved in organized crime, particularly in the drug trade. Many of these groups are considered "new" or "emerging" in that they have become active in recent years. Other groups, such as the outlaw motorcycle gangs, are "new" in the sense that they have only recently been recognized as crime groups, even though they have been operating for many years in organized crime activities and are now well established.

Some of the motorcycle and street gang networks have the appearance of being highly organized, with formal constitutions, elected officers, and regional chapters throughout the United States. On paper, these groups are as tightly structured as LCN; however, informal leaders often emerge to exercise more power than the elected officers. Notably—in contrast with other organized crime groups—the outlaw biker and street gangs do not place much value on secrecy regarding their members' identities. Instead, they publicly proclaim their membership by distinctive colors, uniforms and graffiti. The biker groups engage in a variety of criminal activities, such as theft of motorcycles and prostitution, but the bulk of their criminality today centers around the drug trade.

Black-American criminal organizations have been centered around the traditional vices of gambling (mainly numbers), drugs, prostitution, and to a lesser extent, loan-sharking and theft/fencing (as opposed, for example, to extortion, labor racketeering, and the illicit control of legitimate businesses). Black organized crime groups prey almost exclusively on blacks, and the prepoderance of black organized crime occurs in segregated black neighborhoods, particularly within the inner cities. Since the 1960s, black-run drug distribution organizations have become increasingly common. Most of these are small, fluid groups which continuously evolve and disband because of internal disputes. However, there also have been a number of attempts to form genuine sydicates, including two such instances in Pennsylvania: the Black Mafia (active primarily in the early 1970s) and the Junior Black Mafia (active in the mid-and late 1980s). Both developed out of the street culture of Philadelphia, were modeled on La Cosa Nostra, and were ruined by their own factionalism and violence and by aggressive law enforcement.

Recent immigration to the United States has spawned ethnic crime groups who often direct much of their criminal activity in this country against members of their own ethnic group. For example, the population of Chinese and other Asians has increased, and with it has emerged Chinese organized crime activity revolving around Tongs. Tongs are social and business associations originally established in Chinese communities to help Chinese immigrants adapt to the new country. They also have served as a focal point for community activity. Many Tongs are legitimate but some have been found to be involved in gambling, loan-sharking, prostitution, and smuggling of aliens. Some evidence also suggests that Asian racketeers are expanding their gambling portfolio beyond traditional Asian forms to include sports and video poker gambling.

A number of other ethnic-based immigrant groups also are involved in organized crime, including organizations of Russian emigrés, Cubans, Syrians, and Lebanese. Some of these groups are highly organized, whereas others are not. Similar to other organized crime groups, however, they engage more or less fulltime in a wide variety of crimes including not only drugs and gambling but also counterfeiting, fraud, auto theft, and fencing stolen property. Also, some of these ethnic-based immigrant groups maintain ties to criminal groups in their homelands.

Local Racketeering Syndicates

A largely unrecognized but important dimension of the organized crime phenomenon is the significant and long-standing presence of local racketeering groups that dominate extortion and vice activities in many localities and cities throughout the United States, doing so both through legitimate official structures and by illegal means. As far back as 1951, the Kefauver Committee concluded that much organized crime is localized and indigenous to the community in which it exists.

In the 1960s, John Gardiner wrote about a city he called Wincanton—in reality Reading, Pennsylvania—where for decades organized crime elements worked closely with public officials and local businessmen to dominate gambling and other racketeering activities. Although not necessarily as rife with crime and official corruption, similar racketeering structures apparently exist in many (perhaps most) U.S. cities and towns (see Chambliss, 1978; Steffensmeier, 1986; Pennsylvania Crime Commission, 1990; Potter, 1994;). These studies all show that core membership in these racketeering groups includes not only mafioso and professional criminals but also businessmen (e.g., car dealers, contractors, restaurant owners), police and city officials, attorneys, and other individuals from "respectable" society who are influential in local politics.

These local crime syndicates generally represent distinct entities, although they often overlap and may even be fragments of a large-scale crime organization such as La Cosa Nostra. The syndicates tend to be dominated by a handful of individual entrepreneurs in which the illegal activities of each racketeer are carried out through a network of individuals associated with him in that activity. With this type of operation, the relationship is fostered frequently by the activity rather than the particular people. A number of substantive criminal relationships or partnerships may develop linking joint criminal operations within a network and across other crime networks dominated by other local criminal figures. Overlapping partnerships for specific illegal ventures are stitched together through opportunistic and fluid alliances. In some instances there may be a central racketeering figure but more likely there is shared power and a shifting power structure depending in particular on who at the time is most influential with local law enforcement and city officials.

The majority of local racketeers are well known throughout the community and in many cases represent relationships that have survived for years. Many have been engaged in illegal gambling and the rackets for decades. Those currently active are often offspring or kin (including in-laws) of former racketeers or "old-timers." The core or hub of these local syndicates tends to have a strong ethnic presence—where one or a few ethnic groups dominate (as reflected in designations such as "Irish Mafia," "Polish Mafia," "German Mafia," and "Jewish mob"). In those localities where there is an ample Italian population, moreover, there always appears to be a strong Italian presence within the syndicate's core membership; that is, the main racketeers either are a part of LCN or they form alliances with members or associates of LCN and engage in joint criminal ventures with them. The extent of LCN involvement is sometimes unclear but their influence appears widespread for resolving disputes between competing interests in a particular racket or preventing a dispute from emerging by controlling franchises.

The considerable involvement of LCN (or at least the central participation of individuals of southern Italian background) in a city's rackets is strongly evident in Pennsylvania—probably the only state where the role of local racketeering syndicates as a dimension of organized crime has been fairly adequately researched.[1] LCN refers here not only to the three homegrown Pennsylvania LCN families (LaRocca/Genovese, Bruno/Scarfo, and Bufalino) but also to the New York LCN families who operate in the state. There also has been and continues to be a substantial Jewish involvement in local racketeering in many of Pennsylvania's cities.

The following statement from Sam Goodman—who for many years fenced stolen goods and hobnobbed with people in the rackets in two cities in northeastern United States—clarifies the powerful and influential place of the local clique in local politics and in the local rackets (Steffensmeier, 1986: 63-64):

> There were half-dozen, maybe ten, main ones in American City that were connected one way or another. They all had their fingers into different things, legit and illegit. The main ones were Mafia or connected to it. A couple of others were Italian but not really tied up, even though your ordinary "Joe Blow" is thinking they are. But they [the non-Mafia Italians] were "cut from the same cloth, "know what I mean. The Jewish involvement is there, no doubt about that. But they stay more in the background. If push came to shove I'd say the Italians had the backing to do things their way. But it ain't one boss telling the others what to do. They all more or less worked together, do each other favors, didn't get in each other's way. Who was on top was whoever had the connections with city hall, with the police.
>
> Then you may have another 20-25 guys who are more on the sidelines, like myself. We're doing our own thing but maybe hooking up with the main clique, too, for this or that deal. If the Mafia people and the local clique is pushing for you, that is a very big asset. You are helping them but they are helping you. Put it this way, Angelo [local mafioso in American City] and them, made my path a whole lot easier.

Transnational Criminal Organizations (TCOs)

"Arms, drugs, industrial and military secrets, illegally acquired currency, professional gunmen and agents provocateurs, and human beings reduced to economic or sexual slavery—all now circulate throughout the world more readily and on a larger scale than ever before" (Arlacchi 1986:214). Hardly recognized by many criminologists, criminal organizations are increasingly

2. There are many crime organizations with distinct structures, varying criminal specialties, and distinct modi operandi. Recognition that organized crime groups vary along many dimensions is a prerequisite for tailoring policies or strategies to the specific organization and the political, economic, and cultural contexts within which it operates.

3. Ethnicity typically plays an important role in the formation and function of organized crime groups (Steffensmeier, 1983; Pennsylvania Crime Commission, 1990). Ethnicity contributes to the organization of crime a feeling of camaraderie built on blood ties; a common cultural base; insularity; mutual trust; a distrust of government; and an exclusivity that reinforces bonds and secrecy within the organization.

4. Organized crime and the groups or networks that engage in organized crime differ greatly in geographical scope. Some are based in a single city or region whereas others transcend even national boundaries. Policy initiatives should encompass local, national, and global levels.

Efforts to combat organized crime must take into account both its complexity and variety. The groups operate in different product markets and geographical domains and use a variety of tactics to circumvent law enforcement. There is not a universal panacea for addressing organized crime. Specific policies will depend on which group or product market is targeted. What works for one organized crime problem may not work for another.

Address Roots of Organized Crime

Some of the state's "control" energies should be applied to ameliorate the structural sources that fundamentally fuel organized crime. There are at least four main factors that, singly or in combination, contribute to the rise and persistence of organized crime.

First, a certain level of social-cultural disorganization is an essential precondition for the growth of organized crime. Noteworthy here are the consequences of (1) the industrialization and urbanization that have taken place over the last two centuries in countries in the West, (2) the so-called "modernization" that is presently taking place in certain large Asian, Latin American, and African nations, and (3) the spreading democratization and free-market capitalism in the Eastern European nations. Their effects—growing social injustice, poverty, and violence—create a seedbed in particular for the emergence of large-scale criminal organizations at the global level.

In the United States, these elements of social disorganization are most manifest in the inner cities of large urban areas, where long-term poverty and social disintegration provide fertile ground for drug dealers and other entrepreneurs who market the goods and services supplied by organized crime. In neighborhoods where the most visible symbols of success are the fast cars and flashy clothes and jewels of drug dealers, enterprising youth find it hard to resist the promise of easy riches. Economic and social revitalization of our deteriorating cities is the most urgent need. This will not be cheap, but investment in the future will be more cost-effective in the long run than the continuing escalation in costs of crime, health, welfare, law enforcement, and corrections that are likely to accompany continued neglect of the most vulnerable segment of society.

A second factor is weak goverment—criminal organizations are more likely to emerge and flourish where the government is lacking in legitimacy or is not fully in control of the territory under its jurisdiction. Indeed, organized crime in many countries (e.g., Sicily) has been generated by despotic governments that give rise to groups formed for self-protection and for providing quasi-governmental services. These groups typically involve a common ethnic origin, require loyalty from their members, and during their formative years inspire both fear and respect from their compatriots.

The lack of governmental service and protection, in turn, may foster the growth of an ethos that provides the cultural underpinnings for organized crime. Main tenets of the ethos include distrust of outsiders and government, clannishness, proclivity for sanctioned violence and private revenge, a sense of how to co-opt the law and achieve immunity by corrupting influential persons, and savvy to cultivate the goodwill of local residents while simultaneously exploiting them for personal advantage.

Third, organized crime arises because it is functional either to the community or to large subgroups in the society. These functions are varied but may range from providing desired but illicit goods and services, social control and protection in areas (e.g., against certain predatory crimes) where government or official agencies have failed, opportunities for political and economic participation, and welfare-type assistance (e.g., in finding employment and with short-term loans to prop up precarious small businesses).

Fourth, organized crime is about the exploitation of business or market opportunities. There is an easy affinity between organized crime and market-based economies, as Smith (1980:164) has noted: "[Organized crime] represents in virtually every instance, an extension of a legitimate market spectrum into areas 'normally proscribed.' Their separate strengths derive from the same fundamental considerations that govern entrepreneurship in the legitimate marketplace: a necessity to maintain and extend one's share of the market.

The organized crime phenomenon is primarily *economic* and *institutional* rather than criminal. Control strategies most likely to be effective will target the real structures and seats of power of organized crime—at governmental weakness and official corruption, at financial markets and accumulated capital, and at the institutional degeneration that allows the problems to continue and grow worse:

1. Enhance criminal justice initiatives that better erode the criminal groups' fundamental raison d'être by confiscating their wealth and erecting stronger

barriers between the legitimate financial market and the market in "dirty" capital.

2. Require a larger governmental response—at both the national and international levels—that lessens social disintegration and institutional degeneration by strengthening governmental legitimacy and reducing the economic backwardness of large subgroups of the population.

3. Provide a sustained program of research and intelligence assessment that seeks to better understand the causes and consequences of organized crime, and searches for effective counterstrategies and evaluates them.

The next section elaborates on these essential features of organized-crime control, beginning with the important need for research and the establishment of an external expert community

Research and Assessment

We currently lack the full understanding of organized crime that is needed to build structures and systems to help contain or defeat it. The first step is to establish clearly what we do and do not know about organized crime. To accomplish this will require that we develop a program of research and also institutionalize ongoing assessments of organized crime.

Better Data. A notable feature of organized crime research is the lack of data collection and access. Field research and historical studies are helpful, but, in strictly practical terms, greater access to official agency materials is by far the most crucial element if major advances are to be made in the research on organized crime. Particularly since 1980, considerable information has been available today on a number of organized crime groups (particularly the American Mafia) that is based on electronic surveillance, informant and undercover methodologies, and trial testimony. Most notably, the increasing use of informants in prosecuting organized-crime individuals and groups has resulted in an abundance of intelligence data about organized crime. Access both to the investigative files and the informants would enable the researcher to describe the settings, structure, and activities with a verisimilitude that simply has not been available to date.

First-Rate Scholars. Attracting high-quality scholars to the field is equally important. To do this requires, first, the development of data bases and, second, sufficient economic incentives and opportunities for funded research. Unfortunately, the federal government been stingy in its funding of organized crime, and very little research has been sponsored by the major agencies involved in the organized crime effort.

Foremost is to increase the pool of researchers who are empirically oriented, analytically skilled, and objective in their approach to organized crime. There has been a tendency toward hyperbole—to greatly exaggerate or downplay the significance of this or that crime group in the overall schema of organized crime. With regard to the American Mafia, for instance, just as commentators in the 1950s and 1960s often "puffed up" the power and influence of the American Mafia, writers today frequently engage in considerable "LCN bashing," downgrading its role as being no more powerful or threatening than other ethnic-based crime groups (Kappler, Blumberg, and Potter, 1993) and in some cases even asserting that the "Mafia doesn't exist" (Hawkins, 1969). Some recent writers, in turn, embellish and puff up the power and influence of newly emergent crime groups, such as asserting the dominance of black-run gambling syndicates or characterizing the threat of recent Asian crime groups as "making the Sicilian Mafia look like a bunch of Sunday school kids" and a "fraternity of wimps" (Potter and Jenkins, 1985). These embroidered views lessen the credibility of organized-crime researchers not only among the larger research community but among law enforcement as well.

The Establishment of an External Expert Community. There is a powerful need to develop a research tradition that goes beyond description and makes use of modern social science techniques to develop and test hypotheses about the causes and consequences of organized crime (Reuter, 1987:184). To sustain this will require the establishment of an expert community that is external to law enforcement or government officials and includes specialists from a wide variety of academic and professional fields.

Federal Research. The establishment of a research program, including an expert community, would be greatly enhanced by increased federal support. Historically, such financial support has been limited and sporadic. Among the factors that may account for this is that federal funding agencies such as the National Academy of Sciences and the National Science Foundation place great emphasis on research proposals that are sound both theoretically and empirically (Kenney and Finckenaur, 1995). Organized crime theory is poorly developed and there is a shortage of empirically oriented researchers.

Ongoing National and International Assessment. Intelligence gathering on many facets of organized crime has been ongoing for years, but at present there is very little in the way of national or international assessment of the organized crime problem. Such government assessments should directly address not only what we know about organized crime but also what is *not* known or what we *need* to know. In addition, the assessments should identify the vulnerabilities of organized crime and the opportunities that exist to influence its operations. On the international level, the FBI, CIA, other law enforcement and intelligence agencies, and the military now cooperate and exchange information much more effectively than in the past. What is needed, at present, is to assemble this material into a comprehensive assessment (Godson, 1994).

Enhanced Law Enforcement and More Effective Sanctioning

There has been a considerable advance over the past couple of decades in the investigative and prosecutorial tools that are available to combat organized crime. These include investigative grand juries, grants of immunity, informants, witness protection, electronic surveillance, and auditing of tax returns. In addition, a number of federal (and state) laws now exist that strike more effectively at the structure and assets of criminal organizations.

Chief among these are RICO and CCE (the Continuing Criminal Enterprise or the "drug kingpin" statute). These tools have been applied most successfully against the American Mafia (especially in the eastern United States) but they also are being used increasingly against nontraditional or emerging crime organizations. Indeed, partly because of RICO it is unlikely that these other criminal organizations operating in specific ethnic communities or specific markets will develop the broad-based power that the Mafia has had from the early 1900s to the present.

RICO, and some forty state statutes patterned after it, offer the law enforcement community and crime victims some of the strongest weapons against ongoing organized crime. RICO statutes commonly include both stiff criminal penalties and expansive civil remedies, including lengthy imprisonment, fines, and forfeiture of any interest (e.g., a business, property, or investment) acquired in the named "enterprise."

Designed initially to combat the American Mafia, RICO is a prominent example of "sociological" criminal legislation. It alters law enforcement strategies in a number of critical ways. Whereas traditional law enforcement efforts simply react to apparently isolated crimes, RICO proactively focuses investigations on groups of people engaged in patterns of offenses, placing a premium on identifying and chasing "dirty" money and ruining criminals financially.

What sets RICO apart is that it targets both the organization and the economic foundation of organized criminality more than it does individual wrongdoers. Certain forms of crime are so profitable that they become quasi-institutionalized, and the confederates, especially at the lower levels, become interchangeable. As a consequence, merely disabling individual offenders through incarceration has little impact on the enterprise's vitality or criminal capacity. Besides the leadership, the RICO enterprise approach seeks the identity of members and associates participating in the various crimes as well as the coconspirator businesspeople who financially benefit from the pattern of racketeering activity.

This conception of *expansive criminal enterprise* is novel in American jurisprudence and it has set new standards and requirements for intelligence gathering and police work. First, the effective use of RICO requires a better understanding of the structure and the business-type activities of crime groups. This insight is critical for proving the existence of a criminal enterprise, for identifying and tracing assets for seizure, and for issuing injunctions to remove members of organized criminal groups from positions of power and influence in business and labor organizations. Second, it requires the cooperative effort by local, state, and federal law enforcement agencies to address the organized crime problem at both the local and national levels. To date, local police are hampered by their limited geographic jurisdiction, and law enforcement has not responded by developing sufficient coordination among the agencies. Third, there is an increasingly greater need for entities or units that specialize in developing and coordinating an intelligence base for striking at criminal organizations and not just at individual criminals.

Intelligence allows for a multipronged attack against a criminal organization that incorporates administrative, civil, and criminal sanctions (see discussion below). Another advantage of intelligence programs is that they are a springboard for the collection of data on organized crime that can be used for research purposes and the development of an expert external community.

Greater Use of Civil and Administrative Remedies. Although incarceration is often the ultimate goal of an organized-crime control operation, it often is more feasible and less expensive to employ civil and, if appropriate, administrative remedies. Standards of proof differ—usually less rigorous than in a criminal prosecution—and the penalties may be more effective in diminishing the revenue-generating capabilities of the organization. For example, a criminal organization that uses bars and cocktail lounges to offer illegal gambling, drugs, and prostitution services can be sanctioned both administratively as well as civilly for purposes of shrinking or negating its revenue-generating capabilities. At the global level, moreover, criminal organizations that are involved in large-scale laundering of illicit proceeds through offshore or foreign banking institutions can have their assets attached in civil courts that have jurisdiction. These courts are often more receptive to government claims of illegality and more amenable to returning assets than traditional criminal prodecures.

The advantages of civil and administrative approaches to containing organized crime are particularly evident in government-regulated pariah industries that are most vulnerable to organized crime influence—such as the sanitation industry, state-run lotteries, casino gambling, and construction. The role of government is critical because a well-regulated industry can encourage public confidence and, at the same time, discourage organized crime control and influence. An example is casino gambling, an industry that was once dominated by organized crime. Noteworthy are the regulatory and licensing standards that put the onus on the applicant—since receiving a license from the state is a privilege as opposed to a right—to prove his or her suitability for licensure. The requirements also involve proof of sources of income, so government is able to track monies invested in legitimate businesses. Today, given strict government oversight and the fear of federal intervention, the casino industry has far less corruption and racketeer involvement than a decade or two ago.

Improved Strategies To Control Money Laundering. Money laundering provides the essential link between organized crime and almost limitless commercial and financial options in the legitimate sector. Because of federal and state tax and banking laws and regulations requiring compliance, criminals need to convert illegal income into legal income or at least disguise its illegality. Because hard cash is the preferred medium of exchange among criminals (and their clients), "dirty" money must be turned into "clean" money, for example, deposited into foreign bank accounts, converted into foreign currency, or converted into treasury or bank checks, money orders, or stocks and bonds (Karchmer and Ruch, 1992; Kenney and Finckenauer, 1995).

Policies are needed that allow investigators to more easily follow "money trails" and that erect barriers between the legitimate financial market and the market in "dirty" capital. Helpful actions here would include improved intelligence for gathering and analyzing financial transactions; analysis of money exchanges and check-cashing services; complete data on investment capital, including all sources in "chain" investments, foreign corporations, and offshore banks; full disclosure of trust accounts, including the listing of who has access, the sources of income, allocations, and withdrawals; more rigorous enforcement of reporting laws on bank transactions involving large sums of money; and more effective monitoring and disciplining of licensed professionals involved in financial transactions—including a nationwide data base available to professional licensing, regulatory, and law enforcement agencies. Finally, international action and cooperation are needed since the markets in legitimate finance and "dirty" money are increasingly linked through offshore finance systems (see discussion below).

Circumspect Decriminalization or Nonenforcement. The largest and most profitable organized crime enterprises are those that provide illicit goods and services—drugs, gambling, prostitution, and loan-sharking—to significant segments of the public. Approaches aimed at limiting demand for these goods and services by punishing the consumers or by persuading them noncoercively to avoid these products are obviously important. But these approaches have at best been only marginally successful in reducing the illicit behaviors. Thus, some writers have proposed *decriminalization* as a method of dealing with these crimes.

The argument for decreasing organized criminal opportunity through legalization has been a long-standing one with regard to certain types of gambling, in particular the state lottery. Originally proposed as a way of reducing the income of "numbers"—an illegal lottery game—and capturing those monies for public use, many states now have a variety of lottery games: instant winners, daily drawings, and weekly drawings with payoffs in the millions of dollars (Abadinsky, 1994:508). The lottery has aided some states financially but there is no evidence that the legal lotteries have diminished the revenues of their illegal counterparts.

The issue of decriminalizing drug use is even more complex. Drug trafficking provides the greatest profits for organized crime, especially for the emerging organized crime groups. The decriminalization of powerfully addictive drugs such as cocaine and heroin is unrealistic and may actually enhance the lucrativeness of this market for organized crime (Inciardi 1990). A more middle-of-theroad approach appears feasible, where drugs that are less harmful, such as marijuana are either legalized and regulated or their use is benignly neglected. Already the police and courts in many localities have moved away from enforcement of marijuana laws. The general decline in marijuana use over the past decade or so suggests that this policy of nonenforcement has had few negative consequences and may in fact have had positive effects. Expanded decriminalization of marijuana laws across the United States as a whole as well as decriminalization of some other drug laws on an experimental basis appear warranted. The issue of decriminalization and legalization is complex, however, and more knowledge and evaluation are needed to determine the trade-offs and side effects produced.

Increase in Law Enforcement Resources. Arguably the financial costs and threats to government and institutions posed by organized crime make it the more serious crime problem as compared to delinquency, street crime, and even corporate crime. Indeed, there is growing evidence that as the illegal market in drugs expands and the organized-crime phenomenon grows, juvenile crime and youth gangs are being transformed in some large American cities. The gangs have become older and more entrepreneurial and are increasingly linked to criminal operators who supply them with drugs, employ them in particularly hazardous undertakings, and sometimes protect them from the police.

Yet the bulk of law enforcement resources are directed at ordinary street crimes and at some forms of career criminality—typically the repeat street-crime offender but excluding the organized-crime criminal. Ranking the latter higher in the overall scheme of law enforcement efforts directed at crime requires, among other things, that tax revenue be shifted away from other areas and into law enforcement directed at organized crime. Perhaps more innovative financing of enforcement and research are possible, such as the use of monies produced by legal lotteries.

Strategic Planning at State, National, and International levels

It is difficult to establish organized crime as a top priority given the overloaded condition of the criminal justice system. Effective action against organized crime, therefore, requires priorities in objectives and efficient management of resources. Thus, strategic planning to address organized crime must be part of any effort to contain its growth. More than anything, the planning should include *ongoing government-sponsored assessments* of the nature and scope of organized crime.

At the state level, strategic planning to address organized crime can be accomplished through a variety of mechanisms including a *statewide council on organized crime.* This council, comprised of individuals from a variety of legal and academic backgrounds and utilizing intelligence collected by those agencies responsible for organized crime control, would shape control policies and encourage implementation. Another important predicate for this planning effort is the establishment of state crime commissions tasked to compile intelligence about organized crime activities and publish reports at regular intervals that provide a focus on the problem of organized crime. The statewide council and crime commission not only would aid the law enforcement community but would also contribute to a public that is better informed of the nature and extent of organized crime activity and perhaps aware of how it can assist in prevention control and prevention of organized crime. Former attorney general Robert Kennedy stressed that an informed and insistent public was one of the best weapons available to drive the racketeer into bankruptcy or prison.

Strategic planning at the national level should be pursued in three main ways. First, an advisory task force on organized crime should be established for purposes of providing a comprehensive assessment of the scope and nature of the organized crime problem facing the United States today. Since the 1967 Task Force report on organized crime of the President's Commission on Law Enforcement and Administration of Justice, there has been no serious assessment of organized crime activity in the United States. The proposed task force would review the problem of organized crime from local, state, national, and international perspectives.

Second, a permanent task force or commission should be established that regularly reviews the extent of organized crime activity in the United States and drafts standards that recommend specific state and national actions directed at preventing and controlling organized crime. The task force would also provide comprehensive assessments at regular intervals, perhaps every ten years. The reviews and the comprehensive assessment would be published as reports and made available to law enforcement, researchers, policymakers, and the general public. A federally empowered task force (as compared to local or state commissions) will be better able to combine the expertise of the law enforcement and academic communities, secure intergovernmental cooperation, and gain access to intelligence information from federal, state, and local investigative or enforcement units.

Third, the advisory task force and the permanent commission should be required both to examine the nature and scope of transnational organized crime, particularly as it affects the United States, and to instrument the creation of an international commission or task force for purposes of a broader assessment.

Respond to the Special Threat
of Transnational Criminal Organizations

In April 1994, the Senate Foreign Relations Committee heard testimony from a number of experts about the growing threat to U.S. interests at home and abroad posed by transnational organized crime. International crime organizations were viewed in particular as a major contributing factor to *global ungovernability*.

Several broad measures (and a number of specific steps) should be implemented to improve the U.S. response and the international response to transnational criminal organizations—that is, organized crime groups that have a home base in one state but operate in one or more host states where there are favorable market opportunities (Williams, 1994b).

First, the U.S. government needs to initiate an assessment of the nature and scope of global organized crime. Presently, neither the United States nor any government understands the true magnitude of the problem. For example, there is no firm understanding of the hierarchy and vulnerabilities of the cocaine cartels or of the rapidly emerging groups from the former Soviet Union. In the short-term the United States should undertake this assessment unilaterally and then subsequently provide the leadership to involve other nations to work with to share information and assessments (Olson, 1994).

Second, the United States should take the lead in developing policy responses by the international community, including the creation of multinational task forces. The ability of any government acting alone to make major inroads against criminal organizations that operate transnationally is severely limited. Patterns of cooperation among law enforcement authorities have become stronger and more pronounced in recent years, especially with regard to drugs and money laundering. But more effective forms of international cooperation are needed that aim in particular at the following.

Better Understanding of Transnational Criminal Organizations and More Comprehensive Intelligence. The main emphases here should be on the determination of the factors and conditions facilitating the development of transnational organized crime; the examination of other countries' experiences in regard to controlling organized crime; the creation of centralized location(s) for the collection, storage, and analysis of information pertaining to transnational criminals and criminal organizations; and the sharing and exchange of information.

Reform of the Global Financial System. Transnational criminal organizations have demonstrated considerable entrepreneurial flair for exploiting the many points of access to the global financial market and moving the profits from their illicit activities with relative ease and impunity (Williams, 1994a). Four important initial steps toward reform are: (1) criminalizing money laundering involving specific kinds of organized-crime activity such as narcotics and weapons smuggling; (2) requiring banks and other financial institutions to (a) know and record the identity of customers engaging in significant transactions, (b) maintain, for an adequate time, records necessary to reconstruct significant transactions, and (c) report suspicious transactions; 3) establishing systems for identifying, tracing, freezing, seizing, and forfeiting assets relating to narcotics and other organized-crime activities; and (4) providing incentives for compliance such as receiving a portion of the seized assets.

Elimination of National Sanctuaries and Safe Havens. One of the important approaches here is to enhance both formal and informal cooperation among nations for purposes of facilitating extradition of fugitives and obtaining evidence and witnesses from another country in ways that can be used in one's own courts.

Development of a More Uniform Law Enforcement Environment. an environment is needed that makes it difficult for TCOs to operate with immunity in certain states, to infiltrate other countries, and to move their profits through the global financial system.

These initiatives will require international awareness and cooperation, and in the long term will have to combine with strategies that strengthen weak governments and lessen the poverty and social disintegration that has accompanied post-World War II development. As noted, there are two basic features of some countries that provide congenial environments for the emergence of transnational criminal organizations: where there are sizable economically and socially depressed areas and where the government and/or its officials are weak, acquiescent, collusive, or corrupt.

Conclusion

Just as there has been considerable change in recent decades, there also is much continuity in organized crime. This change and continuity are reflected in the four broad groupings of criminal organizations (or networks) that I have outlined to represent the most serious organized-crime threats to the United States. These groupings are: American Mafia, transnational criminal organizations, emerging or non-traditional criminal organizations, and local racketeering syndicates.

Several key points are worth reemphasizing as important for establishing an agenda for organized-crime control. The first is the recognition that there is not a universal panacea for organized crime. Strategies to combat organized crime must take into account both its complexity and variety. The groups operate in different product markets and geographical domains and use a variety of tactics to circumvent law enforcement. Specific policies will depend on which group or product market is targeted. What works for one organized crime problem may not work for another.

Second, four lines of law enforcement defense are recommended. The first is a vigilant media and an informed public that demands that law enforcement and public officials be held accountable both (1) for treating organized crime as a "serious" crime problem and (2) for corruptive or complicitous behaviors. The second line of defense against organized crime is a research and intelligence program that serves to better understand the causes and consequences of organized crime and that discerns racketeers and their corruptive efforts. A third line is effective coordination and cooperation of criminal justice resources. Fourth, those resources should place a premium on identifying and chasing "dirty" money and ruining the criminals or the organization financially. More than anything, the effective control of organized crime requires legal prohibitions and penalties that are directed against illegal organizations and their economic base, not simply against individual criminals.

Third, organized crime and racketeering do not exist in a vacuum; they are part and parcel of the larger society, and their redress cannot be accomplished solely by a law enforcement response. As noted, the organized-crime phenomenon is as much or more an economic and institutional problem rather than simply a criminal problem. In the long term a strong law enforcement response will have to combine with strategies that strengthen weak or complicitous governments, that lessen poverty and social disintegration, and that alter cultural frameworks that are supportive of organized crime and adaptable to changing circumstances. It is worth noting here that some organized crime groups (e.g., the Sicilian and American Mafia, Chinese Triads, Japanese Yakuza) have demonstrated remarkable adaptation and a dynamic pragmatism that have allowed them to survive and thrive in very different eras and circumstances. For example, the convictions of Mafia leaders in trials during the 1980s in both Italy and the United States might easily lead to the illusion that the decisive blow has been delivered to the "Mafia." But only a few years later its renewed expansion was revealed.

Finally, responding to the problems and dangers posed by organized crime requires a clear understanding of the range of organized crime groups and activities, their roots, their nature, and their likely responsiveness to particular kinds of countervailing efforts. Despite the public attention it sometimes attracts and its pertinence as a veritably serious crime problem, organized crime is a rarely studied and a poorly understood phenomenon. Research should accompany policy formulation. Readily available and accessible data sets, recruitment of first-rate scholars, and development of an external expert community are a sine qua non for informed policy approaches.

Notes

1. This abundance of information is largely an outgrowth of the investigative efforts of the Pennsylvania Crime Commission, which targeted local rackateering in the state. There also are the select reports of the 1951 Kefauver Committee that pertain to several localities in Pennsylvania; Gardener's study of Reading; and Potter's analysis of Scranton. Also, both because of my work with PCC and other ongoing research, I am informed about the local racketeering phenomenon in the state.

2. Prior to World War II, "there did exist...a certain amount of long-distance trade and a series of local drug markets in Asian countries and in some western capitals/ But there was no system of competitive, interdependent national markets, extending into every continent and involving large transactions, such as wee have known in the recent past" (Arlacchi, 1986:217).

References

Abadinsky, Howard. 1994. *Organized Crime*. Chicago, IL: Nelson-Hall.

Albini, Joseph., B. Bajon. 1978. "Witches, Mafia, mental illness, and social reality: A study in the power of mythical belief." *International Journal of Criminology and Penology* 6:285-294.

Arlacchi, Pino. 1986. *Mafia Business: The Mafia Ethic and Spirit of Capitalism*. Guildford, England: Biddles.

Block, Alan. 1983. *East Side-West Side*. New Brunswick, NJ: Transaction Press.

Catanzaro, Raimondo. 1992. *Men of Respect: A Social History of the Sicilian Mafia*. New York: Free Press.

Chambliss. William. 1978. *On the Take*. Bloomington: University of Indiana Press.

Cressey, Donald. 1969. *Theft of the Nation*. New York: Harper and Row.

Fox, Stephen. 1989. *Blood and Power*. New York: William Morrow and Company.

Gardiner, John. 1970. *The Politics of Organized Crime in an American City*. New York: Russell Sage Foundation.

Godson, Roy. 1994. "Crisis of Governance: Devising Strategy to Counter International Organized Crime." Testimony to Senate Foreign Relations Committee. Washington DC, April, 21.

Hawkins, Gordon. 1969. "God and the Mafia." *The Public Interest* 14:24-51.

Ianni, Francis. 1972. *A Family Business*. NY: Russell Sage Foundation.

———. 1974. *Black Mafia: Ethnic Succession in Organized Crime*. New York: Simon and Schuster.

Inciardi, James. 1990. "Legalizing Drugs: A Gormless, Naive Idea." *The Criminologist* 15:1-4.

Jacobs, James. 1994. *Busting The Mob: U.S. v. Cosa Nostra*. New York: New York University Press.

Johnson, Carl. 1993. *Russian Organized Crime: A Baseline Perspective*. Johnston, PA: National Drug Intelligence Center.

Kappler, Victor, Mark Blumberg, and Gary Potter. 1993. *The Mythology of Crime and Criminal Justice*. Prospect Heights, IL: Waveland Press.

Karchmer, Clifford and D. Ruch. 1992. *State and Local Money Laundering Strategies*. National Institute of Justice (Research in Brief). Washington, DC: National Institute of Justice.

Kenney, Dennis, and James Finckenauer. 1995. *Organized Crime in America*. New York: Wadsworth.

Landesco, John. 1929. *Organized Crime in Chicago*. Chicago: University of Chicago Press.

Martens, Frederick. 1987. "The Intelligence Function." In Herbert Edelhertz, (ed.), *Major Issues in Organized Crime Control*. Washington, DC: National Institute of Justice.

Moore, Mark. 1987. "Organized Crime as a Business Enterprise." In Herbert Edelhertz, ed., *Major Issues in Organized Crime Control*. Washington, DC: National Institute of Justice.

Nelli, Hubert. 1976. *The Business of Crime*. New York: Oxford University Press.

Olson, William. 1994. "The Crisis of Governance: Present and Future Challenges. Testimony to Senate Foreign Relations Committee, Washington DC, April.

Pennsylvania Crime Commission. 1990. *The 1990 Report—Organized Crime in Pennsylvania: A Decade of Change*. Conshokocken, PA: Pennsylvania Crime Commission.

Pistone, Joseph. 1988. "Organized Crime: 25 Years after Valachi." Testimony before United States Senate Hearings Before the Permanent Subcommittee on Investigations, Committee on Governmental Affairs, Washington, DC.

Potter, Gary. 1994. *Criminal Organizations: Vice, Racketeering, and Politics in an American City*. Prospect Heights, IL: Waveland Press.

Potter, Gary, and Philip Jenkins. 1978. *The City and the Syndicate*. Lexington, MA: Gini Press.

President's Commission on Law Enforcement and Administration of Justice, Task Force on Organized Crime. 1967. *Task Force Report: Organized Crime*. Washington, DC: U.S. Government Printing Office.

President's Commission on Organized Crime. 1983-1986. *Organized Crime*. Washington, DC: U.S. Government Printing Office.

Reuter, Peter. 1983. *Disorganized Crime: The Economics of the Visible Hand*. Cambridge, MA: MIT Press.

———. 1987. "Methodological and Institutional Problems in Organized Crime Research." In Herbert Edelhertz, (ed.), *Major Issues in Organized Crime Control*. Washington, DC: National Institute of Justice.

Rey, Guido and Ernesto Savona. 1993. "The Mafia: An International Enterprise?" In Ernesto Savona (ed.), *Mafia Issues*. Milan, Italy: International Scientific and Professional Advisory Council of the United States Crime Prevention and Criminal Justice Programme.

Savona, Ernesto (ed.). 1993. *Mafia Issues*. Milan, Italy: International Scientific and Professional Advisory Council of the United States Crime Prevention and Criminal Justice Programme.

Sessions, William. 1988. "Organized Crime: 25 Years after Valachi." Testimony before United States Senate Hearings Before the Permanent Subcommittee on Investigations, Committee on Governmental Affairs, Washington, DC.

Smith, 1980. "Paragons, Pariahs, and Pirates: A Spectrum-based Theory of Enterprise." *Crime and Delinquency* 26: 358-386.

Steffensmeier, Darrell. 1983. "Organization Properties and Sex-Segregation in the Underworld: Building a Sociological Theory of Sex Differences in Crime." *Social Forces* 61:1010-1032.

———. 1986. *The Fence: In the Shadow of Two Worlds*. Totowa, NJ: Rowman and Littlefield.

———. n.d. *Confessions of a Dying Thief*. University Park, PA: Pennsylvania State University. Forthcoming.

Sterling, Claire. 1990. *Octopus: The Long Reach of the Sicilian Mafia*. New York: Simon and Schuster.

Thoumi, Francisco. 1992. "Why the Illegal Psychoactive Drugs Industry Grew in Colombia." *Journal of InterAmerican Studies and World Affairs* 34:37-64.
United States Senate. 1988. "Organized Crime: 25 Years after Valachi." Hearings Before the Permanent Subcommittee on Investigations, Committee on Governmental Affairs. Washington, DC: U.S. Government Printing Office.
White, William. 1943. *Street Corner Society*. Chicago: University of Chicago Press.
Williams, Phil. 1994a. "Threat Assessment." Paper prepared for the UN Secretary General for 1995 World Ministerial Conference on Transnational Organized Crime.
———. 1994b. "Strengthening International Cooperation." Paper prepared for the UN Secretary General for 1995 World Ministerial Conference on Transnational Organized Crime.
———. 1994. "Transnational Criminal Organizations and International Security." *Survival* 36 (1):96-113.

About the Contributors

Robert Agnew is professor of sociology at Emory University in Atlanta. His research focuses on the causes of delinquency, the most recent dealing with his general strain theory of delinquency. Recent publications include "Foundations for a General Strain Theory of Crime and Delinquency" (1992), and "Determinism, Indeterminism, and Crime: An Empirical Exploration" (1995) both in *Criminology*.

John Braithwaite is professor in the Research School of Social Sciences, Australian National University. His recent books are *Crime, Shame and Reintegration*; *Not Just Deserts: A Republican Theory of Criminal Justice* (with Philip Pettit); *Responsive Regulation* (with Ian Ayers); and *Corporations, Crime and Accountability* (with Brent Fisse). His main interests are the development, application, and testing of criminological and regulatory theories and corporate crime.

Robert J. Bursik, Jr. is professor and chair of the Department of Sociology at the University of Oklahoma. His primary research interests concern the relationship between neighborhood dynamics and crime rates, and the formal and informal mechanisms of control at the community level that inhibit illegal behavior. He is the author of *Neighborhoods and Crime* (1993) with Harold Grasmick.

Ronald V. Clarke is professor and dean at the School of Criminal Justice, Rutgers, the State University of New Jersey. He was formerly director of the British government's criminological research department at the Home Office, where he had a significant role in the development of situational crime prevention. He is editor of *Crime Prevention Studies*, and has published widely on diverse criminological topics. His recent books include *The Reasoning Criminal* (1986); *Suicide: Closing the Exits* (1989); and *Situational Crime Prevention: Successful Case Studies* (1992).

Lawrence E. Cohen is professor of sociology and director of the Center for Research in Crime and Delinquency at the University of California at Davis. His primary interests are in criminological theory and qualitative methods, in particular the application of evolutionary game-theoretic models to theoretical criminology.

Ronald P. Corbett, Jr. is deputy commissioner of the Massachussetts Probation department. He currently serves as president of the National Association of Probation Executives, and is adjunct professor at the University of Massachussetts, Lowell. His recent publications include "'Novel' Perspectives on Probation: Fiction as Sociology."

Marcus Felson is professor at the School of Criminal Justice, Rutgers, as well as senior research associate at the Social Science Research Institutute, and professor of sociology, at the University of Southern California. He is author of *Crime and Everyday Life: Insights and Implications for Society* (1995), and co-editor (with Ronald V. Clarke) of *Routine Activity and Rational Choice* (1994). He is currently working on a study of the crime reduction strategy, tactics, and outcomes in the Port Authority Bus Terminal in New York City. He continues his ongoing work linking the routine activity approach, situational crime prevention, and control theory.

Jack P. Gibbs is Centennial Professor Emeritus at Vanderbilt University. His current research interests are in the area of social control theories. He is currently collaborating with Mark Stafford on a control theory of homicide. Recent books include *Control: Sociology's Central Notion* (1989), and *A Theory About Control* (1993).

D. M. Gorman is an assistant professor of urban studies and community health at the Center of Alcohol Studies, Rutgers University. He is also director of prevention at the Center, and has published extensively on the effectiveness of substance abuse prevention strategies. He is currently engaged in spatial analysis research into risk factors and resource allocation in the state of New Jersey.

Harold G. Grasmick is professor of sociology at the University of Oklahoma. In addition to his work with Robert Bursik on neighborhoods and crime, his research interests include the incorporation of social norms and values into a rational choice theory of crime, and the relationship between attribution styles and attitudes toward punishment.

John Hagan recently was named W. Grant Dalhstrom Distinguished Professor of Sociology and adjunct professor of law at the University of North Carolina at Chapel Hill. He is the author or coauthor of many books, including *Crime and Disrepute*, and *Gender in Practice: A Study of Lawyer's Lives* (with Fiona Kay), and he is coeditor with Ruth Peterson of *Crime and Inequality*. A past president of the American Society of Criminology, he is also editor of the *Annual Review of Sociology*. He is continuing collaborative research on the transition to adulthood in Berlin and on lawyers and crime in North America.

Belinda Henderson is a graduate student in sociology at the University of Tennessee, Knoxville. Her current research interest is criminal recidivism.

John H. Laub is professor in the College of Criminal Justice at Northeastern University, and visiting scholar at the Henry A. Murray Research Center of Radcliffe College. He is also editor of *Quantitative Criminology*. His research interests include crime and deviance over the life course, juvenile justice, and the history of criminology. His most recent book is *Crime in the Making: Pathways and Turning Points Through Life* (1993) (with Robert J. Sampson).

Michael Levi is professor of criminology at the University of Wales, Cardiff. His current research interests are social reaction to white-collar crime, money .

laundering and asset forfeiture, and jury decisionmaking in white-collar crime trials. Recent books include *Regulating Fraud: White-Collar Crime and the Criminal Process* (1988), *Customer Confidentiality, Money-Laundering, and Police-Bank Relationships* (1991), and (with Michael Gold) *Money Laundering in the UK: An Appraisal of Suspicion-Based Reporting* (1994). His editorial activities include criminology editor of *Crime, Law and Social Change.*

Richard Machalek is professor of sociology at the University of Wyoming. His major interests include general evolutionary theory and sociobiology. His research pertains to the evolution of social exploitation among a variety of species, including humans. He is currently studying the social structure of spectacled flying foxes in the Australian rain forest.

Robert J. Sampson is professor of sociology at the University of Chicago and research fellow at the American Bar Foundation. His major research interests are the life course and the structural context of crime and its control. His research collaboration with John Laub resulted in the publication of *Crime in the Making: Pathways and Turning Points Through Life* (1993).

Neal Shover is professor of sociology at the University of Tennessee, Knoxville. His book *Great Pretenders: Pursuits and Careers of Persistent Thieves* will be published by Westview Press in 1996. In addition to his work on street-level thieves and hustlers, he also studies corporate crime.

Jinney S. Smith is research fellow at the Institute of United States Studies at the University of London. Her research interests are crime policy, juvenile delinquency, and policing. She is currently conducting a comparative research project on the moral reasoning of juvenile delinquents.

Elizabeth A. Stanko is reader in criminology at Brunel University in Middlesex, England, where she directs the Centre for Criminal Justice Research. She has published widely on gender and crime, policing, prosecutorial decisionmaking, and violence. She is the author of *Everyday Violence* (1995), and *Intimate Intrusions* (1985), and she recently collaborated with Tim Newburn in editing *Just Boys Doing Business: Men, Masculinities and Crime* (1994).

Darrell J. Steffensmeier is professor of sociology at Pennsylvania State University. Current interests include correlates of crime (age, gender, race), courts and sentencing, organized crime and criminal careers, and joint application of qualitative and quantitative methods. From 1990 to 1991 he served as project director and principal writer of the 1990 report, *Organized Crime in Pennsylvania: A Decade of Change.* He currently is completing an update of *The Fence: In the Shadow of Two Worlds* titled *Confessions of a Dying Thief.*

Austin T. Turk is professor of sociology at the University of California, Riverside. A fellow and former president of the American Society of Criminology, as well as a former trustee of the Law and Society Association, he has written extensively on the linkage between legal power and social conflict. Current research interests include community policing, inequality and social control, terrorism, and sociological development in South Africa.

Helene Raskin White is professor of sociology at the Center of Alcohol Studies, Rutgers University. She is currently engaged in longitudinal research on the etiology of substance abuse and delinquency and the consequences of alcohol and other druge abuse from adolescence to adulthood. She has co-edited two books in the alcohol field and has published extensively in the major drug, criminology, and sociology journals.

About the Book and Editor

This book consists of original essays by leading criminologists who were asked to consider the policy implications of prominent theories of crime. The contributors evaluate their own and others' work and present specific policy recommendations in light of their analysis. The main emphasis of the book is on the policy implications of theories that have wide scope or that integrate different perspectives. However, the book concludes with chapters that contemplate theory and policy in their application to specific areas of criminal activity—violence, persistent theft, white-collar crime, and organized crime.

Hugh D. Barlow is professor of sociology and chair of the Department of Sociology and Social Work at Southern Illinois University at Edwardsville. His current research interests include violence, small business crime, and the links between theory and crime policy. In 1993, he was awarded the Herbert A. Bloch Award by the American Society of Criminology for his contributions to the Society and to the profession of criminology. He is author of *Introduction to Criminology*, the 7th edition of which is currently in press, and co-author (with Theodore N. Ferdinand) of *Understanding Delinquency* (1992). He is currently at work on a new book on the criminal justice system to be published by HarperCollins.